COMPUTER
FUNDAMENTALS

COMPUTER
FUNDAMENTALS

Dennis A. Adams

University of Houston

Course Technology, Inc. One Main Street, Cambridge, MA 02142

For Andy and Jenny

Computer Fundamentals is published by Course Technology, Inc.

Publisher	Joseph B. Dougherty
Editor	Pete Alcorn
Production Manager	Thomas E. Dorsaneo
Desktop Publishing	Rosalie Blazej
Cover Design	Darci Mehall
Designers	Rosalie Blazej
Artist	Winston Sin
Copy Editor	Janet Reed
Proofreader	Darlene Bordwell
Indexer	BevAnne Ross
Manufacturing Package Design	Mark Dee
Quality Assurance Specialist	Steve Bayle

Photography Credits

Chapter 1.   Figures 1-2, 1-5, 1-6, 1-8, 1-9, 1-11a, 1-11b courtesy of International Business Machines Corporation. Figure 1-3 © John William Lund. Figure 1-7 courtesy of Cray. Figure 1-10 reprinted from *POPULAR ELECTRONICS*, January 1975, copyright ©1975, Ziff-Davis Publishing Company. Figure 1-11c photo courtesy of Hewlett-Packard Company.

Chapter 2.   Figures 2-1, 2-2, 2-3 courtesy of International Business Machines Corporation. Figures 2-4, 2-5a, 2-5c courtesy of Apple Computer, Inc. Figures 2-5b, 2-5d, 2-7 © John William Lund. Figures 2-6, 2-8 courtesy of Microsoft Corporation. Figure 2-9 courtesy of Hewlett-Packard Company.

Chapter 3.   Figures 3-5, 3-7, 3-14 courtesy of International Business Machines Corporation. Figure 3-12 © John William Lund.

Chapter 4.   Figures 4-4, 4-7, 4-15, 4-19, 4-21a, 4-21b, 4-22a, 4-23 © John William Lund. Figure 4-10 courtesy of Hewlett-Packard Company. Figure 4-17 courtesy Central Point Software, Inc. Figures 4-20, 4-21c, 4-22c, 4-24 courtesy International Business Machines Corporation.

Chapter 5.   Figure 5-10 UPI/Bettmann Newsphoto. Figure 5-16a Bettmann/Hulton. Figure 5-16b The Bettmann Archives. Figure 5-25b © John William Lund.

Chapter 6.   Figures 6-2, 6-3, 6-5, 6-6, 6-7, 6-9, 6-10, 6-14, 6-15, 6-16, 6-17, 6-18, 6-19, 6-20, 6-21, 6-22, 6-23a, 6-23b, 6-24 © John William Lund. Figure 6-8 UPI/Bettmann. Figure 6-9 courtesy Intel Corporation. Figure 6-25 (left) courtesy of International Business Machines Corporation. Figure 6-25 (right) courtesy of Hewlett-Packard Company.

Chapter 7.   Figures 7-8, 7-10, 7-11, 7-27, 7-28 © John William Lund. Figures 7-12, 7-14, 7-16, 7-21a, 7-21b courtesy of International Business Machines Corporation. Figure 7-13 courtesy of Summagraphics Corporation. Figures 7-22a, 7-22b, 7-22c, 7-22d courtesy of Apple Computer, Inc. Figure 7-15 courtesy of Hewlett-Packard Company.

Chapter 8.   Figures 8-6, 8-7, 8-13, 8-14, 8-15, 8-16, 8-17 © John William Lund.

Chapter 9.   Figure 9-3a, 9-3b, 9-6 © John William Lund. Figure 9-11 courtesy of International Business Machines Corporation.

Chapter 10.   Figure 10-8 courtesy Microsoft Corporation. Figure 10-16 courtesy Unix Systems Laboratories.

Chapter 12.   Figures 12-2, 12-3 courtesy of International Business Machines Corporation.

Chapter 13.   Figure 13-9 courtesy Popkin Software & Systems Incorporated. Figure 13-10 courtesy of International Business Machines Corporation.

Brief Contents

Table of Contents

Preface

This book is designed to give you a realistic view of how computers work and how they are used to solve business problems. Several concerns led to the creation of this book.

Organization

Computer Fundamentals uses a unique organization to introduce basic computer concepts. A continuous case — Buena Vista Office Supply (BVOS) — is used throughout to illustrate the essential information that will help make students better decision makers when they are confronted with technology alternatives in their daily lives. The case is combined with a framework for problem solving that is introduced at the beginning of each unit. A detailed overview of BVOS, the example company, and the problem solving framework are described in the Introduction. Unit I provides an overview of the field of computers. Unit II addresses software and its unique role in solving problems. Unit III follows with a discussion of hardware and operating systems that are necessary to support the software. Finally, Unit IV concludes with organizational considerations of using computers and systems as well as databases concepts.

Approach

Purchasing a computer can be a daunting task. This text addresses the basics of computer and information technology from the perspective of the purchaser, both personally and professionally. Because few facts or terms remain constant in the world of computers, we don't pretend that the field is static. What you learn today may not be valid next year, let alone next week! This text stresses the dynamic nature of the computer field.

If there is one paramount message in *Computer Fundamentals* it's that learning how to learn about technology is far more important than memorizing any individual fact or group of facts. To that end, within each chapter and at the end of each chapter the reader is consistently asked to demonstrate comprehension by applying the principles introduced in those chapters. Students are also frequently encouraged to make decisions and investigate information from outside sources.

Features

Software First. Unlike most textbooks with the same aim, *Computer Fundamentals* stresses the needs of the user when developing computer solutions to everyday problems. Meeting the needs of the user involves selecting the software most appropriate to solve the user's problems. This commonly accepted practice requires that the text introduce software before hardware because it is the software that will meet the needs of the user.

Comprehension Questions. Comprehension Questions are spread throughout each chapter. These questions provide an opportunity for students to demonstrate their understanding of the topics discussed before they advance to the next topic.

Using What You Know.   These questions are also interspersed throughout the chapters. Each Using What You Know question challenges the reader to apply newly acquired knowledge to either a real-life situation or a situation at Buena Vista Office Supply.

Summary Points.   The contents of each chapter are summarized in a simple outline format. The outline can serve as a review of the material presented or a quick overview of the entire chapter.

Knowing the Facts.   This end-of-the-chapter exercise section consists of 10 true/false and 10 short answer questions that reinforce the material presented in each chapter. This built-in study guide even includes all the answers.

Challenging Your Understanding.   At the end of each chapter, students are encouraged to go beyond the information presented in the text and draw conclusions, research relevant facts from outside sources like *PC Magazine*, and deal with situations at BVOS. These questions often cover material that has been introduced over more than one chapter, and they often require in-depth analysis.

Unit Projects.   At the end of each of the four units is a Unit Project. These advanced exercises are intended to challenge the student's higher-order thinking skills with in-depth work solving a hypothetical problem.

Glossary and Index.   At the end of the book students will find a comprehensive index and a glossary that provides definitions for all of the key words in the text.

The Supplements

The Instructor's Manual. The Instructor's Manual is written by the author and is quality-assurance tested. It includes:

- Answers or suggested answers to all of the assignments in the text
- Transparency masters of key concepts

Test Bank.   The Test Bank contains 50 questions per tutorial in true/false, multiple choice, and fill-in-the-blank formats, plus two essay questions. Each has been quality-assurance tested by students to achieve clarity and accuracy.

Electronic Test Bank. The Electronic Test Bank allows instructors to edit individual test questions, select questions individually or at random, and print scrambled versions of the same test to any supported printer. In addition, technical support is available from Publishing Innovations at (508) 741- 8010.

Acknowledgments

This book would not have been possible without the insights and technical expertise of several key contributors. First, my thanks go to the following instructors, who helped crystalize the vision and approach used in this book:

Carl Clavadetscher, California State Polytechnic University, Pomona

Pat Fenton, West Valley College

Richard Gilberg, De Anza College

Bob Grill, College of Alameda

John McKinney, University of Cincinnati

Especially warm thanks are due to Professor Bob Grill for his keen and thorough reviews of the entire manuscript, as well as to Beverly Talbot for integrating Professor Grill's suggestions.

I would also like to thank Joe Dougherty at Course Technology for his support and supervision; Steve Bayle at Course Technology for his technical reviews; Pete Alcorn at BMR, in Corte Madera, for his help developing and editing the manuscript; and Tom Dorsaneo at BMR for coordinating the production of the book.

Dennis Adams,
University of Houston
February, 1993

Computer Fundamentals

■   ■   ■

The World of Computing

Unit I

Opening a New BVOS Franchise

In reading this unit, you will get the "big picture." We will discuss computers in the broadest sense: what they are, how they are used, who makes them, and who uses them.

In terms of the problem-solving model, which we will establish in the Introduction that follows, we will principally address step 2: understanding the problem, as shown in Figure I-1. Your problem at BVOS is to research, purchase, and install a computer system that will make your business as efficient as possible. There are two key points here. First, you need more than a computer; you need a computer *system*. Chapter 1 addresses this point in detail. By the end of the first chapter, you will know the various parts of the computer itself, and you will know the parts of the system.

Second, in Chapter 2 you will learn how some well-known companies have used computer systems to become more efficient and more effective. And you will gain some background on a few of the companies that provide the computer products that can help you in your efforts.

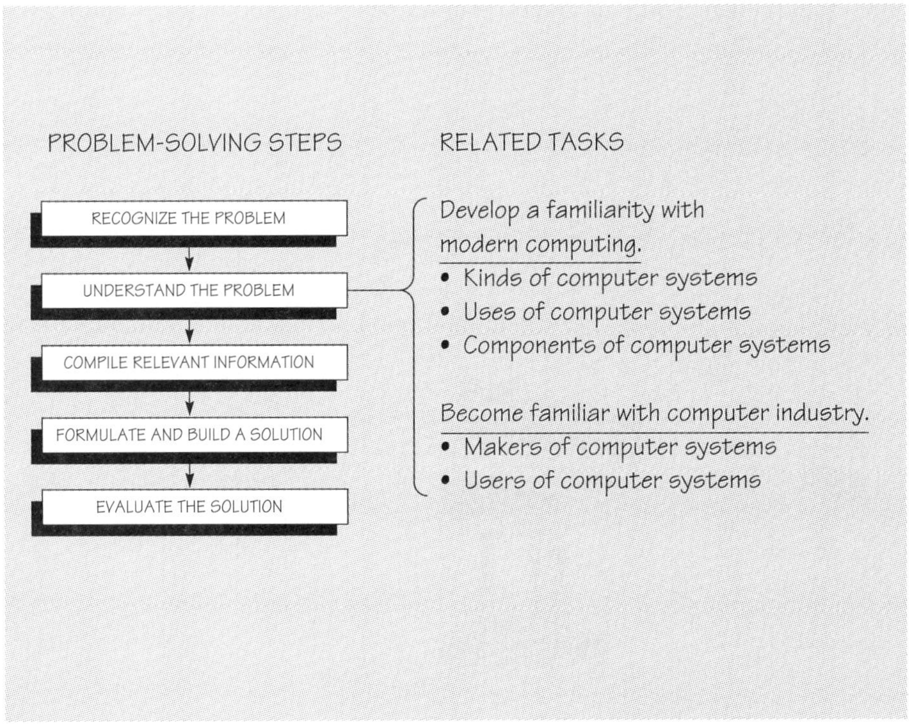

PROBLEM-SOLVING STEPS

- RECOGNIZE THE PROBLEM
- UNDERSTAND THE PROBLEM
- COMPILE RELEVANT INFORMATION
- FORMULATE AND BUILD A SOLUTION
- EVALUATE THE SOLUTION

RELATED TASKS

Develop a familiarity with modern computing.
- Kinds of computer systems
- Uses of computer systems
- Components of computer systems

Become familiar with computer industry.
- Makers of computer systems
- Users of computer systems

Figure I-1   In this unit, we will focus on step 2 of the problem-solving process.

Introduction

The Buena Vista Scenario:
Following a Problem-Solving Approach

In order to show how all of the computer topics presented here are integrated, we have used a single running example throughout the book. The example involves a fictitious business: Buena Vista Office Supply, or BVOS. You, the reader, play the part of an entrepreneur who is opening a branch of Buena Vista in your own community (Figure I-2).

As the owner of the new BVOS branch, you will be faced with a number of problems. Like any good entrepreneur, you want to turn those problems into opportunities, and maybe

Figure I-2
In this book, you will be making decisions related to a business you are opening, a local branch of Buena Vista Office Supply.

even advantages! You ask the question, "How can I use computers to make my business run efficiently?" To solve this central problem, you will follow a standard problem-solving technique, which consists of five steps:

1. Recognizing the problem

2. Understanding the problem

3. Compiling relevant information

4. Designing and building the solution

5. Evaluating the solution

Each step, in turn, requires particular actions and decisions, depending on the problem at hand. Throughout this book, we will provide diagrams similar to Figure I-3 to help you see what is required to accomplish each step.

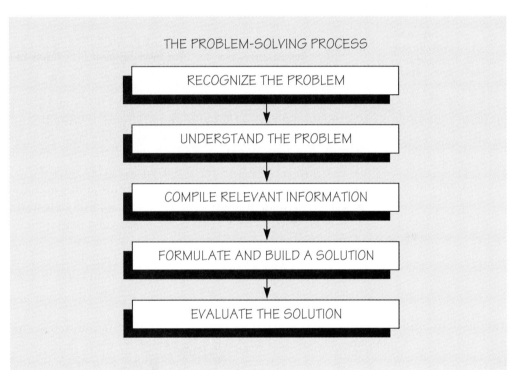

Figure I-3
The problem-solving process. You will find figures similar to this one at key points throughout this book.

Step 1: Recognizing The Problem

Because we have created this scenario for you, the first step is already done. We begin at a stage in which you have researched the office supply market in your area and found that there is a need for an office supply store to service local businesses. You showed your findings to the headquarters of Buena Vista Office Supply in Toronto, Canada, and they agreed that you should open a branch of BVOS in your town.

In your discussions with BVOS headquarters personnel, they outlined to you how most local branches operate. Your customers are local businesses that need office supplies, such as copy paper, office furniture, writing materials, staplers, file folders, and so on. The staff of your branch takes orders from local businesses over the phone or by fax. The staff then fills the orders with the supplies obtained from the regional distributor and delivers the supplies using your delivery vans. A graphic of your merchandise is shown in Figure I-4.

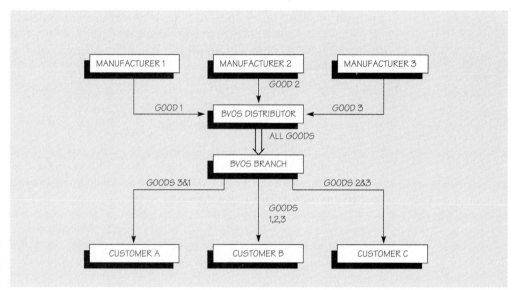

Figure I-4
A flowchart illustrating your role in bringing office supplies to your customers.

To start your new branch, you have estimated that you will need 12 employees:

- Three salespeople will take orders from local businesses.

- Three stockroom workers will fill the orders, box them, and load them onto the delivery vans.

- Five drivers will deliver the supplies to local businesses.

- One inventory manager will monitor your stock of office supplies and, when necessary, order new supplies from the regional distributor. The inventory manager will also be your accountant — billing customers, paying the regional distributor, and paying your employees.

Figure I-5 diagrams your staff members and their functions in your branch office.
To give you a better idea of how valuable computer technology is, executives at BVOS

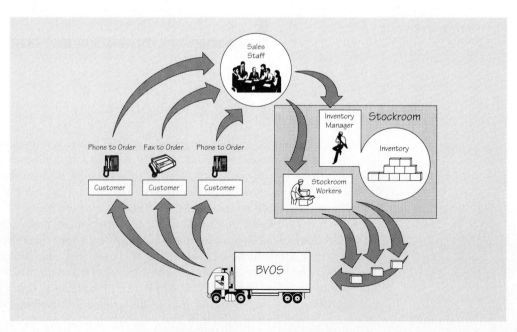

Figure I-5
Your employees and their functions at BVOS.

headquarters showed you profit reports, accounting records, and inventory lists from various BVOS branches before and after computerization. It was obvious that the branches made considerably more money once they implemented computer systems and that their business practices were much more efficient.

Once you saw those financial reports, you saw clearly the task ahead of you. You needed to buy a computer system to make your new business as efficient as possible.

Step 2: Understanding the Problem

Now that you recognize you have a problem worth solving, the next step is to gain a better understanding of that problem. Unfortunately, you don't know much about computers. You have heard a great deal, and you've seen them in many other businesses. But now you will be faced with a lot of purchasing decisions, and you don't have any idea of what you ought to buy.

Fortunately, that's just what you're going to learn about in this book. Each new topic you encounter here begins by covering the basic concepts. You need to master these basic concepts in order to understand what products your new business needs. First, in Unit I, you will get an overview of computers and gain a perspective on the entire computer industry. In Unit II, you will build your understanding of computer software, the most important problem-solving tool of the computer user. In Unit III, you will study the fundamentals of computer hardware — the parts of the computer that you can see and touch. Finally, in Unit IV, you will begin to understand how computers are used to solve business problems.

Step 3: Compiling Relevant Information

After gaining an understanding of each new computer topic, move on to step 3 of the problem-solving process: compiling relevant information. We will provide you with some of the information you need. However, any product data we give you will be out of date by the time you read this book. In order to make an informed decision about what to buy for your new business, you will need to do some current research to find out what computer products are available, the advantages and disadvantages of each product, and how much each costs.

Part of compiling relevant information is knowing where the relevant information is and how to find it. Throughout this book, you will be asked to search magazines, newspapers, and trade catalogs to discover what's available. By the time you get through the book, you will have an excellent sense of the kind of information you will need and where to find it.

Step 4: Designing and Building a Solution

Once you have fully researched the products that are available to you in the computer market, you are ready to enter the fourth step of the problem-solving process: designing and building the solution. As its name implies, this step is divided into two phases. In the first phase, you design your solution; in the second phase, you actually build it.

In the exercises associated with Units II and III of this book, you will become deeply involved in choosing hardware and software for your branch of BVOS. And, in Unit IV, you will examine how the hardware and software work together to solve many of your business problems. In other words, you will design your own solution. This book will provide advice and guidelines, but in the end, the decision about what to purchase will be up to you.

Step 5: Evaluating the Solution

An essential step in any solution is your evaluation. In order to learn from your successes as well as your mistakes, you must always look back at what you have done and make judgments about the job you did.

Summary

Now you understand your challenge as the owner of a new business. Computers will clearly play a large part in setting up the new venture. You have many decisions to make, so don't forget the problem-solving techniques illustrated here. Let's get started with Unit I, "The World of Computing."

An Overview of Computers and Computer Users

Key Terms

automated teller machine (ATM)
communication device
computer
computer system
data
general purpose computer
hardware
input device
laptop
load
mainframe
microcomputer
minicomputer
notebook computer
output device
palmtop computer
point of sale (POS) computer
portable computer
processing device
program
robot
software
special purpose computer
storage device
supercomputer
user
workstation

Objectives

In this chapter, you will learn to:

- Understand what a computer is and name its three essential functions
- Explain the differences between special purpose computers and general purpose computers
- Compare the uses of supercomputers, mainframes, minicomputers, and microcomputers
- Name and describe the four parts of a computer system
- Identify the five types of computer hardware

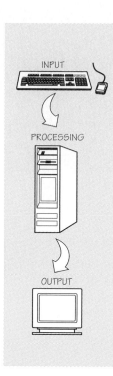

What Is a Computer?

A **computer** is an electronic device for processing data. Its purpose is to accept available data and turn it into useful information.

At the very minimum, a computer must have three parts, as shown in Figure 1-1. At the heart of the computer are **processing devices**, which consist of sets of electronic circuits. Their purpose is to manipulate data using a written set of instructions. Attached to the processing device, there must be at least one input device and one output device. The **input device** accepts data from the person or machine using the computer and transmits it to the processing devices. The **output device** accepts processed data from the processing devices and returns it as information to the person or machine using the computer.

Special Purpose Computers

Computers are everywhere. There are computers on our desks at work, in our televisions at home, in our cars, at the supermarket, at the bank — even in the kitchen (such as those controlling microwave ovens and refrigerators). It is important to realize, however, that the computers that sit on our desktops at work and at home — the machines that we usually think of as computers — are very different from the other examples we just mentioned. The difference between them is that desktop computers are general purpose computers, and most of the others are special purpose computers.

Most of this book is devoted to general purpose computers such as the one in Figure 1-2, and how they are used to solve business problems. Before we turn our attention to the main topic, though, let's take a quick look at some of the other kinds of computers we find in our everyday lives. These computers are referred to as **special purpose computers** because each one is designed to address just one kind of problem.

Figure 1-1
The essence of the computing process is input, processing, and output.

Figure 1-2   A general purpose computer.

Figure 1-3   An automated teller machine, or ATM.

ATMs

Perhaps the most common type of special purpose computer that we interact with directly in our day-to-day lives is the bank's **automated teller machine,** or **ATM** (Figure 1-3). For many years, banking customers had to coordinate their banking around the hours that banks were open. The term "banker's hours," in fact, was used disparagingly in describing the schedule of someone who worked only a few hours a day. Advancements in computer technology and competition among banks led to the development of the ATM. Today, ATMs are so prevalent that a bank has difficulty attracting customers if it doesn't offer an ATM card with each type of account.

An ATM has a small keypad, a video monitor, a card reader, a small printer, and a transaction drawer (Figure 1-4). The keypad and card reader are input devices. The video monitor, printer, and cash tray are output devices. Because the ATM is a computer, we know that there is also a processing device behind the facade that we see.

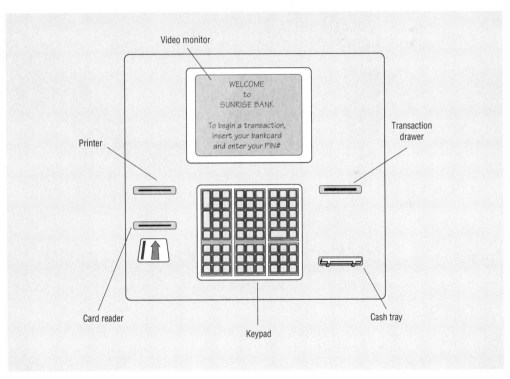

Figure 1-4
An ATM and its input and output devices.

To use an ATM, the bank customer inserts his or her bank card into the card reader and enters a code on the keypad. The ATM's processor checks to see if this code matches the code recorded on the card's magnetic strip. If it does, the processor uses the video monitor to prompt the customer to choose among the options listed. The customer uses the keypad to enter a request for some type of banking transaction.

At this point, the ATM uses a device called a *modem* to call a central computer that keeps track of the customer's account. The central computer checks to see that the requested transaction is acceptable and returns a response to the ATM through its modem. The ATM then prints the results of the transaction using its printer. If the customer is withdrawing cash, the transaction drawer or cash tray gives out cash. If the customer is depositing cash or checks, the transaction drawer accepts them.

Point of Sale Computers

Another common type of special purpose computer is the **point of sale**, or **POS**, **computer**. They were developed to make it easier for large stores to keep track of inventory. POS computers are usually housed in cash registers attached to scanning devices, such as bar-code readers (Figure 1-5). The bar-code reader and the register keys are the computer's input devices. Like the ATM, the POS terminal's output devices include a printer, a small video monitor, and a cash drawer. In this case, however, the POS computer does not directly control the flow of cash, but simply opens the cash drawer at the appropriate time.

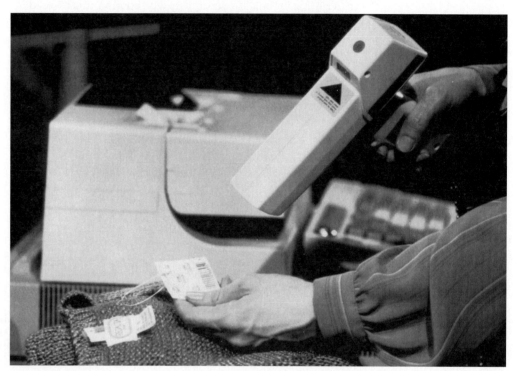

Figure 1-5
POS computers are now found in many retail environments.

Each POS computer is connected to another, more powerful computer somewhere in the store. This central computer acts in much the same way as the computer accessed by the ATM. The central store computer keeps inventories and prices in a computerized file. When the bar code on the item is scanned, the inventory account for that item is decreased by one and the item's price is passed to the cash register.

POS computers have allowed retailers to trim inventories and serve customers better. The scanners get customers through the lines faster, and the charges are more accurate. With ATM systems attached to the POS system, customers can pay for items without ever handling money or a check, thus speeding up the transaction process.

Computers in Manufacturing

From Nike shoes to Chrysler cars, computers are incorporated into the design and manufacture of consumer products. In fact, at companies like IBM and Compaq, computers are used to make computers.

Figure 1-6
Robots like this one have become commonplace in manufacturing.

Employing technologies such as robotics, manufacturers are using computers to decrease production costs and increase the quality of the products they create. A **robot** is a computer that accepts electronic input and performs mechanical output (Figure 1-6). Robots are able to perform hazardous activities, work accurately and consistently, and perform 24 hours a day. The types of activities that are possible with robotics are almost limitless. For example, in the automotive industry, robots are used to paint cars, do spot welding, and put lights in dashboards.

But including computers in manufacturing means much more than robotics. Computers — usually general purpose computers — are also used as high-powered accounting tools to calculate exactly how much raw material is needed to produce a given number of products. They can then be used to manage the whole production process, including ordering materials when necessary.

Comprehension Questions

1. Is the physical movement of a robot's arm considered input, processing, output, or none of the three?
2. A mechanical cash register simply adds numbers that are punched in. Why isn't a mechanical cash register considered a computer?
3. Although a mechanical cash register is not a computer, a pocket calculator is. Explain why a pocket calculator fits the definition of a computer.

Using What You Know

1. Name at least two special purpose computers that were not mentioned in the last section. Identify their input and output devices.
2. Describe a special purpose computer that could be useful to you in your everyday life. Explain what type of data it would accept as input and in what form it would present the output.
3. Which of the special purpose computers mentioned in the last section could be used at BVOS? Explain how and why the computer would be used.

General Purpose Computers

All of the computers mentioned in the previous section are created to perform a specific task. The computers that are used in the office or at home, however, must be able to solve a variety of problems, so they are referred to as **general purpose computers**. These computers can help create everything from documents to art. They can perform mathematical calculations and manage massive collections of data, called *databases*.

Despite the name, different types of general purpose computers are best suited to perform different kinds of tasks. They are therefore categorized by the size of the problems they are designed to address. In general, there are four types: supercomputers, mainframes, minicomputers, and microcomputers. However, you will find that these terms are gradually losing their meaning. You may see references to "mini-mainframes," "super minis," and "super micros," which represent categories that don't fall neatly into the four historical groups.

Supercomputers

Supercomputers like the one shown in Figure 1-7 are designed to solve large, complex mathematical problems. Oil companies use supercomputers to analyze seismic data in their search for oil. The National Oceanographic and Aeronautic Agency uses them to help predict the weather. Researchers in medicine and biochemistry use them to investigate combinatorial DNA in attempting to detect, predict, and cure diseases genetically. Each of these tasks requires a computer that can accept and process huge amounts of numerical data. Supercomputers are not used for common office work, such as creating documents or keeping track of clients, because even though they can perform those functions, it would not be cost effective to do so.

Some of today's supercomputers have thousands of small computers inside them, each of which is more powerful than the typical desktop computer found at home or in the office. They are sometimes called *multiprocessors* or *parallel processors* because of this design.

To protect them from smoke, dust, and other small particles or environmental hazards, supercomputers are often housed in special rooms. The temperature and humidity in these rooms is strictly controlled, and the power supply is filtered to make sure that power surges and dips are smoothed out. Today's supercomputers are smaller than their predecessors, and many no longer need special environments.

The manufacturers of supercomputers include Cray, NEC, Intel, Thinking Machines, and Hypercube.

Figure 1-7 A Cray supercomputer.

Figure 1-8 A mainframe computer, the IBM 370.

Mainframes

Until the mid-1970s, the most common type of computer was the **mainframe** (Figure 1-8). Mainframes are used by large companies and organizations in which many people need access to the company's or organization's files. Mainframes are not as specialized as supercomputers because they must be able to perform many types of business-related tasks. The size of the mainframe is determined by the amount of data it can hold and by the number of people that need access to it at the same time. A small mainframe might be used by only a handful of people, while a large one might be used by thousands.

Like some supercomputers, the processing devices of a mainframe are often housed in a special environment that protects the computer. The biggest manufacturer of mainframes, by far, is IBM. Other companies that make mainframes include Amdahl, DEC, and Groupe Bull.

Minicomputers

The expense of purchasing a mainframe led Digital Equipment Corporation to develop the **minicomputer**, the first of which was released in 1959. These machines were much smaller and easier to use than the mainframes of the time, and they did not require the same sophisticated operating environments. The types of tasks they were used to perform, however, are very similar to that of mainframes. Though they are still known by their original name, they are also sometimes called *departmental computers* because they are inexpensive enough to be purchased by individual departments of large companies. Minicomputers became commonplace in small companies for the same reason. Some minis are designed to be used by a single person; others can be accessed by hundreds of people simultaneously. Figure 1-9 shows a typical minicomputer.

Microcomputers

First appearing on the market in the mid-1970s (Figure 1-10), **microcomputers**, which fit on a desktop, were also known as personal computers because they were intended to be used by individuals, rather than by whole companies or organizations. As these computers became more powerful, they began to enter the business world, taking over at least part of the role that had been played by minis and mainframes. Microcomputers have not completely replaced mainframes in large organizations, however, because micros cannot handle the same volume of data. Because most microcomputers are designed to service the needs of a

Figure 1-9   A minicomputer. The processing components are in the cabinet on the left.

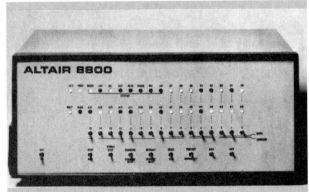

Figure 1-10   The first commercially successful microcomputer, the Altair.

single person, they tend to be less expensive, easier to use, and more flexible than either minis or mainframes. Some of today's micros, however, can be used by more than one person at a time. These new high-powered personal computers have created a new and important category called **workstations**. Workstations that can easily fit on a desktop rival the speed and power of popular minicomputers of the 1960s and 1970s. Engineers are the most common users of workstations.

Today, microcomputers are themselves categorized by size. The original microcomputers, and still the most common size used, are known as *desktop computers* (Figure 1-11a) because they fit on a desk. This term has become a bit of a misnomer, because many full-size microcomputers are now designed to sit on the floor beneath a desk. The first portable microcomputers were released by a company called Osborne. Throughout the 1980s, **portables**, which folded up to the size of a briefcase, remained popular. Today, however, portables have largely been replaced by smaller computers called **laptops** (Figure 1-11b). Laptops weigh less than 10 pounds and fold down to the size of a two-inch-thick pad of paper, though sizes continue to decrease. Small laptops are often called **notebooks**.

As computers become smaller, people are more and more likely to carry them with them all of the time. Today, very small, limited-purpose computers, known as **palmtops** or **personal digital assistants (PDAs)** (Figure 1-11c), can perform a number of applications, such as keeping schedules, storing telephone numbers, taking notes, and so on. Some of these systems will even dial a telephone for you. These computers have several batteries and enough RAM to support whatever applications are built into the system, but they cannot run large programs like Windows or WordPerfect. Many PDAs are still a bit clumsy to use because the keypads are very small, and the LCD screens can be difficult to read. In the future, however, voice and written interaction will provide a more natural interface.

(a)   (b)   (c)

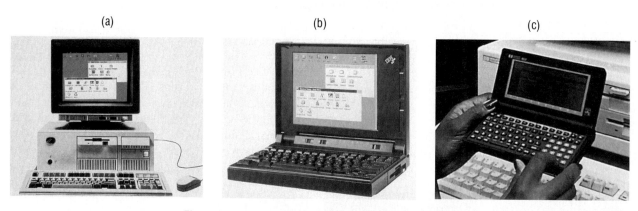

Figure 1-11   (a) A desktop computer; (b) a laptop; (c) a palmtop.

Parts of a Computer System

General purpose computers do not operate on their own like some special purpose computers, such as those found in a car. General purpose computers are interactive devices that must be part of a computer system in order to be useful. As shown in Figure 1-12 (on the next page), **computer systems** include four essential elements: hardware, software, data, and people. So far in this chapter, we have focused on computer hardware, but we must consider the entire system to understand how a computer can be used to perform useful work.

Hardware

The center of any computer system is, of course, the hardware. **Hardware** is the machinery of the computer system. It is what most people think of when they talk about computers. Therefore, when we use the term *computer* in this book, we mean hardware.

Early in this chapter, we defined a computer as "a device for processing data." Because the term *computer*, used alone, means "hardware," hardware is the set of devices that are used to process data. You can think of hardware as the part of the computer you can touch. We also said that a computer must have at least three parts: a processing device, an input device, and an output device.

The "guts" of a computer include the central processing unit (CPU) and memory. In a microcomputer, the CPU is called a *microprocessor*, because it consists of millions of microscopic circuits etched on a silicon chip. The most common input device for a computer is the keyboard. Other input devices can include a mouse, a trackball, a scanner, and a stylus and digitizer tablet. The most common output devices for general purpose computers are the monitor and the printer.

In addition to input, processing, and output devices, most computers contain one or two other important parts. **Storage devices** hold data much the way your brain stores memories. The most common storage devices are hard disk drives and diskette drives. Other storage devices include magnetic tape drives and CD-ROM drives. **Communication devices** enable computer systems to share data. When computer systems need to share data over distances, they do so using telephone lines with the help of a modem. Computers can also share data by connecting them to form a network. Figure 1-13 summarizes the most common microcomputer devices.

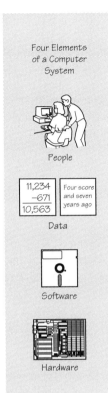

Four Elements of a Computer System

People

11,234
−671
10,563

Four score and seven years ago

Data

Software

Hardware

Figure 1-12
Every computer system must include hardware, software, data, and people.

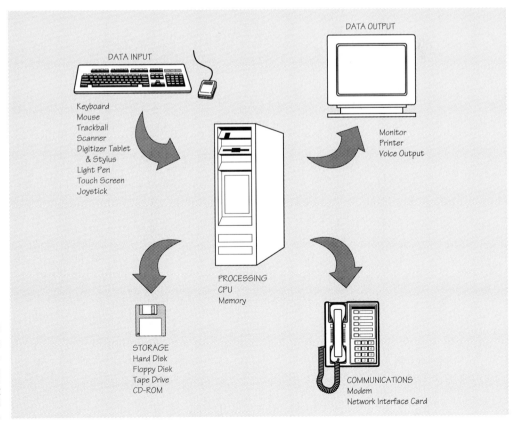

DATA INPUT

Keyboard
Mouse
Trackball
Scanner
Digitizer Tablet
 & Stylus
Light Pen
Touch Screen
Joystick

DATA OUTPUT

Monitor
Printer
Voice Output

PROCESSING
CPU
Memory

STORAGE
Hard Disk
Floppy Disk
Tape Drive
CD-ROM

COMMUNICATIONS
Modem
Network Interface Card

Figure 1-13
Microcomputers include devices for input, processing, output, storage, and communication. The most common devices are listed here under their function.

Software

To be useful for processing data, a general purpose computer needs sets of instructions, which are called **programs**. A collection of programs is called **software**. The two terms are often used interchangeably.

In some special purpose computers, software is not required, because electronic instructions have been built into the circuitry of the hardware. In general purpose computers, however, software is always required. Another way to say this is that general purpose computers are programmable machines. The hardware is built to perform many different types of processing; the software tailors the hardware to perform the type that is needed.

Two main types of software are used in general purpose computers: operating systems and application software. The operating system contains the basic instructions that manage the various hardware devices. The operating system must be loaded before any application software can. To **load** a piece of software is to move it from a storage device into the computer's memory, which is a processing device. Application software is what you use to perform a certain type of task. For example, word processing software is used to create text documents on a computer. Database management software is used to access, manipulate, and organize large amounts of data. Figure 1-14 lists some of the most popular application programs and operating systems.

Data

The third essential element of the computer system is data. For most general purpose computers, **data** consists of numbers, letters, images, and sounds. The type of data that is processed by the computer is determined by the software being used. For example, word

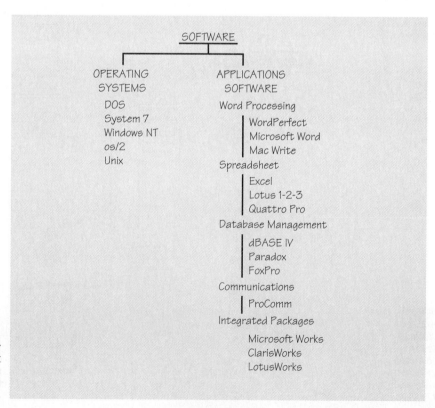

Figure 1-14
Just a few of the most popular application programs and operating systems.

processing software is designed to process text. Spreadsheet software can process text, but it is especially useful in processing numbers. Graphics software is used to process images. Multimedia software can process all three of these types, plus sound and video.

People

Naturally, a computer system isn't going to do much on its own; it generally requires a person to operate it. Because the computer is a tool that is used to accomplish a task, the person operating the computer is often referred to as the **user**.

Comprehension Questions

1. Is a single computer used by 10 people in a small office likely to be a supercomputer, mainframe, a minicomputer, or a microcomputer? Why?

2. Name a type of computer that is appropriate for a businessperson who needs to take a computer along on trips.

3. Is a monitor hardware or software? Is a standard computer monitor a processing device, an input device, or an output device?

Using What You Know

1. General purpose computer systems consist of hardware, software, data, and people, but special purpose computers often do not. Which of the four elements are missing from many special purpose computers? Give three examples.

2. List three reasons why you, as president of BVOS, might want to have a laptop rather than a desktop computer for your personal use.

3. Rather than calling them storage and communication devices, some people refer to disk drives and modems as input/output devices. How can you defend this terminology?

Summary Points

What Is a Computer?

☐ A computer is an electronic device for processing data.

☐ At the minimum, a computer must have an input device, a processing device, and an output device.

Special Purpose Computers

☐ Special purpose computers are designed to address just one kind of problem. Automated teller machines (ATMs) and point of sale (POS) computers are two examples of special purpose computers.

General Purpose Computers

☐ Business and home computers are general purpose computers because they are used to perform a variety of tasks.

Supercomputers

☐ Supercomputers are very powerful computers using many processors working in parallel to solve large mathematical problems.

☐ Supercomputers are often kept in special rooms where they are protected from dust, temperature changes, and electrical surges.

Mainframes

☐ Mainframes are used by large organizations where many people need access to large company data files.

☐ A mainframe must be able to accomplish a variety of business-related tasks.

☐ Many mainframes must also be kept in special rooms.

Minicomputers

☐ A minicomputer is a small, less expensive version of a mainframe.

Microcomputers

☐ Microcomputers were originally intended to be used by individuals, though multiuser micros are now available.

☐ The microcomputer has taken over part of the role of the corporate mainframe.

☐ Most micros are referred to as desktop computers; the smaller models are called portables, laptops, notebooks, palmtops, or PDAs; larger models are referred to as workstations.

Parts of a Computer System

Hardware

☐ The term *computer* generally means hardware.

☐ Hardware devices are categorized into processing, input, output, storage, and communication devices.

Software

☐ Software is the collection of instructions that tell the hardware what to do.

☐ The operating system must be loaded before application software because it is in charge of managing the hardware devices.

☐ Application software turns the computer into a specialized tool capable of performing a specific kind of task.

Data

☐ For general purpose computers, data consists of numbers, letters, images, and sounds.

People

☐ An integral part of the computer system, people interact with computers at all levels.

Knowing the Facts

True/False

1. Some microcomputers can be used by more than one person simultaneously.
2. Disk drives are storage devices.
3. The leading manufacturer of supercomputers is DEC.
4. Software determines the type of data that is processed.
5. Supercomputers are designed to handle large mathematical problems.
6. At the minimum, a computer must have five parts: processing, input, output, communication, and storage devices.
7. Supercomputers and mainframes are often kept in special rooms.
8. Application software must be loaded before any other type of software.
9. Some mainframes can be used by thousands of people at once.
10. Until the mid-1970s, the most common type of computer was the minicomputer.

Short Answer

1. The keypad on the bank's ATM is a(n) _____ device.
2. A computer designed to address just one kind of problem is a _____.
3. The biggest manufacturer of mainframes is _____.
4. Computer systems consist of hardware, software, _____, and people.
5. The terms *software* and _____ are used interchangeably.
6. In a computer system, _____ tailors the hardware to perform the task that is needed.
7. A monitor is a(n) _____ device.
8. In which decade were the first microcomputers released?
9. The Digital Equipment Corporation developed the first _____ in 1959.
10. What type of computer does the National Oceanographic and Aeronautic Agency use to help predict the weather?

Answers

True/False

1. T
2. T
3. F
4. T
5. T
6. F
7. T
8. F
9. T
10. F

Short Answer

1. input
2. special purpose computer
3. IBM
4. data
5. programs
6. software
7. output
8. 1970s
9. minicomputer
10. supercomputer

Challenging Your Understanding

1. How are business users like scientific users? How are they different?

2. Summarize the differences among mainframes, minicomputers, and microcomputers. What do you think the differences among these systems will be in the future?

3. Do you think there will be more general purpose or special purpose computers in the future? Why?

4. Some think that the ATM is an example of a stop-gap technology. A stop-gap technology is something that exists to help an organization or society move from one technological infrastructure to another. The ATM provides relatively quick access to cash which can be used for purchases at stores that for some reason do not accept checks or credit cards. The stop-gap service the ATM provides is to supply currency for transactions that are not yet computerized. The fax, or facsimile machine, may also be a stop-gap technology. Do you think the ATM is a stop-gap technology? Why or why not? What about the fax?

The Computer Industry

Key Terms

Apple II
Apple Computer, Inc.
Borland International
Compaq Computer Corporation
compatible (clone)
competitive advantage
competitive necessity
computer information systems
Digital Equipment Corporation (DEC)
Hewlett-Packard Company
IBM Corporation
IBM PC
Lotus Development Corporation
Lotus 1-2-3
Macintosh
Microsoft Corporation
personal computer (PC)
timesharing
user friendly
WordPerfect
WordPerfect Corporation

Objectives

In this chapter, you will learn to:

- Be aware of the three biggest companies in the micro-computer industry today and give background information on each

- Understand the speed at which computer companies evolve

- Identify the difference between competitive advantage and competitive necessity

- Describe at least three cases in which computer information systems helped companies gain competitive advantages

- Describe the various roles that can be played by computer services companies

Hardware and Software Companies

The computer industry is composed of four parts:
- manufacturers of computer hardware and software
- companies that use computers
- companies that provide computer services
- individual computer users

In the 1960s and 1970s, the computer industry was already huge, but it was relatively stable. Computer hardware and software was made by large companies for large companies. Most computers were mainframes or early minicomputers bought by corporations or organizations that could afford them. During this period mainframe companies sold solutions — hardware and software bundled together for one purpose. It was many years before a separate software industry developed. The biggest mainframe producer by far was IBM, although other companies, such as DEC, Sperry, Hewlett-Packard, NCR, and Control Data, were also important.

Since the introduction of the microcomputer in the mid-1970s, the computer industry has exploded. At the same time, the stability of the business has disappeared. There are now thousands of companies making hardware and software, and many seem to appear and disappear overnight. Nevertheless, several companies have evolved and still maintain influence over the industry. In some cases, such as that of Control Data, the older companies have held on to their role in the large-computer market, choosing (for the most part) to avoid the volatile microcomputer industry. In other cases, such as those of Hewlett-Packard and IBM, the companies have diversified to capitalize on technological improvements and consumer demand for smaller computers. In addition, several important new companies have emerged.

A powerful example of the volatility in the computer industry is a company called Compaq, which we will examine more closely later in this chapter. The company, founded in 1982, quickly grew to challenge the giants, IBM and Apple, as a producer of microcomputers. At one point Compaq was the fastest growing company of all time, in any industry. However, as soon as Compaq undercut its chief rival IBM by establishing a reputation for quality and technological innovation, Compaq was itself undercut. A new breed of companies, led by Dell Computers, offered even lower prices and more innovative sales methods. The quick success of these companies spawns new questions. Will Compaq return to its former prominence? Will IBM? How will Dell counter? We really don't know how the race for domination will turn out. What we do know is that we must acknowledge this market volatility and always consider it when making personal or professional computer-related decisions.

To give you a sense for the industry — how it has evolved and who are the biggest names — here are a few of its most famous success stories.

IBM

Herman Hollerith was an employee with the U.S. Census Bureau during the latter part of the nineteenth century. In those days, all census data was tabulated by hand — a huge, expensive, and time-consuming task. In 1890, it was estimated that the process of counting the census data for that year would take more than 10 years. Because the census was (and is) taken every 10 years, this meant the data for one census wouldn't be available until after the next census was taken.

Figure 2-1

Herman Hollerith and his tabulating machine.

Noting this gross inefficiency, Mr. Hollerith invented an electrical tabulating machine that was capable of reading punched cards the size of a one-dollar bill. Using Hollerith's machine (shown in Figure 2-1), the Census Bureau was able to finish tabulating the 1890 census in two and a half years, thus saving five million dollars on the project. With his invention, Hollerith formed the Tabulating Machine Company and sold the machines around the world. Most of Hollerith's machines were used for accounting purposes.

In 1911, Hollerith's company merged with two clock makers and a company that made scales and food slicers to become the Computing-Tabulating-Recording Company (CTR). In 1914, Thomas J. Watson joined the company. Ten years later, he took over and renamed it **International Business Machines Corporation**, or **IBM**.

IBM began manufacturing computers in 1953 with the 701 model. The company's first major success was the IBM 650 in 1954, and its second, the 1401, in 1959. The System/360, introduced in 1964, was the first family of compatible computers and set a standard for all IBM mainframes still in use today. By the 1970s IBM controlled more than 70 percent of the computer market.

In 1981, IBM entered the microcomputer market with the **IBM PC** (Figure 2-2 on the following page). The IBM PC was designed to be easy to use and expandable. The microcomputer had emerged only a few years earlier when the first successful microcomputer kits were sold to computer hobbyists. Throughout the mid- and late 1970s, a number of manufacturers sold microcomputers, but the industry continued to be dominated by hobbyists and home programmers. These early users envisioned the microcomputer progressing to the point of becoming a valuable tool for the home.

To the surprise of the industry, however, the home computer market did not evolve as quickly as many experts predicted. Instead, the first major users of the PC were businesses, and the first programs that were created for the IBM PC were aimed for business users. As it turned out, this turn of events worked well for IBM. Because businesses naturally needed to communicate with one another, there was an urgent need for standards in the tumultuous microcomputer market. Within 18 months, the IBM PC was a clear market leader and the de facto standard.

In addition to its immediate success, another reason the IBM PC became the market standard was that its design was easily copied. In fact, the computer's specifications were made public. As a result, a number of **clones** or **compatibles** were developed to take advantage of the marketing opportunity IBM had opened up. Ten years after the introduction of the PC, clone makers such as Compaq and Dell have undermined the dominance of IBM, whose market share is less than one quarter of what it once was. The term **personal computer**, or **PC** came to refer to both IBMs and compatibles. In this book, we use this common meaning for PC. When we refer to IBM's machine, we call it the IBM PC.

Despite IBM's diminished market share, the company still had revenue of $64.8 billion in 1991. IBM still controls 33 percent of the large-computer market — twice as much as the second largest manufacturer, Fujitsu. In the personal computer market, IBM, which has just been surpassed by Apple, now controls only 15 percent. One of IBM's most successful microcomputer models, the PS/2, is shown in Figure 2-3. IBM's massive market presence is the reason industry experts say, "When IBM sneezes, the computer industry catches cold."

Figure 2-2   The original IBM PC, released in 1981.

Figure 2-3   One of IBM's biggest sellers, the PS/2.

Apple Computer, Inc.

On April 1, 1976, Steve Jobs and Steve Wozniak (Figure 2-4) founded **Apple Computer, Inc.** to manufacture microcomputers. They started in a garage in Palo Alto, California, in what

Figure 2-4
Steve Wozniak and Steve Jobs, founders of Apple Computer. They are shown holding the system board for the Apple I.

later came to be called Silicon Valley. In six years, Apple was on the Fortune 500 list and earned revenue of almost one billion dollars.

Apple's first computer, the Apple I, was introduced in 1976 at the Palo Alto Homebrew Computer Club. The first Apple Is took 60 hours to build, had no keyboard, power supply, or monitor, and had very little memory. They were intended for computer hobbyists who wanted to write programs. In 1977, Apple released the first **Apple II**, the series that brought the company success (Figure 2-5). The Apple II had an open architecture, which meant that

Figure 2-5 The evolution of Apple's computers, left to right starting with the top row: The Apple II, the Mac SE, the Mac II, and the PowerBook.

as the user's needs changed, the computer could be expanded with hardware from Apple and other vendors. The various versions of the Apple II became especially popular in elementary and high schools, primarily because of grant programs that the company provided as an incentive to use computers. Hundreds of educational programs are written for the Apple II.

The infiltration by IBM into the microcomputer industry was hard on Apple. In just a few years, IBM PCs and compatibles virtually controlled the market. In 1983, the former president of PepsiCo, John Sculley, took over Apple, and a series of new computer products were developed. Most notably, Apple released the Lisa, a graphics-oriented computer that was easy to use. Using a pointing device called a *mouse* to move items around on the screen, the user could learn to use the Lisa in far less time than it took to learn the Apple II. Unfortunately, the Lisa was priced too high and was not a commercial success.

Apple Computer's biggest success, however, came with the **Macintosh**, or the Mac, as it came to be known. The Mac was first released in 1984 and quickly became the epitome of the term **user friendly**, meaning it was easy to use. The first Macs, the Macintosh and the Mac Plus, came in a semiportable unit with a small, built-in monitor, a separate keyboard, and a mouse.

The Mac family of computers steadily diversified. In 1987, Apple introduced the Mac II, which had a larger, separate monitor that was available with color. The original Mac did not gain widespread use in the lucrative business market. With the Mac II, however, which looked more like the PC, the Mac's popularity broadened. Today, the Macintosh line is a strong competitor of the PC, and Apple continues its prominence in the areas of user-friendly design and high-quality graphics output.

Microsoft Corporation

Figure 2-6
The founders of Microsoft, Paul Allen and Bill Gates.

The creation of **Microsoft Corporation** is another legendary success story of the microcomputer industry. The story actually begins at a college prep school in Seattle, Washington, where Bill Gates and Paul Allen began learning to program in the school's new computer lab. The young friends' computer skills became so advanced that they obtained free computer time in return for finding flaws in the minicomputer they were using.

In 1975, Gates saw an article for the new Altair 8800, which was being sold by Micro Instrumentation and Telemetry Systems (MITS). Gates and Allen (shown in Figure 2-6) knew that the new computer was not useful to hobbyists without a programming language — preferably BASIC — that would run on it. The two young men created their own version of BASIC to run on the machine and flew to Albuquerque to sell their product to MITS. After initial success, Gates dropped out of Harvard, moved to New Mexico with Allen, and formed Microsoft to continue work on MBASIC, or Microsoft BASIC. Soon they were adapting MBASIC to run on other new microcomputers, and Microsoft became a highly profitable business.

Gates and Allen got their biggest break, however, when IBM came to them in 1980 to create an operating system for its first microcomputer, the IBM PC. For a small company like Microsoft, the undertaking was enormous, and they were given only one year to complete the whole job. Fortunately, Microsoft was able to purchase another company's operating system and adapt it to IBM's needs. Microsoft met its deadline, and the PC was released with a new operating system called DOS. Although the success of the PC essentially spelled success for Microsoft, the software company made even more money by selling DOS to other microcomputer vendors who make clones.

But Microsoft did not stop with DOS and BASIC, as you can see by the products shown in Figure 2-7 on the following page. Gates was quick to diversify and create other pieces of

Figure 2-7
Some of Microsoft's biggest sellers: DOS, Word, Works. Excel, and Fox Pro.

Figure 2-8
Bill Gates.

software. During the 1980s, Microsoft entered the application software market with Microsoft Works, Word, and Excel. There were two versions of each program: one for the Mac and one for the PC. All three programs were extremely successful. Later, Microsoft introduced Windows, a graphics-based operating environment that runs under DOS and is similar to the Macintosh interface. Two or more applications can be open and running at one time, and users can switch back and forth between them.

With DOS alone, Microsoft could have been the biggest player in the microcomputer software industry. With BASIC and Microsoft's heavy arsenal of application software, there is no contest. Microsoft, still under Gates's direction (Figure 2-8), is now the number one influence on microcomputer software.

Other Important Companies

There are so many makers of computer equipment and developers of computer software that it would be impossible even to list them here. It also would not be appropriate, because we acknowledge the ever-changing landscape of the computer industry as one of the few constants. In the interest of acquainting you with a few more, here is a short list.

DEC. Digital Equipment Corporation, commonly known as Digital or **DEC**, was founded in 1957 by an MIT researcher named Kenneth Olsen. Olsen wanted to build computers that were powerful, yet relatively inexpensive. These computers, which sold for far less than their million-dollar competitors, were controlled with the help of a television monitor and a keyboard. With the success of DEC's PDP series, the minicomputer was born. By the mid-1970s, DEC was a leader in the minicomputer market and posed a significant challenge to IBM's dominance of the computer industry. In 1977, DEC released its first VAX computer. VAX computers come in all sizes, from micro to mainframe, and the same programs can be run on all of them. The VAX achieved widespread popularity during the 1980s. In addition, DEC makes compatibles and printers that compete in the PC market.

Compaq Computer Corporation. Compaq Computer Corporation was founded in 1982 and achieved initial success by making some of the first portable clones. Compaq continues to make both desktop microcomputers and portables. Compaq's success lies in the quality of its systems; the failure rate for Compaq computers is far below the average for clones. Compaq remains one of the largest microcomputer manufacturers. Other major clone manufacturers include Dell, NEC, and Toshiba.

Hewlett-Packard Company.   Hewlett-Packard Company started making computers in the mid-1960s. Much greater customer recognition came, however, when the company released the HP-35, the first pocket calculator, in 1972 (Figure 2-9a). Today, it is a major presence in the microcomputer industry, largely thanks to the HP LaserJet (Figure 2-9b), a desktop laser printer released in 1984, which made high-quality print and graphics available for microcomputers. Other major producers of printers include Panasonic, Epson, Okidata, and Apple.

(a)

(b)

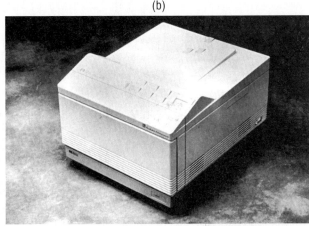

Figure 2-9
(a) Hewlett-Packard's first big success, a pocket calculator called the HP-35; (b) the Hewlett-Packard LaserJet printer.

Lotus Development Corporation.   Lotus Development Corporation created the industry standard for spreadsheet software with **Lotus 1-2-3** (Figure 2-10). Microsoft Excel and Borland's Quattro Pro now pose a major threat to Lotus' domination of the market, but all other spreadsheets are still compared to 1-2-3.

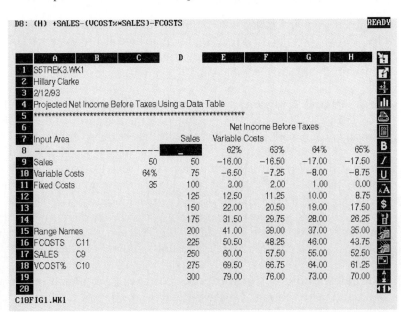

Figure 2-10
Lotus 1-2-3, the industry standard in electronic spreadsheets.

WordPerfect Corporation. During the late 1980s, the equivalent of Lotus in the word processing market was the **WordPerfect Corporation**, with its industry-standard word processor, **WordPerfect** (Figure 2-11). As with 1-2-3, WordPerfect's lead is being challenged, in this case by Microsoft Word.

```
File Edit Search Layout Mark Tools Font Graphics Help        (Press F3 for Help)
                          Shane Miller
                   Total Engineering Concepts
                       42 Scatman Way
                     Cruthers, GA  29987



April 21, 1993


Mark Lakeman
Waste Disposal Inc.
4780 Skypark Drive
Torrance, CA  90505

Dear Mr. Lakeman,

I found last Thursday's meeting to be both productive and
enjoyable.  While investigating your question regarding the
isotopic composition of our nitrogen bath, a number of new issues
have presented themselves.  For example, the need for a catalytic
reagent in Phase III electrolysis may preclude the achievement of
.001M impurity levels in Phase IV separations.  Additionally, the█
C:\CORRES\BFD1PERM\3DVISWP.DOC              Doc 1 Pg 1 Ln 2.5" Pos 3.65"
```

Figure 2-11
WordPerfect.

Borland International. Since its acquisition of Ashton-Tate, **Borland International** has dominated the market for database management software. Ashton-Tate created dBASE II, the first database program for microcomputers. The latest version, dBASE IV, is the market leader. Borland also acquired another popular database program called Paradox (Figure 2-12). In addition, Borland is the leader in the computer language field.

```
System  File  Edit  Database  Record  Program  Window  Browse
                              PERSONAL
   Lastname    Firstname  Mi  Spousename  Address                City          St
   Gossnergan  Ed         Y   Turan       321 Strata Ln.         Boulder       CO
   Mikelk      Warren         Judy        5 Sign Drive           Los Angeles   CA
   English     Jo         G   Richard     12 Davis Plaza         Sausalito     CA
   Mostov      Dave       S   Jill        20 Turbofan Drive      Greensboro    NC
   Fox         Reid       M   Martha      8681 Absence Freya Estat Eureka      CA
   Byron       Peter          Liz         8 Bogota Road          Havelock      NC
   Sine        Marty      N   Nadine      204 Roadside Dr.       New Orleans   LA
   Pecukonis   Ronald     C               869 Linus Melcher Plaza Houston      TX
   Barrett     Judy       R   Leo         3 Regent Saloon Avenue Oak Park      IL
   Casey       Jeff       S   Lee         9692 Hebrew Blvd.      Chicago       IL
   Barkoe      Barbara        Bert        111 Dash Spurn Street  Madison       WI
   Hale        Carol      L   Neal        68 Conspire            Fort Collins  CO
   Barkoe      Martha                     8819 Viscous Tied Lane Newburyport   MA
   Pierson     Michelle       Glenn       145 Downbeat Drive     W. Palm Beach FL
   Bush        Don        S               Mung Drive 712         Saxtus River  UT
   Paretta     Lenny      R   Joan        6 Toward Somber        Hamden        CT
   Mikelk      Pat        K               1409 Unknown Trail     Huntington Bc CA
   Colby       Parky      L   Louis       425 Dollop Pk.         METAIRIE      LA
   Davis       Edward     L   M.          100 Thulium Squibb Junct Chico       CA
   Rasmussen   Mike       S               6622 Conn Trail        Nashua        NH
```

Figure 2-12
Paradox, sold by Borland.

Comprehension Questions

1. Could Compaq claim to make a PC if the original PC was made by IBM? Why or why not?
2. Which was more user friendly, the Lisa or the Apple II?
3. What type of computer do you think kept the price of the IBM PC down?

Using What You Know

1. Why do you think IBM made the specifications for the PC public?
2. Why do you think John Sculley was hired by Apple Computer?
3. Why do you think software companies appear and disappear more quickly than hardware companies?

Major Computer Users

Computers can be used to make a process either more efficient or more effective. In the business world, using computers to increase efficiency or effectiveness is most often done to gain a competitive advantage or as a competitive necessity. If a company uses computers in a new way that its competitors have not tried, the company is pursuing a **competitive advantage**. Innovations in using computers are therefore often associated with gaining competitive advantage. Once one company comes up with an innovative computer solution, though, other companies must eventually adopt the same innovation or come up with their own. Adopting a computer solution to keep up with competitors is a **competitive necessity**. For example, most modern companies have computerized accounting systems as a competitive necessity, because doing it any other way would put them at a disadvantage.

One of the current focuses of corporate management is on computer information systems for competitive advantage. A **computer information system** is an organized means of collecting and processing data to make the data useful to a company. Usually, a computer information system includes one or more computers, a collection of data called a database, and the programs for using the database.

Innovative computer solutions that help gain competitive advantage are often expensive and therefore risky. The following cases are well-known examples of how information can be used for competitive advantage. These cases demonstrate that the strategic value of a computer information system arises from the data that can be collected and made accessible, as well as the creativity with which computers are used to process that data.

American Airlines' Sabre System

Sabre has been highly publicized as one of the most successful examples of a computer information system. In brief, Sabre is the system American Airlines developed to help the company determine how many flights it should schedule and how many passengers must be on a flight for it to be profitable. With Sabre (Figure 2-13 on the next page), American Airlines maintains an accurate and up-to-date accounting of airline seats. The system has allowed the company to fine-tune its daily operations to maximize occupancy and compute load factors affecting the planes.

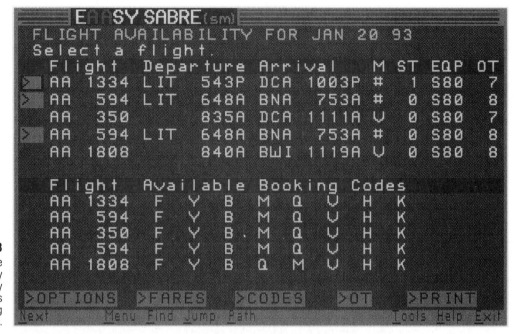

Figure 2-13

American Airlines' Sabre program gave the company a competitive advantage by streamlining its sales operation and maximizing flight occupancy.

One of the major benefits of obtaining this information was discovering that 20 percent of American Airlines' customers were accounting for a far greater percentage of the total seats booked. When the company's marketing personnel saw these statistics, they invented the frequent flyer program. This is an example of changes that were aimed at making a company more efficient, which ended up making it more effective as well.

Sabre's success is measured in more than its 500 percent return on investment. It is also measured by the marketing innovation of the first frequent flyer program and by the information gained about the marketing strategies of competitors.

American Hospital Supply Corporation's ASAP System

Another firm that has been recognized for its innovative use of computer information systems is American Hospital Supply Corporation. Its Analytic Systems Automatic Purchasing (ASAP) system was originally designed to solve its inefficient order-taking and delivery system, which had caused problems with one of the company's major customers.

The ASAP system allowed customers to place their orders directly, using computer terminals located at the hospital. As hospitals realized the ease with which they could order supplies, they tended to switch to American Hospital as their primary supplier. Hospitals saw availability of information and ease of ordering as valuable enhancements in service. Hospital agents were able to scan through up-to-date price lists quickly and conveniently, and then place their orders, which were filled promptly.

The information provided by ASAP to American Hospital Supply's customers, and vice versa, proved to be the competitive edge that ensured the company's success. As a result of ASAP, many of American Hospital's minor competitors suffered significant losses and were forced out of the industry. Other competitors, such as Johnson & Johnson, suffered reductions in their market share.

USAA

USAA is an insurance company that caters to military personnel and their families. In a bold, risky move, USAA decided to use information technology in an effort to reengineer its organizational processes. One notable change USAA made was to adopt what is known as a *document imaging system*.

Insurance companies must manage massive amounts of correspondence — much of it in the form of standardized forms — related to individual clients and cases. Part of USAA's solution to this information management problem was to open all customer correspondence in the mail room and place the letters or forms on a scanning device that looks like a photocopier. The scanner makes an image of the correspondence, which is stored in the company's computer system. The information from the scanned image is then available instantly to anybody using the computer system.

At USAA, insurance agents and claims representatives no longer have to wait while a single copy of an important document makes its way around the office. Now when a customer calls, the telephone system alerts an operator about who is calling, and the customer's information file is automatically presented to the operator before the call is even answered. By having all of the important information immediately available, the operator is able to better serve the customer.

Imaging systems have dramatically changed the ways that companies like USAA operate. In a manual system, information must travel sequentially around an office or from one office to another. Processing of documents must also occur in sequence, and it is difficult to share information. An imaging system allows several employees to use information at the same time, and the whole processing job happens much more quickly. USAA's system made the company far more effective because customers had their claims settled in far less time than it took using the manual system.

American Express

The American Express card operates without a preset credit limit. Instead, American Express (AMEX) uses a computer system to make decisions about credit approval each time a card member makes a purchase. The store salesperson swipes the card through a special card reader that translates information contained on the card's magnetic strip to a central American Express office. Potential card purchases are analyzed to determine whether they are consistent with previous purchases. If they are, then the purchase is automatically approved. If the purchase is large and inconsistent with previous purchases, an AMEX representative will pick up the phone and gather more information.

Before AMEX adopted its new computer information system, all authorizations were made manually by a set of authorizers — a time-consuming and expensive process. The automated authorization process was created to speed authorization and to save AMEX the cost of hiring authorizers. The rules for AMEX authorization were created by interviewing the authorizers. The criteria the authorizers used were programmed into the automatic authorization program. Now most credit approvals are made without human intervention. Other credit card issuers have followed American Express's lead in the credit authorization procedure.

Computer Services Companies

In between the organizations using computers and the companies making hardware or developing software, there is a third group that has emerged: computer services companies.

Timesharing

The meaning of the term *computer services* has changed over the years. During the 1960s and 1970s, most computers were mainframes and minicomputers. Because these large computers allowed many employees to use them simultaneously, companies could often address many of their problems by buying a single computer.

Still, buying a single computer was expensive. Companies with computers looked for any way possible to recoup the cost of the machine. One common method they used was the timesharing system. In general, **timesharing** refers to multiple users sharing a single central processing unit (CPU). As a computer service, timesharing is something that companies with computers offer to companies without computers. Large computer systems are not turned on and off, so there is usually a lot of time when a company is not using its computer. If the company offers timesharing, other companies or individuals can pay the company for the privilege of using the unused computer time. Timesharing in this sense has become less common as microcomputers have gained in popularity and power.

You will also hear the word *timesharing* used as a generic term for the practice of many individuals within a single organization sharing the resources of the mainframe computer. Timesharing is the process of dividing the computer's attention among many users, one user after another. Because a mainframe computer can execute hundreds or even thousands of instructions in the time it takes a human to execute two keystrokes, it seems as if every user is getting the computer's complete attention.

Consulting

Almost every industry uses computers in one way or another. In many cases, the way companies use computers has become quite exotic. In most of the situations described in the last section, the company using the computer solution is not entirely responsible for the development of the solution. In some cases, a computer services company has been responsible for masterminding and setting up the computer information system that fostered the competitive advantage.

Many modern computer services companies are a type of consulting firm that specializes in setting up computer information systems for other companies. Some of the best-known computer services companies are Andersen Consulting, Perot Systems, EDS, Businessland, Systematics, and Computer Sciences Corporation. Some larger companies such as IBM, McDonnell Douglas, and Martin Marietta have computer services branches. One of the more famous firms, Electronic Data Systems, or EDS, was founded by H. Ross Perot, who mounted a much publicized presidential candidacy in 1992.

The employees of computer services companies are often the graduates of MIS (Management Information Systems) departments. In fact, some of the most common employers of MIS graduates are computer services companies.

Software Developers

Some computer services companies are considered software developers rather than consulting firms. Similarly, some software developers are considered computer services companies. Sometimes a company is both. The reason is that developing computer information systems can involve either writing a new program or tailoring an existing program to meet a particular need.

For example, the software that is sold as database management software is normally very open-ended, meaning you can use the software to manage data in a variety of ways. The software is so open-ended, in fact, that using it to manage data just the way you want may take a considerable investment of time. As a result, many programs have emerged that manage databases for specific purposes, such as accounting, project management, and so on.

The companies that develop such software are considered computer services companies. Depending on the way they define the term, some people describe all software developers as computer services companies, simply because they are providing business tools.

Comprehension Questions

1. If you were starting an airline company today, would installing a computer system to track reservations be a competitive advantage or a competitive necessity?

2. Does the creation of a customer service department make a company (primarily) more efficient or more effective?

3. Why aren't innovations in computer information systems associated with competitive necessity?

Using What You Know

1. Explain how a system similar to Sabre might be used at BVOS.

2. If you, as an entrepreneur, are seeking a competitive advantage, why might it be better to find a computer services company that is not also a software developer?

3. How might a system like ASAP be used at BVOS?

Summary Points

Hardware and Software Companies

☐ The introduction of the microcomputer destabilized an industry that had been dominated by a few large companies, especially IBM.

☐ Some of the most important hardware companies in the microcomputer industry today are Apple, Digital Equipment Corporation (DEC), Compaq, and Hewlett-Packard.

☐ The most influential software companies in the microcomputer industry include Microsoft, Lotus, Word-Perfect, and Borland.

Major Computer Users

☐ Companies try to gain a competitive advantage with innovation in computer information systems; they adopt widely used techniques as competitive necessity. Examples of such systems are American Airlines' Sabre system, American Hospital Supply Corporation's ASAP system, the image processing system adopted by USAA, and the automated credit approval system used by American Express.

Computer Services Companies

Timesharing

☐ The original computer service was timesharing, in which companies with computers sell the unused time on their large-computer systems to companies that lack such systems.

☐ Timesharing also refers to the process of dividing a mainframe computer's attention among many users while appearing to serve them all simultaneously.

Consulting

☐ Many modern computer services companies are consultants that help other companies set up computer information systems.

Software Developers

☐ Companies that create computer information systems can very easily become software developers because they often create programs to solve their clients' problems.

☐ Some people consider all software development companies to be computer services companies.

Knowing the Facts

True/False

1. Timesharing as a computer service is an arrangement between a company with a computer and one without.

2. A document imaging system can be part of a computer information system used to gain competitive advantage.

3. At one point, Compaq was the fastest growing company of all time.

4. IBM is the biggest player in the microcomputer hardware industry.

5. Innovations in computer information systems are usually associated with competitive necessity.

6. Hewlett-Packard gained widespread recognition by making the first pocket calculator.

7. DEC initially gained success by manufacturing minicomputers.

8. Compaq initially gained success making portable PCs.

9. Microsoft's first product was DOS, the operating system for the IBM PC and the compatibles.

10. The first computer by Apple had no keyboard and no monitor.

Short Answer

1. The introduction of the _____ in the mid-1970s destabilized the computer industry.

2. _____ created an electronic tabulating machine for the U.S. Census Bureau.

3. Although they do not all do consulting or work for individual clients, some people consider all _____ to be computer services companies, because their products help businesses and organizations.

4. Dividing a computer's attention among many users is known as _____.

5. Some of the most common employers of MIS graduates are _____.

6. The term _____ can include IBM microcomputers and compatibles.

7. When a computer information system is adopted by most of the firms in a given type of business, the system becomes a _____.

8. The product that sealed Microsoft's success was _____.

9. Two of the leading database programs, dBASE IV and Paradox, are both owned by _____ _____.

10. Jobs and Wozniak were the founders of _____ _____.

Answers

True/False

1. T
2. T
3. T
4. F
5. F
6. T
7. T
8. T
9. F
10. T

Short Answer

1. microcomputer
2. Herman Hollerith
3. software developers
4. timesharing
5. computer services companies
6. PC
7. competitive necessity
8. DOS
9. Borland International
10. Apple Computer

Challenging Your Understanding

1. In 1992, Bill Gates, CEO of Microsoft, was the richest American. What are the components of his success? What can Microsoft do in the future to maintain its power in the software market?

2. Is the term "clone" appropriate these days? Why or why not?

3. During the 1960s and 1970s, IBM spent more money on research and development (R&D) than its closest competitors made in revenues. What part does R&D play in the profitability of a computer company?

4. Most computer manufacturers have begun marketing their services as much or more than their products. Why do you think this is happening?

5. Do you think a computer can give a company a sustainable competitive advantage or just a temporary advantage?

Unit I Project

Identifying Market Leaders in the Computer Industry

Yamamoto and Company (Y&C) is a world-renowned business consulting company that monitors, analyzes, and forecasts worldwide issues related to the law, energy, technology, medicine, finance, demography, and culture. Yamamoto boasts the services of Nobel laureates, leading economists, and well-known scholars.

Your broad background, education, and quick intelligence have landed you an attractive junior analyst position in the U.S. office of Y&C. Your first assignment is in technology. When you report to work, you are assigned to Jennifer Andrews, senior technology analyst. Ms. Andrews is preparing an analysis of the computer industry.

Your job is to prepare a report detailing the major companies in the computer industry. Use any resources you feel are necessary to show market share, revenues, and other indicators for mainframe, minicomputer, and microcomputer manufacturers, as well as software developers and computer services companies. Your report should include graphs and tables detailing your findings.

Because you want to impress your boss, you are going one step further than requested. Using the data and your best guesses, forecast the future of the computer industry in the next decade. Be sure to tell Ms. Andrews what you found, how you arrived at your forecast, and what assumptions you made in order to create the forecast.

Solving Problems with Software

Unit II

Understanding the Needs of BVOS Staff

Recall from the Introduction that the problem-solving process can be broken into five stages:

1. Recognizing the problem
2. Understanding the problem
3. Compiling relevant information
4. Formulating and building the solution
5. Evaluating the solution

In the last unit, we looked at the big picture and tried to understand the problem of purchasing a computer system in general terms by giving an overview of the entire computer industry, both the producers and the users of hardware and

PROBLEM-SOLVING STEPS	RELATED TASKS
RECOGNIZE THE PROBLEM	Determine what processes should be computerized. • Writing memos, reports, correspondence • Analyzing financial data • Keeping records of customer transactions • Communicating within branch and with Toronto
UNDERSTAND THE PROBLEM	Determine software needs. • Word processing, spreadsheet, database, and communications packages.
COMPILE RELEVANT INFORMATION	Find appropriate sources of information. • Computer magazines • Colleagues and friends Determine what is relevant. • Decide which software features are necessary to meet your needs.
FORMULATE AND BUILD A SOLUTION	Take action. • Compare prices and features for popular packages in each of the four application areas needed.
EVALUATE THE SOLUTION	

Figure II-1 Steps 2, 3, and 4 of the problem-solving process involve several tasks that relate to software.

software. Now that you have a better idea of how Buena Vista Office Supply (BVOS) relates to other companies using computers, it's time to look more closely at the specific needs of your new company, do some research on the software market, and make some purchasing decisions. In other words, you will be moving through steps 2, 3, and 4 of the problem-solving process, focusing exclusively on software. Figure II-1 on the previous page details the tasks required by each step. We will add to these tasks when we repeat steps 2, 3, and 4 in the next unit, which focuses on hardware.

Dear _____,

As we agreed in our telephone conversation on Friday, you will be installing a computer system in your new branch office. The figures showing the difference between the revenue achieved by branches with and without computer systems speak for themselves.

The most important advantage of installing a computer system is the ability to automate the process of keeping track of inventory and taking customer orders. Branch owners who have switched from manual inventory methods to computerized methods will attest to greater efficiency, fewer errors, and even better job satisfaction among employees.

Automating your record keeping consists mainly of creating a database that contains:
- an itemized listing of your current inventory of office supplies
- a record of the inventory you have on order from the regional distributor
- a record of current orders from customers

All of this data is accessed automatically by your accounting system, which can keep track of accounts payable (essentially, money due to the regional distributor plus payroll) and accounts receivable (money due from your customers).

Because most of our branches use dBASE IV, that is the database software you should buy. Using dBASE will make it easier for you to trade information with the other branches. You have more leeway in other software-purchasing decisions, since compatibility with headquarters will not be as critical as with the database software. We will be more than happy, however, to give you advice about which products we like, which we don't, and which products our in-house system experts are familiar with.

I understand that you probably don't have much experience in setting up a computer system, much less an inventory database. Don't worry. As soon as you have your system running, we'll send down our in-house system experts, Diane Lindstrom and Mary Soriano, to help you set up the database and get you moving in the right direction. Essentially, they'll design the database for you and train your people how to use it. Lisa Yep, your accountant and inventory manager, will need to spend quite a bit of time with Diane and Mary while they are there, since Lisa will naturally become your local expert on the system.

Figure II-2   A letter from Elmer Phillips, the vice president of BVOS in Toronto.

The reason for focusing on software before hardware is that software is the real problem-solving tool of the computer system. You should find the software program that best fits your specific needs in terms of both function and final output format. Whatever gap exists between what your software can do and what you want it to do must be bridged by the most expensive element of the problem-solving process — human labor. Also, your system hardware will limit the kind of software you can choose. Since you don't yet own any hardware and you want the greatest possible freedom when choosing software, you should pick the software first. Once you have chosen the appropriate software to solve your business problems, you can make informed decisions about purchasing the right hardware to run your software.

What Your Computers Are For

Let's look now at the things you need software to do for you at BVOS.

The Inventory Database

When Elmer Phillips, the vice president of BVOS in Toronto, first introduced the idea of purchasing a computer system for your BVOS branch, he mainly talked about the advantages of keeping track of inventory and customer orders. Figure II-2 (on the previous page) is the first part of a letter he sent to you regarding the advantages of computerizing your office. Figure II-3 is a graph that shows the average BVOS revenue at branches with and without computer systems.

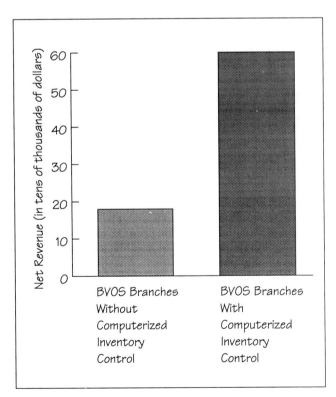

Figure II-3   Average revenue at BVOS branches with and without computer systems

Analyzing Financial Data

As president, your primary concern will be making sure your new enterprise is profitable. Therefore, another important advantage to having a computer system is the ability to keep track of your accounts, analyze financial data and create budgets like the one shown in Figure II-4 (on the next page). You will want to know what products are selling best, which are generating the most revenue, and how much revenue you need to turn a given profit. You can use your computer system to calculate, for example, how many dollars per square foot of floor space per year of profit must be figured and balanced with the needs of customers for low-profit items. There are numerous money-related questions that you will want to answer as your business gets moving.

Sending Correspondence to Clients and Associates

Another basic need you foresee is the ability to send letters to customers, potential customers, and headquarters. Rather than write letters by hand (which is unprofessional) or on a typewriter (which is cumbersome and slow), you would like to create, edit, and store your correspondence on your computer. Lisa, your manager, also wants to correspond with customers and headquarters using a computer.

Sending and Receiving Data Over the Phone Lines

You will need to obtain a great deal of data from headquarters on a regular basis. BVOS headquarters constantly adjusts prices, and you will need to keep abreast of these changes to keep your books straight. To serve their existing branch offices, headquarters has created a link to the BVOS mainframe in Toronto. The computer systems at your branch will be able to share information with the main computer system hundreds of miles away.

Finding Software Solutions

These four tasks — maintaining inventory and customer orders, analyzing financial data, sending correspondence, and exchanging information — can be accomplished with the aid of software. In order to solve these problems for BVOS, you will need to decide what software products are the right tools for the job. When you reach Chapter 4, you will make several purchasing decisions. Before you do so, however, we will first explain what software is and describe the various types that exist. Next, we will describe the most common software tools that are used in business today and look at a few of the most popular products. Finally, we will explain what programming is and how software is made.

When you are done with this unit, not only will you know what software is, you will understand the process of choosing software for a given type of problem, and you'll know how software is developed.

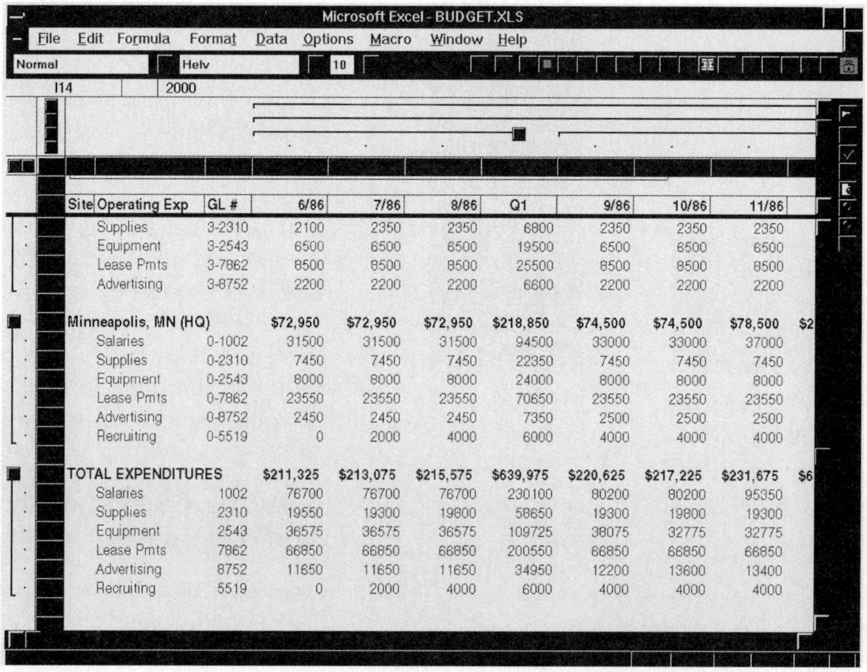

Site Operating Exp	GL #	6/86	7/86	8/86	Q1	9/86	10/86	11/86	
Supplies	3-2310	2100	2350	2350	6800	2350	2350	2350	
Equipment	3-2543	6500	6500	6500	19500	6500	6500	6500	
Lease Pmts	3-7862	8500	8500	8500	25500	8500	8500	8500	
Advertising	3-8752	2200	2200	2200	6600	2200	2200	2200	
Minneapolis, MN (HQ)		**$72,950**	**$72,950**	**$72,950**	**$218,850**	**$74,500**	**$74,500**	**$78,500**	**$2**
Salaries	0-1002	31500	31500	31500	94500	33000	33000	37000	
Supplies	0-2310	7450	7450	7450	22350	7450	7450	7450	
Equipment	0-2543	8000	8000	8000	24000	8000	8000	8000	
Lease Pmts	0-7862	23550	23550	23550	70650	23550	23550	23550	
Advertising	0-8752	2450	2450	2450	7350	2500	2500	2500	
Recruiting	0-5519	0	2000	4000	6000	4000	4000	4000	
TOTAL EXPENDITURES		**$211,325**	**$213,075**	**$215,575**	**$639,975**	**$220,625**	**$217,225**	**$231,675**	**$6**
Salaries	1002	76700	76700	76700	230100	80200	80200	95350	
Supplies	2310	19550	19300	19800	58650	19300	19800	19300	
Equipment	2543	36575	36575	36575	109725	38075	32775	32775	
Lease Pmts	7862	66850	66850	66850	200550	66850	66850	66850	
Advertising	8752	11650	11650	11650	34950	12200	13600	13400	
Recruiting	5519	0	2000	4000	6000	4000	4000	4000	

Figure II-4
Budgets help managers keep their businesses profitable.

C H A P T E R   3

Introduction to Software

Key Terms

application
application package
application software
batch processing
command-line interface
game software
graphical user interface (GUI)
icon
interactive program
menu-driven interface
operating system software
program
real-time processing
simulation software
software
tutorial software
user interface
utilities
overview

Objectives

In this chapter you will learn to:

- Understand in general terms what software is and the decision-making process involved in selecting software
- Compare the three main types of software used in business
- Name and describe at least five other software applications
- Compare the three types of user interface
- Describe the difference between real-time and batch processing

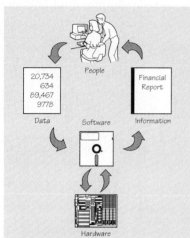

Figure 3-1
Software is the crucial link among people, the data they must process, and the hardware they use to do so.

Software and the Computer System

Software forms the link among people, hardware, data, and information, as shown in Figure 3-1. Specifically, software is what people use to manipulate data on a computer in order to obtain information.

To understand how software makes this interaction possible, this chapter will give you a comprehensive sense of what software is. We will start with a general definition, then fill it out by describing the major types of software that are available. Finally, we will explain briefly how software works.

What Is Software?

Software is the term used to describe the sets of instructions that control the computer. A piece of software — a series of instructions that perform a particular task — is commonly called a **program**. A group of program instructions is shown in Figure 3-2. Because most software products are created for accomplishing specific tasks, we refer to software as the main problem-solving component of the computer system.

In general, no matter what the task, software is designed to accept data and process it so it becomes useful and appears as information. The instructions that comprise the program tell the hardware how to interpret the data, how to manipulate or process it, and how to present it.

Types of Software

There are three main types of software discussed in this book: application software, utility software, and operating system software.

```
 System  File  Edit  Database  Record  Program  Window
                        W-ICITEM.PRG
 close data
 use inmprodt in 1 alias old
 use icitem-w in 2 alias new
 sele old
 go bottom
 m_oldrec=recno()
 sele new
 dele all
 pack
 go bottom
 m_newrec=recno()
 sele new

 if m_oldrec <> m_newrec then
     for i = 1 to (m_oldrec - m_newrec) + 1
         append blank
     endfor
 endif

            |<E:>|          |              |           |Ins  |Num
```

Figure 3-2
Each line in this program is an instruction that tells the computer what to do.

Application Software

Application software refers to any program the user employs to accomplish a specific type of task, as shown in Figure 3-3. The most common **applications** (tasks) that these programs accomplish are creating documents through word processing, creating spreadsheets, managing databases, creating graphic images, and communicating with other computers. There are, however, many other applications for which programs have been written. For a program to be called application software, the tasks it accomplishes must exist independent of the computer. For example, word processing is an application because the need to create documents would still exist even if there were no computers available to help us. Application programs are often characterized by enabling the user to obtain formatted output.

Some application software products you may have heard of are WordPerfect and Microsoft Word (word processing), Lotus 1-2-3 (spreadsheet), dBASE (database management), Harvard Graphics (graphics), and ProComm (communications).

Specific pieces of application software are often referred to as **application packages**, or simply as applications. Thus, the term *application* is sometimes used to mean the task, but it can also mean the software. A piece of application software is referred to as a package because it is capable of performing a number of different functions.

There are actually many other types of application software. Another type of application especially familiar to young people is **game software**, an example of which is shown in Figure 3-4 on the next page. Video game systems for the home, such as Nintendo and Sega, require software to operate. In fact, the software represents a bigger source of income for these companies than the hardware. Game software is also available to run on microcomputers.

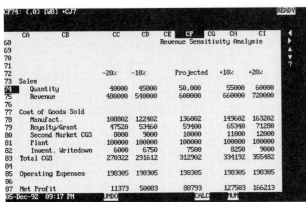

(a)

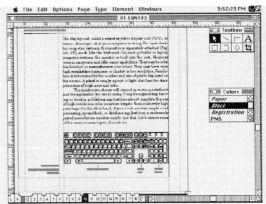

(b)

(c)

Figure 3-3
Three pieces of application software:
(a) a spreadsheet program;
(b) a desktop publishing program;
(c) a program for composing music.

Although the topic is not often discussed in computer textbooks, it isn't uncommon to find game software on computers that people use at work. If you watch your employees at BVOS, you may find that, over time, they will collect a few games to entertain themselves during their free time or when things are slow around the office.

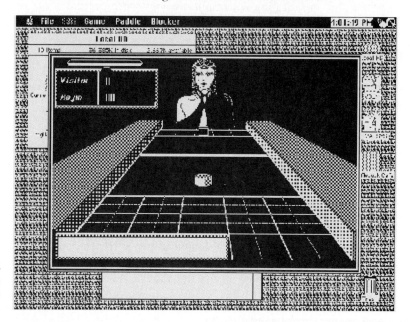

Figure 3-4
The computer game shown here is a type of application software.

The field of education has adopted some of the previously mentioned types of application software and added a few more, as shown in Figure 3-5. **Tutorial software** teaches a subject by directing the student through a series of steps — instructions that appear on-screen. In the more advanced tutorials, the program actually tests the student's comprehension during the program and reteaches material that the student did not properly understand. (Many application programs come with their own tutorials that teach you how to use the software.) At the other end of the scale in terms of complexity, businesses and government have developed simulation software to train employees. **Simulation software** uses the computer to imitate the interaction of real-world objects and activities, such as designing, building, operating, or repairing a car, jet, or forklift. Perhaps the best-known simulation software is the flight simulator. Extremely complex flight simulators are used to train astronauts and pilots, while scaled-down simulators are used as game software on microcomputers and home video game systems.

An exreme outgrowth of computer simulation, known as **virtual reality**, is in its infancy. This new field attempts to replace reality and fool our human senses. In the field of medicine, doctors can put on special headgear and visors with gloves in order to "operate" on the simulation of a real patient. The computer generates a stimulus that allows the doctor to experience the sight and touch of an operation — all without picking up a scalpel.

Utility Software

A second type of software are programs called **utilities**. Utilities accomplish specific tasks that relate to the internal functioning of the computer. Utility programs sort, copy, compare, search, and list files; they also perform diagnostic routines that gauge the condition and performance of the computer system. Operating systems, which we dicuss next, incorporate

Figure 3-5
Tutorial and simulation
software are types of
application software used
in education.

some utility functions. Other utilities are packaged separately. Some utility programs that you may have heard of are the Norton Utilities, Stacker, and FastBack. A screen from the PC Tools utility package is shown in Figure 3-6.

Programmers still use other types of utility programs called compilers and interpreters. These programs translate the material that the programmer writes into instructions the computer can understand. By doing so, these programs save today's software developers countless hours of work that previously had to be done by hand.

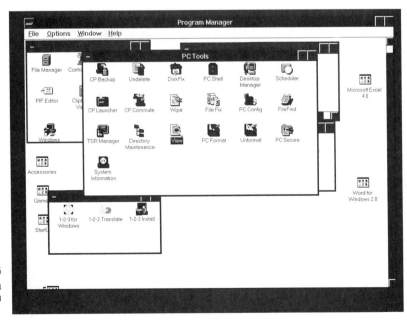

Figure 3-6
The PC Tools packages a
set of utility programs in
Macintosh or IBM versions

Operating System Software

The third type of software that you will learn about in this book is **operating system software** (usually referred to as simply **operating systems**, but also sometimes called **system software**). Before a microcomputer can load any other piece of software, it needs to load an operating system, or **OS**. The OS of a microcomputer contains basic instructions that help all the hardware components work together and help other software interact with the hardware. Some common operating systems are DOS, the Macintosh's System 7, OS/2, Windows NT, and Unix.

Although we will cover application and utility software in this unit, we will not cover operating systems until Unit III. The reason for this sequence is that understanding operating systems requires understanding the hardware that the OS controls.

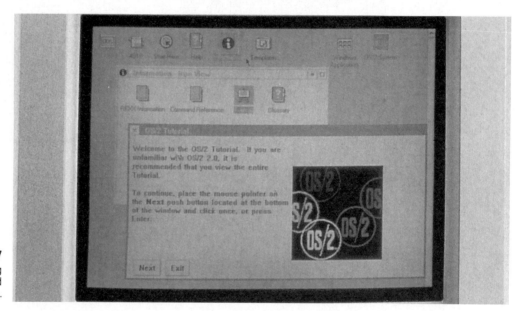

Figure 3-7
OS/2 2.0, an operating system for IBMs and compatibles.

Comprehension Questions

1. Autodesk, Inc., makes a software package that helps you design houses. What type of software do you think it is? Why?

2. Microsoft Windows includes a program that displays a clock on the screen. What type of software do you think the program is? Why?

3. Broderbund makes a program for the Macintosh that reviews an entire year of geometry and tests your understanding as you go. What type of software do you think the program is? Why?

Using What You Know

1. See if you can find out what types of software the following are: AfterDark, Quattro Pro, AutoCAD, Mathematica, and Where in the World Is Carmen Sandiego?

2. Can you think of how and why BVOS could use Lotus 1-2-3, Paradox, and WordPerfect?

3. Using a computer magazine, find 10 pieces of software that you haven't heard of. Using the information in the magazine, try to describe what the software does and what type of software it is.

How Software Works

When software is loaded into the computer's memory, it does its job by controlling the central processing unit (CPU) that is the brains of any microcomputer. Once the software is loaded, the sets of instructions that comprise it take over and control the hardware, which reads the instructions and carries them out. In general, software instructions tell the hardware how to do one of two things:

- Some instructions tell the computer how to handle input and output.
- Other instructions tell the computer how to process and store the data it receives.

Input and Output Through User Interfaces

The computer is a machine for processing data in what is called the **processing cycle**. Let's expand on this definition a bit. People, whom we call users, provide data — in one form or another — to computers. This process is called **input**. Computers process the data by carrying out software instructions and the commands issued by the user. Computers then present the processed data back to users. This process is called **output**. The software controls how the computer accepts data and commands as input, and to some degree, controls how it presents data as output through its **user interface**.

In general, there are three basic kinds of user interface: command-line interfaces, menu interfaces, and graphical user interfaces. The most important differences among the three lie in how the user issues processing commands.

Command-Line Interfaces. In a **command-line interface**, the user controls the program by typing commands at the keyboard. The earliest microcomputer programs all used command-line interfaces, primarily because this type of interface is the easiest to create. But many programs that are popular today still use command-line interfaces. The best example is DOS, an operating system created by Microsoft Corporation that is the most widely used piece of software in the world.

An example of the DOS command-line interface is shown in Figure 3-8 on the next page. The "C:\" at the beginning of some lines is the command prompt. The characters that follow the prompt, such as "ver" and "dir," are commands that have been entered by the user. Lines that do not begin with a command prompt are the computer's responses to the commands, that is, output. For example, when you enter "ver," this is input that tells the computer to output the DOS version number on the screen.

Menu-Driven Interfaces. A command-line interface requires the user to know what commands are available and how to use them. **Menu-driven interfaces** relieve some of the burden by providing lists of options from which the user can choose. A given menu option can either invoke a command or bring up another menu that allows the user to further clarify the option selected in the previous menu. Moving from one menu to another is known as "navigating through the menu system."

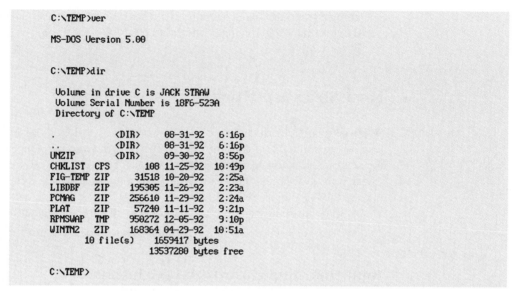

```
C:\TEMP>ver

MS-DOS Version 5.00


C:\TEMP>dir

  Volume in drive C is JACK STRAW
  Volume Serial Number is 18F6-523A
  Directory of C:\TEMP

.               <DIR>       08-31-92   6:16p
..              <DIR>       08-31-92   6:16p
UNZIP           <DIR>       09-30-92   8:56p
CHKLIST  CPS        108     11-25-92  10:49p
FIG-TEMP ZIP      31518     10-20-92   2:25a
LIBDBF   ZIP     195305     11-26-92   2:23a
PCMAG    ZIP     256610     11-29-92   2:24a
PLAT     ZIP      57240     11-11-92   9:21p
RPMSWAP  TMP     950272     12-05-92   9:10p
WINTN2   ZIP     168364     04-29-92  10:51a
       10 file(s)      1659417 bytes
                      13537280 bytes free


C:\TEMP>
```

Figure 3-8
In DOS command interface, characters following the command prompt, C:\, are commands input by the user.

CompuServe, an information service users can access through telephone lines, uses a menu-driven interface (although users can also type commands at a command prompt). Figure 3-9 shows a WordPerfect 5.1 menu for formatting text.

Graphical User Interfaces. The Apple Macintosh popularized a third kind of interface, the **graphical user interface**, or **GUI** (pronounced "gooey"). With a graphical user interface, the user usually controls the program by using a pointing device called a **mouse** to select actions, objects, and programs that are represented on the screen. In addition to text and menus, a graphical user interface often includes little pictures, called **icons**, that are used to represent programs, data files, and commands.

```
Format: Line

    1 - Hyphenation                        No

    2 - Hyphenation Zone - Left            10%
                          Right            4%

    3 - Justification                      Full

    4 - Line Height                        Auto

    5 - Line Numbering                     No

    6 - Line Spacing                       1

    7 - Margins - Left                     1"
                  Right                    1"

    8 - Tab Set                            Rel; -1", every 0.5"

    9 - Widow/Orphan Protection            No



Selection: 0
```

Figure 3-9
A menu-driven interface in WordPerfect 5.1.

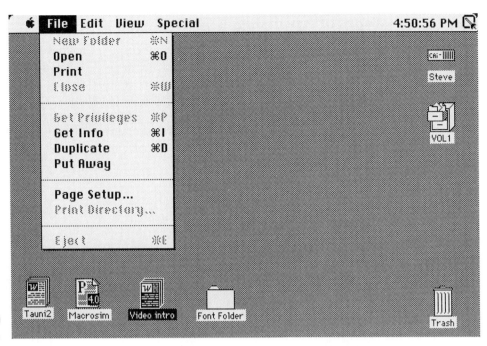

Figure 3-10
The Macintosh's GUI.

Figure 3-10 shows the Macintosh's GUI. The words along the top of the screen are the names of "pull-down menus," which the user accesses with a mouse. In the figure, the File menu is currently open. Below the menus are several icons.

Advantages and Disadvantages of Each Interface.   Since the introduction of the original Macintosh in 1984, computer users have been debating the advantages and disadvantages of these interfaces. From a novice's point of view, the advantages of the GUI are obvious: Pointing to parts of the screen and selecting menu options or icons is a far more intuitive process than typing commands at the keyboard. With a GUI, it is often possible to start using a new piece of software without ever touching a software manual. For this reason, GUIs are often referred to as "user friendly." Simple menu-driven interfaces are less intuitive than GUIs but more intuitive than command-line interfaces. Some people choose menu-driven interfaces over GUIs because they prefer working entirely from the keyboard, without using a mouse.

The advantages of a command-line interface may not be as obvious, but they can be equally compelling. One advantage cited by the command-line advocates is that issuing a command from the keyboard — even a complex command — is usually more efficient than navigating through a system of menus. Naturally, this advantage is true only if you are a competent typist and are familiar with the commands. Another advantage of the command line is that the programs that use them tend to be smaller and therefore faster. Finally, command-line allies will tell you that having to learn something about a program from the manual before you sit down at the computer will make you a more informed and more efficient user in the long run.

In evaluating the various user interface options, the focus must always be on understanding the skill and experience of the intended user.

Types of Processing

There are two basic ways that computers process the data they receive: real-time processing and batch processing.

When you use a microcomputer, you generally require real-time processing. **Real-time processing** means that you give the computer a command and it is carried out immediately, as demonstrated in Figure 3-11. The same user is the source of input and the recipient of output. The user gets a response from the computer in a time frame that is relevant for a user sitting at a computer. Real-time processing is often associated with **interactive programs**, which require user input to function.

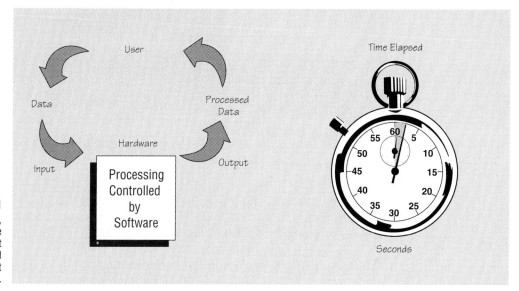

Figure 3-11
In real-time processing, the hardware and software process data as soon as it is input by the user, and generate output immediately.

A bank ATM such as the one shown in Figure 3-12 is an example of an interactive program that uses real-time processing. When you use the machine, you enter your identification number, access your account, and withdraw or deposit money in just a few seconds. Your account information is updated immediately. If it weren't, you could drive from one ATM to another and withdraw the maximum amount of money from each one with no regard for how much money was actually in your account.

The alternative to real-time processing is batch processing. **Batch processing** does not require user input while the program is running. Instead, the program collects data over a period of time and then processes the data all at

Figure 3-12
This bank's ATM uses real-time processing so your account balance can be figured immediately each time you perform a transaction.

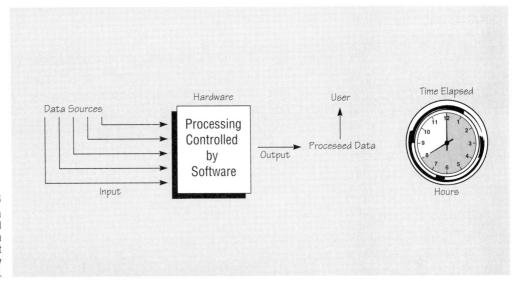

Figure 3-13
In batch processing, data is collected over a period of time, often from a variety of sources; output is generated only periodically.

Figure 3-14
Mainframes like this one are often used to perform batch processing.

once, as demonstrated in Figure 3-13. The user of the processed data is not necessarily the source of input data. Although almost everything done on microcomputers uses real-time processing, it is important to realize that mainframes often use batch processing, as shown in Figure 3-14. Mainframes tend to stay on 24 hours a day. Batch processing is an efficient way to use a mainframe when most of the users are not at work.

Banks use batch processing to enter checks into accounts. When the bank has collected enough checks, it processes them all in sequence and updates the accounts. Batch processing is very efficient because the computer can be used for other activities while the batches of data are being collected.

Comprehension Questions

1. The DOS command A:\DIR gives a directory listing of all files in drive A. The same command in a command-line Unix operating system is A:\LS-A. Which do you think is more intuitive? Why?

2. What types of interfaces are illustrated in Figure 3-5?

3. Imagine that you are not limited by current technology. Describe an advanced user interface that is more intuitive and user friendly than any of the three types mentioned.

Using What You Know

1. Pick which interface your salespeople will use, and justify your choice with three reasons.

2. Of the three most popular interfaces available, which would you pick to win the battle over types of interfaces? Why?

3. Name two examples of batch processing that are not mentioned in this chapter.

Summary Points

What Is Software?

☐ A piece of software, also known as a program, is a set of instructions that controls the computer and makes it useful for accomplishing a specific task.

☐ Software is the primary problem-solving tool of the computer system.

☐ Software instructions tell the computer how to interpret data, how to process it, and how to present the processed result.

Types of Software

Application Software

☐ Application software refers to any program that is used to accomplish a user-defined task that exists independent of the computer.

☐ Common applications are word processing, creating spreadsheets, managing databases, creating graphic images, and communicating with other computers.

☐ Application packages consist of sets of interconnected programs that work together to perform the desired task.

☐ Game software is played on microcomputers or on special video game systems.

☐ The field of education has created tutorial software and simulation software.

☐ Modern programming requires programs called compilers and interpreters.

Utility Software

☐ Utility programs are used to accomplish tasks that relate to the internal functioning of the computer system.

Operating System Software

☐ The operating system is the first program loaded into the computer.

☐ The OS contains basic instructions that allow the hardware to work and that help software interact with the hardware.

How Software Works

☐ Software instructions must be loaded into memory to be carried out.

Input and Output Through User Interfaces

Command-Line Interfaces

☐ With a command-line interface, the user directs the computer by typing commands from the keyboard.

Menu-Driven Interfaces

☐ With a menu-driven interface, the user directs the computer by choosing from a menu of options. If the option is a complete command, the computer carries it out. If the option needs further clarification, the user is shown a different menu.

Graphical User Interfaces

☐ With a GUI, the user directs the computer by using a pointing device to select text, menus, and icons.

Advantages and Disadvantages of Each Interface

☐ Menu-driven interfaces are less intuitive than GUIs but more intuitive than command-line interfaces. They do not require a mouse.

☐ GUIs are more intuitive than command-line interfaces.

☐ Command-line interfaces tend to be more efficient once the user becomes familiar with the commands.

☐ GUIs will win out in the end because they are preferred by new users.

Types of Processing

☐ Interactive programs that use real-time processing require user input and give responses in a time frame that is relevant for the user.

☐ Programs that use batch processing collect data over a period of time and process it all at once without requiring user input.

Knowing the Facts

True/False

1. Application software supports tasks related to the internal functions of the computer.
2. An operating system must be loaded into a computer before any other type of software is loaded.
3. The instructions that comprise any program tell the computer how to accept data, process it, and present it.
4. The most intuitive type of interface is the graphical user interface, or GUI.
5. Game software requires a computer designed for games, such as a Nintendo or an arcade machine.
6. An ATM at a bank uses real-time processing.
7. Application packages are generally smaller than utility programs.
8. Simulation software is usually more complex than tutorial software.
9. The first user interfaces were menu-driven interfaces.
10. DOS includes a command-line interface.

Short Answer

1. Small pictures called _____ are often used in GUIs.
2. Name two types of software used in education.
3. Sets of instructions that control the computer are called _____.
4. The added efficiency of a command-line interface may be lost if the user cannot _____.
5. Mainframe systems use _____ processing to take advantage of times when few users are present.
6. What are the three main types of software?
7. What line of computers popularized the graphical user interface?
8. Which type of software is best described as problem-solving software?
9. Real-time processing is generally associated with _____ programs, while batch processing does not require user input while the program is running.
10. Of the three main types of software, understanding _____ requires the most knowledge of computer hardware.

Answers

True/False	*Short Answer*

True/False

1. F
2. T
3. T
4. T.
5. F.
6. T
7. F
8. T.
9. F.
10. T

Short Answer

1. icons
2. tutorial, simulation
3. software or programs
4. type
5. batch
6. operating system, software, application software, and utilities
7. Macintosh
8. application software
9. interactive
10. operating system software

Challenging Your Understanding

1. We described two types of educational software. But the field of education might also use some of the other types we described. How might other kinds of application software and utility programs be used in education?

2. We claimed that "software forms the link among people, hardware, and data." Support this idea by explaining why software, rather than hardware or data, forms the link.

3. See if you can find out what type of software Windows 3.0 or 3.1 is.

4. During the 1980s, the most common type of computer in elementary schools was the Apple II. Much of the educational software written for the Apple II uses menu-driven interfaces. Is a menu-driven interface the best type for elementary school students? Why or why not?

5. Virtual reality involves the use of computers to create artificial worlds that allow humans to explore, create, learn, and work in environments that would normally be hostile or difficult to create. How might virtual reality be used in business applications?

6. What kind of computer interface do you prefer? Why?

C H A P T E R   4

Application Software and Utility Software

Key Terms

analytic graphics
antivirus software
artificial intelligence
backing up (archiving)
bitmap
bulletin board service (BBS)
communications software
computer-aided design (CAD)
context-sensitive help
query
copy-protected software
database
database file
database management
    system (DBMS)
data compression
desktop publishing (DTP)
documentation
downloading
draw program
edit
electronic mail (E-mail)
expert system
field
file management
    (hard disk management)
font
font manager
graphics
graphics software
help features

hot links
hypermedia software
installation
integrated application package
knowledge base
knowledge engineer
modem
modules
multimedia
paint program
presentation graphics
public domain software
query
record
screen saver
shareware
site license
software piracy
spreadsheet
telephone support
typeface
upgrade
uploading
utility package
vector graphics
version
virus
what-if capability
word processing
WYSIWYG

Objectives

In this chapter you will learn to:

- Have an understanding of the most popular types of application software and explain the function of each
- Understand the important capabilities of a DBMS
- Briefly explain the difference between paint and draw programs
- Name four activities that communications software can help you perform
- Describe the advantages and disadvantages of integrated software
- Name five types of utility software and explain the function of each
- List at least three periodicals that cover computer products
- Explain the advantages of getting information from friends and business associates
- Name the six criteria you should consider when shopping for a software package
- Describe the three principal types of software support
- Describe the four steps of software installation
- Explain the significance of software piracy and describe the steps software companies are taking to deter it

Applications Software

Recall the four basic problems that you, as president of the new BVOS branch, need to solve:

- Setting up and maintaining your inventory database

- Analyzing financial data

- Sending correspondence

- Communicating via computer with Buena Vista headquarters

Since the term *application software* refers to a program that solves a particular type of task, you will be addressing these four problems with application software. In this chapter, we will cover the various types of application software. Then we will cover some popular types of utility software, which you may also want to purchase for BVOS. Finally, we will look at the issues involved in selecting an application package.

Common Applications

Most users have very similar computing needs. They need to collect and analyze data, and they need to communicate their findings. Software producers have responded to these needs by creating a wealth of certain types of application packages.

Database management systems were created to help users collect and organize data. To analyze data, you might use either a database manager or a spreadsheet package.

Several types of application packages are available for communicating ideas. For text communication, the most common type of software is the word processor. If the text requires complex formatting and integration of graphics, you might use desktop publishing software. If you want to communicate your ideas graphically, there are many graphics packages to choose from. And if you need to communicate your ideas to someone through the phone lines, you will use a communications package. All of these appplications can be performed on the same microcomputer, as demonstrated in Figure 4-1.

Let's look at the most common types of application software in greater detail.

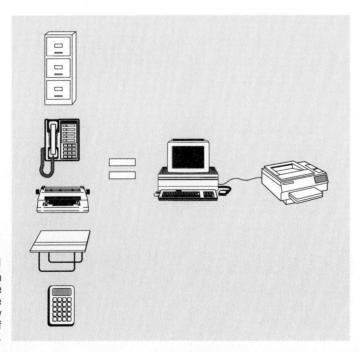

Figure 4-1
With the right application software, a single microcomputer can take the place of many cumbersome pieces of office equipment.

Database Software

A **database** is a collection of data that is stored and ordered to help users answer certain questions. A database can include all kinds of digital data, text, graphics, numbers, full-motion video, and sound. Databases used for business, however, generally include only text and numbers. A text-based database is organized into fields, records, and files. A **field** is a relatively small unit of text. Each field lists a certain type of data. For example, in your position at BVOS, you might want a personal database that includes data on business contacts, such as last name, phone number, and so on. Fields are grouped into records. A **record** contains a set of data about a particular person, place, or event. For example, the fields for the name, department, Social Security number, and address of one of your employees could be listed in a database as a record. A group of related records, such as those pertaining to the the illustrations in this book, can be grouped together in a **database file** such as the one shown in Figure 4-2.

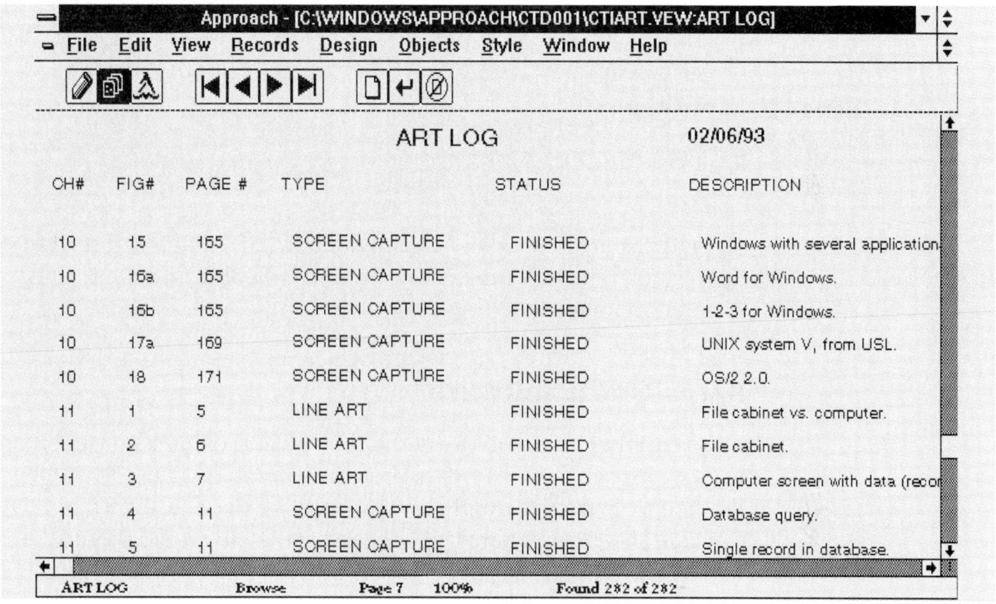

Figure 4-2
A small database file: each column of data is a field, and each row is a record.

A database comprises a group of related database files. In order to be related, each file in the database must share at least one field with one other file.

Database software is an informal term for a program that manages a database. The formal term is **database management system**, or **DBMS**. Database management systems on microcomputers began in 1981 when George Tate and Hal Lashlee, owners of a software marketing firm, received orders for a software package written by Wayne Ratliff. The three men formed a company, Ashton-Tate, and began marketing dBASE II, the DBMS that revolutionized the industry. The most popular DBMSs for microcomputers are compatible with dBASE III+, a product written by Ashton-Tate and now sold by Borland International. Another DBMS sold by Borland is Paradox (Figure 4-3 on the next page).

Modern DBMSs have several important capabilities that make them valuable tools. A DBMS should allow you to:

- Sort records according to the contents of fields.

- Ask certain questions, called **queries**, about the data in the database. Queries generally list files that meet certain criteria, count files, or make computations based on numerical data.

- Ensure the security of the data. With a password system, for example, only certain users are allowed to view or change certain fields.

```
 System  File  Edit  Database  Record  Program  Window  Browse
                          CLIENTS                                    ≡
  Company              Address                City         State Zip ▲

 California Beauty Inc.  900 Tenable Court      Woodsboro    TX   78393◆
 Carolina Systems        5 Mention Trail        Washington   NC   27889
 Citibank Communication  7930 Rhubarb Towers 6  Bakersfield  CA   93309
 City Greeley            6 Zing Rd.             Richardson   TX   75080
 Commercial Room         45 Ports Font Drive 93 Golden       CO   80401
 Computer Directions     9603 Befallen Typhoon  Long Beach   CA   90805
 Computer Services       378 Phillips Plaza     Morehead City NC  28557
 Computing Consultants   3710 Scramble Blvd.    Los Angeles  CA   90048
 Control Services Computin 40 Inside Nicosia Pk. 3 Bryan     TX   77802
 Cox Computer Gaucher    426 Hubert Dr.         Cupertino    CA   95014
 Cubinets & Opera        774 Saracen Circle     Camden       NJ   08103▼
  ⁗◄◆                                                            ►.

                                          run cls
                                          set disp to mono
                                          run rpm
                                          run cap
                                          run cls
```

Figure 4-3

Paradox is one of the latest DBMSs for microcomputers.

DBMSs are one of the most widely used and yet most difficult to understand of the application types. Because they are both valuable and confusing, we will devote an entire chapter, Chapter 12, to them.

Spreadsheet Software

A **spreadsheet** is a grid divided into rows and columns. Data entered into this grid is used to perform calculations on large sets of numbers. Until the 1980s, most accountants and bookkeepers used manual spreadsheets like the one shown in Figure 4-4, which they kept on large sheets of paper. The concept of the electronic spreadsheet was created by Daniel Bricklin in 1979 while he was a student at the Harvard Business School. He and Robert Frankston developed VisiCalc (the "visible calculator") to solve accounting problems they were assigned in school. More than a means for organizing numerical data, VisiCalc allowed the user to enter a formula into a spreadsheet cell (the intersection of a row and a column) that would compute an error-free result based on the numerical values of other cells. Thus, for instance, totals of columns of numbers could be calculated automatically. The spreadsheet program will recalculate the formulas each time the data changes.

Figure 4-4

Before the electronic spreadsheet was invented, accountants kept their records on manual spreadsheets.

Electronic spreadsheets have revolutionized modern business with their simplicity, flexibility, and **what-if capability**. *What-if* means that you can ask a hypothetical question and consider alternatives simply by entering new data or changing a formula. For example, say you have constructed a spreadsheet to keep track of expenses, revenues, and net profit. If you wanted to see the impact on net profit of an across-the-board employee salary increase, you could add a column that computes a given percentage increase for each salary and creates a new total for all the salaries. The spreadsheet automatically computes a new total expenses figure that reflects the total salary figure, then computes a new net profit to reflect the new total expenses.

Another valuable characteristic of modern spreadsheet packages is their ability to generate graphs of the spreadsheet data using 3-D effects, color, and multiple typefaces. For instance, given a column of numbers that lists the total revenue for each month, you could select the entire column and automatically generate a pie chart that illustrates each month's total as a part of the year's total. The spreadsheet and line graph shown in Figure 4-5 were created with Microsoft Excel.

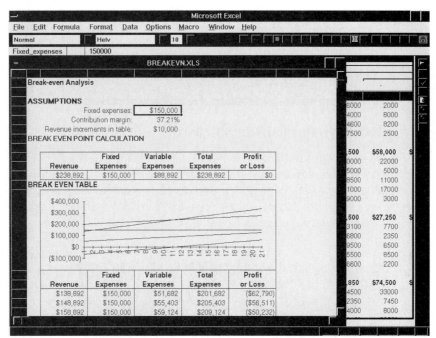

Figure 4-5
Many modern spreadsheet packages, such as Microsoft Excel, allow you to generate graphs and combine them with data.

Word Processing Software

Word processing is the process of creating text documents on a computer. Word processing software, commonly called a word processor (although the same term can also refer to the person using the software), is designed to make it easier to draft and edit text. With a word processor like the one shown in Figure 4-6 on the next page, you can move and delete text, check spelling, create tables and columns, modify margins, draw lines, change the appearance of text, and view how a document will appear before you print it.

The first word processing software was conceived as an improvement on the typewriter. The most striking advantage of creating documents on a computer is that the process of creating the document is separated from printing the document. This makes it possible to **edit**, or make changes to, a document without retyping the entire text. As word processors have become more sophisticated, many features have been added, so that word processing software can hardly be compared to a typewriter any longer.

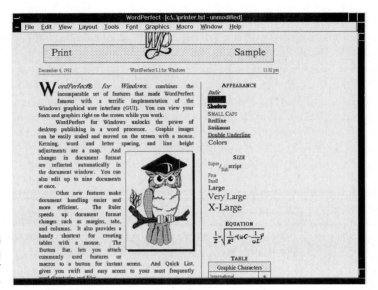

Figure 4-6
This document was created using WordPerfect for Windows.

Desktop Publishing Software

Desktop publishing (also known as **DTP**) is the use of a computer to create high-quality documents that are ready to be sent to a printer. Although desktop publishing software shares many of the same capabilities as modern word processing software, DTP software specializes in the most advanced features, especially the ability to incorporate a wide variety of typefaces and the ability to combine text and graphics. The goal of DTP is to allow the greatest possible flexibility in how the printed page will look, as shown in Figure 4-7.

Many businesses find DTP to be a cost-efficient way to produce publications, because it requires fewer people, less equipment, and less time than the traditional publishing production process.

Although it is often possible to create graphics and text in a DTP program, it is far more common to import text from a word processing program and graphics from a graphics program to combine them in a DTP file. For example, as Figure 4-8 illustrates, the pages of this book were composed using a DTP package called Ventura Publisher. The text, however, was originally input using Microsoft Word for Windows.

Figure 4-7
These complex pages were created with DTP software.

Graphics Software

Graphics software allows you to create **graphics** — illustrations, diagrams, graphs, and charts — on a computer. Research shows that most people can understand and retain more

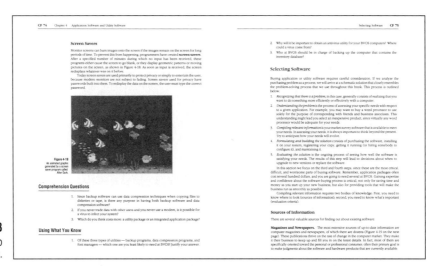

Figure 4-8
A page of this book set up
with DTP software.

information when it is presented in a graphical format. Consequently, most business presentations and many of those made in school are most effective when they include graphics that support the message. The purpose of a graphic is primarily communication.

Analytic graphics are used to display numerical information. They include such formats as pie charts, line graphs, and bar graphs. The graphical capabilities of spreadsheet software, for example, are referred to as analytic graphics. **Presentation graphics** packages are separate pieces of software that provide sophisticated capabilities for creating professional quality analytic graphics using color, multiple typefaces, and 3-D effects. Figure 4-9 is an example of a presentation graphics package.

In addition to analytical software and presentation graphics software, there are many paint and draw programs that allow you to create images from scratch using a mouse or a graphics drawing tablet. **Draw programs** enable you to create pictures by manipulating and combining graphic elements, such as straight lines, circles, and curves. In a vector graphics program — which includes draw programs and **computer-aided design (CAD)** programs — an image is stored as a pattern of lines. CAD programs are similar to draw programs. However, draw programs usually provide effects and capabilities for creating illustrations, while CAD programs are used to create highly specialized designs requiring

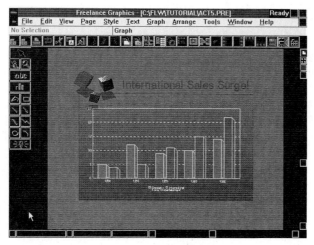

Figure 4-9
A graphic created using a
presentation graphics
program.

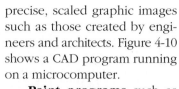

Figure 4-10
This microcomputer is equipped with CAD software.

precise, scaled graphic images such as those created by engineers and architects. Figure 4-10 shows a CAD program running on a microcomputer.

Paint programs such as MacPaint, shown in Figure 4-11, allow the user to produce the effect of painting on the screen using a graphics tablet or mouse and a range of colors, known as the palette. A computer displays an image as a set of tiny dots, set close to each other. The simplest types of output equipment uses one bit to control each dot. The image can therefore be stored as a map that shows which bits are supposed to be on and which are off. An image stored in this way is appropriately named a **bitmap**. Paint programs form images using bitmaps.

Figure 4-11
An illustration created with MacPaint.

Communications Software

Communications software manages the transmission of data, usually over telephone lines, with the help of a hardware device called a **modem**. Communications software and a modem allow a computer user to:

- Transfer files to and from another computer equipped with communications software and a modem. Sending a file to another computer is called **uploading**. Retrieving a file is called **downloading**.

- Access electronic **bulletin boards services**, or **BBS,** which are an electronic means for information exchange. Users can see and respond to messages from other users. They can also upload or download entire files and, in some cases, entire software programs. There are hundreds of BBS around the country. Some cater to special interests, hobbies, or particular industries; others are more general. Around the world there are literally thousands of BBS. A few examples are Boston Citinet (information

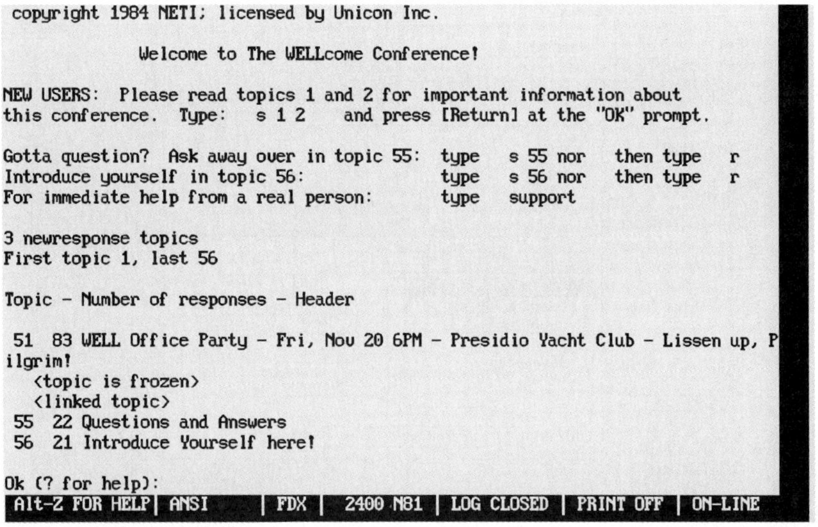

Figure 4-12
An electronic bulletin board.

about Boston), the Federal Job Information Center, OSprey's Nest (discussion of birdwatching), Take 3 (reviews of movies, video, and film), and OCRWM Infolink (information about radioactive waste).The BBS shown in Figure 4-12 is The Well, a general-interest service located in Sausalito, California.

- Access information services. By going on-line with an information service, subscribers can perform a wide range of activities, including shopping, getting news, posting want ads, obtaining up-to-the-minute stock quotes, playing games, and ordering airline tickets. Some information services charge by how many minutes you are on-line; some bill a flat monthly fee. Prodigy and CompuServe are examples of information services.

- Send **electronic mail**, usually called **E-mail**. E-mail systems allow you to send electronic messages to other users who are not necessarily on line when you leave the message. When the other user accesses the E-mail system, the system will automatically tell the user that he or she has a message.

With special communications software and a fax modem, it is possible to send faxes to and receive faxes from a facsimile machine through a microcomputer. Fax modems are less expensive than stand-alone fax machines and, given the right equipment, can deliver higher quality output.

Integrated Application Packages and Their Alternatives

Integrated application packages combine a collection of applications in one package with a common interface. Common applications found in an integrated package include a word processor, a database, a spreadsheet, a graphics system, and a communications system. When included in integrated packages, the individual applications are usually called **modules**. Figure 4-13 on the next page shows the opening screen for Microsoft Works for the Mac. Here you can choose which of the five applications you want to use.

Integrated packages have several advantages. The first is price; integrated packages often cost significantly less than purchasing all the applications separately. Another is the advantage of a single interface, which makes it more comfortable — especially for new users — to switch between applications. Third, these packages allow data to be transferred from one application to another, a process that can be difficult for some operating systems. With such a package, data from a database can be easily graphed in a spreadsheet and then incorporated

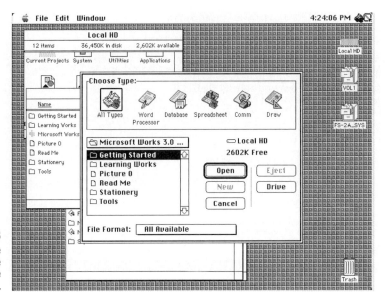

Figure 4-13
In Microsoft Works for the Mac, the user can choose from among five applications.

into a report on the word processor. Some of these packages allow a data change in the database or spreadsheet modules to be reflected in word processing documents or wherever that data may be used. The automatic updates of files between modules are called **hot links**.

The primary disadvantage of integrated software is that a specialized package offers more advanced capabilities. For example, the spreadsheet component of an integrated package may not provide as large a grid as a stand-alone package such as Lotus 1-2-3.

There are alternatives to integrated packages. Some stand-alone programs have the ability to pass data back and forth. For example, in Windows you can create a spreadsheet and a graph in Lotus 1-2-3, import them to a WordPerfect document to add text, and then merge that document with information in Paradox, provided the applications have been designed for use with Windows (Figure 4-14). However, this capability tends to be more cumbersome with stand-alone packages than with the integrated package.

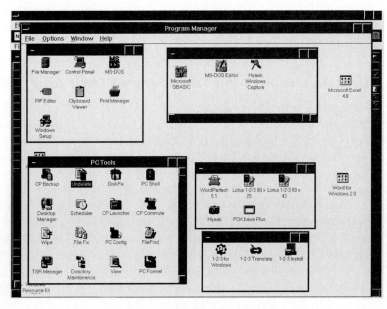

Figure 4-14
All Windows environment applications can trade data easily.

Hypermedia

Hypermedia software such as HyperCard, shown in Figure 4-15, is a subset of the database family that incorporates the advantages of multimedia for conveying information. **Multimedia** refers to the use of several communications media within a single presentation. Multimedia generally includes text, audio, graphics, animation graphics, and full-motion video. Both hypermedia and multimedia are appealing because they encourage nonsequential exploration of the various media.

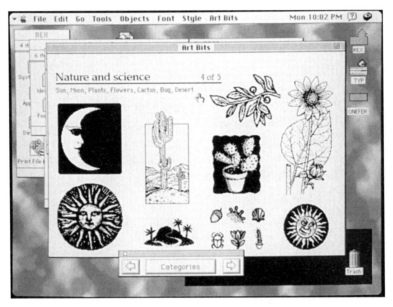

Figure 4-15
A screen from HyperCard, a hypermedia application for the Macintosh.

A hypermedia database of the War of 1812, for example, might contain audio recordings of battle recreations, maps, and text describing the war and important battles. Certain words or phrases could be selected from the text for more information about the subject. While reading about the War of 1812, you could highlight the name Napoleon and read a short biography of the emperor of France. Or while reading about the battle of Waterloo you might highlight the word Waterloo and see a map of where that battle was fought. You might also run across a reference to Tchaikovsky's *1812 Overture* and listen to part of that music. Hypermedia aims to bring life to the text and numbers in a database.

Artificial Intelligence and Expert Systems

Computers have long been used to help humans solve problems. Given precise instructions, a computer can repeatedly and consistently provide a predictable answer. The computer is not thinking; it is simply reproducing the actions that were programmed into it. **Artificial intelligence** is a broad field that attempts to endow computers with the ability to think and reason in ways that are similar to human thought processes. The term *artificial intelligence* was coined in 1956 by John McCarthy, a key figure in the development of the field.

One of the advancements in the field of artificial intelligence has been made in the area of expert systems. An **expert system** is a system that has been created to mimic the human decision-making process in a very narrow problem area. For example, a medical expert system called MYCIN helps physicians diagnose medical problems. MYCIN allows the physician to enter a patient's symptomology and receive suggestions for further testing. If enough information is given, MYCIN suggests a diagnosis and in some cases a series of procedures for treating the problem. The physician using MYCIN can also ask the system how it made its diagnosis. MYCIN will then produce the set of logic it used. From this the physician can learn from the system or choose to interpret the results differently.

MYCIN was created by asking expert diagnosticians how they did their job. By capturing this expertise, the MYCIN programmers, called **knowledge engineers** (a generic term for expert systems programmers), were able to create a program that mimicked the actions of many experts. The coded knowledge or expertise is entered into a **knowledge base**, a database of computer logic and rules based upon human expertise.

Comprehension Questions

1. Why do you think integrated packages usually include word processing, spreadsheet, database, communications, and graphics applications?
2. Is a DBMS a type of hypermedia software, or is it the other way around?
3. The ability to format text is generally associated with word processing software, but it is included in many other packages. What other types of application software might include text-formatting capabilities?

Using What You Know

1. The computers at your school probably have access to certain application packages. Find out what they are.
2. At the beginning of this unit, we outlined four tasks that you will face at BVOS. What four types of application software will you need to purchase to accomplish these tasks?
3. How might you use DTP software at BVOS? How could you use hypermedia software?

Utility Software

Software applications and the computers on which they run are selected to help users solve problems. For many users, this is all that is required. However, at times additional software tools are needed to make the computer easier to use, more efficient, more effective, or safer. Utility software supplies functionality that is not included in the set of applications that run on the computer. For example, software developers have created utility programs to protect display monitors, to facilitate making backup copies of data, and to protect against computer viruses — all functions not commonly performed by a word processing or spreadsheet application package. Most utility software programs are optional and must be purchased separately; however, utility functions are becoming increasingly available as part of operating systems. Utility software can make a substantial difference in how a computer is used and how well hardware, software, and data are preserved.

Utility Packages

Some developers, such as Symantec and Central Point, offer **utility packages**, which include a set of useful programs that either act as conveniences or protect the computer system.

Probably the most famous utility package is the Norton Utilities. This package lets the user perform such tasks as maintaining the hard disk, restoring files that have been deleted or damaged, formatting disks, and searching for files.

Backup Systems

Backing up or **archiving** your data is nothing more than copying data and software from the computer's hard disk (the large storage area built into most microcomputers) and storing the copy in a safe location. It seems that we all understand the importance of backing up: Data is vulnerable to loss or damage from countless causes. But we don't all practice what we preach. Part of the problem is that the process of creating a backup copy is time consuming, especially if we are simply using the operating system to copy data and software to diskettes. Backing up a 100 MB hard disk this way could easily take several hours. Consequently, software companies have written utilities that help create backups quickly and relatively painlessly.

These tools first read a portion of the software or data from the hard disk. Then the files are compressed. **Data compression** is a technique of logical and mathematical methods to minimize the amount of storage space that the software or data occupies. Data compression has been compared to moving furniture using a moving truck. It doesn't make sense to arrange the furniture in the truck the same way it is arranged in your living room. It is much better to eliminate the excess space between the items. Programs that use data compression work in a similar way.

After data compression, the backup software copies the data to a tape or diskette. The process of backing up a hard disk with data compression is illustrated in Figure 4-16. The user then stores the tape or diskette in a safe place. If the data on the hard disk is ever damaged, the backup copy can be used to restore the hard disk.

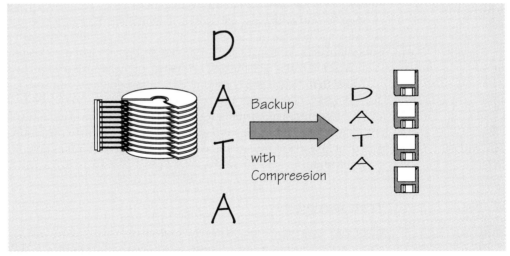

Figure 4-16
The backup process.

Data Compression Software

The amount of room that software takes up on a computer is increasing at an astounding pace. It seems that every new release of a program requires more and more space. Although the size of hard disks is also growing, users often find that their hard disks are full long before they are ready to buy a new one.

One solution — at least a partial solution — is proper file management. **File management**, sometimes called **hard disk management**, means organizing your software and data in a meaningful way on your hard disk, making frequent backups, and eliminating old files. Improper file management can cause a hard disk to fill quickly.

Even with proper file management, however, hard disks can become crowded. To address this issue, many users turn to data compression software that will squeeze as much data and information into a computer as possible, as discussed in the preceding section. Some data compression mechanisms can effectively double the amount of disk space that you have. Unfortunately, data compression software can slow down your computer, because it must first decompress the files before you can use them.

It is now common practice for software companies to ship their software in compressed format. The software is decompressed when it is installed.

Antivirus Software

During the 1980s, some computer users began to notice that their computers were acting strangely. Computers would fail to start one day, or would begin to lose files, or would display odd messages on the screen. These computers had been "infected" by a rogue program, called a **virus**, that attached itself to legitimate programs and automatically copied itself into other programs. This copying process occurs indefinitely, with the virus replicating itself wherever it can. Viruses are also called Trojan horses, logic bombs, or worms.

Although viruses that cause colds in humans occur naturally, computer viruses don't. Every virus must be created by a programmer. Also, a virus doesn't just appear on a computer. It is introduced into a computer when a user inserts an infected disk or when a modem is used to connect to an infected computer via telephone lines.

A virus can cause substantial harm. One virus created by Robert Morris, a student at Cornell University, infected more than 6,000 computers nationwide and reportedly caused millions of dollars's worth of damage. Other viruses are more benign, displaying messages or causing odd effects on the screen. The Michelangelo virus — so named because it was scheduled to activate on the artist's birthday — did minimal damage because people found out about it ahead of time. Some people elected not to use their computers on Michelangelo's birthday. Others changed the date on their computer's internal clock to the day after his birthday.

Antivirus software is used to detect and eradicate viruses. An advertisement for one such program, along with a few of the viruses that it can detect, is shown in Figure 4-17. It can protect computers from infection by inspecting all data and software that are used on the system, or just new files. An important practice is "safe computing" — check all software and data for viruses before you use them. Very few computer environments are totally safe from infection.

Font Managers

If you pick up a typical magazine and look at the ways that characters can appear on a printed page, you will find a wide variety of typefaces. A **typeface** is a complete set of printed characters (all the letters, numbers, punctuation marks, and special characters, such as dollar signs and asterisks) that are created with a single style. Common typefaces are Courier, Helvetica, and Times Roman. A typeface can be any size. One set of characters in a specific typeface, in a specific size, is called a **font**. Fonts are measured in points; one point equals 1/72 of an inch. For example, typewriter characters are usually 10-point or 12-point Courier. Table 4-1 shows several of the most common fonts.

Figure 4-17
Antivirus software detects
and eradicates viruses.

Computers use sets of fonts that can be displayed on the screen and printed. Because the resolution of a screen and a printer almost always differ, computers must work with separate screen fonts and printer fonts. The appearance and size (proportionally speaking) of screen fonts and printer fonts must be properly matched in order to achieve *WYSIWYG* (meaning What You See Is What You Get and pronounced *wiz-ee-wig*). **WYSIWYG** refers to the ability to display text and graphics on-screen the same way they will be printed. To control the fonts that are available for use — which ones can be displayed and which can be printed — software developers have created **font managers**, utilities that tell the computer how to display and print each font.

Courier

Garamond

Helvetica

Times

AvantGarde

Palatino

Bookman

Century Schoolbook

Zapf Chancery

Table 4-1
Some common fonts.

Screen Savers

Monitor screens can burn images onto the screen if the images remain on the screen for long periods of time. To prevent this from happening, programmers have created **screen savers**. After a specified number of minutes during which no input has been received, these programs either cause the screen to go blank, or they display geometric patterns or moving pictures on the screen, as shown in Figure 4-18. As soon as input is received, the screen redisplays whatever was on it before.

Today screen savers are used primarily to protect privacy or simply to entertain the user, because modern monitors are not subject to fading. Screen savers used for privacy have passwords built into them. To redisplay the data on the screen, the user must type the correct password.

Figure 4-18
An animated graphic generated by a screen saver program called AfterDark.

Comprehension Questions

1. Since backup software can use data compression techniques when copying files to diskettes or tape, is there any purpose in having both backup software and data compression software?

2. If you never trade data with other users and you never use a modem, is it possible for a virus to infect your system?

3. Which do you think costs more: a utility package or an integrated application package?

Using What You Know

1. Of these three types of utilities — backup programs, data compression programs, and font managers — which one are you least likely to need at BVOS? Justify your answer.

2. Why will it be important to obtain an antivirus utility for your BVOS computers? Where could a virus come from?

3. Who at BVOS should be in charge of backing up the computer that contains the inventory database?

Selecting Software

Buying application or utility software requires careful consideration. If we analyze the purchasing problem as a process, we will arrive at a schematic solution that closely resembles the problem-solving process that we use throughout this book. This process is outlined below.

1. *Recognizing that there is a problem,* in this case, generally consists of realizing that you want to do something more efficiently or effectively with a computer.

2. *Understanding the problem* is the process of assessing your specific needs with respect to a given application. For example, you may want to buy a word processor to use solely for the purpose of corresponding with friends and business associates. This understanding might lead you select an inexpensive product, since virtually any word processor would be adequate for your needs.

3. *Compiling relevant information* is your market survey of software that is available to meet your needs. In assessing your needs, it is always important to think beyond the present. Try to anticipate how your needs will evolve.

4. *Formulating and building the solution* consists of purchasing the software, installing it on your system, registering your copy, getting it running (or hiring somebody to configure it), and maintaining it.

5. *Evaluating the solution* is the ongoing process of seeing how well the software is satisfying your needs. The results of this step will lead to decisions about when to upgrade to new versions or replace the software.

In this section we focus on the third and fourth steps, since these are the most critical, difficult, and worrisome parts of buying software. Remember, application packages often cost several hundred dollars, and you are going to need several at BVOS. Gaining expertise and confidence about the software-buying process is critical, not only for saving time and money as you start up your new business, but also for providing tools that will make the business run as smoothly as possible.

Compiling relevant information requires two bodies of knowledge: First, you need to know where to look (sources of information); second, you need to know what's important (evaluation criteria).

Sources of Information

There are several valuable sources for finding out about existing software.

Magazines and Newspapers. The most extensive sources of up-to-date information are computer magazines and newspapers, of which there are dozens (Figure 4-19 on the next page). These publications thrive on the rate of change in the computer market. They make it their business to keep up and fill you in on the latest details. In fact, most of them are specifically oriented toward the personal or professional consumer; often their primary goal is to make judgments about the software and hardware products that are currently available.

Figure 4-19
Computer industry periodicals are some of the best sources of information about software.

PC Magazine is often the heftiest publication on a magazine rack. It comes out every two weeks and often runs to 600 pages. As the name implies, its focus is on the family of computers and software that are compatible with the IBM PC. Each issue contains numerous evaluations of new products and comparisons of similar hardware or software. As you might imagine, there are a lot of ads in 600 pages of text, but when you're faced with a purchasing decision, the ads can be as valuable as the articles.

PC World is another popular magazine oriented toward new products available for IBM-compatible machines. *PC World* is very similar to its main competitor, *PC Magazine,* although *PC World* costs slightly more. Like *PC Magazine,* information and even software are available through the on-line service the publication offers through CompuServe.

Macworld is published by the same company as *PC World* and is based on a similar format. The difference, of course, is that *Macworld* focuses on hardware and software available for the Apple Macintosh line of computers.

Infoworld and *PC Week,* both of which are tabloid-format newspapers, are good sources for software reviews and are especially popular with larger business organizations.

Other publications that are worth looking at when faced with a purchasing decision are *MacUser,* which competes with *Macworld; Byte,* which addresses the entire microcomputer industry rather than limiting itself to a single type of platform; and another computer newspaper, *Computerworld.*

Friends and Associates.   Another valuable source of information about computers is your friends and business associates who are computer users. Although the people you know may not have as much information as the periodicals mentioned above, there are a few advantages of word-of-mouth advice:

- Usually, it's free.

- It is easier to ask specific questions.

- Your friends are likely to be more candid about their feelings than magazines can be.

- These are the people with whom you will be trading data. If they have good things to say about the products they are using and you buy the same ones, you will have no compatibility problems (discussed in the next section).

Computer User Groups.   A user group is an organization of users who share experiences, ideas, and advice about a particular piece of hardware or software. User groups are excellent sources of information, and they are free. Some groups invite vendors to demonstrate and discuss new products. In fact, user groups can be influential in getting vendors to change or enhance their products (Figure 4-20).

Other Sources of Information.   If you can afford their cost, many firms provide consulting services regarding software, as well as other computer issues. For example, EDS and Andersen Consulting help their clients solve computer-related problems.

Evaluation Criteria

Knowing how to evaluate a given software product is the crucial component of making a wise purchasing decision. Several issues must be considered, no matter what type of software you are looking for.

Compatibility. First, if you own the hardware for your computer system, the field of software choices has already narrowed. This is because most software products will run on only one type of machine. For example, the perfect application package for your needs may exist, but only for a computer you don't have.

Although this sounds like a serious problem, it rarely is, at least from a purchasing standpoint. A wide variety of quality software exists for many different kinds of computers, especially for PCs (and compatibles) and Macs.

Figure 4-20
A vendor demonstrating a new application package to a user group.

Software Features. This evaluation criterion is the most obvious. Every competing software product has a slightly different set of features or capabilities. When deciding which product to buy, you need to consider several scenarios and decide which one best describes your situation. First, can you buy an application off the shelf that is designed to meet your particular needs? There are specialty software programs for all kinds of businesses (Figure 4-21). For example, although you can manage a payroll with a DBMS program, it's cheaper and easier to buy a program, such as QuickPay, that already has payroll functions set up. If you manage an apartment building, you can buy apartment manager software with fields predefined for tracking rents, maintenance costs, tenant histories, and other relevant matters.

Second, if a specific application does not exist, can a software package such as dBASE IV, Lotus 1-2-3, or WordPerfect be configured to solve your problem?

The third scenario is the most problematic. If the appropriate application does not exist, you must write it from scratch, or more realistically, hire someone to do so. To understand

Figure 4-21
Businesses must often choose from among (a) a specific software package such as SBT Accounting Systems, (b) a general application like Lotus 1-2-3, or (c) hiring someone to create a custom-made program.

(a)   (b)   (c)

this process you need to understand computer programming, which we cover in the next chapter.

User Interface.   As we discussed in Chapter 3, one important factor affecting all software is the user interface. Programs can be built with a command-line interface, a menu interface, or a graphical user interface (GUI). In some cases, as with the Macintosh and programs written to run under Microsoft Windows, the interface is predetermined. With programs that run under DOS, however, the nature of the user interface may be a deciding factor in your choice.

Reputation.   As with any product purchase, the reputation of the manufacturer is an issue. Over time, a software developer establishes a certain reputation. If you ask experienced users or professionals in the computer industry, they will be able to give you their opinions of all the major software companies. You can count on the big ones — Microsoft, Lotus, WordPerfect, Borland, and several others — to put out quality products, because their reputations depend on it. Nevertheless, even among these companies, you will discover nuances of behavior that may affect your purchasing decisions.

Software Support.   One of the biggest factors affecting a company's reputation is the support it offers for its software. Software support comes in three basic forms: documentation, help features, and telephone support (Figure 4-22). **Documentation** is the printed material that comes with the software. Sometimes there are several booklets that are packaged with

(a)

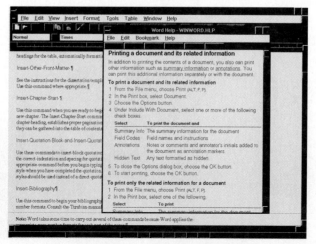

Figure 4-22
Software support:
(a) software manuals,
(b) on-line help screen,
and (c) telephone support.

(b)

(c)

the diskettes, but the most important single item is the manual. The quality of the manual can determine how well you are able to learn and use the software.

Help features are files, built into the software package, that you can access while you are using the software. Normally they can give you information about all of the commands and procedures that you can use. The major factors affecting the quality of the help features are how informative the help screens are and how easy it is to find the relevant help. Some programs have **context-sensitive help** that will automatically display the relevant help screen, depending on the part of the software that the user is working on.

In addition to documentation and help features, many software manufacturers offer **telephone support**, through which users can ask questions directly of the manufacturer's employees. The quality of phone support can vary dramatically. The time it takes to reach an employee is one issue, and the cost of the call is another. Some companies have 800 numbers, so the call is free. Others do not charge for the support, but you must pay for the phone call. Still others have 900 numbers, so you must pay directly for the phone call and support.

Upgrades. The software market is constantly evolving. As years go by, word processors, spreadsheet software, and database management systems add features and become more sophisticated. When one software company adds features to its product, companies with related products feel pressure to add similar features to their own packages. This phenomenon leads software companies to create upgrades to their existing software. An **upgrade** is simply a new version of the software, generally with additional features.

The **version** of a piece of software is generally indicated by a number; an upgrade has a higher number than the previous version. For example, in 1992, Autodesk upgraded its computer-aided drafting program, AutoCAD, from Release 11 to Release 12. Many companies signal a major change by adding a whole unit to the version number; they signal a minor change by increasing the version number by one tenth or one hundredth. For example, when Microsoft made minor improvements to its integrated package, Works 2.0, it released version 2.01. When it upgraded Windows 3.0, the new version became Windows 3.1. The company's 1991 upgrade to Word for Windows changed the program from Word for Windows 1.1 to Word for Windows 2.0.

When looking at a company's policy concerning upgrades, the most important consideration is the price charged users of the previous version. Once you own one version of a software program, most companies offer you upgrades for a fraction of the cost of the original program. A few companies even offer upgrades for free. Others, however, charge the full cost of the software for each upgrade.

Purchase and Installation

Once you finally choose a product and purchase it, there are still a few important steps.

Register Your Copy. First, as soon as you take a new piece of software out of the box, you should register your copy with the software manufacturer. Usually this step requires filling out and mailing a 3"x5" card. The purpose of registering your copy is to inform the software company that you own a legal copy of its software. Once you register, the company will inform you by mail of upcoming upgrades and other products. In some cases, you will not be able to obtain phone support unless you have registered.

Make a Backup Copy. The next step after registering your copy is to make a backup copy of the software because disks can become damaged. The best way to safeguard your valuable

Figure 4-23
This user is installing a new application onto his computer's hard disk.

new software is to create an extra copy of the original diskettes before you install the program on your hard disk. Most software manuals remind you to do this as part of the installation process.

Install the Software. With software, **installation** means copying the program files from the original diskettes to the computer's hard disk (Figure 4-23). In years past, this process was done manually, issuing copy commands to move the files. Now the process is often automated by an installation program. The user simply types "INSTALL" or "SETUP" or selects an icon with a mouse and then answers the questions asked by the installation program. In any case, the software usually comes with an installation guide that tells you what to do.

Read the Manual. When you are learning a new program — especially one with an intuitive GUI — there is a natural temptation to dive right in and try to accomplish your goals without any guidance. Exploring and experimenting is a valuable way to learn about software. Nevertheless, it is almost always worth your while to read at least the first few chapters of the software manual immediately after you purchase the software. There are two good reasons for doing so. First, time is money. In most cases, reading how a task is supposed to be accomplished is less time consuming than attempting to figure it out on your own. Second, there are often multiple methods for accomplishing the same task. Most of the time, one method is better than the others. If you experiment and find a way to do what you want, you will probably stick with that method, even though better options may be available. The manual is more likely to point you in the right direction the first time.

Software Piracy

When trying to solve a problem, it is often tempting to borrow someone else's software. **Software piracy** is the illegal copying or duplication of software. Software pirates cost the software industry billions of dollars every year and drive up the cost of the software to consumers.

Most software is licensed for use on a particular type of computer. Software is protected by the same type of copyright that protects this book. A copyright is a right that an author has to protect the expression of an idea and to control its publication. With respect to software, a copyright means that software cannot be shared. The problem is that software is very easy to copy and share, and the copy works just as well as the original (except that the person with the copy can't register with the company and doesn't have the documentation). The Software Publishers Association is a group of software companies that have joined together to protect software copyrights and to fight software piracy. The group conducts audits of computers in organizations and files lawsuits if it finds examples of software theft.

Copy Protection. Some software companies have tried to curb software piracy by modifying the software so that it will not run properly unless an authorized copy of the software is being used. By requiring that a special diskette is used or that a device is installed into the computer, these companies are attempting to combat software piracy. These systems are called **copy-protected software**. One problem with copy-protected software is that it makes it very difficult for legitimate users to create a legal backup copy of the software.

Site Licenses. Many organizations ask software companies to sell them site licenses to simplify the process of obtaining copies of software for a number of computers (Figure 4-24). A **site license** is a written document detailing the purchasers' right to copy and use a software product on a specified number of computers at a single time. For example, a school may purchase a 20-copy license of WordPerfect so it can install the program on all 20 computers in its computer lab. Such a site license is less expensive than purchasing 20 separate copies of the software. The advantage of the site license is that the purchaser can make an honest attempt to curb software piracy by purchasing, at a discount, a relatively large number of copies. This also provides software tools to many individuals in the organization and creates a standard for a particular application.

Figure 4-24
Many businesses purchase site licenses so they can use the same program on a set number of machines.

Shareware and Public Domain Software. A relatively new concept in the purchase of software is the notion of shareware. **Shareware** is reasonably priced software that is distributed free of charge or for a nominal fee. If after using the software you find it useful, you are asked to send in a payment. There are thousands of shareware titles encompassing applications from games to accounting systems.

There are also programs that are in the public domain. **Public domain software** is very similar to shareware in that you can obtain it legally without paying for it. When something is in the public domain, that indicates that the item can be used by the public without a fee. In some cases, the author of the public domain software will list a name and address and request a fee, but users are not required by law to pay.

Comprehension Questions

1. Which is probably a more significant upgrade, version 3.01 to 3.10 or version 2.2 to 3.0?

2. If you operated a computer lab at a school and needed 25 copies of WordPerfect, what type of license would you buy?

3. Who do you think are the main targets of Software Publishing Association lawsuits? Why?

Using What You Know

1. Of the sources of information given in this chapter, which is most valuable to you as president of BVOS? Why?

2. Say you own a piece of software and a new version has just been released. What factors will affect your decision whether to buy the new upgrade?

3. What do you think are the advantages and disadvantages of distributing a program as shareware?

Summary Points

Common Applications

Most users have similar computing needs, including collecting and analyzing data and communicating ideas.

Database Software

☐ A database is a collection of related data, organized into fields, records, and files.
☐ Modern DBMSs allow the user to sort records, create queries, and secure data.

Spreadsheet Software

☐ A spreadsheet is a grid of columns and rows used to perform calculations on sets of numbers.
☐ The what-if capability of spreadsheet software allows the user to ask hypothetical questions related to numerical data.
☐ Most modern spreadsheet packages include graphing capabilities.

Word Processing Software

☐ A word processor makes it possible to edit text, because the printing process is separate from the process of creating the document.

Desktop Publishing Software

☐ DTP software shares many of the same capabilities as word processing software, but it specializes in advanced formatting features and the ability to integrate text and graphics.

Graphics Software

☐ Analytic graphics are used to display numerical information.
☐ Presentation graphics packages combine analytic graphics with sophisticated formatting capabilities.
☐ Draw programs, including CAD software, use vector graphics to create images with sets of straight lines called vectors.
☐ Paint programs use raster graphics to create bitmapped images.

Communications Software

☐ Communications programs manage the transmission and receipt of data using a modem.
☐ Communications software allows the user to upload and download files, access bulletin boards, subscribe to information services, and send electronic mail.
☐ With a fax modem, some communications packages allow the user to send and receive faxes via computer.

Integrated Application Packages

☐ Integrated packages combine several applications into one package that has a common interface.
☐ Applications in integrated packages usually include word processing, spreadsheets, databases, communications, and graphics.
☐ Integrated packages are generally less expensive than buying each application separately, but they do not provide all of the advanced capabilities.

Hypermedia
□ Hypermedia is a subset of the database family that incorporates the advantages of multimedia.

Artificial Intelligence and Expert Systems
□ Artificial intelligence attempts to endow computers with the ability to think and reason like humans.

□ Expert systems mimic the human decision-making process in a narrow problem area.

Utility Software
Utility software programs supply software functionality that is not included in the set of applications that run on the computer.

Utility Packages
□ Utility packages include a set of popular utilities.

Backup Systems
□ Backing up data consists of copying the contents of a hard disk and storing the copy in a safe place.

□ Software companies have created backup software to simplify the process of backing up data.

□ Most backup programs include data compression techniques that pack the data together and save storage space.

Data Compression Software
□ Data compression software is used to pack as much data onto a hard disk as possible.

□ Data compression can slow down a computer system.

Antivirus Software
□ A virus is a program that automatically copies itself from one host program to another. Viruses can be benign or dangerous.

□ Antivirus software detects and eradicates viruses.

Font Managers
□ A typeface is the complete set of printed characters that conform to a particular style; a font is a typeface of a specific size.

□ Font managers work to match screen fonts and printer fonts.

Screen Savers
□ Screen savers protect display monitors by replacing, after a specified interval, a still screen with a blank screen or a screen showing moving images.

Selecting Software
The process of selecting a piece of software conforms to our problem-solving model.

Sources of Information
□ There are several valuable sources of information, but the most extensive are computer industry periodicals.

Magazines and Newspapers
□ Worthwhile publications include *PC Magazine, PC World, Macworld, MacUser, Byte, PC Week*, and *Computerworld.*

Friends and Associates
□ Word-of-mouth advice is free, can include candid opinions, and can help ensure compatibility.

Computer User Groups
□ Organizations of users share free information and advice about a particular software product.

Other Sources of Information
☐ Consulting firms are available for computer advice.

Evaluation Criteria

Compatibility
☐ Most programs will run on only one type of machine; if you own hardware, your software choices are already narrowed.

☐ Plenty of software is available for most hardware platforms.

Software Features
☐ Every competing program has a slightly different set of features.

User Interface
☐ If the user interface has not already been determined by your operating system or environment, you should take it into account when comparing products.

Reputation
☐ Each software manufacturer has a reputation; as you come to know them, they will affect your choices.

Software Support
☐ The value of a given program's software support is determined by the documentation that comes with the product, the on-line help features, and the telephone support offered by the manufacturer.

Upgrades
☐ A company's pricing policy on upgrades should be considered when buying a package.

Purchase and Installation

Register Your Copy
☐ Registering your ownership of a program with the manufacturer will keep you informed of upgrades and, in some cases, allow you to obtain telephone support.

Make a Backup Copy
☐ Just in case your original program disks become damaged, you should make a backup copy of them.

Install the Software
☐ Installing the software consists of copying the files to the system's hard disk.

☐ Many modern packages have installation programs that automate the installation process.

Read the Manual
☐ Reading the manual saves time in the long run and ensures that you use the most efficient method to perform tasks.

Software Piracy
☐ The illegal copying of software hurts the software industry and raises the costs of software.

Copy Protection
☐ Some software companies protect their copyrights by requiring that a special disk is used or that a device is installed into the computer.

Site Licenses
☐ Site licenses allow customers to purchase the rights to run a program on a set number of machines.

Shareware and Public Domain Software

☐ Shareware is distributed free; if users continue to use the software, they are asked to send a fee to the owner.

☐ Programs in the public domain are free; the programmer can request a fee, but there is no legal responsibility for users to pay.

Knowing the Facts

True/False

1. The advantage of data compression is that it speeds up your use of the computer.

2. Sending a file to another user through the phone lines is called downloading.

3. Artificial intelligence is an attempt to endow computers with the ability to think and reason.

4. Hypermedia software is a subset of the database family.

5. Most spreadsheet packages include analytical graphics programs.

6. Expert systems are able to mimic the human decision-making process, but only in a narrow problem area.

7. VisiCalc was the first electronic spreadsheet.

8. Every computer system should have antivirus software, because viruses occur naturally in data.

9. Paint programs use vectors to create graphics, while draw programs use bitmaps.

10. Text used in a DTP program is generally created in a word processing program.

Short Answer

1. What are the three types of software support?

2. In a spreadsheet, a _____ is the intersection of a row and a column.

3. The formal term for a piece of database software is a _____.

4. When considering a company's policy concerning _____, the most important factor is the price they charge to users of the previous version.

5. Name three magazines that report on the computer industry.

6. Name three advantages of asking friends and business associates for advice about software products.

7. CAD stands for _____.

8. The _____ capability of spreadsheets allows users to obtain answers to hypothetical questions involving numbers.

9. _____ is the term used to describe a specific size of a typeface.

10. Most backup utilities employ _____ techniques that minimize the amount of space required by the data being backed up.

Answers

True/False

1. F
2. F
3. T
4. T
5. T
6. T
7. T
8. F
9. F
10. T

Short Answers

1. help features, documentation, phone support
2. cell
3. database management system, or DBMS
4. upgrades
5. *PC Magazine, PC World, Byte, MacWorld, Mac User,* etc.
6. it's free; you can ask specific questions; you'll get candid answers
7. computer-aided design
8. what-if
9. Font
10. data compression

Challenging Your Understanding

1. When patients go to a doctor, they often complain that they have to wait too long to see the physician, but fully expect the doctor to spend a great deal of time with them in the examination room. The same phenomenon occurs in telephone support. What can a software company do to provide cost-effective telephone support in a timely fashion?

2. Spreadsheet programs are becoming very powerful. What are the characteristics of a problem that can be effectively addressed using a spreadsheet? What kinds of problems are ill suited for spreadsheets?

3. What are the key distinctions between word processing and desktop publishing? As word processing software becomes more powerful, will there be much of a distinction?

4. How do electronic mail, faxes, and bulletin boards differ? It would seem that they all serve very similar purposes.

5. Do you think that in the future the difference between artificial intelligence and natural intelligence will be noticeable?

6. How often should you back up your data? How often do you want your bank to back up data concerning your balance? Where should you store your backed up data?

7. Is utility software just a type of application software? What kinds of problems does it solve?

8. What kind of person do you think creates computer viruses? Are these people criminals? If so, what laws are they breaking?

9. What are some good sources to consult before buying application software? What are some bad sources?

10. List the important factors to consider when purchasing software. Rank these factors from most important to least important.

11. Would you bet your business on shareware or public domain software? Why or why not?

Programming and Programming Languages

Key Terms

Ada
alpha version
analog device
ANSI
ASCII
assembly language
BASIC
beta version
binary code
binary numbering
   system
bit
bug
byte
C
COBOL
code
compiler
data
digital device
EBCDIC
executable file
debugging
fifth-generation
   language (5GL)

file
first-generation
   language
flowchart
FORTRAN
fourth-generation
   language (4GL)
high-level language
information
instruction explosion
interpreter
kilobyte (K)
knowledge
logic error
logic structure
loop structure
low-level language
machine language
megabyte (MB)
natural language
   processing (NLP)
nonprocedural
   language
object code

object-oriented
   programming
Pascal
portability
program
programming
pseudocode
query
second-generation
   language
selection structure
sequence structure
source code
spaghetti code
SQL
structured
   programming
subroutines
syntax error
third-generation
   language
top-down design
transistors

When Is Programming Necessary?

As we saw in the last chapter, you will solve several of your business problems by purchasing application software. Sometimes, though, you will run into a problem that could be solved using a computer, but no application software exists to help you do so. At this point, you may have to create the software yourself or have it made for you. To know what this process entails, you need to understand what computer programming is, how programmers create software, and what programming languages they use.

Before we delve into these topics, however, you must first understand how data differs from information, and how information differs from knowledge. The distinction is vital to your appreciation of programming — and even of software in general — because computers can work only with data, but people generally want to gain information or knowledge. Once this distinction is clear, we can move on to describing first how the computer represents data, and finally to the process of programming.

As president of a small company, you might ask why you need to know anything about programming. One reason is that, as president, part of your job is to provide the best tools for your employees so they can work efficiently. For the problems we are addressing in this book, the tools are pieces of application software. Since all software is the product of programming, it is important to have some notion of programming in order to understand software; software simply makes more sense if you know something about the process of creating it.

Another reason for knowing about programming is that programmers from the head office are going to visit your branch. Using the programming capabilities of dBASE IV, they will tailor your application software to meet the needs of your inventory database. By doing so, these programmers will save you and your employees countless hours of work. As president, you don't need to know how to create these programs yourself, but you do need to know why the company programmers are coming and what they are doing.

Data, Information, and Knowledge

A computer is a device for processing data. A computer user, however, is generally interested in obtaining information, with the ultimate goal of increasing knowledge. Understanding the differences between data and information, and between information and knowledge, will help you get the most out of your computer.

Data is facts without a context. Data can come in many forms: Numbers, letters, sounds, images, smells, and tastes are all data. Humans derive an overall impression of the world around them (reality) by obtaining data through the senses (sight, sound, touch, taste, and smell). By combining the data we get through our senses, we add meaning to the data and thereby turn the data into **information**. For example, yellow, sphere, and fuzzy, taken individually, are pieces of data. Put this data together and you have information about a tennis ball. In short, information is data plus meaning, or data in context.

Here's another example. The number .357 is a piece of data. Taken alone, it has no meaning — it's just a number. We don't know if it refers to a gun (a .357 Magnum) or the humidity of the air. But if .357 is data found in a table of batting averages, it becomes information about a batter. In this context .357 means that the batter has gotten a hit almost 36 percent of the times that he has been to bat.

When found in a table of batting averages, .357 is information. Understanding the significance of this batting average is **knowledge**. In other words, knowledge is information plus significance. We gain knowledge by collecting information over time and assimilating it with what we already know. If you have a knowledge of baseball, you know that .357 is an excellent batting average and might well earn a player several million dollars a year. Knowledge provides a perspective on how to use information and data, as illustrated in Figure 5-1.

Another way to compare data, information, and knowledge is to look at how much each is worth. In general, data isn't worth anything. After all, what good are numbers, words, or sounds if we don't know what they refer to? As soon as this data is put in context, though, it can have value. If you find a post-it note on your floor that says 4:30 P.M., it probably isn't worth anything. But if that same post-it is stuck to your calendar next to a note that says "Meet with bank loan officer," that post-it could be worth thousands. Thus, information is value-added data. Knowledge, however, is generally worth even more than information, because knowledge represents an entire body of information.

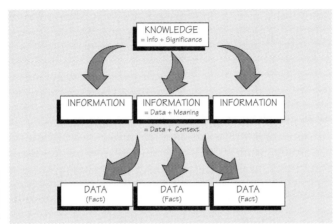

Figure 5-1
The relationship among data, information, and knowledge.

When you think about how a computer works, it's important to remember that humans tend to work with information and knowledge. The data we receive is almost invisible to us because it is usually received in context. Thus, data becomes information for us before we even think about it. A computer, on the other hand, works exclusively with data (though it does its work incredibly well). If the computer is used properly, it can present data in such a way that the data has immediate meaning for the user and is perceived as information. But the computer is none the wiser (Figure 5-2).

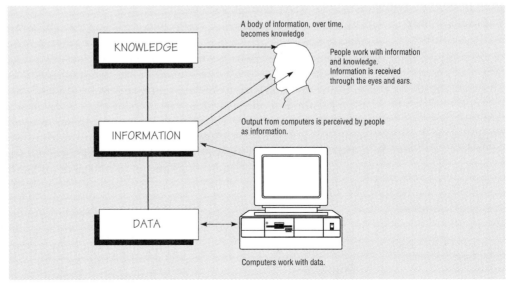

Figure 5-2
Computers work exclusively with data; humans tend to work with information and knowledge.

Comprehension Questions

1. From the user's point of view, what is the purpose of processing data?
2. Is a photograph a piece of information or a piece of data? Explain your answer.
3. Of data, information, and knowledge, which can be owned? Which is easiest to sell?

Using What You Know

1. List 10 types of data that you might keep in your customer database.
2. List five pieces of information that might prove useful in your efforts to make a profit in your new enterprise.
3. Name three areas of knowledge you will look for when hiring delivery drivers.

How the Computer Represents Data

A computer is an electronic device that processes and stores data in the form of electricity. It contains millions of **transistors**, which are tiny electronic switches. These transistors recognize only two states: on and off. Thus, all the data that is held in the computer must be represented by a series of switches that are either on or off. Computers are referred to as **binary** because they use only two electrical states.

Over time, computers will probably evolve from using electrical charges to using units of light called photons. Theoretically, at least, photon-based computing can be far more powerful and efficient than electron-based computing. As technology catches up with theory, the computer industry will move in this direction.

Analog and Digital Data

You might think that there is not much you can do with a series of on and off switches. As it turns out, though, you can create an approximate representation of just about anything, provided you have enough switches.

Base 10	Binary Code
0	0000
1	0001
2	0010
3	0011
4	0100
5	0101
6	0110
7	0111
8	1000
9	1001

Table 5-1

Counting from 0 to 9 using base 10 and binary code.

Because the computer is a binary device, we can use a **binary numbering system** to represent any series of switches. The binary numbering system works the same way as our base-10 numbering system, but instead of having 10 digits (0 through 9), we have only two (0 and 1). In this system, a 0 represents a switch that is off, and a 1 represents a switch that is on. Thus, any data that is held in the computer can be represented by base-2 numbers (see Table 5-1). **Binary code** is the term used to refer to computer data that is represented using a series of binary numbers. Because all data in a computer is represented with numbers, a computer is referred to as a **digital device**.

The opposite of a digital device is an **analog device**. An analog device is one that represents data with continuously variable physical quantities. The human ear, for example, is described as an analog device because it translates the physical phenomenon of sound using the physical movement of the eardrum.

The simplest example to illustrate the difference between the terms *analog* and *digital* is to look at the difference between an analog watch and a digital watch. The analog watch represents the rotation of the earth with rotating hands. The method of representation is directly related to the phenomenon being represented. A digital watch, however, displays the time in numbers by breaking the time it takes the earth to rotate into numbered intervals of hours and minutes. At any given instant, the time shown on the digital watch is just an approximation, because the numbers display an exact time for a whole second or a whole minute. The digital watch can display more accurate times by breaking the time into smaller units, but the time shown is always an approximation.

Another way to explain the difference between analog and digital is to compare a phonograph record to a compact disk. On a phonograph record, which is an analog device, sound is translated into a wavy line, which is etched into the record as a groove (see Figure 5-3a). The waves in the groove correspond directly to the frequency of the sound that is recorded. In theory at least, any frequency of sound can be represented accurately by the physical characteristics of the groove.

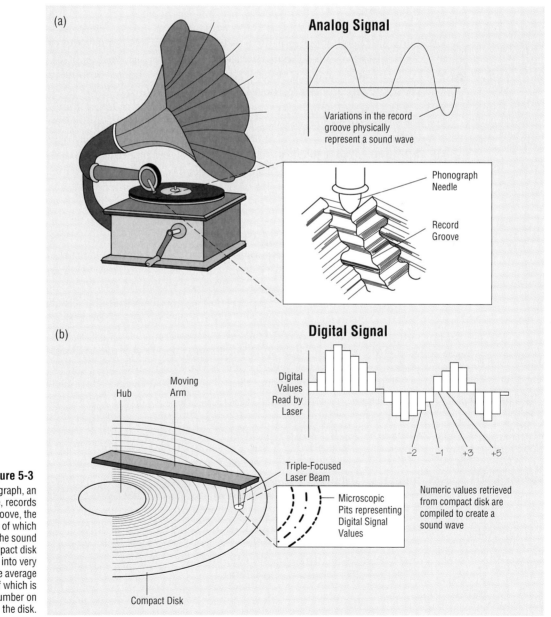

Figure 5-3

(a) The phonograph, an analog device, records sound with a groove, the shape of which corresponds to the sound wave; (b) a compact disk breaks the sound into very short intervals, the average frequency of which is recorded as a number on the disk.

A compact disk, on the other hand, represents sound as numbers, and is therefore a digital device. To do this, the compact disk must divide the sound into discrete intervals and then use a number to represent the average frequency of the sound within that interval (see Figure 5-3b). Even though the sound is constantly changing, the compact disk can store an excellent approximation of the sound with a very rapid sequence of numbers.

Bits and Bytes

When discussing computers, it is often important to talk about quantities of data: How much data can a computer hold? How much data can a computer process in one second? Because data in a computer consists of electrical switches, the smallest quantity of data is a single electrical on-off switch. The name for a single switch is one **bit**, which is a contraction of **bi**nary dig**it**.

Because a single bit can't represent very much data, bits are grouped into sets of eight. Eight bits together comprise one **byte**. When discussing quantities of data, bytes are actually a much more useful standard of measurement than bits, because it takes one byte to represent each character on the keyboard. For example, on a microcomputer, the uppercase letter "A" is usually represented by the following byte of data: 01000001.

As you can see, one byte still isn't a very big unit of measurement, especially when you consider that a single software program or data file can consist of thousands or even millions of bytes. For this reason, computer users often refer to kilobytes and megabytes. One **kilobyte** (abbreviated **K**) equals 1,024 bytes, and one **megabyte** (abbreviated **MB** or **meg**) equals 1,024 kilobytes, or 1,048,576 bytes. For extremely large measurements, one billion bytes is a gigabyte (one gig), and one trillion bytes is a terabyte.

ASCII

As noted above, it takes one byte to represent a single keyboard character. However, the system one uses to represent letters as numbers is entirely arbitrary. In other words, each computer maker could devise a different system. If they did, though, transferring data between one type of computer and another would be difficult. Over time, computer makers saw the advantage of a standard code for representing characters. The one used in microcomputers is called **ASCII** (pronounced *ask-ee*), which is an acronym for the American Standard Code for Information Interchange. A portion of the ASCII table, translating keyboard characters into bytes of binary code, is shown in Table 5-2.

The most widely used encoding scheme outside of ASCII is called **EBCDIC** (pronounced *eb-see-dick*), an acronym for Extended Binary Coded Decimal Interchange Code. This scheme is used primarily on large IBM computers. A third and increasingly popular code, produced by the American National Standards Institute, is called **ANSI** and is used in programs such as Microsoft Windows and Word. ANSI codes are very similar to ASCII codes; in fact, the first 128 characters are almost identical. The remaining characters, which are used for graphics, indentations, and other formatting characters, are different.

Normally, the difference between ASCII (or ANSI) and EBCDIC is not very important because so many of us only use microcomputers. However, if we want to send information from a microcomputer to an IBM mainframe, the difference can be troublesome. For example, on a PC, the character "L" is 01001100, which, when sent to a mainframe, is interpreted as "<". In order to transfer the data, it must be translated using a device or software package called a protocol converter.

	EBCDIC	ASCII		EBCDIC	ASCII		EBCDIC	ASCII
A	193	65	a	129	97	0	240	48
B	194	66	b	130	98	1	241	49
C	195	67	c	131	99	2	242	50
D	196	68	d	132	100	3	243	51
E	197	69	e	133	101	4	244	52
F	198	70	f	134	102	5	245	53
G	199	71	g	135	103	6	246	54
H	200	72	h	136	104	7	247	55
I	201	73	i	137	105	8	248	56
J	209	74	j	145	106	9	249	57
K	210	75	k	146	107			
L	211	76	l	147	108			
M	212	77	m	148	109			
N	213	78	n	149	110			
O	214	79	o	150	111			
P	215	80	p	151	112			
Q	216	81	q	152	113			
R	217	82	r	153	114			
S	226	83	s	162	115			
T	227	84	t	163	116			
U	228	85	u	164	117			
V	229	86	v	165	118			
W	230	87	w	166	119			
X	231	88	x	167	120			
Y	232	89	y	168	121			
Z	233	90	z	169	122			

Table 5-2
ASCII and EBCDIC equivalents for numbers and letters.

Files

A set of data that the user has given a name to is called a **file**. Files can consist of text (alphanumeric characters), pictures, or sound. Anything that can be represented with binary code can be a file. Normally, a file is a group of data that goes together (see Figure 5-4).

A **program** is a special kind of file that the computer can execute. For this reason, programs are sometimes referred to as **executable files**.

```
D:\>cd dos

D:\DOS>dir

 Volume in drive D is JACK STRAW
 Volume Serial Number is 18F6-523A
 Directory of D:\DOS

 .             <DIR>        12-07-92  12:14a
 ..            <DIR>        12-07-92  12:14a
APPEND   EXE     10774 04-09-91   1:00p
ASSIGN   COM      6399 04-09-91   1:00p
ATTRIB   EXE     15796 04-09-91   1:00p
BACKUP   EXE     36092 04-09-91   1:00p
CHKLIST  CPS       297 12-07-92  12:17a
DISKCOMP COM     10652 04-09-91   1:00p
DISKCOPY COM     11793 04-09-91   1:00p
NLSFUNC  EXE      7052 04-09-91   1:00p
       10 file(s)        98855 bytes
                       3919872 bytes free

D:\DOS>
```

Figure 5-4
A directory of files listed using DOS. The column on the far left lists the names of each file; the next column lists the file extensions (files with extensions COM or EXE are executable files).

Comprehension Questions

1. Why is it more logical that a byte is composed of 8 bits, rather than some round number such as 5 or 10 bits? (*Hint:* The computer is a binary device.)

2. Why do you think ASCII code is not widely used by microcomputer software in Japan?

3. Is a glass thermometer that you use to take a person's temperature a digital device or an analog device? Why?

Using What You Know

1. Of the three coding schemes discussed in the last section, which one will be used the most by BVOS computers? Justify your answer.

2. How many bits of data does it take to spell out Buena Vista Office Supply?

3. If a double-spaced page of text includes about 250 words that average six characters each (including spaces), how many kilobytes of memory are required to hold the 10-page status report to headquarters that you have written?

What Is Programming?

All data and software must be reduced to binary code for a computer to be able to use them. In order for software to be understood, the instructions that make up each program must be stored in **machine language**, a particular kind of binary code, illustrated in Figure 5-5. **Programming** is the process of creating the instructions that the computer can use. Most of this process is done by programmers who write software using programming languages. A second part is done by interpreters and compilers, which are pieces of software that convert programming languages into machine language that the computer can understand.

There are two ways to translate a program (known in this context as **source code**) into machine language. The first way is to use a **compiler**, which translates the language all at once into machine language. After one pass, the compiler will inform the user of pieces of code that it cannot understand. When the programmer has solved all of the problems, the compiler generates what is called **object code**, which is just a machine language version of the program.

Some computer languages use interpreters instead of compilers. Rather than creating the object code in advance, an **interpreter** translates the language while the program is running. For this reason, an interpreted language must always be accompanied by the interpreter program. To fix errors in the program, the programmer must attempt to run it. When the interpreter runs into a line of code that it can't interpret, it stops, and the programmer fixes that line (or whatever line caused the problem).

As you might expect, programs written with interpreted languages are slower than those written in compiled languages. Just as a diplomat must speak more slowly when an interpreter is standing next to him, the interpreted program runs more slowly because the interpreter must first translate the program, then carry out its instructions.

The Five Generations of Programming Languages

Programming languages have evolved as the languages have become less like machine language and more like the languages we use in speech and writing.

Low-Level Languages

Programming languages are referred to as low level or high level, depending on how similar the language is to machine code. **Low-level languages** are all the first- and second-generation languages. Machine language is considered the lowest level of programming language because it is closest to the actual requirements of the hardware platform. Sometimes this is called "programming on the bare metal." Machine languages are known as **first-generation languages** because they were the first to be used by programmers. Although common in the 1940s, machine language is still written today, though sparingly.

In **second-generation languages**, programmers began using mnemonics or symbols (usually words) to represent commonly used strings of machine language. All languages from the second generation forward are referred to as symbolic languages. The symbols are translated into machine language using an assembler. A hallmark of the 1950s, **assembly language** is widely used today because it allows programmers to better control the operation of the computer. Many high-level programs use portions of assembly language programs to speed processing. An example of assembly language is shown in Figure 5-6 on the next page.

Low-level languages require a great deal of programming experience because the languages have very few English-like statements and most of the instructions are in very detailed code. Although they are very fast, low-level languages have a disadvantage: They have almost no **portability** between computers. In other words, there is a different machine language and assembly language for each type of microprocessor. Thus, if a programmer writes an assembly language program for a particular model of PC, it will not work on any model that uses a different CPU, much less on a Macintosh or a NeXT computer.

```
58 10 C 054
58 40 1 024
D2 02 4 011 C 00D
50 10 D 234
92 00 D 234
96 80 D 234
41 10 D 234
D2 03 D 060 C 06A
58 F0 C 010
05 EF
58 10 C 054
D2 03 D 060 C 06E
58 F0 C 010
05 EF
58 70 D 200
58 10 C 054
18 21
D2 03 2 098 C 024
58 F0 2 0C8
05 EF
95 00 2 088
58 20 C 040
07 72
50 10 D 200
58 70 D 200
58 50 C 028
07 F5
92 E8 6 000
58 00 D 22C
50 00 D 228
58 00 C 02C
50 00 D 22C
58 20 C 030
95 E8 6 000
07 82
58 10 C 01C
07 F1
58 00 D 228
50 00 D 22C
58 10 C 054
```

Figure 5-5
An example of machine code that can be understood by the computer.

High-Level Languages

The third, fourth, and fifth generations of computer languages are all referred to as **high-level languages**. Three features of these languages distinguish them as high level. First, the code used in high-level languages is much more like English than the code used in low-level languages. High-level languages

```
START       EQU     *
            L       1,054(0,12)             DCB=1
            L       4,024(0,1)
            MVC     011(3,4),00D(12)                            V(ILBOEXT1)
            ST      1,234(0,13)             SAV3
            MVI     234(13),X'00'           SAV3
            OI      234(13),X'80'           SAV3
            LA      1,234(0,13)             SAV3
            MVC     060(4,13),06A(12)       WC=01           LIT+10
            L       15,010(0,12)            V(ILBOQIO0)
            BALR    14,15
            L       1,054(0,12)             DCB=1
            MVC     060(4,13),06E(12)       WC=01           LIT+14
            L       15,010(0,12)            V(ILBOQIO0)
            BALR    14,15
            L       7,200(0,13)             BL =1
            L       1,054(0,12)             DCB=1
            LR      2,1
            MVC     098(4,2),024(12)                            GN=01
            L       15,0C8(0,2)
            BALR    14,15
            CLI     088(2),X'00'
            L       2,040(0,12)             GN=08
            BCR     7,2
            ST      1,200(0,13)             BL =1
            L       7,200(0,13)             BL =1
```

Figure 5-6
An example of assembly
language.

use words like WHILE, IF, THEN, ELSE, FOR, IN, DO, and END. Second, high-level languages are machine independent, meaning that their programs are much more portable than those of low-level languages. The compiler or interpreter is, of course, machine dependent, since the machine language is not portable. Third, high-level languages exhibit **instruction explosion**. This means that when an assembly program is translated into machine language, each line of assembly — each instruction — becomes one machine language instruction. A single line of a high-level language, however, may be compiled or assembled into several (or many) machine language instructions. Often a good compiler or interpreter can be judged by how few lines of machine language it creates from single lines of the high-level code.

There are scores of high-level programming languages. Each of these languages was created to address a certain set of programming problems. For example, there are languages designed to help teach other languages. Some languages are most often used in business data processing, and others are most often used in scientific work. Table 5-3 contains a list of some popular high-level programming languages and their strengths. As you can see, there is no shortage of programming languages. You might also note that most of the names of programming languages, such as FORTRAN, are capitalized because they are acronyms.

Most high-level languages are **third-generation languages**. All of the languages listed in Table 5-3 are of the third generation. In general, a third-generation language is a general-purpose symbolic language that is machine independent.

Fourth-generation languages are often called **4GLs**. As we move from the third generation to the fourth and fifth generations, computers become easier and easier to use. 4GLs are more English-like than previous languages and allow users to concentrate more on what they want the computer to do rather than how to do it (Figure 5-7). This is what makes fourth- and future-generation languages **nonprocedural languages**. The result is that users with little computer training can become effective programmers. Fourth-generation

Language	Strengths
Ada	A multipurpose, structured language used by the U.S. government.
BASIC	An easy-to-learn, yet relatively powerful language used in home computers as well as in business. (Beginner's All-Purpose Symbolic Instruction Code)
C	Creates very portable, structured programs in a variety of areas. C is widely held as the most popular programming language in the world.
COBOL	A language suited to business data processing and sophisticated file processing. More business programs are currently written in COBOL than in any other language. (COmmon Business-Oriented Language)
FORTRAN	A language created for complex mathematical computations. FORTRAN is the programming language of choice for many scientific and engineering application. (FORmula TRANslator)
Pascal	A language used to create structured programs. Pascal was designed to teach structured programming and as such is very popular among student programmers.

Table 5-3
Some popular high-level languages and their strengths.

languages are often less flexible than third, because most 4GLs are created for specific purposes. Some products that are usually considered application packages, such as dBASE, are also considered 4GLs because they can be programmed to carry out specific kinds of tasks.

Fifth-generation languages, or **5GLs**, combine the easy-to-use aspects of 4GLs with artificial intelligence and expert systems to make the computer even easier to use. Although very few 5GLs are available, one of their primary characteristics is **natural language processing (NLP)**. Natural language processing allows the user to instruct the computer just as he or she would instruct a human assistant. For example, an instruction to display yesterday's sales for the southeast region, organized by sales territory, can be typed "DISPLAY YESTERDAY'S SALES FOR THE SOUTHEAST REGION, ORGANIZED BY SALES TERRI-TORY". As you can see, there is no difference between what we wanted to do and how we told the computer to do it. It is predicted that future 5GLs will help create computers that we can actually talk to.

```
SELECT LAST_NAME FIRST_NAME FROM EMPLOYEE_FILE
    WHERE SSN IS IN
            (SELECT SSN FROM JOB_LIST, PROJECTS
            WHERE JOB_LIST.JOB_NUMBER = PROJECTS.JOB_NUMBER
            AND PROJECTS.TYPE = "SOFTWARE")
```

Figure 5-7
Instructions written in SQL, a 4GL used to query databases.

Comprehension Questions

1. Why are symbolic languages easier to use than machine languages?
2. Of the three differences cited between low- and high-level languages, which do you think is most important to software manufacturers?
3. Why do you think students learning programming are more likely to be trained in a third-generation language than a fourth-generation language?

Using What You Know

1. As president of BVOS, if you were to learn a programming language, what type would you learn and why?
2. From the evolution of programming languages described in this section, what might you expect from sixth-generation languages?
3. For what types of jobs would it be useful to know first-generation languages? Why?

Common Programming Languages

Although many programming languages exist, there are several that are frequently encountered in business. These languages are used to create programs that help users solve business and other kinds of problems.

BASIC

One of the easiest programming languages to learn is **BASIC** (**B**eginner's **A**ll-Purpose **S**ymbolic **I**nstruction **C**ode). BASIC was developed in 1964 at Dartmouth College by John Kemeny and Thomas Kurtz to teach students the logic of programming without the programming complications that often came with other languages of the day. At one time, the BASIC programming language was a standard feature that came with the IBM PC. Although BASIC was conceived as a tool to help students learn another programming language (FORTRAN), today it is a powerful, well-supported language in its own right. There are different versions of BASIC depending on the computer being used. BASIC is commonly implemented using an interpreter. Figure 5-8 shows a short BASIC program.

FORTRAN

FORTRAN (**FOR**mula **TRAN**slator) is a third-generation language known for being able to perform extensive mathematical manipulations. Developed in 1957 by John Backus, FORTRAN is the oldest high-level programming language. Prior to its creation, programs were written in assembly or machine language. FORTRAN was the first programming language that could be used to write programs on one computer for subsequent use on another computer. Program portability has since become a standard feature of high-level programming languages. A short FORTRAN program is shown in Figure 5-9.

```
'December 8, 1992
'File:  HILOW.BAS
'Programmer:  D. Adams
'
'This program reads in a set of test scores from the file  STU-
DENT.DAT.
'It then print the largest and smallest test scores and the students
'who earned those scores.
'
'INPUT variables:  std$          is the student's name
'                  grade         is the student's test score
'OUTPUT variables: highest       is the highest test score
'                  lowest        is the lowest test score
'                  hstd$         is the student with the highest test
score
'                  lstd$         is the student with the lowest test
score
'
OPEN "STUDENT.DAT" FOR INPUT AS #1
highest = 0                                'Initialize the variables
lowest = 100
ON ERROR GOTO printit
DO UNTIL EOF(1)
        INPUT #1, std$, grade         'Read data
        IF grade  highest THEN        'Check for the largest value
                highest = grade       'Remember the highest grade
                hstd$ = std$          ' and the corresponding student
        END IF
        IF grade  lowest THEN         'Check for the smallest value
                lowest = grade        'Remember the lowest grade
                lstd$ = std$          ' and the corresponding student
        END IF
LOOP
'
'Print out the values.
'
printit:
PRINT "The highest grade was"; highest; "earned by "; hstd$; "."
PRINT "The lowest  grade was"; lowest; "earned by "; lstd$; "."
CLOSE (1)
END
```

Figure 5-8
A short but complete
program written in BASIC.

```
      REAL GPA
      CHARACTER STDNAME*20
      INTEGER I
      OPEN(5,"STUDENT.DAT"
 100 READ (5,200,EOF=500)NAME, GPA
 200 FORMAT(A20,F4.3)
      IF (GPA .GE. 3.0) WRITE (6,400) NAME, GPA
 400  FORMAT(IX,A20,7X,F5.2)
      GOTO 100
 500 CONTINUE
      CLOSE
      STOP
      END
```

Figure 5-9
The same program as
Figure 5-8, but written in
FORTRAN.

Figure 5-10
Grace Murray Hopper, the "mother of modern programming."

COBOL

COBOL (**CO**mmon **B**usiness-**O**riented **L**anguage) is a language frequently used for developing business applications. COBOL was formally defined in 1959 by Grace Hopper. Hopper, who retired as a Rear Admiral from the U.S. Navy (see Figure 5-10), is affectionately known as the "mother of modern programming." COBOL, the first language developed specifically with portability in mind, was a consortium effort among business, government, and academia. COBOL's portability caused the price of software to decrease because a software company could write a payroll program, for example, then sell it to several companies. The buyer was able to purchase a program without the substantial development costs normally associated with software, and the seller was able to recoup development costs and make a profit. COBOL encouraged business use of computers. A sample COBOL program is depicted in Figure 5-11.

```
IDENTIFICATION DIVISION.
PROGRAM-ID.          GRADES.
ENVIRONMENT DIVISION.
CONFIGURATION SECTION.
SOURCE-COMPUTER.    IBM-370.
OBJECT-COMPUTER.    IBM-370.
INPUT-OUTPUT SECTION.
FILE-CONTROL.
    SELECT INPUT-FILE ASSIGN TO UT-S-SYSIN.
DATA DIVISION.
FILE SECTION.
FD  INPUT-FILE
       LABEL RECORDS ARE STANDARD
       RECORD CONTAINS 80 CHARACTERS
       DATA RECORD IS INPUT-CARD.
01     INPUT-CARD.
       05   STUDENT-NAME    PIC X(20).
       05   GPA             PIC 9V999.
       05   FILLER          PIC X(56).
WORKING-STORAGE SECTION.
77     EOF                  PIC X VALUE 'N'.
01     OUTPUT-LINE.
       05   STUDENT-NAME    PIC X(20).
       05   FILLER          PIC X(10) VALUE SPACES.
       05   GPA             PIC 9.999.
PROCEDURE DIVISION.
       READ INPUT-FILE AT END MOVE 'Y' TO EOF.
       PERFORM PRINT-DATA UNTIL EOF = 'Y'.
       CLOSE INPUT-FILE.
       STOP RUN
PRINT-DATA.
       IF GPA GREATER THAN OR EQUAL TO 3.0 THEN
            MOVE CORRESPONDING INPUT-CARD TO OUTPUT-LINE
            DISPLAY OUTPUT-LINE.
       READ INPUT-FILE AT END MOVE 'Y' TO EOF.
```

Figure 5-11
The same program as Figure 5-8, but written in COBOL.

Pascal

Developed in the early 1970s by Swiss scientist Niklous Wirth, **Pascal** is a general-purpose high-level language named after the French mathematician Blaise Pascal. Pascal uses the principles of structured programming, which require that a program be written according to a logical structure. Larger routines are broken down into smaller ones (called "modules"), each of which performs a specific activity.

Pascal first gained popularity in academic circles as a teaching tool. It has strongly influenced other structured languages such as Ada and dBASE. Figure 5-12 shows a short Pascal program.

```
program students;
type    student_rec   = record
            name          : string[20];
            gpa           : real;
        end;
        student_file  = file of student_rec;
var     student       : student_rec;
        datafile      : student_file;

begin
        assign(datafile,"STUDENT.DAT");
        reset(datafile);
        while(not Eof(datafile)) do
                begin
                        if (student.gpa = 3.0) then begin
                                writeln(student.name, stu-
dent.gpa);
                        Read(datafile,student);
                        end;
                end;
        end;
        close(datafile);
end.
```

Figure 5-12

The same program as Figure 5-8, but written in Pascal.

C

In 1972 Dennis Ritchie of Bell Laboratories created a programming language that was designed, like COBOL, to be portable across several types of computers. The difference between COBOL and **C** was the way the programmer controlled the structure of the program. Programmers use a set of rules to help them create programs that will be easy to read, understand, and fix. The C programming language specifically incorporates these constructs of "structured programming"; other languages such as COBOL do not. C has been called the most portable programming language available. Therefore, many application packages have been written in C. The C language is one of the most popular programming languages in the world. (As an aside, the predecessor of C was B, a low-level assembly-like programming language; the predecessor of B was an assembly language.) A sample C program is shown in Figure 5-13 on the next page.

SQL

SQL (**S**tructured **Q**uery **L**anguage) was developed in the 1970s at IBM San Jose Research Laboratories by D. Chamberlain and others. SQL is a 4GL that allows users to ask questions

```
#include <stdio.h>
#include <conio.h>

void main()
{
    FILE *s_file;
    char  student_name[20];
    float gpa;
    s_file=fopen("STUDENT.DAT","r");
    while (! feof(s_file)) {
        fscanf(s_file, "%20s %e",&student_name, &gpa);
        if (gpa >= 3.0)
            printf("%s\n",student_name);
    }
    fclose(s_file);
}
```

Figure 5-13
The same program as
Figure 5-8, but written in C.

of, or **query**, a database. SQL also lets users put data into a database and change data that is already in a database. A database query is created when a user has a question that needs to be answered or a problem to be solved. SQL is also called "structured English" because of the way it "forces" users to write its commands. SQL is the standard language for interacting with a database.

SQL can be incorporated directly into some third-generation languages to increase the power of these older languages. SQL is used in dBASE IV as a standard interface language for creating dBASE programs. Figure 5-14 shows an SQL query of a database.

Figure 5-14
A database query written in
SQL.

```
SELECT STUDENT_NAME GPA FROM STUDENT_RECORDS WHERE GPA = 3.0
```

Ada

The United States government has long been in the business of establishing standards for computer hardware and software. Collectively, the federal government is the largest consumer of computer hardware and software. The government writes programs to fly missiles, print paychecks, audit tax forms, monitor jet fighters, conduct air-traffic control, monitor satellites in space, launch space shuttles, and keep track of the citizenry. **Ada** was originally developed for and by the U.S. Department of Defense. The government selected the Ada programming language to be the standard programming language for all major federal systems projects. Ada is a high-level, third-generation programming language that was designed to work well in both real-time and batch systems. Figure 5-15 shows a short Ada program.

Ada was named after Ada Byron King, the Countess of Lovelace (Figure 5-16). Ada Lovelace, daughter of the English romantic poet, Lord Byron, was a contemporary of Charles Babbage, the "father of computers." Babbage was a mathematician at Cambridge University who developed the "analytical engine," a calculating device that used punched cards as input data. In 1842, at the age of 27, Lovelace began working with Babbage and making significant changes to the control sequences of the engine. Ada Lovelace is credited for being the first programmer, because she described programming concepts that are the heart of all computer programs today.

```
with TEXT_IO;
use TEXT_IO;
with SEQUENTIAL_IO;
procedure STUDENT_READ is
        type STUDENT_RECORD is
                record
                            STUDENT_NAME : STRING(1..20);
                            GPA          : FLOAT;
                end record;
        package STUDENT_IO is new SEQUENTIAL_IO(STUDENT_RECORD);
        use STUDENT_IO;
        SRECORD : STUDENT_RECORD;
        SFILE   : STUDENT_IO.FILE_TYPE;
begin
        OPEN(SFILE,IN_FILE,"STUDENT.DAT");
        READ(SFILE,SRECORD);
        while not END_OF_FILE(SFILE)
                loop
                        if SRECORD.GPA not  3.0 then
                                PUT(SRECORD.STUDENT_NAME);
                                NEW_LINE;
                        end if;
                        READ(SFILE,SRECORD);
                end loop;
        CLOSE(SFILE);
end STUDENT_READ;
```

Figure 5-15

The same program as Figure 5-8, but written in Ada.

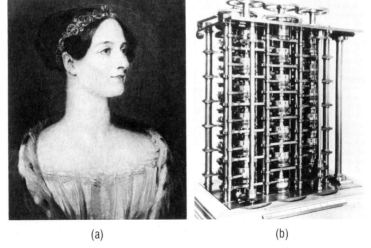

Figure 5-16

(a) Ada Byron King, the Countess of Lovelace; (b) Charles Babbage's analytical engine.

(a)   (b)

Other Languages

It is at times difficult to separate a programming language from application software. For example, the database package dBASE is an application package that allows users to design and use databases (which will be discussed later). However, dBASE has a programming language that will allow a programmer to create an application to solve a problem. Likewise, the spreadsheet program Lotus 1-2-3 is an application that allows users to analyze data in spreadsheet form. However, Lotus 1-2-3 contains a kind of programming language called a **macro** that allows programmers and users to create Lotus 1-2-3-based applications (see

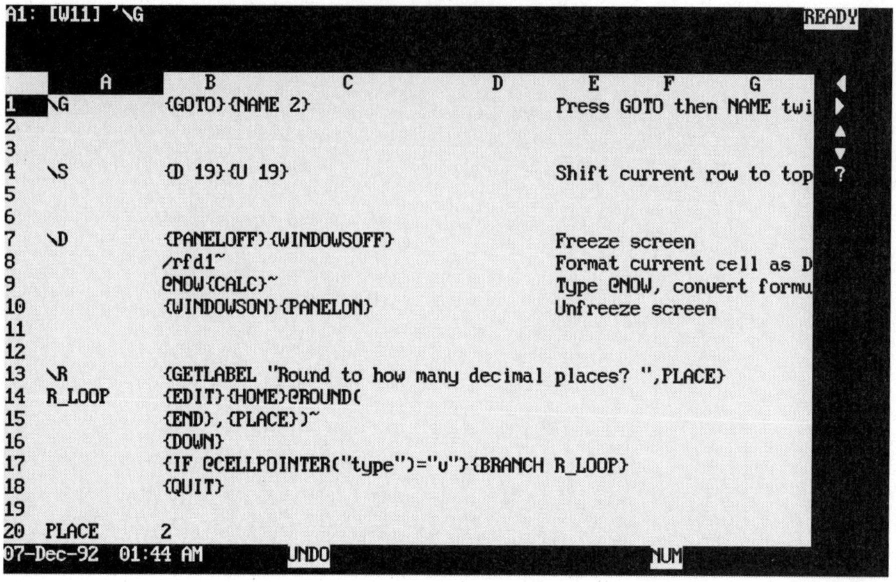

```
A1: [W11] \G                                                        READY

          A         B            C         D        E      F      G
1   \G          {GOTO}{NAME 2}                      Press GOTO then NAME twi
2
3
4   \S          {D 19}{U 19}                        Shift current row to top
5
6
7   \D          {PANELOFF}{WINDOWSOFF}              Freeze screen
8               /rfd1~                              Format current cell as D
9               @NOW{CALC}~                         Type @NOW, convert formu
10              {WINDOWSON}{PANELON}                Unfreeze screen
11
12
13  \R          {GETLABEL "Round to how many decimal places? ",PLACE}
14  R_LOOP      {EDIT}{HOME}@ROUND(
15              {END},{PLACE})~
16              {DOWN}
17              {IF @CELLPOINTER("type")="v"}{BRANCH R_LOOP}
18              {QUIT}
19
20  PLACE       2
07-Dec-92  01:44 AM           UNDO                            NUM
```

Figure 5-17
A Lotus 1-2-3 macro, an example of programming with an application.

Figure 5-17). As programming languages become more English-like, the difference between a program and a programming language will be difficult to pinpoint.

Object-Oriented Programming

Traditional programming focuses on the function of a program. Creating the program is a process of emulating how people carry out a task, and data is organized so the computer can execute the instructions as quickly as possible. **Object-oriented programming**, which has gained popularity in the past few years, is an alternative to the traditional programming strategy. Rather than seeing a task purely as a means for accomplishing an end, object-oriented programming looks at the various elements as having certain attributes and as performing certain actions.

For example, a programmer creating the BVOS customer billing system might create "customer" and "account" objects. The attributes of each customer object are its name, address, and so on. The attributes of each account object include its balance and date due. A customer object that needs an account balance could send a message to the account object that reads "tell balance."

The strategies used in object-oriented programming allow programmers to create, use, and reuse programs more easily than do more traditional strategies. Object oriented programming therefore decreases programming costs and increases the quality of programs. Symantec's C++ and Borland's Pascal with Objects are two well-known object-oriented languages.

Comprehension Questions

1. Which language is more likely to be used to calculate satellite orbital paths, FORTRAN or COBOL?

2. What language might be best for developing accounting software?

3. Name an advantage of learning Pascal rather than BASIC.

Using What You Know

1. Use computer magazines to find five companies that market programming software. What are the companies and what languages do they use?

2. Find at least two competing prices for C compilers. How much do they cost?

3. If you had only one programmer at BVOS, what language would you want him or her to learn, and how might you use that person's skills?

The Programming Process

The very first computing machines were entirely hardware; no software was needed. Computing devices were the tools of mathematicians and engineers who needed to calculate mathematical equations quickly. A hardware approach to computing systems is very limiting, however, because this inflexible device affects the way problems are viewed. As the old saying goes, "If all you have is a hammer, soon all your problems begin to look like nails."

Through the work of legendary figures in computing such as John Von Neumann and Grace Murray Hopper, we began to focus on the sets of instructions that control the computer. This software approach, which only became popular in the 1940s and 1950s, is far more flexible for solving problems. It allows a single computer to be used for a wide range of tasks. It also means that the process of creating a set of instructions — a program — is completely separated from designing the hardware.

When a programmer sets out to create a program, all he or she is really doing is solving a problem. The process for creating a program, therefore, is just a special case of the problem-solving process. The two processes, programming and problem solving, are compared in Figure 5-18.

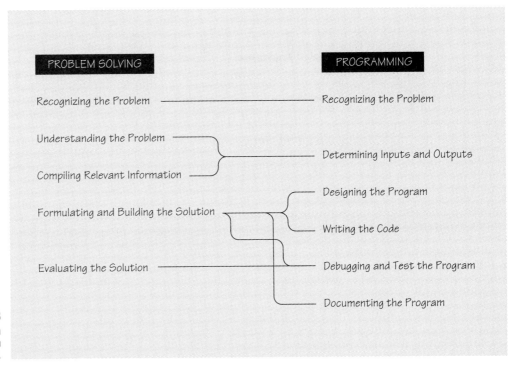

Figure 5-18
The steps involved in programming and problem solving are very similar.

Recognizing the Problem

As with all problem solving, programming begins with recognizing that there is a problem. Often this step occurs when a computer user realizes that a problem cannot be solved with any software products that are currently available. Once the user has come to this conclusion and decides that a program must be created, the final part of this step is to create a clear statement of the objectives that the program needs to meet.

Determining Inputs and Outputs

Step 2 is to determine what output is desired and what input is necessary to produce that output. This step can be thought of as "pre-design." As you can see from Figure 5-18, specifying input and output is a combination of understanding the problem and compiling relevant information. In this step, the programmer may also decide on the programming language that will be used.

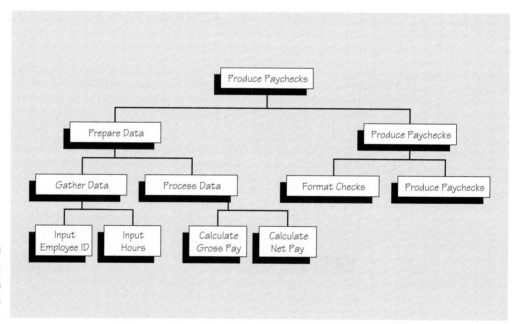

Figure 5-19
Top-down design involves breaking the overall problem into a set of subroutines, which can be programmed separately.

Designing the Program

Next we come to the all-important design step. For the most part, the longer a programmer spends on the design step, the less time he or she will spend writing the program. The object of this stage is to create the most efficient method for producing the desired output from the available input, given the types of processing that the computer is capable of.

During the past few decades, a great deal of attention has been paid to how programs are designed. Over the years, programmers have found that the most effective way to make good software is to build a logical framework for the program. This general approach and the techniques that are used in it are known as **structured programming**.

Top-Down Design. The most fundamental technique used in structured programming is to break the overall objective into smaller tasks and keep doing this until the smaller tasks are relatively simple. This "divide and conquer" approach is called **top-down design**. The result of top-down design is that programming consists of writing a series of **subroutines**, which can be put together to accomplish the original objective (Figure 5-19). Subroutines are also sometimes called modules, procedures, functions, or routines.

Pseudocode.　One relatively informal method for creating a top-down design is to write **pseudocode**. Pseudocode gets its name because it looks like code that has been written in a real computer language, but it isn't. Pseudocode is a way for the programmer to go through the motions of writing a program without worrying about the exact syntax of the computer language. This allows the programmer to concentrate on the logic of a program.

　　The degree of detail incorporated into the pseudocode is entirely up to the programmer. He or she may, in fact, start with a very rough pseudocode that summarizes the entire program in just a few lines. The programmer might then develop and polish his or her work until it is very similar to the actual language in which the program will be written. Figure 5-20 shows pseudocode for part of the top-down design developed in Figure 5-19.

```
Produce paychecks

Enter employee ID number
Enter hours worked by employee.
Calculate employee's net pay
Calculate employee's gross pay.
Ensure that information has been entered
    and calculated for all employees.
Format paychecks.
Print paychecks.
```

Figure 5-20

Pseudocode written to address part of the top-down design shown in Figure 5-19.

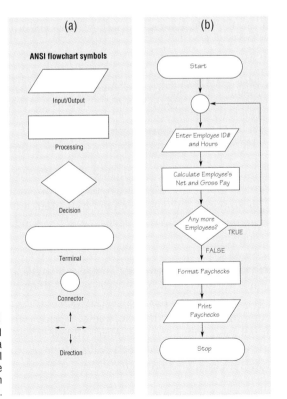

Figure 5-21

(a) The standard ANSI flowchart symbols; (b) a flowchart, a formal representation of the top-down design shown in Figure 5-19.

Flowcharting. Another, more formal, technique for structured programming is to create a logical **flowchart** of the desired program. Figure 5-21 shows a flowchart of the same top-down design you saw in Figures 5-19 and 5-20. Notice the different shapes used in different steps of the chart. Each of these shapes tells you something about the function of that step.

Logic Structures. Unlike pseudocode, the flowchart provides a graphic representation of how the input data becomes output. Notice that the program does not always move in a straight line down through the chart. In addition to sequential steps, there are branches where selections must be made, and there are loops that force the program to repeat a series of steps. These are the three basic **logic structures** that are used in programs: sequence, selection, and loop.

The **sequence structure** is, of course, the simplest (see Figure 5-22). When the program gets done with one step or one subroutine, it moves on to the next. Because the computer reads the steps of the program in sequential order unless it is told to do otherwise, no special statement needs to be made to create a sequential structure.

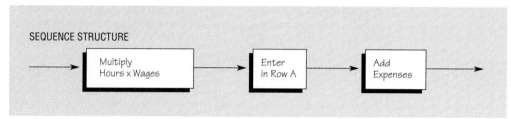

Figure 5-22
A sequence structure.

A **selection structure** (Figure 5-23) is used when the type of processing depends on the nature of the input data. Selection structures are sometimes referred to as IF-THEN-ELSE structures because these are the programming terms normally used to create the structure. The condition, or IF statement, is the one in the diamond-shaped decision box in the flowchart. This is where a certain condition is evaluated. If the condition is true, the program moves to the THEN statement and carries out the processing instructions. If the condition is false, the program moves to the ELSE statement and carries out those processing instructions. The flowchart here shows just two processing possibilities (THEN or ELSE), but there is no reason why there couldn't be more than two.

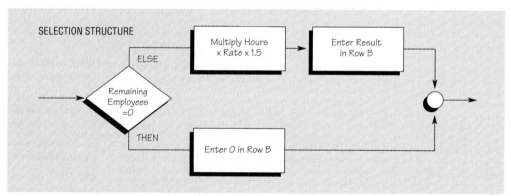

Figure 5-23
A selection structure.

A **loop structure** is similar to a selection structure but uses one of two statements, either DO WHILE or DO UNTIL. In the DO WHILE statement, the loop statement is repeated *while* the condition is true. The program will keep looping back until the condition is no longer true. In a DO UNTIL statement, the loop is repeated *until* the condition is true (see Figure 5-24).

The Opposite of Structured Programming. You might think that giving a program a logical, top-down design is the obvious way to proceed, and all programmers would follow that course. Unfortunately, there are lots of illogical ways to proceed, and there are plenty of bad programs out there to prove it. Often the sign of a badly written program is lots of GOTO statements that tell the computer to jump to a different place in the program. The result of too many GOTO statements is **spaghetti code**. The reason for the term is obvious if you try to create a flowchart of such a program.

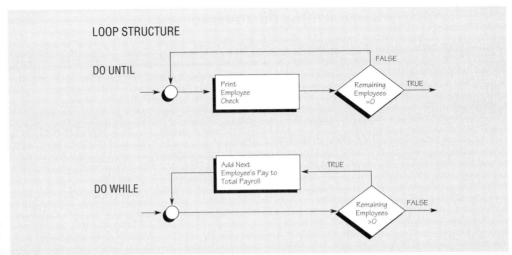

LOOP STRUCTURE

Figure 5-24
The DO WHILE and DO UNTIL loop structures.

Writing the Code

Once an efficient design has been created for a program, the next step is to sit down at the computer and actually write the instructions, or **code**. In structured programming, writing the code is the process of rebuilding the pseudocode or flowchart within the constraints of the programming language being used.

Debugging the Program

Rarely has a program been written that did not contain errors. An error in a program is known as a **bug**, and fixing errors is known as **debugging**. This quaint term has a perfectly logical explanation. As you've learned, Admiral Grace Hopper was one of the first programmers. In 1945, she was trying to find the source of a problem she was having with an IBM Mark I computer, a 51-foot contraption that weighed 5 tons. She eventually discovered the problem: A moth had been caught in one of the electronic relays. Ever since then, hardware and software malfunctions have been called bugs.

Software errors generally fall into one of two categories. **Syntax errors** are mistakes that violate the rules of whatever program the language is written in. The first phase of debugging is running the program through the compiler or interpreter. One of the responsibilities of the compiler or interpreter is to identify syntax errors.

Logic errors most often occur when the programmer has made an unfounded assumption. When you are creating a program, it is important to remember that a computer is absolutely literal, meaning that it does exactly what the program tells it to do. One common type of logic error is writing an endless loop. A DO WHILE loop might include a condition that is always true, or a DO UNTIL loop a condition that is always false. In either case, the computer will become stuck in the loop.

Once the software has been debugged, it must be tested. For commercial software, the testing process often takes months. The first version of the software, known as the **alpha version**, is usually tested only by an in-house audience. The second, and hopefully last preliminary version, is the **beta version**, which goes to an outside test audience. When a new version of a program is about to be released, you will often see reports on the beta version in trade magazines such as *PC World, Macworld,* and *PC Magazine.*

Documenting the Program

Documentation is a final important step in the programming process. Every program needs to be documented; the process should begin in the design stage. A program's internal documentation should include comments within the code itself, such as a preliminary

```
DECLARE SUB loademup (n, sum)            'This program reads test scores
DECLARE SUB sortem (n)                   'and prints the n, mean, median,
DECLARE SUB variance (n, var, mean)      'variance and standard deviation.
DIM SHARED x(200)

CALL loademup(n, sum)                    'Read STUDENT GRADES
CALL sortem(n)                           'Sort the grades for the median
mean = sum / n                           'Calculate mean
CALL variance(n, var, mean)              'Calculate variance
median = x(INT((n / 2) + .5))                'Locate middle value
PRINT "# tests ="; n
PRINT "mean    ="; mean
PRINT "median  ="; median
PRINT "variance="; var
PRINT "std dev ="; SQR(var)
END

SUB loademup (n, sum)
  sum = 0                                'Initialize sum variable
  n = 0                                  'Initialize number of grades
  OPEN "TEST.GRD" FOR INPUT AS #1
  WHILE NOT EOF(1)
        n = n + 1                        'Accumulate number of grades
        INPUT #1, x(n)                   'Read file
        sum = sum + x(n)                 'Accumulate sum of grades
  WEND
  CLOSE (1)
END SUB

SUB sortem (n)                           'This routine uses the common
 flag = 0                                'BUBBLE Sort to sort the grades
 FOR i = 1 TO n - 1                      'in an ascending fashion.
  FOR j = 1 TO n - i
   q = j + 1
   IF x(j)  x(q) THEN                    'This logic swaps the places of
      hold = x(j)                        'two test scores that are out of
      x(j) = x(q)                        'order (i.e. not in ascending order)
      x(q) = hold
   END IF
  NEXT
 NEXT
END SUB

SUB variance (n, var, mean)
 sumvar = 0                                     'Initialize variance sum
 FOR k = 1 TO n
     sumvar = sumvar + (x.k - mean) ^ 2         'Calculate variance
 NEXT
 var = sumvar / (n - 1)
END SUB
```

Figure 5-25
Documentation consists of (a) annotations in the source code and (b) separate printed documents.

(a)

description and line-by-line explanations (Figure 5-25a). External documentation should include flowcharts for use by programmers in understanding the logical structure of the program, and manuals to facilitate use of the program (Figure 5-25b).

(b)

Comprehension Questions

1. Suppose a program is compiled successfully, but the print command causes output to be sent to the monitor. Is this a syntax error or a logic error?

2. Is top-down design part of structured programming, or is it the other way around?

3. Which is the more formal process: creating a flowchart or writing pseudocode? Justify your answer.

Using What You Know

1. Programming software is often much more than just operating an interpreter or a compiler. What might such software packages include to help the programmer?

2. Besides using it as a programming tool, how might you use flowcharting software around the office?

3. How is choosing an application program similar to programming? What parts of each process are related?

Summary Points

Data, Information, and Knowledge

☐ Data is abstract descriptions of reality.

☐ Information is data plus meaning, or data in context.

☐ Knowledge is information plus significance.

☐ Data has no inherent worth. Information and knowledge have value.

☐ Computers process data but cannot create information. If the data is presented well, we can interpret it as information.

How the Computer Represents Data

☐ Today's computers process electrical signals.

☐ Computers are binary because they represent data with on/off switches.

Analog and Digital Data

☐ Computers are referred to as digital devices because they represent all data as numbers.

☐ Analog devices represent data with continuously variable physical quantities that are related to the phenomenon being represented.

☐ A digital device can only approximate a physical phenomenon.

Bits and Bytes

☐ A bit, which is the smallest quantity of digital data, represents one on/off switch.

☐ Eight bits make a byte.

☐ It takes one byte to represent each character on the keyboard.

☐ A kilobyte is 1,024 bytes. A megabyte is 1,024 kilobytes.

ASCII

☐ The most common binary coding scheme used on microcomputers is called ASCII.

☐ EBCDIC is used on mainframes.

☐ ANSI is similar to ASCII and is gaining popularity on microcomputers.

Files

☐ A group of data that the user has given a name to is called a file.

☐ Programs are also files.

What Is Programming?

☐ Programming is the process of creating instructions that the computer can understand and execute.

☐ Compilers and interpreters are programs that translate the instructions written by the programmer into machine language instructions.

☐ A compiler translates the code all at once and reports syntax errors.

☐ An interpreter translates the code while the program is running.

☐ Programs written in interpreted languages are slower than those written in compiled languages.

The Five Generations of Programming Languages

Low-Level Languages

☐ Low-level languages include the first and second generations.

☐ The first generation is machine language.

☐ The second generation, assembly languages, uses mnemonics to stand for sets of machine language instructions.

☐ Low-level languages have almost no portability between machines.

High-Level Languages

☐ The third through fifth generations are high-level languages.

☐ High-level languages look more like English, are machine independent, and exhibit instruction explosion.

☐ Third-generation languages are general-purpose symbolic languages, also known as procedural languages.

☐ Fourth-generation languages (4GLs) are nonprocedural, are easier to use than third-generation languages, and are created for specific purposes.

☐ Fifth-generation languages combine 4GLs with artificial intelligence, expert systems, and natural language processing.

Common Programming Languages

BASIC

☐ BASIC was originally developed as a tool to teach programming.

FORTRAN

☐ FORTRAN is the oldest high-level language; it is the first portable language.

☐ FORTRAN is used for mathematical manipulations.

COBOL

☐ Developed by Admiral Grace Hopper, COBOL was a consortium effort among business, academia, and government.

☐ COBOL is popular for business applications.

☐ COBOL was designed with portability in mind, a feature that made software development economically feasible.

Pascal

☐ Pascal is noted for its structured programming.

☐ It was initially popular in academia.

C

☐ C includes the constructs of structured programming.

☐ It is known as the most portable language and is one of the most popular languages in the world.

SQL

☐ SQL is a 4GL that allows the user to ask questions of a database.

Ada

☐ The government selected Ada as the standard language used in federal programs.

Other Languages

☐ Application packages such as Lotus 1-2-3 and dBASE include 4GLs to tailor the application. It can be difficult to distinguish a flexible application from a programming language.

Object-Oriented Programming

☐ Object-oriented programming represents a departure from the strategies of traditional programming. The programmer's focus is on the elements of the program and what they do; the result is a reuseable code.

The Programming Process

☐ The programming process is a special case of the problem-solving process.

Recognizing the Problem

☐ This step begins with recognizing that existing software will not meet a given need; it ends with a clear statement of the program's objectives.

Determining Inputs and Outputs

☐ This "pre-design" phase combines understanding the problem with compiling relevant information.

☐ The programmer picks the programming language in this phase.

Designing the Program

☐ Proper design uses the techniques of structured programming.

☐ Top-down design is a "divide and conquer" strategy. The result is that programming consists of writing a series of subroutines.

☐ Pseudocode is a strategy in which the programmer writes the logic of the program without worrying about the syntax of the language.

☐ Flowcharting diagrams the logic of the program.

☐ The logic of a program can include sequence, selection, and loop structures.

☐ Unstructured programming is characterized by numerous GOTO statements.

☐ The result of unstructured programming is spaghetti code.

Writing the Code

☐ In structured programming, writing the code is the process of rebuilding the pseudocode or flowchart within the constraints of the language's syntax.

Debugging the Program

☐ Debugging the program consists of eliminating syntax and logic errors from the instructions.

☐ Commercial software goes through a long process of debugging that includes preliminary alpha and beta versions of the software.

Documenting the Program

☐ Documenting the program, both within the code and in print, is often considered a part of the programming process.

Knowing the Facts

True/False

1. Programs written in third generation languages tend to be more portable than those written in assembly language.

2. Compilers and interpreters are pieces of software.

3. The most common code used for representing alphanumeric characters on a microcomputer is ANSI.

4. Only high level languages exhibit instruction explosion.

5. The result of top-down design is that programming consists of writing a series of subroutines.

6. The simplest logic structure is the selection structure.

7. Information can be thought of as data plus meaning.

8. BASIC, C, and FORTRAN are third-generation languages.

9. Programs that use an interpreter tend to be faster than those that use a compiler.

10. A digital device represents data as a series of numbers.

Short Answer

1. IF THEN ELSE statements initiate _____ structures.

2. Name a 4GL that allows users to ask questions of a database.

3. A _____ translates a program into machine language while the program is running.

4. An endless loop is a common type of _____ error.

5. Computers are referred to as _____ devices because they use only two electrical states.

6. _____ bytes equals approximately one megabyte.

7. _____ is a language originally created by Admiral Grace Hopper for developing business applications.

8. _____ is a language that was originally created to help teach programming.

9. _____ is the process of creating instructions that the computer can execute.

10. DO WHILE and DO UNTIL are used in _____ structures.

Answers

True/False	*Short Answer*
1 T	1. selection
2. T	2. SQL
3. F	3. interpreter
4. T	4. logic
5. T	5. binary
6. F	6. One million
7. T	7. COBOL
8. T	8. BASIC
9. F	9. programming
10. T	10. loop

Challenging Your Understanding

1. Do cassette tapes that store music encode the music as analog data or digital data? If you answered "analog," is it possible to store music on tape digitally? If you answered "digital," is it possible to store music on tape analogically?

2. The prefix "kilo" means 1,000. Why do you think a kilobyte equals 1,024 bytes rather than 1,000 bytes?

3. When we get to the point where we can talk to computers, will we need programmers?

4. Programs go through many, many revisions. When do you think a program is ready to be used? Who makes that determination?

5. Some research indicates that workers in an already stressful environment can be further stressed out when they use a computer program that does not adequately solve the user's problem. Should programmers be held accountable for the programs they write or is it the responsibility of the user to make appropriate use of the software?

6. Some estimates indicate that maintaining a program can cost as much as developing a program. What can programmers do to make maintaining a program as inexpensive as possible?

7. Give an example of a syntax error and a logic error arising from writing a short paragraph.

Unit II Project

Comparing Leading Word Processors for Gonzalez Legal Services

After graduating from a secretarial school as a legal secretary, Marcia Gonzalez was hired by Lopez, Nguyen and Porra, a well-established legal firm in a large city. Marcia started out as a filing clerk and over an eight-year career progressed from that position to senior legal secretary for Patricia Stokowski, a junior partner in the firm.

Marcia had learned the legal business quite well. She noted that a great deal of the day-to-day work in a law office involved the formatting and creation of standard legal documents. It occurred to her that Lopez, Nguyen and Porra could save a lot of money if they outsourced much of the secretarial support to an outside company whose business was the creation of legal documents. Marcia eventually got up the courage to present her idea to Patricia, who thought it was a great idea and encouraged Marcia to seriously consider it.

Patricia put up part of the seed money and Gonzalez Legal Services was formed. Patricia convinced the other junior partners to send as much work to Marcia as possible. In ten months, Lopez, Nguyen and Porra were able to reduce personnel costs by $35,000. On the anniversary of the partnership formation, Marcia got a contract with Lopez, Nguyen and Porra to handle all the routine legal transactions for the firm for the next five years. Soon three other large firms were also using Gonzalez.

Now Marcia had a problem. Her labor costs were beginning to significantly climb. Each additional work order actually was decreasing the after tax profit she made. Something had to be done to automate her business. The natural place to start was to computerize the creation of the legal documents.

You have been hired by Gonzalez Legal Services to help select a word processing system to support the creation, storage, retrieval and printing of large legal documents. Use whatever resources are available to you, but keep in mind that the system must be able to work in a legal environment and must have the ability to create and implement standard legal documents and form letters. Provide Ms. Gonzalez with a list of three word processing packages that would suit her needs. You should detail the strengths and weaknesses of each.

Hardware and Operating Systems

Unit III

So far, we've said a great deal about software without saying much about hardware. We wanted to discuss software first because, when buying a new computer system, the hardware should be chosen to support the applications you have purchased and will purchase in the future. Compatibility between present and future applications is vital; you don't have the luxury of buying a new computer when you need a new application! Now that you know how to purchase software, we need to look at the equipment that supports it.

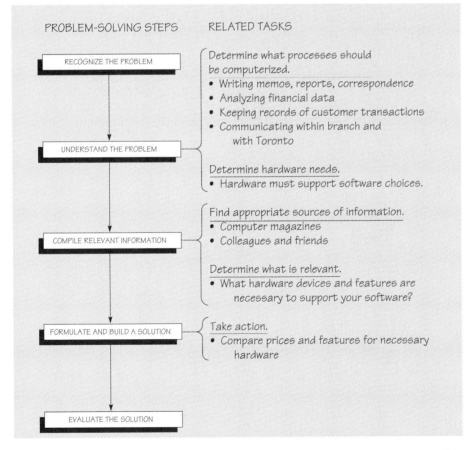

Figure III-1 In this unit, you will again be executing steps 2, 3, and 4 of the problem-solving process. This time, you will focus on hardware and operating systems.

Purchasing Hardware

In setting up your branch of BVOS, you have followed steps 2, 3, and 4 of the problem-solving methodology with respect to software. You have taken measures to understand the varied needs of your staff, your customers, and the central office in Toronto. You isolated important applications, used computer magazines to compare them, and selected appropriate programs. Now it's time to repeat these steps to choose the right hardware. Figure III-1 on the previous page shows what steps 2, 3, and 4 will include this time around.

Kinds of Hardware

As we explained in Unit I, computer systems are made up of hardware, software, data, and people. Software is a set of instructions and procedures that tell the computer what to do. Hardware is the physical manifestation of the computer system. If you can touch it, it is hardware. Thus a diskette is hardware, but the program contained on it is software. Often when users think about computer systems, they visualize the hardware that makes up the system.

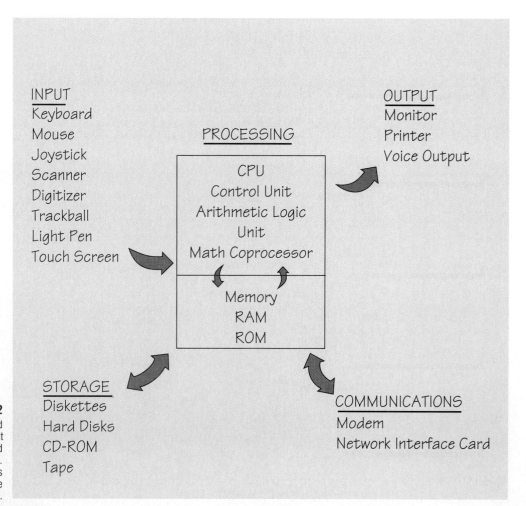

Figure III-2
A standard input-processing-output diagram, with storage and communication added. The most common devices are listed under the function they serve.

INPUT
Keyboard
Mouse
Joystick
Scanner
Digitizer
Trackball
Light Pen
Touch Screen

PROCESSING
CPU
Control Unit
Arithmetic Logic Unit
Math Coprocessor

Memory
RAM
ROM

OUTPUT
Monitor
Printer
Voice Output

STORAGE
Diskettes
Hard Disks
CD-ROM
Tape

COMMUNICATIONS
Modem
Network Interface Card

Microcomputer hardware consists of a collection of electronic devices that can help the user process data. These devices are broadly categorized into two functions: processing and input/output (I/O). Processing devices enable the computer to evaluate, manipulate, and store data for the user. Memory chips and CPUs are examples of processing devices. I/O supports communication between the processing devices and the world outside. I/O devices (1) provide interfaces so humans can interact with computers; (2) allow for the long-term storage of data; and (3) facilitate communication with other computers.

Although all three of these functions are part of I/O, we typically refer to input devices and output devices as those hardware components that serve the first function, that is, input from users and output to users. A mouse and a scanner are examples of input devices. Monitors and printers are output devices. Components that serve the second I/O function, allowing for the storage of data, are commonly referred to as storage devices. The third function, communication, is served by modems, fax modems, and network hardware. Figure III-2 summarizes the relationships among input, processing, output, storage, and communication devices.

Processing Devices

Key Terms

286
386
486
arithmetic logic unit (ALU)
bit
bus
byte
cache memory
central processing unit (CPU)
chassis
chip
clock speed
clones
compatibles
control unit
data bus
desktop model
expansion board
expansion slot
footprint
kilobyte (K)
math coprocessor

megabyte (MB)
megahertz (MHz)
memory
memory chip
MIPS
motherboard
nonvolatile memory
parallel port
peripheral
port
power supply
RAM
register
resistor
ROM
serial port
SIMM
surge suppresser
system unit
tower model
transistor
upward compatibility

Objectives

In this chapter you will learn to:

■ Define the two main parts of the central processing unit (CPU) and describe the purpose of each

■ Differentiate between the most common CPUs used on IBMs and compatibles

■ Name two important factors that affect the processing speed of the CPU

■ Explain the purposes of RAM and ROM and explain why ROM is nonvolatile and RAM is volatile

■ Describe how the CPU and RAM work together to compute simple arithmetic problems.

■ Explain how to calculate the amount of memory a computer requires

■ Differentiate between the two types of cache memory

■ Identify the main choices that are available when buying a chassis for a system unit

■ Name the main computer components found within the system unit

■ Explain how peripherals are connected to the CPU using expansion slots, expansion boards, data buses, and ports

■ Explain the importance of a surge suppresser

Processors: The Computer Engine

Each family of computer— Mac, IBM, NeXT, and so on — has a different set of processing equipment. In fact, more than their brand names, their processing differences are what separate computers into these families. So, choosing what type of computer to buy is really a processing decision. Even within a particular family, deciding which model computer to buy is a processing decision, because each model a company makes has different processing capabilities.

In this chapter, you will learn about the two basic processing components: microprocessors and memory chips. In addition, you will learn about the way the processing components are connected to the rest of the hardware devices. At the end of the chapter, you will look at computer magazines for new products, their processing capabilities, and their prices.

The System Unit: All the Hardware You Need

In most microcomputers, all of the processing components, including the central processing unit (CPU) and memory chips, are part of the **system unit** (Figure 6-1). The primary components of the system unit are the ports, the power supply, and the **motherboard**, which contains the bus, the CPU, all of the chips for controlling system peripherals, and slots for additional circuit boards. We will discuss these components in the sections that follow.

In addition, the system unit may include one or more storage devices, such as diskette drives or a hard disk drive. It can even include the display monitor. Therefore, the system unit itself is not a processing device; it is a catch-all term for the set of components that are housed together.

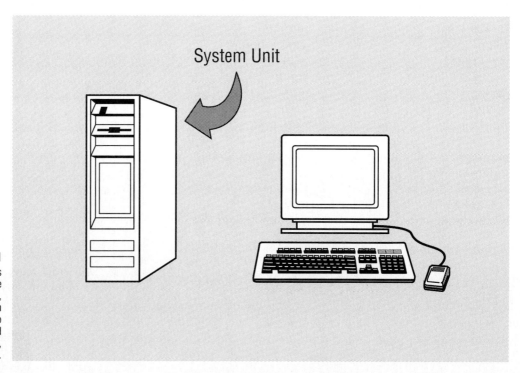

System Unit

Figure 6-1

The system unit of this computer houses the motherboard with the CPU, memory chips, expansion slots, and bus. It also includes the ports, the hard disk, one diskette drive, and the power supply.

When speaking to computer users or even salespeople, it is important to realize that many people refer to the entire system unit as the CPU. This usage is not accurate, because the CPU is just a small part of the system unit. Nevertheless, the usage is common and you should be familiar with it.

The Computer Chip: The Computer's Core

At the heart of every microcomputer is a set of integrated circuits, usually called *chips*. A **chip** is a small piece of silicon, often no bigger than your smallest fingernail, that is etched with electrical pathways (Figure 6-2).

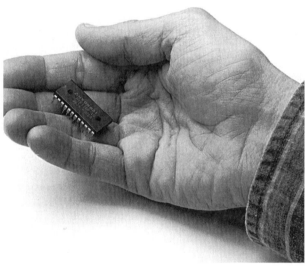

Figure 6-2
A computer chip.

As you learned in Chapter 5, computers represent data with a series of on-off switches called *transistors*. The earliest computers — those created before 1947, when the transistor was invented — used vacuum tubes instead of transistors. A vacuum tube is an electronic device that controls the flow of electrons in a vacuum. Each vacuum tube, which was several inches tall and an inch or more in diameter, acted as a single switch. Computers made with vacuum tubes, such as the one shown in Figure 6-3 on the next page, were gigantic and often weighed several tons. The ENIAC (Electronic Numerical Integrator and Calculator), developed for the U.S. Army in 1946, occupied 1800 square feet and contained 18,000 vacuum tubes (Figure 6-4 on the next page).

In 1947, researchers at AT&T's Bell Laboratories invented the **transistor**, a semiconductor device that operates as an electronic switch. When activated, it opens a circuit, bridges the gap between two wires, and allows current to flow. The transistor was made of solid materials instead of hollow tubes: This was the birth of "solid-state" electronics. During the 1950s, the size of computers shrank dramatically because the transistors used were much smaller than vacuum tubes (Figure 6-5b on the next page). Nevertheless, each transistor had to be individually soldered onto a circuit board, and a powerful computer of the day needed thousands of transistors.

Figure 6-3
A vacuum tube can act as a single electronic switch.

Figure 6-4
The ENIAC computer was big enough to fill a medium-sized house.

About 10 years after the invention of the transistor, Jack Kirby and Robert Noyce invented the integrated circuit, which combined a set of transistors and **resistors** (electronic components that resist the flow of current) on a single chip. Since that time, the size of the integrated circuit, or chip, has steadily shrunk, and the number of transistors on a single chip has multiplied. Modern chips like the one shown in Figure 6-5 pack millions of transistors onto a piece of silicon that is smaller than the earliest transistor.

Figure 6-5
(a) The tiny chip on the right contains millions of electronic switches; (b) the transistor is a single switch.

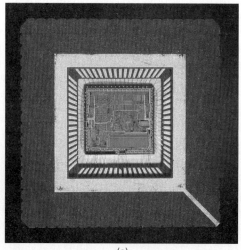

(a)

(b)

The CPU

There are actually many types of computer chips. The two types that make up the processing components of a microcomputer are called microprocessors and memory chips. **Memory chips** hold programs and data. Memory will be discussed later in this chapter.

The term *microcomputer* comes from the fact that processing is controlled by a microprocessor. The main microprocessor in a microcomputer is the **central processing unit** or **CPU**. The CPU, known as the computing part of the computer, is responsible for controlling the flow of data throughout the computer and for executing program instructions (Figure 6-7).

CPU

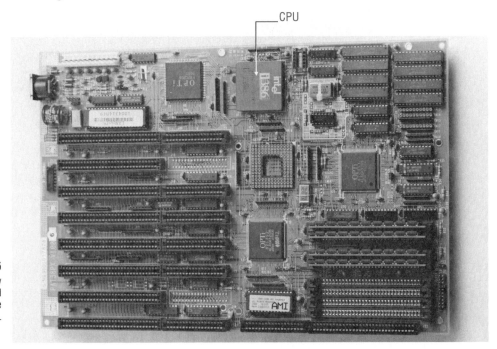

Figure 6-6
The CPU controls the flow of data on the motherboard and throughout the computer.

Every CPU has at least two parts: a control unit and an arithmetic-logic unit (Figure 6-7 on the next page). The **control unit** retrieves program instructions from memory, evaluates them, and retrieves data from memory. It then coordinates the processing that takes place in other parts of the CPU. The control unit is the "switchboard" of the computer, making connections between other hardware components.

The **arithmetic-logic unit**, or **ALU**, works in conjunction with the control unit by handling all of the arithmetic and logical functions required by the control unit. Numbers are transferred from memory to the ALU for calculation, and the results are sent back to memory. The ALU performs addition, subtraction, division, and multiplication, and it evaluates equality or inequality. Actually, the ALU performs addition to do all of this. For example, to determine the product of 4 and 3, the computer starts with 0 and adds 4 three times (4 + 4 + 4) to get 12. **Registers**, part of the ALU, are high-speed memory circuits. Small sets of data are moved from memory to the registers when the ALU is to perform arithmetic or logical operations on the data.

A **math coprocessor**, an optional extension to the control unit and the ALU, can help speed up processing. Some mathematical computations can be very time consuming for an ALU to handle (see Figure 6-8 on page CF 128). Although we can easily look up a logarithm

Figure 6-7
A typical CPU contains a control unit and an arithmetic logic unit.

in a table, the computer must calculate, to the desired numerical precision, the value. Because the CPU was designed to manipulate a wide variety of data types (numbers, text, and graphics), it could not be tuned to perform a single type of activity. However, by adding a math coprocessor to the CPU, we add a special purpose chip that will perform mathematical routines extremely quickly. This speeds up programs that use mathematics or sophisticated, vector-generated graphics.

We should note, however, that the software must be able to detect the presence of the math coprocessor in order to use it. Some microprocessors, such as the 486DX, have incorporated a math coprocessor in them. With others, it is possible to add a coprocessor.

Popular Microprocessors

Microcomputers are often differentiated by the type of CPU they use. For example, the IBM PC, first sold in 1981, used the 8088 chip, manufactured by Intel Corporation. As software requirements have grown and computer manufacturers compete with more powerful and faster machines, more advanced chips have been packaged with new computers. Today, the most popular IBMs use 80286, 80386, and 80486 chips, also manufactured by Intel. A machine with one of these CPUs is commonly referred to as a **286**, **386**, or **486**. Software is constantly getting faster, easier to use, and more powerful. Processing power races to keep pace with the ever-improving software. Because of these proven patterns, it is safe to say that the 386 microprocessor has become a business standard. Of course, as soon as anything becomes a standard in the computer industry, change can't be far behind. The 386 should probably be a minimum for all machines at BVOS.

If you plan to run DOS programs or Windows programs, a 386SX processor is sufficient, although a 386DX is faster and not much more expensive. The difference between these two CPUs is the speed with which the CPU can send and receive data. If you run a lot of Windows programs and want good performance, get at least a 486SX. However, if you plan to run CAD programs, spreadsheets, and anything else that would work better with a math coprocessor, a 486DX performs best.

In addition to the computers actually constructed by IBM, a large number of **clones** or **compatibles** are made by other companies and conform to the design standards of IBM machines. The compatibles market grew during the 1980s, primarily because (1) the microprocessors used by IBM machines were made by another company (Intel), and (2) because the IBM did not prosecute companies that copied its design. By the mid-1980s, IBMs and compatibles were the most common type of microcomputer in the world. As a result, although *PC* can simply mean "personal computer," the term usually means IBMs and compatibles, that is, any machine that conforms to the standards set by the IBM PC. Intel was the first, but is no longer the only, company to develop CPUs for IBM-compatible PCs. Advanced Micro Devices (AMD) chips cost PC makers less (enabling them to pass on consumer savings), plus AMD's top-of-the-line 386 chip outperforms Intel's highest rated 386 chip.

Unlike the IBMs and compatibles, the Macintosh line of computers, made by Apple Computer, Inc., uses chips made by Motorola. The original Macintosh used the Motorola 68000. More recent Macintosh machines use the 68020, the 68030, and the 68040. As with Intel's 286, 386, and 486, higher numbers translate into more processing power and speed (Table 6-1).

Manufacturer	Chip number	Computers using the chip
Intel	8088	IBM Personal Computer
	8086	AT&T Personal Computer 6300
	80286	IBM PC/AT, Compaq Portable II
	80386	IBM Personal System/2 Model 80
		Compaq Deskpro 386
	80486	IBM PS/2 Model 70
Motorola	68000	Apple Macintosh
	68010	AT&T Personal Computer 7300
	68020	Apple Macintosh II
	68030	Apple Macintosh IIcx
		NeXT computer
	68040	Hewlett-Packard workstations

Table 6-1
Chip manufacturers, numbers, and computer users.

Measuring the Speed of a CPU

All microprocessors are not created equal. They vary most in the speed at which they carry out their tasks and the volume of tasks they can do. The speed of the CPU is controlled by the electronic clock that is connected to it. This clock generates electrical "ticks" millions of times per second. The number of ticks is called the **clock speed** of the computer. Because one tick is actually an electrical cycle, clock speeds are measured in millions of cycles per second, or **megahertz (MHz)**.

The best way to think about clock speed is to remember that one cycle is the amount of time it takes to turn a transistor on and off again. Therefore, the faster the clock speed of a computer, the faster the computer can process data. All other factors being equal, a microprocessor working at 50 MHz operates twice as fast as one operating at 25 MHz.

The original IBM PC, which used the Intel 8088 chip, operated at 4.77 MHz. Most 286 computers operate at 16 MHz, though some run slower. 386 chips can operate at 16, 20, 25, or 33 MHz. 486 machines usually operate at 25, 33, 50, or 66 MHz, or even faster. By the time

Figure 6-8
A motherboard and the
math coprocessor.

you read this book, the 486DX2 may be available, at 100 MHz. Clock speed is a central factor affecting the performance of the computer, so there is constant pressure from consumers who want computers operating at faster clock speeds.

Because these CPUs can operate with different system clocks, the clock speed is often included with the CPU number to indicate the type of machine. For example, someone might tell you, "I use a 386 25," meaning the person uses a 386 processor operating at 25 MHz.

Note that, although the higher the number of MHz the better (faster), you can't compare speeds from different generations of CPUs. A 486 running at 25 MHz is faster than a 386 running at 33 MHz, for example. At the time this book was written, the fastest IBM-compatible performance on the market was the 486 CPU running at 66 MHz.

Another unit of measure used when talking about microprocessors is the number of instructions per second the chip can execute. The unit used to measure instructions per second is **MIPS**, which stands for Millions of Instructions Per Second. An **instruction** is a statement that specifies what operation a CPU is to perform. In this case, the term *instruction* refers to a machine language instruction, so each one is very rudimentary. For example, a single instruction might tell the control unit only to access a byte of data in memory and give the data to the ALU. A subsequent instruction might tell the ALU what to do with the data. The number of instructions per second that a computer can execute is a more difficult figure to determine than the clock speed, because several factors are taken into account. MIPS, however, is a more accurate gauge of the computer's processing speed than clock speed.

Word Size

Before discussing word size, let's review the definitions of bit and byte. Computer input is converted into binary members (0 or 1), and a **bit** is one of these digits. Eight bits make a **byte**, which is the common unit of computer storage and is equivalent to one alphanumeric character.

Most microprocessors in use today are 16-bit or 32-bit processors. The number of bits refers to the microprocessor's **word size**, which is the amount of data it can accept at one time. A 16-bit microprocessor, such as Intel's 8088 or 80286, accepts data two bytes (16 bits) at a time. A 32-bit microprocessor, such as Intel's 80386 or 80486 and Motorola's entire 68000 line, accepts data four bytes at a time. All other factors being equal, a 32-bit microprocessor processes data twice as fast as a 16-bit microprocessor. Word size is another factor affecting a computer's MIPS rating. Table 6-2 summarizes the clock speeds and word sizes of the most popular CPUs from Intel and Motorola.

Chip number Intel	Clock Speed	MIPS	Word size
8088	5 Mhz	.33	16
	8 Mhz	.75	
8086	8 Mhz	.66	16
	10 Mhz	.75	
80286	10 Mhz	1.5	16
	12 Mhz	2.66	
80386SX	16 Mhz	2.5	32
	20 Mhz	4.2	
80386DX	16 Mhz	5-6	32
	20 Mhz	6-7	
	25 Mhz	8.5	
	33 Mhz	11.4	
80486SX	25 Mhz	20	32
	33 Mhz	27	
80486DX	25 Mhz	20	32
	33 Mhz		27

Table 6-2 Clock speeds and word sizes for Intel and Motorola processors.

Comprehension Questions

1. If the only arithmetic function the ALU really uses is addition, how is it able to compute division problems?

2. Why is it acceptable to speak of a PC made by Compaq when the original PC was created by IBM?

3. Using only the information we have provided regarding word size and clock speed, how much faster is a 386 operating at 32 MHz than a typical 286?

Using What You Know

1. On which computer systems in the new Buena Vista Office Supply branch will it be most advantageous to have a math coprocessor? Why?

2. When a word processing program performs a word search, the user types in a word, and the computer tells the user where that word occurs in the current document. What type of operation is the ALU performing to accomplish this task?

3. Why is it not possible for MIPS to be greater than MHz?

Memory

In addition to the type of CPU, its clock speed, and its word size, the other major factor affecting the processing power of a computer is the amount of memory it has. **Memory** (sometimes called primary storage) is the set of electronic "cubbyholes" where data and program instructions are stored when the CPU needs quick access to them (Figure 6-9). Each one-byte cubbyhole is assigned a unique address so that the CPU can store and retrieve data by location.

There are two kinds of memory chips in every microcomputer: ROM chips and RAM chips.

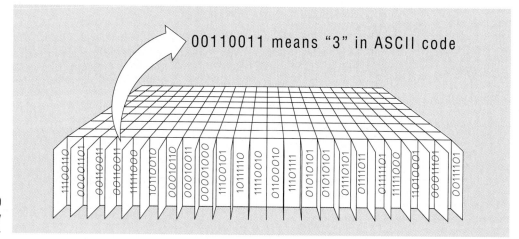

00110011 means "3" in ASCII code

Figure 6-9
Each cubbyhole in memory can hold one byte of data.

ROM

ROM stands for read-only memory (you'll catch some people saying "ROM memory," but the term is redundant). ROM permanently stores data and instructions frequently needed by the computer. It includes the basic instructions needed to start the computer and utility programs needed to maintain the computer. ROM is referred to as **nonvolatile memory** because the user cannot change what is stored there. Nonvolatile memory retains the data and instructions it contains, even when the computer's power is turned off. That way, when the computer is turned on again, those instructions and data are ready and waiting to tell the computer what to do.

RAM

ROM represents only a small fraction of the total memory in a computer. The computer needs far more space to hold all of the other items that the CPU needs ready access to: The operating system, the application program being used, and data that the application program is manipulating are all stored in memory (Figure 6-10). These programs and data are held in another type of memory called **RAM**, which stands for random-access memory. All program execution and data processing take place in RAM. Other common terms for RAM are *memory*, *main memory*, *primary storage*, and *read/write memory*.

The usefulness and the dangers of RAM lie in the fact that RAM stores data as tiny electrical charges, which must be kept alive by the computer's power supply. The advantage of storing

Figure 6-10
ROM and RAM on the motherboard.

data in this way is that it can be processed very quickly, and it can be changed. Thus, when a program or data is no longer needed, the RAM holding it can be erased, allowing space for new programs and data to be loaded. The danger of RAM is that all data and instructions held there must receive a constant supply of current. If the power supply is interrupted for even a fraction of a second, the data and instructions in RAM disappear. This is why RAM is referred to as **volatile memory**. Because RAM doesn't "remember" once you turn off the power to your computer, it's important to save your work frequently. When you do this, your work is saved to a storage device, which we will discuss in Chapter 8.

Like the other parts of the CPU, memory is also compared in terms of speed. However, memory is not regulated by the electronic clock that governs the ALU and control unit. Instead, the speed of memory is discussed in terms of how quickly the specific memory contents can be located and transmitted to the CPU. Because memory chips are extremely fast, retrieval time is usually measured in nanoseconds. (One nanosecond equals one billionth of a second.) The smaller the value, the faster the memory can be used. Memory speed is another factor affecting the MIPS rate. You should look for a memory speed of 60 to 80 nanoseconds. Another factor is the wait state, the amount of time that passes before an operation takes place.

How the CPU and RAM Work to Process Data

To give you an idea of just how the CPU and RAM work together to process data, let's look at a short set of instructions you might use at BVOS. Say you have used your spreadsheet software to set up the electronic spreadsheet shown in Figure 6-11 on the next page, which calculates total revenue and total expenditures for a one-month period. The last cell in the spreadsheet calculates total profit by subtracting total expenditures from total revenue. You have entered a formula in this cell, so the calculation is performed automatically.

As shown in Figure 6-12 on the next page, to calculate total profit the computer must execute the cell formula, which is held in memory, step by step:

1. The control unit of the CPU finds the memory address of the data held in the cell linked to the "Total Revenue" label and sends the data to a register in ALU. The ALU is then holding the number $40,903.

2. The control unit finds the address of the data held in the cell linked to the "total expenditures" label and sends the data to another register in the ALU. The ALU is now also holding the number $36,934.

	A	B	C	D	E
1	BVOS PROFIT/LOSS for APRIL 1995				
2					
3	Expenditures			Revenue	
4					
5	Labor	$15,568		Furniture	$11,937
6	Overhead	$8,833		Paper Goods	$12,776
7	New Equipment	$2,389		Computer Supplies	$10,456
8	Cost of Goods	$10,144		Filing and Misc.	$5,733
9					
10	Total Expenditures	$36,934		Total Revenue	$40,903
11					
12				**Total Revenue**	**$40,903**
13				**Total Expenditures**	**$36,934**
14				**Profit**	**$3,969**
15					
16					
17					
18					
19					

Figure 6-11

You created this spreadsheet at BVOS to calculate total revenue and total expenditures for a one-month period. The last cell contains a formula that automatically calculates total profit by subtracting total expenditures from total revenue.

3. The control unit tells the ALU to subtract 36,834 from 40,903.

4. Because the ALU computes all arithmetic with addition, it adds the opposite of 36,834 to 40,903 and returns the result, 3,969, to the control unit.

5. The control unit stores 3,969 in the memory address that is linked to the cell next to the "Total Profit" label.

6. The control unit sends $3,969 to the monitor with instructions about where to place the data. The result of the calculation is displayed on the screen.

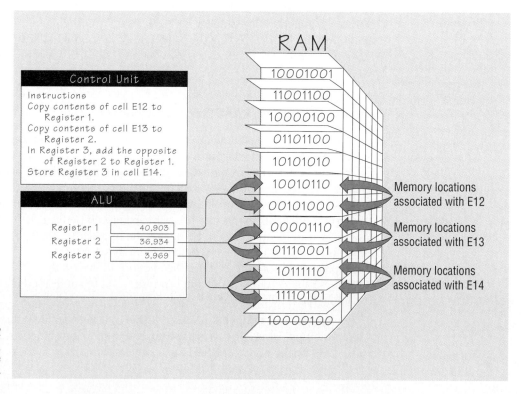

Figure 6-12

How the control unit, ALU, and RAM process a simple formula.

Measuring RAM

The amount of memory in your computer is a crucial factor affecting what software you will be able to run. During the early and mid-1980s, most of the IBM PCs sold were packaged with a maximum of 640 kilobytes (K) of RAM. (A **kilobyte** is equal to 1024 bytes.) At that time, 640 K was sufficient to run most of the programs that were on the market, and memory was generally measured in kilobytes.

As software became more powerful, however, it required more and more available RAM. To meet the requirements, microcomputers started being packaged with more RAM, and RAM is now often measured in megabytes (MB). (A **megabyte** is equal to a million bytes.) Today, it is difficult to find a computer with less than 1 MB of RAM. Even laptop and notebook models are more often sold with at least 2 MB. Many desktop models come with much more: They range from 1 to 64 MB of RAM.

The total amount of memory that a computer can access is dependent on the CPU. Some microprocessors can manipulate or address millions or billions of bytes of memory, while others can address only thousands. For example, most of the PCs that came with 640 K of RAM could address only 1 MB of memory. 386 and 486 computers, however, can address 4 gigabytes (about 4 billion bytes). Figure 6-13 shows the maximum addressable memory for the most popular PC microprocessors.

Chip	Addressable Memory
8086	1 megabyte
8088	1 megabyte
80286	16 megabytes
80386SX	16 megabytes
80386DX	4 gigabytes
80486SX	4 gigabytes
80486DX	4 gigabytes

Figure 6-13
Maximum addressable memory for Intel's most popular CPUs.

Cache

Cache is a reserved section of high-speed memory that can run up to five times the speed of RAM. It stores the most recently used information in fast memory (cache) on the assumption that the most recently accessed information will be used next. This is true 85 percent of the time. The CPU, which moves the data back and forth between cache and RAM, can access the data faster when it's in cache.

Most systems with cache have 64 K of it, but some come with 256 K or more. However, the incremental benefit is negligible once you pass 256 K. All 486 CPUs come with an 8 K cache, and many are designed to supplement that. If you want cache, you must buy a machine that's designed for it.

A disk cache is a portion of RAM that acts as a buffer between the CPU and the disk and thereby minimizes the time required by programs that frequently require storage.

Deciding How Much Memory to Buy

How much RAM is enough? Quite often the amount of RAM needed is related to how fast you want your computer to operate. With many software packages, when enough RAM is not available, disk storage is used. Using disk storage slows down processing because it cannot be accessed as quickly as RAM. Check the applications that you will be running to see how much memory they can take advantage of.

To decide how much memory to buy when you purchase a computer, you should first estimate your minimum memory requirements. To determine the minimum memory requirements, you must look at the RAM requirements for the largest program you are going to use, then you must add enough bytes to fit the largest data file that you might need to access through your largest piece of software. These numbers, however, are just your minimum requirements. You will probably want to buy significantly more memory for some machines for several reasons:

- Upgrades of software almost always require more memory than the previous version. For example, WordPerfect 4.2, the best-selling word processing software during the late 1980s, required 256 K of RAM. WordPerfect 5.1, however, requires 384 K of RAM, and WordPerfect for Windows takes up 2 MB of RAM. If you want to keep up with the current versions of your software, you may need more memory with each upgrade.

- Microcomputer users tend to accessorize their systems with helpful utility programs, such as screen savers, virus protection, font managers, and so on. While such programs can be helpful, they take up space in RAM. Consequently, it's a good idea to plan on some extra space to handle any utility programs you might want to install.

- If you buy an IBM or compatible and want to keep open the option of running Windows or OS/2, you will need much more memory than you would for a DOS machine. Just to run Lotus 1-2-3 for Windows on the Windows 3.1 platform requires 3 MB of RAM, as opposed to 512 K to run Lotus 1-2-3 R2.2 on a pure DOS platform.

If you can afford it, it is always a good idea to buy extra memory. The pace of software innovation is staggering, and the only way to factor it in is to buy a computer that gives you room to grow. If necessary, you can expand your RAM with **SIMMs** (single in-line memory modules), which are narrow printed circuit boards that hold memory chips (Figure 6-14).

Figure 6-14
A SIMM, used to add memory to a microcomputer.

SIMMs come in 1, 2, 4, 8, and 16 MB increments and connect to the motherboard. Some motherboards have room for as many as 16 SIMMs — that's a maximum of 256 MB of extra RAM.

Comprehension Questions

1. Explain why the basic instructions used to start the computer can't be held in RAM.
2. Briefly explain why memory speed affects the MIPS rate.
3. Explain how the CPU and RAM might process the problem of determining which is larger, 3 or 4.

Using What You Know

1. Using newspaper advertisements, find two comparable computers with different amounts of memory. Using the information you have found, how much more would you say it costs to have 8 MB of RAM rather than 4 MB?

2. What is the minimum memory requirement to run Windows NT and Lotus 1-2-3 for Windows?

3. Compare the memory requirements for the following products:
   - The latest version of WordPerfect on the Mac
   - The latest version of WordPerfect for Windows
   - The latest version of WordPerfect for DOS

Connecting Peripherals

The CPU and memory comprise the computer's processing components, but they need a way to communicate with the other hardware components. Both the CPU and the memory chips are mounted on the motherboard. The other hardware devices are connected to the motherboard through expansion slots, ports, and the data bus.

Ports

A **port** is an I/O device interface in which an external peripheral can be plugged into the system unit. Ports can be connected directly to the motherboard or to expansion boards. A computer uses ports to communicate with its peripherals (Figures 6-15 and 6-16).

There are many types of ports that a computer can use. On IBMs and compatibles, you will usually find two types of ports mentioned in computer literature and ads: parallel ports and serial ports. While both of these types transfer data using circuits, they differ in the way the data is transferred. In a **parallel port**, a series of parallel wires allow a group of bits to be transmitted at once. Parallel ports are sometimes called *centronics ports* after the connector that is often used to attach printers to expansion boards. Parallel ports are most often used to connect output devices, especially printers.

A **serial port** transmits data one bit at a time. Serial ports generally have fewer wires in their connectors than do parallel ports. Modems are always attached to serial ports, mice often are, and printers sometimes are.

Figure 6-15 Parallel, serial, and SCSI ports.

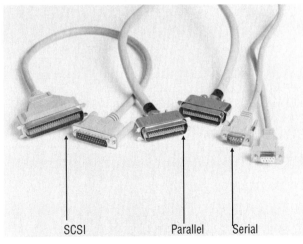

SCSI   Parallel   Serial

Figure 6-16 Cable connectors for SCSI, parallel, and serial ports.

Both types of ports have advantages. Parallel ports are able to transmit faster, while serial ports are better suited to transmit over long distances.

Macintosh computers use a special type of port interface known as a **SCSI** (pronounced "scuzzy"). SCSI stands for Small Computer System Interface. In the Mac, the SCSI design is built into the motherboard. SCSI boards can also be installed in PCs. A SCSI design allows peripherals to be connected in sequence, creating a daisy chain.

Expansion Slots and Boards: Built-in Flexibility

Peripherals are hardware devices, such as modems, printers, and so on, that connect to the computer. Many peripherals require an expansion board, which plugs into an **expansion slot** on the motherboard (Figures 6-17 and 6-18). **Expansion boards** are printed circuit boards similar to the motherboard. They provide a hardware interface between the peripheral and the motherboard. On one edge of an expansion board, there is a gold strip. This strip is the part that fits into the expansion slot on the motherboard.

Expansion boards are used to add many types of devices, including additional disk drives or RAM, communication devices such as modems or fax boards, input devices such as scanners, or output devices such as printers or display adapters. The number of expansion slots on your motherboard determines the maximum number of expansion boards that can fit in your computer. PCs have from three to eight slots. What's important is the number of slots left over after your system is configured. If you run out of slots, you can no longer expand your system.

Data Buses

The motherboard uses electronic pathways called **data buses** to transfer data between the CPU and the peripherals, as well as between the CPU and the memory chips (Figure 6-19).

Figure 6-17 Expansion slots on the motherboard.

Figure 6-18 Expansion boards plugged into expansion slots on a motherboard.

Figure 6-19
The data bus on the motherboard.

The kind of bus used in a computer is important for two reasons. First, the size of the bus affects how fast data can flow through it. The CPU determines what size bus can be built onto the motherboard. For example, the 8088 chip uses an 8-bit bus, the 286 uses a 16-bit bus, and the 386DX and 486 use 32-bit buses (Figure 6-20). The wider the bus, the more data can move through it in a given amount of time.

Second, the way a motherboard and its buses are constructed also affects the computer's capabilities. Among IBMs and compatibles, there are four competing architectures. It's important to know which bus architecture a computer has before purchasing any peripherals. The Industry Standard Architecture (ISA) type of bus was the first and dates to the original IBM PC. The ISA architecture allows for 8-bit and 16-bit bus lines. When IBM began making machines with 386 processors, it needed a new architecture that could handle the 32-bit bus. IBM created the MicroChannel Architecture (MCA), which requires special, more sophisticated peripheral expansion boards. The problem with MCA was that the old 8-bit and 16-bit boards wouldn't work. The companies that manufactured those boards were understandably upset, since IBM had broken the trend of upward compatibility. **Upward compatibility** means that new machines can use the same software and hardware used in older, less powerful machines. Without upward compatibility, every advancement in hardware would require users who want to take advantage of the advancement to buy an entirely new system.

Chip	Bus size
8088	8 bits
8086	16 bits
80286	16 bits
80386SX	16 bits
80386DX	32 bits
80486SX	32 bits
80486DX	32 bits

Figure 6-20
Intel and Motorola have gradually expanded their bus sizes.

To solve the problems created by MCA, a group of hardware manufacturers came up with the Extended Industry Standard Architecture (EISA), which is compatible with ISA-based peripherals, but can transfer 32 bits (Figure 6-21 on the next page). Under certain circumstances, EISA is not as fast as MCA, but only EISA is upward compatible.

The newest bus architecture is called the *local bus*. A machine with the new 32-bit local bus architecture is faster than those with MCA, ISA, or EISA. A computer with a local bus and a 33 MHz CPU can transfer 132 MB of data per second. MCA with 33 MHz transfers at 40 MB per second, EISA at 33 MB per second, and ISA at 8.33 MB per second.

Power Supplies

A critical component in all computers is the power supply (Figure 6-22). The **power supply** is the device that takes ordinary household AC power and transforms it into DC current, on which the computer operates. It is important to match the power supply with the power consumption of the peripherals and the motherboard. In some older PCs, it is not possible, for example, to install a second hard disk, because the power supply is insufficient to power the device.

For many computers, the power cable is the only electronic pathway between the computer and the outside world. Unfortunately, the quality of electrical power to your home or office can vary substantially. Unlike refrigerators and incandescent lamps, computers cannot easily withstand such environments. If a power surge (a wave of voltage) or spike (a very short, sharp blast of voltage) hits your computer, it can burn out the power supply, burn through the connections between the power supply and the motherboard, and destroy the motherboard. From the motherboard, the electrical surge or spike can proceed to the monitor, the disk drives, and keyboard. This short burst of electricity could reduce your computer to a high-tech paper weight.

Consequently, computers need devices that protect them from electrical problems associated with blackouts, brownouts, sags, and other power level inconsistencies. A **surge suppressor** (or surge protector) will keep electrical surges and spikes from passing from the electrical system to the power supply. A surge suppressor, such as the one illustrated in

Figure 6-21
ISA and EISA expansion boards.
ISA boards can fit into EISA slots.

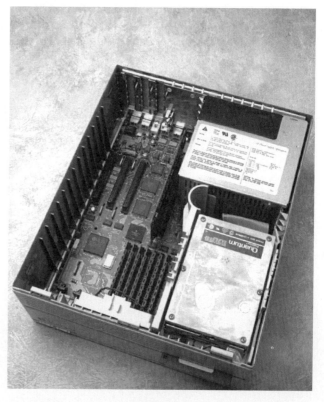

Figure 6-22
An open system unit showing the power supply.

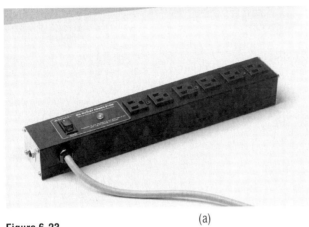

(a)

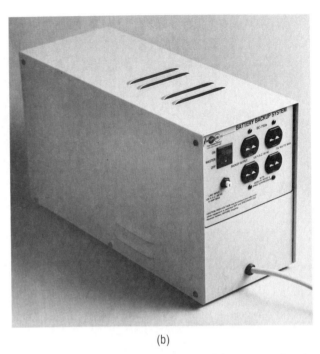

(b)

Figure 6-23
(a) A surge suppressor;
(b) an uninterruptable
power supply.

Figure 6-23a will detect an unusual increase in the level of electricity and then immediately break the electrical connection. The faster it breaks this connection, the better the protection.

Other power protection devices, such as **uninterruptable power supplies**, can keep the computer operating several minutes after the loss of power, giving you time to save your files and power down (Figure 6-23b). Because of the tremendous amount of electrical power, no power protection mechanism can protect against a lightning strike. There are two types of uninterruptible power supplies: one switches to a battery supply when the power goes out; the other runs the computer off a battery and is always recharging the battery, so there is no switching delay.

Always make sure the outlets you use to plug in your computer and peripherals are three-pronged, grounded outlets. An electrician can tell you whether an outlet is grounded.

The power supply in the computer generates heat, which requires the chassis to contain a fan for cooling the computer. The chassis has air holes through which cooler air outside the computer is drawn and warmer air inside is pushed out. It is critical that these airways remain open when the computer is on. It is also important to remember that having too many air holes in a computer is undesirable. While installing a peripheral device in a computer, it is tempting to leave the cover of an expansion slot open. When this happens, however, the air flow that was created in the chassis design is disrupted, and the computer becomes improperly cooled because the air does not flow over the appropriate parts of the motherboard. In addition, having too many open airways encourages dust and moisture to accumulate in the microcomputer.

The Chassis

The outside of the system unit is called the system cabinet or **chassis**. A chassis must conform to certain Federal Communicatons Commission regulations regarding the amount of radio interference that emanates from the computer. These regulations (termed the Class B rule) are designed to provide reasonable protection against electrical interference in a residential installation. A device that did not conform to this rule might cause interference with radios

Figure 6-24
Desktop models in the
Macintosh line. The
compact machine on the
right has a smaller
footprint than the one on
the left.

and televisions. In addition, just as radio waves can escape from a computer, these same waves can intrude on the computer. When this happens, data loss can occur.

When you purchase the system unit of a computer, you may have to decide on a chassis design. During the early and mid-1980s, most of the computers sold were **desktop models**, meaning that the chassis was designed to lie flat on a desk. Whether the monitor was an integral part of the chassis or not, it tended to sit on top of the system unit. These chassis were often compared by the size of their **footprint**, or the amount of space they occupied on the desk. For example, the less expensive models in the Macintosh line — the Mac Plus, the SE, and later the Mac Classic — featured a small footprint, with the monitor built into the chassis (Figure 6-24). The more powerful machines in the line — the Mac II, the LC, and several others — had separate monitors and chassis with larger footprints. This configuration was typical for PCs.

Gradually, chassis started appearing in another configuration, the tower model, which provided an alternative to the desktop model. **Tower models** stand on one end, as shown in Figure 6-25. This design frees desk space, either by allowing the chassis to stand on the floor (either under or next to a desk) or simply by taking less space on the desk. Tower models often come in three sizes: full towers, mid-towers, and mini-towers.

The chassis design of a computer can affect the number of expansion boards that can be connected to the motherboard. Full tower and large desktop models generally provide the most room for expansion boards. Mini-towers and small footprint models usually have fewer slots to fit boards into. When shopping for a computer, it is always important to think about what peripherals you may want to attach and how much room a given model or chassis gives you for growth. Also, be aware that some expansion boards are longer than others. Some are full length; others are half length. When you compare two computer designs, look at the number of full-length and half-length boards that will fit in the system unit.

Some companies, such as Apple and IBM, tend to package the system unit, monitor, keyboard, and mouse together in a few different configurations. When purchasing one of

Figure 6-25
Chassis designs for PCs.

these packages, you often don't choose the type of chassis — it's determined by the model you want. When purchasing a clone, however, you can often determine the exact specifications of your computer and can choose whatever chassis design you prefer.

Comprehension Questions

1. Why is the difference between MCA and EISA less relevant for new computer users than for experienced users who are upgrading to new processing equipment?

2. Describe a situation in which you might want to purchase a mini-tower model for your system unit.

3. Why does a printer require a parallel port, while a modem requires a serial port?

Using What You Know

1. You have decided to buy a full tower system unit for the network server. You have the choice of putting it in the stockroom, the sales room, or a small closet off of the sales room. Which would you choose and why?

2. Why must a 286 have a 16-bit bus rather than a 32-bit bus?

3. What type of chassis is most appropriate for the computers in the stockroom and why?

Summary Points

Processors: The Computer Engine

☐ Choosing what type of computer to buy is a decision about processing.

The System Unit: All the Hardware You Need

☐ The system unit includes the motherboard, the ports, and the power supply. It often includes the disk drives, and it sometimes includes a monitor.

☐ Many users say *CPU* when they mean *system unit*.

The Computer Chip: The Computer's Core

☐ A computer chip is a piece of silicon etched with electrical pathways.

☐ The invention of the transistor in 1947 allowed computer makers to replace vacuum tubes with solid-state electronics.

☐ Millions of transistors now fit on a chip that is smaller than the earliest transistor.

The CPU

☐ The two main types of chips found in microcomputers are microprocessors and memory chips.

☐ The main microprocessor in a microcomputer is the CPU.

☐ The CPU consists of the control unit and the ALU.

☐ A math coprocessor may also be added to the CPU to speed up mathematical processing. A 486 CPU includes a math coprocessor.

Popular Microprocessors

☐ Today, the most popular PCs use the 286, 386, and 486 CPUs.

☐ The term *PC* includes both IBMs and compatibles or clones.

☐ Macs use the 68000 line of Motorola chips.

Measuring the Speed of a CPU

☐ The speed of a CPU is controlled by an electronic clock; the number of ticks per second is measured in MHz.

☐ MIPS is a more complete measurement of the computer's speed because more factors are included.

Word Size

☐ Word size, which measures the number of bits that a computer can accept at once, is another factor affecting MIPS.

Memory

☐ The speed of memory also affects the MIPS rate.

ROM

☐ ROM, which is nonvolatile, stores the basic instructions needed to start the computer.

RAM

☐ All of the programs and data to which the CPU needs ready access are stored in RAM, which is volatile.

How the CPU and RAM Work to Process Data

☐ The control unit passes data back and forth between RAM and the ALU.

Measuring RAM

☐ Most early PCs had 640 K of RAM.

☐ Today, RAM is often measured in megabytes because the requirements of modern software have pushed manufacturers to supply more RAM with new computers.

Cache
- ☐ Cache can speed up processing by providing a buffer between the CPU and RAM.
- ☐ A disk cache can speed up certain types of processing that require storage by providing a buffer between the CPU and storage.

Deciding How Much Memory to Buy
- ☐ Minimum memory requirements are figured by adding the memory requirements of your operating system, your largest application program, and the largest data file you will access with your largest application program.
- ☐ You may need to buy more than your minimum requirements to allow for software upgrades, utilities, or moving from DOS to a GUI.

Connecting Peripherals

Ports
- ☐ Ports are the I/O device interface into which peripherals are plugged; they can be directly connected to the motherboard or connected to an expansion board.
- ☐ Parallel ports allow a group of bits to be transmitted at one time.
- ☐ Serial ports allow data to be transferred only one bit at a time.

Expansion Slots and Boards: Built-in Flexibility
- ☐ Many peripherals require expansion boards, which are plugged into expansion slots on the motherboard.

Data Buses
- ☐ The CPU is connected to memory and all the peripherals through the data bus.
- ☐ The size of the data bus affects the MIPS rate.
- ☐ The design, or architecture, of the data bus also affects performance.

Power Supplies
- ☐ The power supply converts household AC current to DC current.
- ☐ Surge suppressors protect computer equipment from electrical surges and spikes.

The Chassis
- ☐ The box that forms the outside of the system unit can come in several different configurations.
- ☐ Chassis models are compared by their footprints, by whether they are desktop or tower models, or by what size tower model they are.

Knowing the Facts

True/False

1. The ALU uses addition to perform multiplication, division, subtraction, and comparison.

2. MCA motherboards cannot be connected to expansion boards that are designed for ISA motherboards.

3. Data can be transmitted more quickly through parallel ports than through serial ports.

4. A computer operates on DC current.

5. One way to help keep your system cool is to remove as many of the expansion slot covers as possible.

6. RAM stores programs needed to start the computer.

7. The size of the data bus affects the MIPS rating.

8. Modems usually require parallel ports.

9. The data bus connects the CPU to the RAM chips.

10. In some computers, the monitor is inside the system unit.

Short Answer

1. A memory cache is a buffer between _____ and the CPU.

2. What are the two basic types of computer chips used in processing?

3. The processing components of the computer are mounted on the _____.

4. ROM is referred to as _____ memory, because it retains its contents even when the computer is turned off.

5. What 1947 invention eventually led to the development of the computer chip?

6. What are the two main components of the CPU?

7. Hardware devices connected to the motherboard through expansion slots or ports are known as _____.

8. The word size of the 386 and 486 chips is _____ bits.

9. The most accurate measurement of a computer's processing speed is _____.

10. IBMs and compatibles are collectively referred to as _____.

Answers

True/False

1. T
2. T
3. T
4. T
5. F
6. F
7. T
8. F
9. T
10. T

Short Answer

1. RAM
2. memory chips and microprocessors
3. motherboard
4. nonvolatile
5. the transistor
6. the control unit and the ALU
7. peripherals
8. 32
9. MIPS
10. PCs

Challenging Your Understanding

1. Using whatever resources are available to you, find prices for a Dell 486 33 MHz with 8 MB of RAM. Find the price for the same configuration from IBM. How do you explain the difference?

2. On ISA-bus PCs, the 8 MHz data bus is the slowest device on the motherboard. It is slower than RAM and slower than the CPU. What are the implications of this (if any) for computer users?

3. It is generally possible to upgrade a PC by purchasing additional memory. Find out approximately how much it costs to add each MB of RAM.

4. After using a Mac LC with 2 MB of RAM for a year, your accountant wants to increase the RAM to 8 MB. Is this change possible? If so, how much does it cost?

5. If BVOS is immediately successful, you may need to hire a secretary to handle some of your correspondence and cover general work around the office. This person's computer needs would be strictly limited to word processing. What kind of processing components would you buy for this new employee, and why?

6. Say you are buying computers with 386 microprocessors running at 16 MHz with 2 MB of RAM for each of the stockers and salespeople. Use a popular computer magazine, such as *PC Magazine* or *PC World*, to find the minimum that you will be able to spend for each of these computers.

C H A P T E R   7

Input and Output Devices

Key Terms

alphanumeric keys
bar-code readers
cathode ray tube (CRT)
CGA
characters per second (cps)
click
cursor (text cursor)
cursor-movement keys
digitizer tablet
dot matrix printer
dot pitch
double-click
drag
EGA
ergonomics
flat-panel display
function keys
gray scale
hard copy
impact printer
ink-jet printer
internal fonts
laser printer
letter-quality print

light pen
liquid crystal display (LCD)
monitor
monochrome
mouse
near letter-quality (NLQ) print
numeric keypad
optical character recognition
   (OCR)
pages per minute (ppm)
pixel
pointing device
PostScript
printer driver
QWERTY
resolution
scanners
soft copy
soft fonts
SVGA
toggle switch
touch screen
trackball
VGA

Objectives

In this chapter you will learn to:

- Define the four major areas of the keyboard
- Explain the importance of keyboarding skills
- Name and describe the three common mouse techniques
- Explain the differences among the mouse, the trackball, and the pen
- Describe how scanners differ from manual input devices
- Define the capability of OCR software
- Explain why voice input is difficult and how it is currently accomplished
- Name the two basic types of monitor and differentiate between them
- Name the three types of flat-screen monitor
- Explain how monitors create multiple shades of gray or colors
- Describe the most important factors to consider when purchasing a monitor
- Name the four types of graphics card used on the PC and explain the differences among them
- Name the three most common types of printers and describe how each works
- Compare the three types of printers in terms of resolution and speed

Getting Data "In" and Information "Out"

Input refers to data being retrieved by processing devices from peripherals, such as a disk drive, modem, or keyboard. *Output* means data sent from processing to a peripheral. This is the formal, and more technically accurate, use of these terms. However, an *input device* more often means a device that a computer user employs to give data to the computer. *Output device* usually means the monitor or the printer, that is, a device that is used to present processed data to the user. When people need only to see processed data, it is sent to the monitor. When people want printed output, it goes to the printer. These are the meanings that we use in this chapter.

This chapter covers several types of input devices, including keyboards, pointing devices, and scanners. The second half of the chapter covers monitors and printers.

The Keyboard and Its Parts

The most widely used input device for microcomputers is the keyboard. In fact, the first microcomputers to gain widespread acceptance in the market used keyboards as the sole input device. As processing power and user interfaces became more sophisticated, other devices were added. The keyboard, however, remains the most versatile input device, though it isn't always the easiest one to use.

As shown in Figure 7-1, a keyboard can include as many a five separate areas: the alphanumeric keys, the function keys, the cursor-movement keys, the numeric keypad, and the toggle-switch lights.

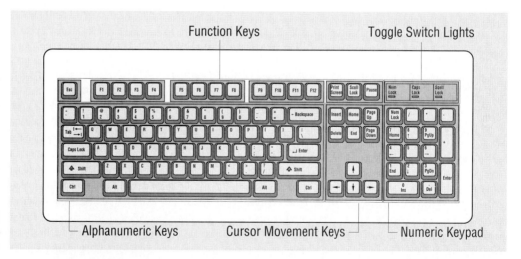

Figure 7-1
The IBM 101 keyboard, the standard for many PCs.

Alphanumeric Keys.   The area of the keyboard that includes all the letters of the alphabet consists of the **alphanumeric keys** (Figure 7-2). The term *alphanumeric* comes from the fact that this part of the keyboard includes all of the ALPHAbet and all of the NUMERICal digits. This area looks very similar to the keyboard of a standard typewriter. Like a typewriter, this area includes punctuation marks, the Tab key, Backspace key, Spacebar key, Enter key (usually called the Return key on a typewriter), and the Shift and Caps Lock keys. This part of the keyboard is sometimes called the **QWERTY** (pronounced "kwer-tee") keyboard, a name derived from the first six characters on the left in the top row of letters.

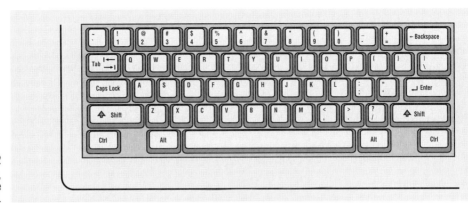

Figure 7-2
The alphanumeric keys, also known as the QWERTY keyboard.

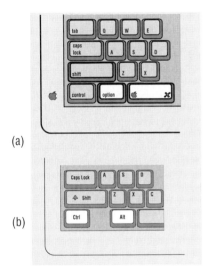

(a)

(b)

Figure 7-3
Modifier keys on
(a) the Mac keyboard and
(b) the IBM keyboard.

In addition to the typewriter keys, the alphanumeric area of a keyboard usually includes two other keys (actually four, since both keys are found on both sides of the keyboard). On the Apple keyboards used with the Macintosh (Figure 7-3a), they are the Command and Option keys. The Command key usually has a four-petaled, flowerlike image on it, as well as an apple symbol on it. On the IBM keyboard (a keyboard design, not necessarily made by IBM), the two extra keys are the Ctrl and Alt keys, which stand for "control" and "alternate" (Figure 7-3b). All of these keys are used in the same way as the Shift key. The user holds down one of these keys while typing another alphanumeric, function, or cursor-movement key. The function of these additional keys is determined by the program being used.

Function Keys. IBM and compatible computers all have **function keys** that enable a software developer to assign a specific software function to a single key (Figure 7-4). Once again, the function of the particular key, or key combination, varies with the program being used. For example, the F3 key in WordPerfect for the PC tells the computer to display the Help menu. In DOS, F3 tells the computer to repeat the last command typed at the keyboard.

A few special keys are located in the same row as the function keys. To the left of the function keys on most keyboards, you will find the Escape (Esc) key. The Escape key allows you to cancel a command that is about to be executed. To the right of the function keys are Print Scrn, Scroll Lock, and Pause or Break. If your printer is set up to do so, Print Scrn will print everything that appears on your monitor. Scroll Lock holds the cursor in one place on the screen as the text scrolls by. In some programs, Pause or Break allows you to cancel a command that is currently being processed.

Figure 7-4
The function keys. On older IBM keyboards, they are located to the left of the alphanumeric keyboard.

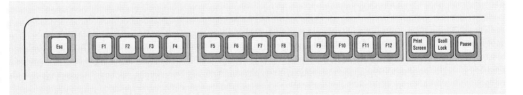

Cursor-Movement Keys. The **cursor** is the point on the screen where letters, numbers, or punctuation symbols typed at the keyboard will be entered. The **cursor-movement keys** (Figure 7-5) allow the user to use the keyboard to move the cursor around the screen. The

Figure 7-5
The cursor movement keys.

arrow keys simply move the cursor one character, cell, or field to the right, left, up, or down. The Home and End keys can be used to move the cursor to the beginning or end of a document, but their functions vary depending on the program. Page Up and Page Down (PgUp and PgDn) cause the cursor to jump to the top of the previous or subsequent screen or page. The Delete key works just like the Backspace key, except it deletes the character at the cursor (or to the right of the cursor when it is displayed as a vertical line), rather than the character to the left of the cursor. Finally, the Insert key is a **toggle switch**, meaning that pushing it once turns the Insert mode on, and pushing it again turns the feature off. When Insert mode is on, new characters typed in the middle of a line of text will make room for themselves and will not erase existing characters. When Insert Mode is off, the keyboard is in Overwrite mode, also called Typeover. With Typeover on, new characters typed in the middle of a line of text will overwrite existing characters.

The Numeric Keypad. The **numeric keypad** (Figure 7-6), located on the right side of the keyboard, allows for quick entry of numbers. The keypad is more useful than the numbers across the top of the alphanumeric keyboard for entering a large set of numerals. The numeric keypad includes arithmetic function keys (+, −, *, and /), a well as an Enter key. The cursor-movement keys may be combined with, or repeated on, the keypad. To use the cursor control keys on the keypad, turn off the numbers by pressing the Num Lock key.

Lights on the Keyboard. Keyboards often have three toggle-switch lights on them: Num Lock, Caps Lock, and Scroll Lock (Figure 7-7). Each light is connected to a toggle switch on the keyboard. The Num Lock light is controlled by the Num Lock key on the numeric keypad. When the light is on, typing the keys on the numeric keypad will display numbers. When the light is off, the keys on the keypad can be used for cursor movement. The Caps Lock key is connected to the Caps Lock key on the alphanumeric keyboard. When it is on, alphabetic characters you type will appear capitalized. The Scroll Lock light is connected to the Scroll Lock key, which is located in the same row as the function keys. In some programs, turning on Scroll Lock will hold the cursor in one place on the screen and force the data to scroll past the cursor. When Scroll Lock is off, you can move the cursor around the screen.

Figure 7-6
The numeric keypad.

Figure 7-7
Toggle-switch lights.

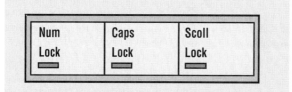

Data Entry with the Keyboard

When business people speak of *data entry*, they usually mean typing numbers and letters at the keyboard. A data entry job at a company usually entails typing documents or entering numbers into a company database. But data entry personnel are not the only ones entering data at the computer. Financial analysts, department managers, and other company personnel also enter data at computers. Therefore, virtually every microcomputer user needs to know how to use a keyboard (Figure 7-8). This means that typing or keyboarding skills have become more and more important as computer use has grown. Learning to type with all 10 fingers without looking at the keyboard has become a valuable asset in the job market.

You probably already know how painfully slow keyboarding can be if you can't type. To make you feel better, you should know that there is a historical reason for the level of dexterity required for typing. The QWERTY keyboard was designed when the manual, nonelectric typewriter was the only kind that existed. If two keys are pressed at the same time on a manual typewriter, the arms that reach up and hit the paper tend to get stuck. The QWERTY keyboard was originally designed to slow typists down and thereby keep typewriters from getting jammed. Those of us who have learned to type on QWERTY keyboards don't want to learn again. As a result, no redesign of the standard layout has ever gained acceptance.

Figure 7-8
Being able to type with all 10 fingers and not look at the keyboard has become a valuable skill for all business people.

A Few Words About Ergonomics: The Human Factor

Most of the keyboard illustrations in this chapter show keyboards we're all familiar with. However, there is a special kind of keyboard that folds in the middle in order to angle the user's hands into what is, for some people, a more comfortable and natural position. This keyboard was developed in response to a marked increase in chronic wrist and hand injuries suffered by people who spend a lot of time at the keyboard.

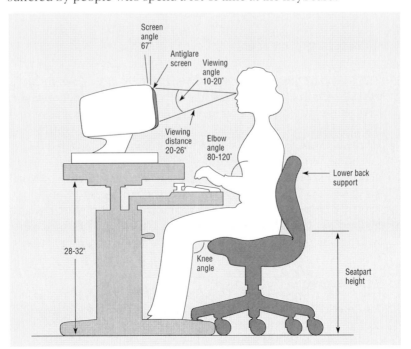

Figure 7-9
Proper body position when working at a computer can help prevent strain and injury.

The keyboard is an ergonomically designed product. **Ergonomics** is the study of people-machine relationships. An ergonomically designed product accommodates a person's body or actions. There are optimum kinds of equipment and optimum ways to adjust this equipment. Adjusting your sitting position so that you are comfortable is important as well. Figure 7-9 on the previous page shows a good posture for sitting at the keyboard, along with proper heights and distances for equipment. Additional ergonomic equipment can include wrist rests, an adjustable desk chair, and a foot rest. Bear in mind that regardless of how ergonomically designed your work area is, you may need to take periodic brief breaks to stretch your neck, shoulders, and back muscles.

Comprehension Questions

1. Some keyboards, such as those that came with the original Macintoshes, don't have numeric keypads. Who at BVOS would appreciate a keyboard with a numeric keypad?

2. Within a given program, how many different actions can be assigned to a single function key on the computer?

3. What kinds of application programs absolutely require input devices other than the keyboard?

Using What You Know

1. Are there any computers at BVOS that do not need keyboards? If so, which ones? Why?

2. Which of your employees need typing skills the most? Why?

3. From the advertisements you can find in magazines, see if you can tell whether keyboards are typically included when you buy a computer or are typically purchased separately. What does an average computer keyboard cost?

Pointing Devices

The keyboard provides one important way to interact with the computer. However, as anyone who can't type knows, the keyboard can be an unnatural mechanism for human interaction. Another family of devices, which attempts to make up for the shortcomings of the keyboard, is broadly classified as pointing devices. A **pointing device** allows the user to interact with the computer simply by pointing to parts of the screen.

Some form of pointing device — most often a mouse — is a standard component of almost every prepackaged microcomputer available today. The reason is that more and more programs are incorporating graphical user interfaces (GUIs). In a GUI, commands can be executed by selecting the command name using the pointer (though there are often keyboard methods for doing the same thing). In addition to GUIs, which are generally easier to use with a pointing device, modern graphics software virtually requires the use of one.

The Mouse

A **mouse** (Figure 7-10) is a pointing device that enables the user to identify a position on the screen by moving a tool around on a horizontal surface, such as a desktop or a mouse pad.

As the mouse is moved across the surface, the cursor on the screen moves correspondingly. The mouse can be used to select icons or commands on a menu, to move text and data in a program, or to move the text cursor around the document. A mouse is used in graphics programs to mark parts of graphic images and to create illustrations. Many programs — especially those that incorporate a graphical user interface — are beginning to require the use of a mouse.

The mouse was developed at the Stanford Research Institute. Apple popularized the device by packaging it with the Macintosh, beginning with the first Macs sold in 1984. The mouse, in fact, was a major part of Apple's original advertising campaign. In the ad they used, they encouraged users to "test drive" the Mac. Their claim that the mouse made the Mac easier to use than the PC was hotly contested by PC users, but the Mac and its mouse-dependent GUI were a big hit. Over time, many developers of software for the PC began to tap into the popularity of the mouse in an effort to make the PC more user friendly.

Figure 7-10
A Mac mouse, a trackball, and a PC mouse.

A mouse controls a mouse pointer, or mouse cursor, on the screen. To use the mouse, you push it around the desktop or mouse pad to move the mouse pointer to the desired position on screen. You then initiate some action with a mouse button. A mouse has one, two, or three buttons on it. To select something on the screen, such as a command, a graphic object, or a GUI icon, you move the mouse pointer to the command, object, or icon, then **click** once with the main mouse button (with two- and three-button mice, this is usually the leftmost button). To move an item across the screen, you move the pointer to the item, press and hold the mouse button, and **drag** the item to the new location. Finally, you can **double-click** (click twice in rapid succession) to select an item and initiate an action at the same time. Clicking, dragging, and double-clicking are the three basic techniques used with a mouse.

A **trackball** is a device that provides the functionality of a mouse, but doesn't roll around on the desk. A trackball is like an upside down mouse. It is a ball that rolls around in a base, and it controls the pointer on the screen. Buttons, which work much like mouse buttons, are located on the side of the unit.

Trackballs are especially popular with portable and laptop computers like the one shown in Figure 7-11, because an appropriate surface for a mouse is not always available when using a laptop or portable computer.

Light Pens and Digitizer Tablets

A **light pen** (Figure 7-12) is a light-sensitive, pen-shaped instrument that is connected to a video terminal. The user puts the light pen against the desired point on the screen and presses a button on the pen to identify the screen location. Pressing this button causes the pen to sense light. The place being illuminated identifies the screen location. Light pens are used in place of keyboards to select menu items and to draw. They are especially popular in environments such as auto shops, where dirt and grease make keyboards impractical.

Some other systems use a pen that is connected by a wire to a **digitizer tablet**, which acts as a surface for the pen to "write" on while the screen cursor creates a corresponding image. The digitizer tablet allows the user to write, draw, select command choices, or just replace the cursor with the pen. This technology is used in point of sale entries, warehouse inventory, and with graphics software (Figure 7-13).

Touch Screens

Touch screens can only loosely be defined as pointing devices, because the "pointing device" is actually the user's finger. Such screens permit the user to touch certain areas of a monitor to give commands. For example, instead of typing a command to view market information, the user can simply touch a menu item called MARKET INFORMATION with a finger. Touch screens are important components in the new technology called multimedia, where computers incorporate video, voice, graphics, and text into applications. Although few software packages currently utilize touch screens, they are gaining popularity quickly

Figure 7-11 The Macintosh PowerBook includes a built-in trackball.

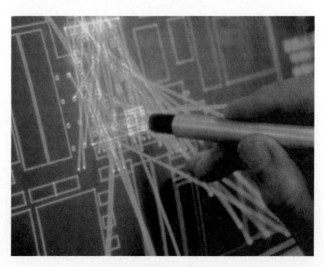

Figure 7-12 A light pen.

for applications in retail stores. They help customers find items, receive coupons and information about products, access bridal registries, take blood pressure, and even buy lottery tickets (Figure 7-14).

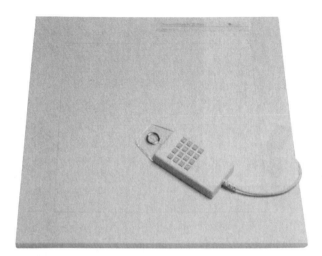

Figure 7-13 A digitizer tablet used as part of a graphics workstation.

Figure 7-14 Touch screens like this one are becoming common in department stores, supermarkets, and other retail stores.

Comprehension Questions

1. Can you think of a reason why mice are more popular than trackballs, even though trackballs take up less room on the desk?
2. Why are function keys used less often than they used to be?
3. What arguments can be made for using keyboard commands rather than mouse commands?

Using What You Know

1. On which computers at BVOS would it be most advantageous to have a mouse? On which would the mouse be dispensable?
2. Why is a pointing device an important part of a desktop publishing system?
3. How might a pen and digitizer tablet be used to streamline data entry in a stockroom?

Scanning Devices: Automating the Input Process

Both keyboards and pointers are used when data must be entered manually. Sometimes, though, the data that we need to input already exists on paper or in some other printed form. **Scanners** automate the process of data entry by reading an image and translating it into digital code. They do this by shining a light at the image and recording the intensity of the light that is reflected. With this technique, scanners can be used to digitize text, photographs, graphics, and bar codes to create binary code.

Figure 7-15
The results of digitizing a
photo with a flat-bed
scanner.

Most of the scanners used with microcomputers are two-dimensional image scanners. The images most frequently digitized are pages of text and graphic images. These scanners are classified as flat-bed or hand-held, and as color or gray-scale. With a flat-bed scanner, the image is placed on a flat piece of glass in much the same way a piece of paper is placed on a photocopier (Figure 7-15). Hand-held scanners are much smaller, with scanning fields usually no wider than 4½ inches. Gray-scale scanners reduce both color and black-and-white images to shades of gray. Color scanners are able to record the color of the image being scanned.

Optical Character Recognition

Using a scanner requires application software that can interpret the image that is created. Normally, when an image is scanned, graphics software is used to save the image as a bitmap file. If text is scanned, however, the computer requires software with **optical character recognition** (**OCR**) capabilities to regenerate text from a bit-mapped image that was created by a scanner. Once the text is read by the OCR software, it can be manipulated, edited, and printed by word processing or DTP software. The IRS uses OCR to convert the bit-mapped files created from scanning completed 1040 forms back to text.

As OCR software becomes more advanced, more and more types of print can be recognized. Advanced OCR software is becoming better and better at recognizing handwriting and converting it into ASCII text. Thus, a page of notes that you take for class can be turned into a document without your retyping the text.

Bar-Code Readers

Although the most common type of scanner used with microcomputers is the image scanner, bar-code readers are actually much more prevalent items, though they are generally used with larger computer systems. **Bar-code readers**, such as the one shown in Figure 7-16, are used to read bar codes, such as the universal product code, or UPC, symbol used on products in grocery and retail stores. Bar-code readers are faster than human data entry and are far more accurate. Using bar codes, a photo-electric scanner converts the succession of stripes into a code. The code identifies the product and data related to it. In the supermarket, the data is usually a brief description of the item and the price. Because the point of sale software that interprets the bar code is normally connected to an inventory database, this data can be used to track inventory. Thus, when an item is purchased, the item is automatically deducted from the store's inventory. When a number of items have been purchased, the software can automatically order new stock and relay financial data to the store's accounting system.

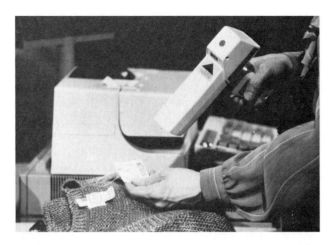

Figure 7-16
The most common type of scanner is the bar-code reader.

Voice Input

Science fiction writers have been writing for half a century about machines that can understand our spoken commands. Today fact is meeting fiction. **Voice input** systems scan the sound of your voice, digitize the data, and compare the digitized sound to a set of commands. If there is a match, the action associated with that sound is performed. With voice input, you can quickly and easily accomplish tasks such as telling the computer to save your current document. Voice input systems are invaluable to people whose physical handicaps would otherwise prevent them from using computers.

Interpreting digitized sound is a difficult problem. There are vast differences in the way people pronounce words. Consequently, we need to train the computer to understand how we say certain sounds. To do this, we initialize the voice system by saying certain key words and sounds into a microphone when the computer tells us to. This information is captured in a voice template that is then used to interpret what we say. Each subsequent statement is compared to the template before it is converted into text.

Comprehension Questions

1. What do you think are the most important sounds to record on a voice template? Why?
2. What skill is no longer required by sales clerks in stores that have bar-code readers?
3. If OCR software is not used, what type of application is most likely to use scanned images?

Using What You Know

1. How is optical character recognition like scanning your voice?
2. If headquarters printed bar codes on all their packaging, which of the BVOS computers would you want to equip with bar-code readers?
3. How might a gray-scale flat-bed scanner with OCR software be used at BVOS?

Monitors

A **monitor** is simply a device that displays output on a screen. The monitor in a microcomputer is generally the default output device. In other words, if you don't tell the CPU to send data somewhere else, it sends the data to its monitor and the output is displayed on your computer screen. There are a wide variety of monitors available, varying in type, size, resolution, ability to display color, and several other factors.

Monitor screens are made up of pixels, which are tiny dots (Figure 7-17). A **pixel**, which stands for *picture element*, is the smallest graphic unit on the screen. A pixel consists of one dot on a monochrome screen and three dots (red, green, and blue), or clusters of these dots, on a color screen. The density of the pixels on the screen determines the resolution of the

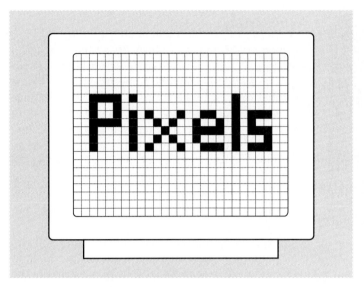

Figure 7-17 A computer screen contains a grid of pixels similar to the ones shown here but much smaller and closer together. In a color monitor, each pixel is composed of three dots: one blue, one red, and one green. The shade of each pixel is determined by combining these three colors.

monitor. **Resolution** refers to the degree of sharpness and clarity of the images displayed. Factors affecting the resolution include the overall dimensions of the screen, the total number of pixels, and, for color monitors, the **dot pitch**, the distance between the three colored dots that make up a single pixel. (Dot pitch does not apply to monochrome monitors.) The lower the dot pitch the sharper the image. For example, if you see an ad for a monitor that reads "15-inch, .28mm, 1024 x 768," this monitor measures 15 inches diagonally, the dot pitch is .28 mm, and there are 768 rows of pixels, with 1024 pixels in each row.

Types of Monitors

There are two main types of monitors: CRT monitors and flat-panel monitors. The types are differentiated by the methods they use to display an image.

CRT Monitors.   The **cathode ray tube,** or **CRT**, works just like your television. As shown in Figure 7-18, a special type of vacuum tube sprays a stream of electrons, which are directed onto a piece of glass that is coated with phosphor. When the electrons hit the phosphor, the phosphor glows.

The phosphor on the piece of glass, or screen, is organized into pixels. The phosphor in each pixel quickly fades after the electron beam passes. Consequently, the pixels need to be refreshed frequently by the beam. If they are not refreshed frequently enough, the screen appears to flicker. To give you an idea of how noticeable flicker is, manufacturers sometimes list how many times the screen is refreshed each second. The unit provided is Hertz (Hz), which measures cycles per second. Monitors generally operate at at least 60 Hz.

CRT monitor manufacturers go to great pains to eliminate flicker. The most popular method currently available for reducing flicker is a noninterlaced screen. Televisions use interlaced screens, which means that the electron beam starts at the top of the screen and scans every other row in each vertical pass — the odd rows on the first pass and the even rows on the second. The screen appears to be refreshed

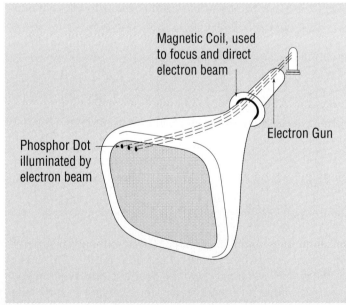

Magnetic Coil, used to focus and direct electron beam

Electron Gun

Phosphor Dot illuminated by electron beam

Figure 7-18
How an image is created by a cathode ray tube.

about 60 times per second. But in fact, each line of pixels is refreshed only 30 times per second; each line is refreshed every other cycle. Noninterlaced screens refresh every row with every pass. A computer can more easily refresh every other row because each pass requires only half as much information. Noninterlacing requires more data, but flicker is less noticeable. Monitor ads usually indicate if a screen is noninterlaced, or NI, because the reduced flicker is a selling point. Noninterlacing can add significantly to a monitor's price.

Flat-Panel Monitors. The main limitation of CRT screens is that they must be at least several inches deep and often weigh several pounds. Furthermore, CRTs require a lot of power. As a result, they cannot be used in laptop computers, where everything must be light, compact, and energy efficient. These machines use **flat-panel displays** (Figure 7-19). There are currently three competing technologies in flat-panel monitors.

The most popular form of flat-panel display so far is the LCD monitor, which uses the same technology as digital watches. **LCD** stands for **liquid crystal display**. The pixels in an LCD are composed on liquid crystal and are suspended between two panes of glass with wires running through them, as shown in Figure 7-20. Usually, there is a light behind the back glass. In its normal state, the liquid crystal material is clear, and the light shines through. But when current shoots through the wire that runs through a pixel, the liquid becomes solid looking, and the light is blocked.

The two other techniques used in flat-panel displays are *gas-plasma* and *electroluminescence* (EL). Both tend to be easier to read than LCD monitors because, like a CRT, the screen itself emits light and therefore does not need to be backlit. **Gas-plasma displays** use gas that glows when it is electrically charged. **Electroluminescent displays**, like CRT displays, use phosphor, but they cause the phosphor to glow with perpendicular sets of wires (Figure 7-21 on the next page).

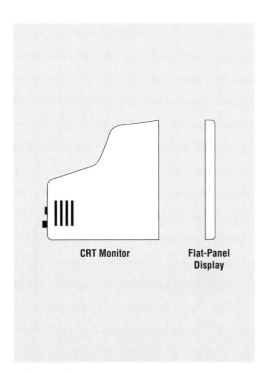

Figure 7-19 CRT monitors are at least several inches deep and often weigh several pounds. Flat-panel monitors are thinner, lighter, and require less power.

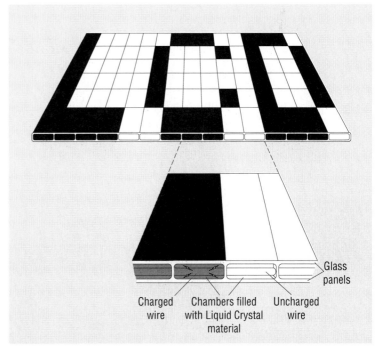

Figure 7-20 How an image is created with an LCD monitor.

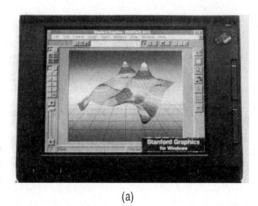 

Figure 7-21
The two leading types of flat-panel monitors: (a) LCD; (b) gas-plasma.

(a)   (b)

Monitor Size

Just like the televisions in our homes, monitors differ in size. Some monitors have very small screens; others can display two full pages of information at a time. Studies show that the bigger the screen, the less eye strain accompanies computer work. Large screens are becoming popular in graphical user interface environments and in desktop publishing applications.

Single-page monitors do not vary much in size. The average CRT screen for PCs is 14 inches, measured diagonally. Increasingly, users are choosing 16-inch or larger monitors. If you're planning to use your computer for desktop publishing, graphic design, or large spreadsheets, you should consider a screen that is larger than 14 inches. A 20-inch monitor, for example, allows you to display two facing 8-inch pages. Unfortunately, large screen monitors are significantly more expensive than their 14-inch counterparts. Be sure that your software can adjust the amount of information it places on the screen to take advantage of the larger screen. Figure 7-22 compares some of the monitors available with the Macintosh.

Monochrome and Color Monitors

The first characteristic that buyers usually consider when purchasing a monitor is whether or not they need the screen to display color. A **monochrome** monitor displays images in one color against a background of a different color. The most common colors are black, amber, or green characters on white or black backgrounds. Amber is considered easiest on the eyes. Many early PC monitors could display only 25 lines of type at one time, with 80

(a)   (b)   (c)   (d)

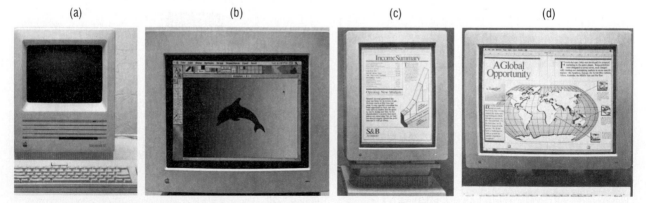

Figure 7-22   Macintosh monitors: (a) the compact 9-inch screen; (b) the 13-inch screen, standard on the Mac II and other large footprint models; (c) the full-page monitor; and (d) the dual-page monitor.

characters in each line. However, today most monochrome monitors can display graphics, too. Resolution tends to be better on monochrome monitors than on color monitors. They are very suitable for many home or office applications. By linking more than one bit to each pixel, **gray-scale** monitors are able to create varying darknesses in a single pixel. Monitors that are not gray-scale approximate shading with a checkerboard (or some other pattern) of light and dark pixels.

Color monitors provide more variation in the way information is presented. After all, color has a significant impact on the way information is perceived by the user. In addition, because human eyes differ in their ability to see certain colors, allowing the user to change the color of information that is presented can improve productivity and decrease eye strain.

A color monitor creates all other colors by combining red, green, and blue. For this reason, color monitors are sometimes referred to as *RGB monitors*. Color monitors are similar to gray-scale monitors in that each pixel must be linked to a number of bits. The number of colors a pixel can display is determined by the number of bits linked to each pixel. The most primitive color monitors can display only four colors (red, green, blue, and black), using just two bits for each pixel. At the other end of the scale, 24-bit color monitors can display over 16 million colors with each pixel.

Graphic Cards for the PC

When using a PC or compatible, the type of graphics adapter or graphics card (the expansion board that must accompany the monitor) distinguishes monitors from each another. Macintosh machines all come with high-quality, high-resolution graphics capability and do not require an additional graphics adapter. A PC or compatible monitor, however, may be labeled CGA, EGA, VGA, or SVGA.

The Color Graphics Adapter (**CGA**) was the first type of color graphics monitor that was released with the IBM PC. CGA systems display 320 x 200 pixels (320 horizontally and 200 vertically) in four colors on the screen when the monitor is in graphics mode. CGA provides relatively primitive graphics capability, at least by today's standards. Enhanced Graphics Adapters (**EGA**) were the next generation: They can produce 16 colors on the screen, with 640 x 350 resolution. Video Graphics Array (**VGA**) monitors create even more vivid and clear images. As the name indicates, they are ideal for video graphics because they allow the user to choose from among over 200,000 different colors in 640 x 480 resolution, though only 16 colors can be displayed on the screen at once. With their high resolution, VGA monitors are appropriate for computer-aided design applications, business graphics, and video games. Super VGA, or **SVGA**, is capable of 1024 x 768 resolution, with 16 colors on the screen at any given time. At lower resolutions, SVGA adapters can display much higher numbers of colors at once.

The minimum standard resolution for IBM-compatible systems is 640 x 480. This standard is VGA. However, more users are turning to SVGA, which is 800 x 600 or 1024 x 768, depending on the software. SVGA is priced competitively with VGA. For 14-inch color monitors, the dot pitch should be .28 mm or lower.

Trying to select a video card can be perplexing. In general, the newer technology in VGA cards can produce sharper images more quickly than CGA or EGA cards, though the older monitors can be obtained for much less money. The more you use the monitor, the more you should be concerned with how the text and graphics look. If they are sharp and easy to read, then your eyes will tire less quickly. Moving to a graphical user interface will certainly encourage the use of higher resolution color monitors.

When purchasing a VGA or SVGA adapter card, it is important to make sure that it has enough internal memory. If you are using Windows or any graphics programs, insufficient memory may cause your system to slow down. Modern adapter cards often contain 1 MB of their own memory. If the memory on your card is not sufficient, it may be possible to buy an accelerator card to speed up your system.

Purchasing a Monitor

When purchasing a monitor, you must decide what kind of resolution and color you want, then select the hardware that will support those specifications. If you are planning to use your computer primarily for word processing and some spreadsheet work, a medium-resolution monitor will do. If you plan to perform desktop publishing and will be using multiple fonts and graphics, a screen with higher resolution will display those fonts and graphics more accurately.

The decision whether to purchase a color or monochrome monitor is based upon personal preference and economics. For example, GUIs can be easier to interpret in color, but the added convenience may not warrant the added cost. Although color is very desirable when doing graphics work on the screen, it is of little use when you print the graphics if you don't have a color printer.

Buying a monitor involves the purchase of two pieces of equipment: the monitor itself and the video graphics card that goes inside the computer. You should make sure that the card and the monitor are compatible, because some cards cannot communicate with some monitors. In general, a VGA card can communicate only with a VGA-compatible monitor.

When you shop for a monitor, ask the dealer to demonstrate how it displays text and graphics in several applications. Check the clarity of small type; this is an important test for a monitor.

Comprehension Questions

1. How many bits must be connected to each pixel to display 256 colors or 256 shades of gray?
2. When you do graphics work, why might it still be appropriate to have a color monitor even though you don't have a color printer?
3. How many more pixels are there on an SVGA screen than on an EGA screen?

Using What You Know

1. Who at BVOS (or which group) will be least concerned with the resolution and color on the screen?
2. Compare the cost of a high-resolution (1024 x 768) monochrome monitor with that of a high-resolution color monitor. If you were using the monitor on a daily basis, would the difference in cost deter you from buying the color monitor? Why or why not?
3. Describe, in detail, the kind of monitor you, as president of BVOS, have on your laptop. More important, why do you have such a monitor?

Printers

Besides monitors, the only other standard output device is the printer. Printing is the creation of text or graphic images on paper. Printed output is often referred to as **hard copy**, while output on the screen is known as **soft copy**.

There are three types of printers to which microcomputers are commonly connected: dot matrix printers, ink-jet printers, and laser printers.

Dot Matrix Printers

The most prevalent type of printer used with microcomputers is the dot matrix printer. **Dot matrix printers** create images with a set of pins that push an inked ribbon against the paper. Dot matrix printers are often compared by the number of pins they use to impact the paper. The most common kinds are 9-pin and 24-pin printers. The larger the number, the higher the print quality. As shown in Figure 7-23, a 24-pin printer creates characters that are smoother and more fully formed than a 9-pin printer. A popular dot matrix printer is shown in Figure 7-24.

Although dot matrix printers do not produce the highest quality print, they are very popular, primarily because they are the least expensive type of printer. Another advantage is that, among the three main printer types, dot matrix printers are the only ones to physically strike the paper. As a result, they are called **impact printers**. The only other type of impact printer is the daisy wheel printer, which works like some typewriters, with letters on a spinning wheel that are pushed against the paper. Daisy wheel printers are still found in many schools and offices, though few are now being sold. Impact printers are necessary when printing on multicopy forms, such as bills and receipts. One disadvantage of impact printers is that when in operation, they are louder than other types.

Similar to a dot matrix printer is a thermal printer. This printer burns small dots onto special paper to create an image. Again, the more dots, the better the print. Thermal dot matrix printers are also popular in fax machines.

INTERNATIONAL

INTERNATIONAL

Figure 7-23
Magnified letters from 9-pin and 24-pin dot matrix printers.

Figure 7-24
A popular dot matrix printer.

Ink-Jet Printers

Ink-jet printers create images by shooting tiny droplets of ink at the paper (Figure 7-25). The aim of the spray is much more precise than the pins of a dot matrix printer, so the resolution of the image is far better. Color ink-jet printers are able to create color images by combining red, green, blue, and black ink. Ink-jet printers are usually about twice as fast as dot matrix printers. However, they often require coated paper; even good-quality bond paper makes the ink look fuzzy.

Laser Printers

The preferred printer among microcomputer users is the laser printer. A **laser printer** uses laser beams to project an image onto a photosensitive drum, where powdered ink called *toner* is bonded to the paper with heat (Figure 7-26). The technology used is very similar to that used in photocopiers.

Although laser printers cannot achieve the quality of print normally found in books, their output is more than sufficient for most business and personal applications. When used at the office, a laser printer is generally shared by several employees due to its cost. However, the cost of laser printers is dropping. Figure 7-27 shows a popular laser printer.

Color laser printers combine colored toner to create their images. Color printers are used primarily for desktop publishing. Base your selection of a color printer on speed, resolution, the number of colors needed, and the ease and cost of ink replacement.

Comparing Printers

There are several factors to take into account when comparing printers. Printers vary in the quality of print, speed, software compatibility, available fonts, and of course, cost.

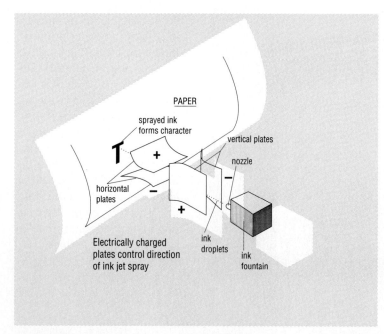

Figure 7-25   Ink-jet printers create images by spraying tiny drops of ink onto the paper.

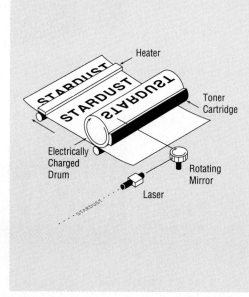

Figure 7-26   How a laser printer creates an image.

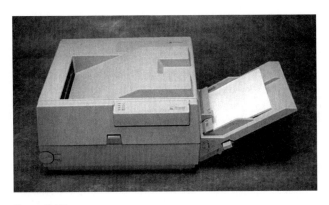

Figure 7-27
A typical laser printer.

Quality of Print.   Print quality is measured in various ways. The simplest comparison is between letter-quality and near letter-quality print. A printer that can produce **letter-quality print** creates characters that are comparable in quality to typewriter print. Printers that produce **near letter-quality (NLQ) print** create characters that are less sharp. Dot matrix and thermal printers are known for being near letter quality, while laser and ink-jet printers are known for their letter-quality type. Figure 7-28 shows the difference between near letter-quality and letter-quality output.

As mentioned, the near letter-quality output of a dot matrix printer is measured by how many pins the printer uses. Letter-quality printers are often compared by the number of dots per inch (dpi) they create. A higher number means higher quality text. Typically, laser printers operate at a minimum of 300 dpi, though 600 dpi is common and much higher numbers are available. Ink-jet printers are able to print up to about 300 dpi.

Dot matrix printers are often purchased when the user is concerned with the content of what the computer produces rather than how the printed copy looks. Dot matrix printers are also necessary for printing on multiple-copy forms. They will provide adequate output for most users. In addition to being less expensive than a laser printer, a dot matrix printer requires less periodic maintenance. Also, those with a large number of pins and fresh ribbons can produce near letter-quality output. However, when presentation of the output is a major concern, such as a presentation to a client, letter-quality printers are more desirable.

Printer Speed.   Another major factor distinguishing one printer from another is the speed with which it creates characters or images. There are two methods for measuring printer speed, depending on how the printer creates a page of text. Dot matrix and ink-jet printers print one character at a time and are therefore measured in terms of **characters per second (cps)**. Dot matrix printers commonly print about 100 cps, though modern ones may print faster. Ink-jet printers often print twice that fast. Cps figures are useful for comparison, but

(a)   (b)   (c)

made his
work
basis for
from the

made his
work
basis for
from the

Figure 7-28   (a) A close-up of NLQ output from a 24-pin dot matrix printer; (b) output from a 300 dpi ink-jet printer
(c) output from a 600 dpi laser printer.

are often misleading, because they are calculated based on the time it takes to print one line. The figure does not take into account the time it takes to move the paper to the next line.

Laser printers use a more reliable figure, known as **pages per minute**, or **ppm**, because they lay out an entire page and print it with a rolling drum that is as wide as the page. Laser printers range between 4 and 25 ppm, though most operate at about 6 ppm. By comparison, ink-jet printers can print about three pages per minute. In general, the faster the printer, the more expensive it is, regardless of how the letters are printed on the page. Naturally, the speed of a printer becomes more of an issue if several people are going to share a single printer.

When considering the speed of any printer, you must remember that the figures given by the manufacturer are for printing pages of text and for printing in black and white. As soon as you begin to add graphics and color to your document, your printing speeds will drop dramatically. This is because graphics and color require far more memory than text. For example, one page of text, even if it is dense and complicated, is not likely to require more than 10 K of memory. One page of bit-mapped graphics, however, can occupy more than 200 K. The length of time it takes the printer to print the page is closely related to the amount of memory that the page requires.

Software Compatibility. When you use a printer, you have to make sure that your application or operating system software knows what kind of printer you want to use, because different printers are controlled with different codes. To use a printer, your software needs a **printer driver**, which is a small piece of software that translates the CPU's output into codes that the printer understands.

With so many printers on the market, creating and maintaining drivers can be overwhelming. Adobe Systems has attempted to solve this problem by suggesting that printers be supplied with special purpose CPUs that can do the work of the printer driver. The computer is then able to send the printer a standard set of control codes, so all software can send the same output to any printer. The Adobe standard is called **PostScript** (Figure 7-29). PostScript printers are usually more expensive because of the increased processing capabilities of the printer. Some non-PostScript printers can be converted by installing a PostScript printer cartridge into the printer. Although not as prevalent, another standard for laser printers is Hewlett-Packard's Printer Control Language, PCL.

Figure 7-29
Three standard PostScript fonts: Times, Palatino, and Helvetica, all in 16-point type.

TIMES   PALATINO   HELVETICA

Available Fonts. A printer needs instructions about how to print various fonts. These instructions may come from software that is stored in the computer, or they may come from a ROM chip in the printer. Fonts that are built into the printer are called **internal fonts**. Fonts that are downloaded from the computer are called **soft fonts** (because they come from software). You can increase the number of soft fonts by purchasing additional fonts, either individually or as font libraries. Internal fonts can be supplemented by adding a cartridge to the printer.

The number of fonts available to you will affect the versatility of the printer. For most business and personal applications, you can get by with just a few fonts. However, if your work involves DTP, you might always be pushing for new fonts. In this case, you should consider buying a printer with a large supply of internal memory; each font that you need to download will take up space in your printer's memory. Having a PostScript printer can solve some of your font problems because many PostScript printers come with 35 internal fonts, each of which can be scaled to different point sizes.

Comprehension Questions

1. Of dot matrix, ink-jet, and laser printers, which type prints the fastest?
2. Are thermal printers useful for printing on multiple-copy forms? Why or why not?
3. Say a dot matrix printer can print at 100 cps. How long would it take the printer to generate a page with 250 words of six characters each? How many pages per minute is this? Does this figure seem believable?

Using What You Know

1. Which is higher resolution, a 300 dpi laser printer or a 1024 x 768 SVGA monitor?
2. Which computers at BVOS should be linked to dot matrix printers and why?
3. Does anyone at BVOS need a laser printer? Why or why not?

Summary Points

Getting Data "In" and Information "Out"
☐ In common usage, an input device is hardware that the user employs to give data to the computer, and an output device is hardware used to present information to the user.

The Keyboard and Its Parts
☐ The keyboard was the first input device widely used with microcomputers.
☐ It remains the most versatile input device.

Alphanumeric Keys
☐ The alphanumeric keys form the QWERTY keyboard, which resembles the standard typewriter keyboard.

Function Keys
☐ The function keys accomplish tasks that are determined by the program being used.

Cursor-Movement Keys
☐ The cursor-movement keys are used to move the cursor around the screen or document.

The Numeric Keypad
☐ The numeric keypad is a convenient alternative to the numbers that run across the top of the alphanumeric keys.

Lights on the Keyboard
☐ Many keyboards have three lights to indicate the condition of three toggle switches: the Num Lock, Scroll Lock, and Caps Lock keys.

Data Entry with the Keyboard
☐ *Data entry* can refer to a job that requires typing or entering numbers, or it can simply refer to keyboard input.

A Few Words About Ergonomics: The Human Factor

☐ There are optimum kinds of equipment and optimum ways to adjust the equipment to maximize your comfort and minimize the risk of injury when you use the computer.

Pointing Devices

☐ Pointing devices have become more common as GUIs have gained popularity.

The Mouse

☐ The three basic mouse techniques are clicking, dragging, and double-clicking.
☐ The Macintosh popularized the mouse.
☐ A trackball is essentially an upside-down mouse that is especially useful in laptop computers.

Light Pens and Digitizer Tablets

☐ A pen is applied directly to the screen or a digitizer tablet to write, draw, or select command choices.

Touch Screens

☐ Touch screens, which allow the user to use a finger as a pointing device, are becoming popular in many retail stores.

Scanning Devices: Automating the Input Process

☐ Scanners automate data entry by reading a printed image.
☐ Scanners can be color or gray-scale, hand-held or flat-bed.

Optical Character Recognition

☐ OCR software enables the computer to regenerate text by scanning a printed document.

Bar-Code Readers

☐ Bar-code readers are used primarily in point of sale systems to keep track of inventory and speed sales.

Voice Input

☐ Voice input systems are becoming more adept at understanding spoken commands.

Monitors

☐ The monitor is usually the default output device.

Types of Monitors

CRT Monitors

☐ The cathode ray tube is the same technology as used in televisions.
☐ The resolution is determined by the density of pixels.
☐ The amount of flicker is determined by the refresh rate and whether the screen is interlaced or non-interlaced.

Flat-Panel Monitors

☐ Flat-panel displays are useful in portables and laptops because they use less power, weigh less, and take up less space than standard monitors.
☐ The three common types of flat-panel displays are LCD, gas-plasma, and electroluminenscent.

Monitor Size

☐ Bigger screens are useful in DTP work and cause less eye strain.
☐ The average monitor is 14 inches, measured diagonally.

Monochrome and Color Monitors

☐ Monitors can generate shades of gray or color by linking each pixel to more than one bit.

☐ Color monitors generate all other colors by combining red, green, and blue.

Graphic Cards for the PC

☐ Graphics monitors require a CGA, EGA, VGA, or SVGA graphics card that is compatible with the monitor.

Purchasing a Monitor

☐ The kind of monitor you purchase should depend on economics and how you will use it.

Printers

Dot Matrix Printers

☐ Dot matrix printers create an image by striking the paper with inked pins; the number of pins determines the resolution.

☐ Because their pins strike the paper, dot matrix printers can be used for multiple-copy forms.

☐ Thermal printers burn small dots onto special paper.

Ink-Jet Printers

☐ Ink-jet printers shoot tiny drops of ink at the paper.

Laser Printers

☐ Laser printers work much like photocopiers.

Comparing Printers

Quality of Print

☐ Dot matrix and thermal printers can be NLQ, while ink-jet and laser printers can be letter quality.

☐ Letter-quality printers measure their resolution in dpi.

Printer Speed

☐ Dot matrix and ink-jet printers measure speed in cps.

☐ Laser printers measure speed in ppm, a more accurate measurement than cps.

☐ Printing graphics and color will slow down any type of printer.

Software Compatibility

☐ Printers require printer drivers.

☐ PostScript printers have extra processing power built in to alleviate the need for printer drivers.

Available Fonts

☐ Internal fonts are built into the printer.

☐ Soft fonts are downloaded from the computer.

Knowing the Facts

True/False

1. OCR is capable of reading handwriting but not printed text.
2. In a color monitor, each pixel is controlled by a single bit.
3. Bar-code readers are most often used in point of sale systems.
4. The layout of the keys on the keyboard was originally designed to slow down typists.
5. Strictly speaking, the numeric keypad on a keyboard is not a necessity, because it provides no additional functionality.
6. Cps is a more accurate measurement than ppm.
7. Interlaced screens are less prone to flicker than non-interlaced screens.
8. Color monitors create all other colors by combining red, yellow, and blue.
9. Because of the popularity of GUIs, the keyboard is quickly being replaced by the mouse.
10. The mouse is the most common pointing device packaged with laptops because of the limited space available on the keyboard.

Short Answer

1. PostScript printers help alleviate the need for including a wide variety of _____ with each software package.
2. _____ fonts are downloaded from the computer to the printer each time they are used.
3. Refresh rate is measured in cycles per second, also known as _____.
4. LCD monitors are popular in _____ computers because they require less space and power than CRT monitors.
5. A _____ provides the functionality of a mouse, but doesn't need to roll around on a horizontal surface.
6. _____ printers create an image with a technique similar to that of a photocopier.
7. _____ printers are effective for printing on multiple-copy forms.
8. The Caps Lock, Scroll Lock, and Insert keys are referred to as _____ because they control features that can be turned either on or off.
9. What family of computers popularized the mouse?
10. To translate a printed page into ASCII text, a scanner must be used with _____ software.

Answers

True/False

1. F
2. F
3. T
4. T
5. T
6. F
7. F
8. F
9. F
10. F

Short Answer

1. printer drivers
2. Soft
3. Hertz or Hz
4. laptop or portable
5. trackball
6. Laser
7. Dot matrix
8. toggle switches
9. Macintosh
10. OCR

Challenging Your Understanding

1. Look at *PC Magazine* or *PC World*. What is the price of laser printers? How does this compare with a dot matrix printer that can print near letter quality?

2. Laser printers use toner cartridges. How much do they cost? Does their price affect your laser printer decision? How long do they last?

3. If we could talk to computers, would we need any of the input devices discussed in this chapter? Why?

4. Try to determine how much a printer should cost as a percentage of the cost of the entire computer system. What types of applications require the cost of the printer to be a higher percentage of the total?

5. What are some of the legal and ethical issues associated with using image scanners?

Storage Devices

Key Terms

CD-ROM
directories
disk crash
diskette
diskette drive
folder
formatted (initialized)
hard disk
hard disk drive
nonremovable storage
optical disk
read-write head
removable storage
storage device
storage media
subdirectories
tape drive
write protect

Objectives

In this chapter you will learn to:

- Differentiate between storage devices and storage media
- Describe how diskettes are formatted
- List the storage capacities of double-density and high-density diskettes
- Explain how diskettes can be write protected
- Understand important ways to take care of diskettes
- Describe what happens in a disk crash
- Describe two advantages of hard disks over diskettes
- Name the most important advantage diskettes have over hard disks
- Name and describe two common schemes for creating hierarchical file structures
- Define the three magnetic alternatives to internal hard disks
- Describe how tape drives can be used to back up hard disks
- Define CD-ROM and name three other emerging storage technologies

Storage Devices and Storage Media

All of the hardware components we have talked about up to this point have been "devices": processing devices, input devices, and output devices. In this chapter we discuss storage devices, but we will also be discussing storage *media*. **Storage devices** are used to put the data on and take the data off of storage media. **Storage media** are passive pieces of hardware that merely hold data. For example, as shown in Figure 8-1, a diskette *drive* is a storage device. It is connected, via the data bus, to the CPU, and is therefore an I/O device. It is used to read data from and write data to a diskette, which is a storage medium. (*Medium* is the singular form of *media*.)

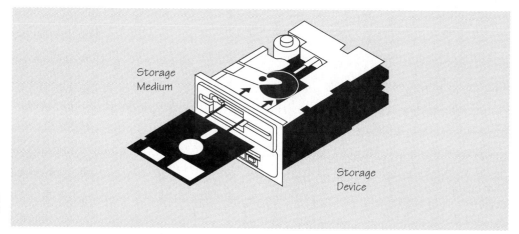

Storage
Medium

Storage
Device

Figure 8-1
A diskette drive is a
storage device. A diskette
is a storage medium.

Diskettes and Drives

The first type of storage device widely used with microcomputers was the diskette drive, and the first storage medium was the diskette. A **diskette**, sometimes called a floppy disk, is a round piece of mylar (plastic) coated with a magnetic substance called ferrous oxide and encased in a square plastic envelope or shell. The first standardized diskette was 8 inches in diameter. Today there are two common kinds of diskette: the 5¼-inch diskette and the 3½-inch diskette (Figure 8-2). The older of the two is the 5¼-inch diskette, which is encased in a flexible plastic envelope. This type is gradually being replaced by the 3½-inch diskette, which comes in a hard plastic case with a sliding cover. The 3½-inch type is winning the popularity contest not just because it is smaller, but because it can hold more data and, because of its case, is less vulnerable to damage and loss of data.

A **diskette drive** (also known as a floppy disk drive or

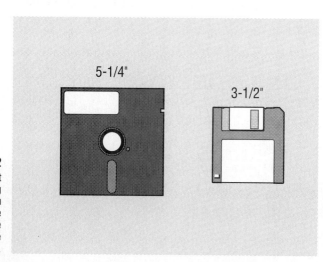

5-1/4"

3-1/2"

Figure 8-2
The 5¼-inch diskette at
left is gradually being
replaced by the 3½-inch
diskette. The 3½-inch type
is smaller, holds more
data, and is less vulnerable
to damage.

floppy drive) is the I/O device used to access the data on a diskette. The diskette drive (Figure 8-3) consists of a drive bay, where the diskette is inserted; the drive, which rotates the disk; and the most important part, the read-write head. A **read-write head** works like the recording and play heads of a cassette tape recorder. It reads the magnetic charges on the disk, records new charges when necessary, and erases old charges.

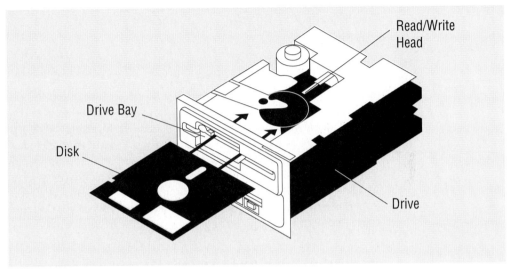

Figure 8-3
A 5¼-inch diskette drive.

How Data Is Organized on a Diskette

When you buy a new diskette, it is just what we have described: a piece of plastic with magnetic material on it. In order to be used, the diskette must be formatted. **Formatting** (**initializing** is the Mac term for the same process) is the process of mapping the magnetic surface into an arrangement of tracks and sectors that would look something like a dartboard if the arrangement were visible (Figure 8-4). First, the read-write head creates concentric circular tracks. Then the drive divides each track into sectors. This mapping enables the diskette drive to quickly locate any spot on the diskette.

Early diskettes held data on only one side. All modern diskettes, however, use both sides. The total number of tracks, sectors, and therefore bytes, on a diskette depend on the size of the diskette, the quality of the diskette material, and the capabilities of the diskette drive.

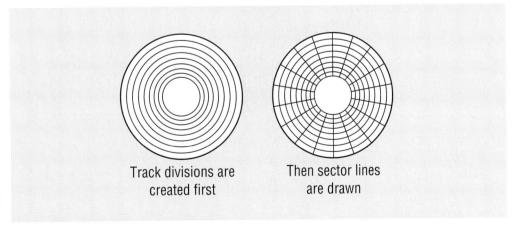

Track divisions are
created first

Then sector lines
are drawn

Figure 8-4
Organization of a formatted
diskette.

Table 8-1

Summary of diskette
capacities for PCs and
Macs.

FLOPPY DISK CAPACITIES		
Macintosh	5 1/4"	3 1/2"
Double Density	N/A	800 KB
High Density	N/A	1.44 MB
IBM		
Double Density	360 KB	720 KB
High Density	1.2 MB	1.44 MB
Extra Density*		2.88 MB
*requires Extra Density drive		

Most 5¼-inch diskettes hold either 360 K or 1.2 MB, depending on whether the diskette is double density or high density. Double-density diskettes have less capacity than high density. If used on a Macintosh, 3½-inch diskettes hold either 800K or 1.44 MB. On a PC or compatible, 3½-inch diskettes hold 720 K or 1.44 MB (Table 8-1).

Even with 3½-inch diskettes, PCs and Macs format diskettes differently. As a result, a PC cannot read a diskette that has been initialized on a Mac unless the PC has a special device that lets it do so. To address this compatibility problem, some Macs are equipped with a SuperDrive. With a utility program, the Mac can use the SuperDrive to read 3½-inch diskettes formatted on a PC.

Protecting Data: Just in Case

Although in general diskettes can be read or written to, it is possible to protect the data on the diskette from being written over by the read-write head. As shown in Figure 8-5, 5¼-inch diskettes have write-protect notches, and 3½-inch diskettes have write-protect tabs. If the notch is covered with a piece of tape or the tab is pushed so that a hole shows through the case, the drive's read-write head will not write data to the diskette. The data can then be read but not changed. The diskette is said to be **write protected**.

Figure 8-5

Data on 5¼-inch diskettes is protected by putting a piece of tape over the write protect notch. Data on 3½-inch diskettes is protected by pushing the write protect tab so a hole appears through the case.

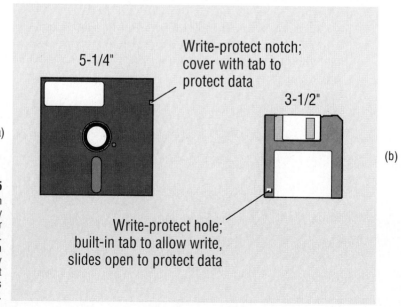

(a)

5-1/4"

Write-protect notch;
cover with tab to
protect data

3-1/2"

(b)

Write-protect hole;
built-in tab to allow write,
slides open to protect data

Taking Care of Diskettes

When data is moved from memory to storage, it is translated from electrical charges into magnetic charges. The data is therefore more durable, because it no longer requires current from the power supply. It is by no means permanent, however. Not only can data be written over by the drive's read-write head, it can be destroyed by any number of environmental hazards. The following is a list of dos and don'ts for taking care of your diskettes:

- Do not touch the surface of the diskette. This is a common danger with 5¼-inch diskettes, because some part of the diskette is always visible. With 3½-inch diskettes, it's best simply to avoid sliding the protective cover.

- Don't remove a diskette from a drive when the drive light is on. The drive light tells you that the diskette is spinning and the read-write head may be reading or writing to the diskette. Removing the diskette when this is happening is likely to damage the data currently held on the diskette. It can also damage the head.

- Don't expose diskettes to any magnetic fields. In addition to real magnets, common problem items include paper clips, poorly insulated wires, and music speakers.

- Don't expose diskettes to excessive heat or excessive moisture.

- Do store diskettes upright when they are not being used.

- Do use diskette labels and label your diskettes carefully with descriptive names. It often helps to include the date that data was written on a diskette, and, if appropriate, the program that was used to create the files. If it isn't already obvious, you should also include the storage capacity of the diskette.

In addition to the above rules, 5¼-inch diskettes need added care because they do not have a hard protective shell. With 5¼-inch diskette

- Use only felt-tip pens when writing on diskette labels that are already attached to the diskette. Pencils, erasers, and ball-point pens require too much pressure and can damage the diskette surface.

- Do not stack anything on top of the diskette. The pressure may damage the data surface.

- When not in use, keep the diskette in a paper or plastic diskette envelope. The plastic envelopes that come with 3½-inch diskettes don't add much protection, but the 5¼-inch envelopes protect the exposed diskette surface.

- Don't ever force the diskette into the drive. If it doesn't fit easily, something is in the way.

- Don't bend or fold the diskette, and don't try to attach it to anything with a clip or staple.

With proper care, diskettes can last a long time, though you should never rely heavily on a diskette. If data is important, make sure there are at least two copies of it — more than two, if the data is truly vital.

Purchasing Diskette Drives

Computers used in homes and businesses generally have either one or two diskette drives. Having two drives is common on PCs because of the conflict between 3½ and 5¼-inch diskettes. Many IBMs now come with a single 3½-inch drive. Clones, however, tend to have one of each size. Although the 3½-inch drives are gaining popularity, there are still a lot of 5¼-inch drives out there. If you need to trade diskettes with someone who has only the older type of drive, you must have that kind of drive as well. Moreover, some PC software is provided only on 5¼-inch diskettes, though most developers make their products available on both sizes. If you are buying a PC with only one drive, you probably want the 3½-inch drive. If you are getting two, it's safest to have one of each.

When purchasing a Mac, the decision of how many drives to have installed is a simple one, since all Mac diskettes are 3½ inches. If you want to copy data between two diskettes in one step, you might want two drives. Otherwise, one is usually sufficient.

If you ever find that you need another diskette drive, you can probably add it. If there is room in your system unit, PCs can generally be upgraded with an additional internal drive. If there isn't room, you may be able to attach an external diskette drive like the one shown in Figure 8-6.

Figure 8-6
If you want to add another diskette drive but there is no room in your system unit, you can add an external drive like the one shown here.

Comprehension Questions

1. Diskette drives tend to be upward compatible. What does this tell you about high-density drives?

2. Is a RAM chip a device, a medium, or both?

3. Why can a paper clip be a hazard around a diskette?

Using What You Know

1. What is the difference in cost between a 10-diskette box of high-density 3½-inch diskettes and a 10-diskette box of double-density 3½-inch diskettes?

2. What is the difference in cost between an external and an internal 3½-inch drive?

3. For what kind of data is it a good idea to write protect your diskettes? What kind of data is best left on unprotected diskettes?

Hard Disks and Hard Disk Drives

Although most microcomputers made during the early 1980s relied on diskette drives as their sole storage device, it didn't take computer manufacturers long to realize that a more convenient method was needed. With entirely diskette-based systems, users had to switch diskettes in and out of drives constantly. First the diskette containing the operating system was inserted, the data was read into memory, and the diskette was removed. Then the application diskette was inserted. If a second diskette drive was available, a diskette could be put in the second drive to store data. Otherwise, the data diskette and application diskette had to be swapped in and out of the single drive as needed.

Figure 8-7
An internal hard disk inside the system unit

The solution to the problem was the internal **hard disk**, a large magnetic storage area built into the system unit (Figure 8-7). The **hard disk drive** is the I/O device that accesses data on the hard disk. The hard disk is sealed inside the hard disk drive. As a result, hard disks are known as **nonremovable storage**. By contrast, diskettes are **removable storage**, because the diskette can be taken out of the drive and placed in a different one.

Although it is often important to distinguish between diskettes and drives, the terms *hard disk* and *hard disk drive* are often used interchangeably. This rarely causes any confusion, since the disk is nonremovable.

In their early days, hard disks allowed users to keep at least the operating system and the application packages in one handy place. The diskette drive was always free for data files. Early hard disks were often 20 MB, which seemed like a lot when users were accustomed to nothing but diskettes. As program size grew and users began keeping their data files on the hard disk, however, 20 MB became woefully inadequate. Today, hard disks of 10 times that size are becoming the norm. As an example, consider that Windows 3.1, a popular graphical user interface for PCs, takes up 10 MB, and you need to add another 4 to 15 MB for each application. And that's just for the software programs; you also need to store data, of course, and that requires more memory.

Hard Disks Compared to Diskettes

A hard disk is actually not one but a stack of rigid aluminum disks, called platters (Figure 8-8 on the next page). The hard disk is able to store more data than diskettes can because several disks are used, and because data can be packed on the metal far more densely than on mylar. The hard disk drive works the same way as the diskette drive, though there are some important differences in design.

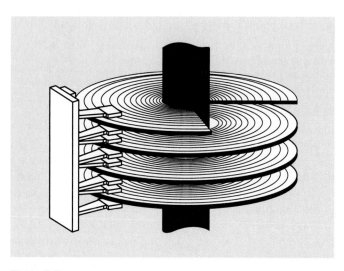

Figure 8-8
A hard disk is usually a stack of aluminum platters. The same tracks on different platters define a cylinder. Locations on the hard disk are defined by cylinder, side (which side of which platter), and sector.

First, there are a number of read-write heads, one for each side of each platter. Second, the drive and read-write heads are attached to the disk differently because the disk is never removed from the drive. Third, and most important, the read-write heads travel very close to the disk surface, but never touch the disk. Diskette drive read-write heads are designed to touch the diskette surface. If any contact occurs between a hard disk and the head, the system experiences a **disk crash** (also called a head crash). In a disk crash, data is lost and the disk and head often have to be replaced. Sometimes it's cheaper to just buy a whole new hard disk.

Preventing a disk crash is a tricky business, considering the disk spins at about 3000 revolutions per minute — about 45 miles per hour — and the head travels only 15 millionths of an inch above the platter. On a diskette, the residue from a fingerprint might be enough to obscure the data so the diskette drive's read-write head can't read it. But on a hard disk, a fingerprint can actually bridge the gap between the disk and the head and cause a crash. Figure 8-9 gives an idea of how close together the head and disk are. Now you know why the hard disk has to be sealed in a metal case.

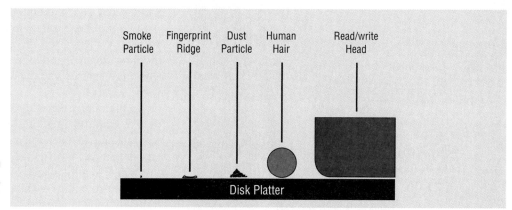

Figure 8-9
Hair, dust, even a fingerprint is enough to cause a hard disk crash.

There are two major advantages of hard disks over diskettes: lots of storage capacity and fast access times. On the other hand, diskettes have the advantage of easy portability. Let's look at these factors one at a time.

Capacity.   Hard disks can have several hundred times the storage capacity of diskettes. With respect to data files, this added capacity is a huge convenience. With respect to modern applications packages, a hard disk's capacity is a necessity.

Access Time.   Hard disk drives work like common compact disk players. When we want to listen to song number seven on a CD, we must instruct the CD player to play the song. After receiving the command, the player must position the laser over the correct spot on the CD (Figure 8-10). In computer terms, this is called a *seek*. Next, we have to wait for the beginning of the song to rotate under the laser. This is called *rotational delay.* Finally, we wait while the player reads the digital data off the CD using the laser and sends it to the amplifier. This is the *transfer time.* Therefore, a hard disk's access time is the sum of the seek time, the rotational delay, and the transfer time.

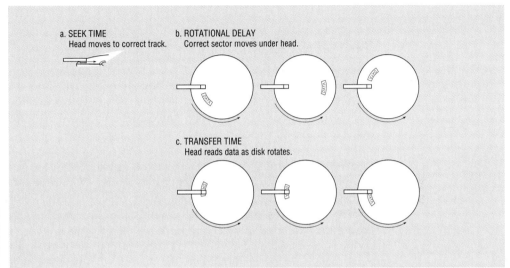

Figure 8-10
Access times for disk drives are the sum of (a) seek time, (b) rotational delay, and (c) transfer time.

In a hard disk, speed is the second most important feature, after storage capacity to consider. The speed at which your hard disk stores and retrieves data greatly affects your system's performance.

Portability.   The biggest advantage of diskettes over hard disks is easy portability. Data can be copied to a diskette and then taken home, passed to another user at the office, or even sent through the mail. Although programs are usually installed on a hard disk, they are originally supplied on diskettes because buyers must purchase them and bring them home before they can be installed. Software developers, in fact, are some of the biggest consumers of diskettes.

No matter how much a user may plan to depend on a hard disk, having a diskette drive is still a necessity for a standalone machine, because it's the usual way to get new software onto the hard disk.

Formatting a Hard Disk

Despite the differences in design, a hard disk is used just like a diskette. Before a hard disk can be used, it needs to be formatted. Formatting a hard disk divides it into tracks and sectors. With some computers, it is possible to partition the hard disk so that it can be treated as two or more smaller disks. This technique is just a method for organizing data, though, because the disk is still a single physical unit. As with diskettes, different operating systems format hard disks in different ways. This is generally not an issue, however, because hard disks are not normally exchanged between systems.

Types of Hard Disks

The least expensive and most popular hard disk is the IDE (integrated drive electronics). Some users who need a large-capacity drive or who want to expand their system with CD-ROM or tape drives prefer the SCSI (small computer systems interface, pronounced "scuz-ee") drive.

Organizing Files

Besides losing data from a disk crash, the biggest pitfall when using a hard disk is lack of good organization. On a disk, whether diskette or hard, files are listed in **directories**. The problem is that a large hard disk can easily store several thousand files. Without organization, all of these files would be listed in a single directory. Finding a single file among thousands could be almost impossible.

Subdirectories and Folders.   To solve the problem of disk organization, operating systems allow users to create hierarchical file structures. With a hierarchical structure, the user can break down the main directory (often called the root directory) into a group of **subdirectories**. In some operating systems, these subdirectories are referred to as **folders** because they are used in much the same way file folders are used in a filing cabinet. Each subdirectory or folder can contain files, other folders, or both. Except that they take up disk space, there is no logical limit to the number of subdirectories, so the user is free to create as intricate a hierarchy as he or she needs.

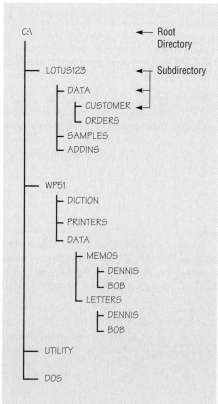

Figure 8-11

A hard disk directory structure, organized by application. The root directory contains the subdirectories LOTUS123, WP51, UTILITY, and DOS. The first two of these directories contain their own subdirectories.

Common Organizational Models.   On computers used in businesses, there are two common organizational models for storing files. The first could be called "organization by application" (Figure 8-11). When applications are installed on a hard disk, all the program files (the factory-created files that come with the software) for a single package are generally put in one subdirectory. Some users like to organize their data files according to the structure that these applications create, so that all of the documents created using a given application can be found in subdirectories within that application's subdirectory. For example, say you typically use two programs, WordPerfect and Lotus 1-2-3. The WordPerfect subdirectory might contain subdirectories called "Letters" and "Memos." The Letters and Memos subdirectories could, in turn, be subdivided according to the addressees of the letters and memos. Likewise, the Lotus 1-2-3 subdirectory might contain subdirectories for "Budgets" and "Forecasts."

Another popular organizational model might be called "organization by project" or "organization by client." In this scheme, an

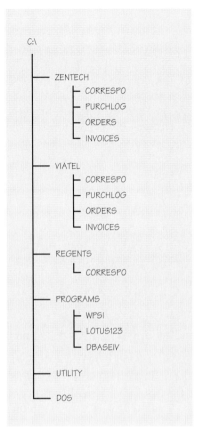

Figure 8-12
A hard disk directory structure, organized by client

example of which is shown in Figure 8-12, the program files for each application are still placed in their own directories, but no other files are stored there. Instead, data file subdirectories are created for each client or each project in progress. For example, at BVOS, the main directory of a disk might contain subdirectories with the names of companies that often buy supplies from you, such as Zentech, Viatel, and Regents. Each of these subdirectories could contain several types of application documents. Rather than being organized by application, they are grouped according to the nature of four smaller subdirectories: "Correspondence," "Purchase Logs," "Orders," and "Invoices."

These two organizational schemes are the most common, but there are plenty of others some perhaps even more effective or more efficient. Every user has different needs. Above all else, the structure should fit the need.

Alternatives to Internal Hard Disks

Throughout this section we have described the internal hard disk. There are, however, several other options for high-volume magnetic storage devices. An older computer that doesn't have an internal hard disk and doesn't have room to have one installed can be upgraded with an external hard disk (Figure 8-13). External disks work exactly the same way as internal ones, except that they are outside the system unit and are therefore somewhat more portable. An external hard disk can also be used to supplement the storage space of a computer that has an internal hard disk that is not large enough for the user's needs.

A second option is the hard card (Figure 8-14). Every disk drive requires a disk controller card, which is just a special type of expansion board connected to the motherboard. A hard

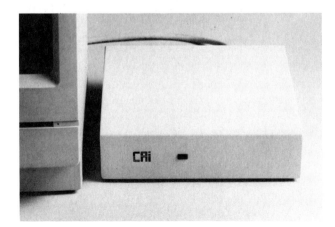

Figure 8-13 An external hard disk.

Figure 8-14 A hard card, which is plugged into an expansion slot in the motherboard.

Figure 8-15 A hard disk cartridge.

card combines the disk drive and the card by mounting a small hard disk directly on the controller board. Hard cards are now available as large as 105 MB, and they are growing quickly. They allow users with extra expansion slots to add storage without taking up space anywhere else.

A third option is the removable hard disk cartridge (Figure 8-15). The cartridge bridges the gap between the hard disk and the diskette by allowing the hard disk to be removed from the system unit. Disk cartridges allow the user to have virtually unlimited storage space, divided into large chunks of, say, 40 MB.

Comprehension Questions

1. Data access for CD players and disk drives requires the same three steps. So what is the basic difference between these two types of devices?
2. A hard disk cartridge is not truly a removable storage medium. What does this tell you about what is inside the cartridge?
3. In addition to transporting data, what other uses can you think of for diskettes?

Using What You Know

1. How large are hard disk cartridges now, and how much do they cost?
2. Compare the cost of a 200 MB hard disk and a comparable amount of hard disk cartridges.
3. What is the difference in price between a 200 MB external hard disk and a 200 MB hard internal disk?

Magnetic Tape

When you've got all your programs and data on one hard disk, one perpetual fear is that you'll experience a disk crash and lose everything. The fear is not unfounded; disk failures are regrettably common, and every user should back up his or her hard disk. As we explained when we covered utilities, software is available to make the process easier.

If you are backing up data onto diskettes, the process can be painful. Backing up a 100 MB hard disk, even with data compression techniques, can require 50 diskettes and take a great deal of time. To cure this inconvenience, hardware manufacturers have adapted cassette tape technology to computer storage needs. Using a cassette that looks very much like a music cassette, a **tape drive** (Figure 8-16) can copy the contents of an entire hard drive onto one tape. With such a device, you can tell your system to back itself up on the tape drive and then leave your computer to finish the process on its own. As with diskettes, you

Figure 8-16
Magnetic tape and a tape drive used for backup purposes.

can also back up designated files or groups of files — by name or by date created, for example — rather than backing up the entire hard disk.

Backing up with tape drives still requires backup utility software, but the software gives you added flexibility. Some software for tape drives allows you to schedule a backup when you aren't even present. As long as the computer is on and the cassette is in the drive, the tape drive will start backing up at a specified time. On the other hand, you might want to back up your hard disk while you continue to work with some other program. This may also be possible.

You might ask, "If cassettes can hold so much information, why don't we use them instead of hard disks?" The answer lies in the difference between sequential media and random-access media. A backup tape, like a cassette music tape, is a sequential medium. To find a particular piece of data on the tape, the tape drive must scan the tape sequentially, in forward or reverse, until it encounters the data. If you have ever looked for a song on a cassette, you know this can take some time.

A hard disk, however, is like a CD in that it is a random-access medium. When a CD player looks for a song, it only takes a second or two. The CD is mapped (formatted), and the player can use the map to jump directly to the right spot. After all, the distance between any two places on a CD can't be more than about five inches, whereas two spots on a cassette can be 100 yards apart. A hard disk is like a CD: Its surface is mapped and the read-write head can move to any point very quickly.

Other Forms of Tape

Cassettes are by far the most common type of tape used with microcomputers. Other types of tape are available, however. If you watch movies from the 1960s and 1970s, scientific and governmental computers are often shown with reel-to-reel tapes. Although reel-to-reel tape is not often used with microcomputers, it is still the standard means for backing up large amounts of data on minis and mainframes and for transferring data between the two.

How Often Should I Back Up?

Think about how much time and money you will spend if you cannot get a computer back to the state it was in before a hard disk failure in a reasonably short time. For example, if you spent three days creating a spreadsheet for a class or for work, would you mind spending another three days recreating that spreadsheet? What is that time worth to you? If you were writing a report that was printed two weeks ago, but was changed several times since the last time you printed it, how important were those changes?

No one is going to force you to back up your data. You have to decide how often to back up based upon how valuable your time is. Keep in mind that backing up is not a costless activity. It takes a while to back up a large disk drive. If you don't have the time to spare, this could be a tough decision. The answer to the question "How often should I back up?" is "Just often enough."

Also consider what you need to back up and when. You may not need to back up the entire hard disk every time you do a backup.

Optical Storage Technology

A disk that is written to and read by light is an **optical disk**. Although optical disks can store 600 MB or more of data and software, they are removable, like ordinary diskettes. The increased capacities of these devices are encouraging software manufactures to incorporate many more features into their systems than they did previously. In addition, users of small computers have access to a substantial amount of data that they previously could not store. Although optical disk technology is now considerably slower than its magnetic counterpart, changes in technology will improve this problem.

Some optical disks, like compact disk read-only memory, or **CD-ROM**, can only be read from. As the name implies, CD-ROM is a read-only media. CD-ROM disks can be read by a laser in the CD-ROM drive (Figure 8-17), but they cannot be written to — at least not yet. The advantage of CD-ROM technology is the amount of data that can be stored on a single disk. One disk can hold as much as 650 MB of data.

CD-ROMs are used to store data that rarely, if ever, changes. For example, a CD-ROM that contains zip codes and road maps would not need to be updated as frequently as a file with payroll information. Entire encyclopedias are available on a single disk, as are complete sets of street maps for the major (and not-so-major) metropolitan areas of the United States. CD-ROM is also used to store multimedia presentations, which require vast amounts of memory. Despite the storage capacity of a CD-ROM disk, however, one disk can hold only about 10 minutes of full-motion video with sound.

Other optical disks can be written on a single time and then read many times. These are called write-once, read many, or **WORM**, disks. These disks are used to store archival information such as end-of-the-year financial data for a business. Once this data has been created, legally it cannot be changed, so WORM technology is a perfect storage medium for it.

Floptical disks (removable optical diskettes) are optical disks that can be written to and read over and over again. This gives users the ability to store and use millions and millions of bytes of data and software. The NeXT computer was one of the first computers to incorporate the optical disk.

Figure 8-17
A CD-ROM disk and drive.

Comprehension Questions

1. Is it seek time, rotational delay, or transfer time that makes cassette tapes slower than hard disks?
2. Is a diskette a sequential medium or a random-access medium?
3. Why can't a microcomputer back up to a CD-ROM disk?

Using What You Know

1. What data might headquarters provide to BVOS branches on CD-ROM?
2. If you had a 200 MB hard disk, can you think of any reason that you might want two 100 MB cassettes or even four 50 MB cassettes for backing up?
3. Since the time this book was published, what new storage media have emerged?

Summary Points

Storage Devices and Storage Media

☐ Storage devices are I/O peripherals used to write to and read from storage media.

Diskettes and Drives

☐ Diskettes, which are made of flexible mylar, come in two sizes: 3½ inches and 5¼ inches.

☐ The 3½-inch model is becoming more prevalent than the 5¼- inch model.

☐ A diskette drive consists of the drive bay, the drive, and the read-write head.

How Data Is Organized on a Diskette

☐ To be used, new diskettes must be formatted, a process that maps the surface into tracks and sectors.

☐ 5¼-inch diskettes store either 360 K or 1.2 MB, depending on whether they are double density or high density.

☐ 3½-inch diskettes initialized on a Mac can store either 800 K or 1.44 MB.

☐ 3½-inch diskettes formatted using DOS can store either 720 K or 1.44 MB.

Protecting Data: Just in Case

☐ Both sizes of a diskette can be write protected by covering the write-protect notch or sliding the write-protect tab.

Taking Care of Diskettes

☐ Diskettes must be protected from pressure, heat, and magnetic fields.

☐ Diskettes must not be removed from the drive while the drive light is on.

Purchasing Diskette Drives

☐ If you are buying a PC with one drive, you should probably get a 3½-inch drive; if you are getting two drives, get one of each size.

Hard Disks and Hard Disk Drives

☐ The hard disk allows the user to have access to a large, nonremovable storage device.

Hard Disks Compared to Diskettes

☐ A hard disk consists of a set of aluminum platters.

☐ In a hard disk drive, the read-write head never touches the media; if it does, the system experiences a disk crash.

Capacity

☐ Hard disks can store hundreds of times more data than a single diskette.

Access Time

☐ Though seek time and rotational delay are negligible factors, transfer time is much better with hard disks than with diskettes.

Portability

☐ Diskettes are portable; hard disks — especially internal ones — are much less so.

Formatting a Hard Disk

☐ To be used, a hard disk must be formatted — a process of dividing the disk into tracks and sectors.

Types of Hard Disks

☐ Two available hard disks are the IDE and the SCSI.

Organizing Files
☐ Operating systems list files on disks in directories.

Subdirectories and Folders
☐ Operating systems allow users to establish hierarchical file systems by creating subdirectories or folders.

Common Organizational Models
☐ The two most common ways to organize files are organizing by application and organizing by client or project.

Alternatives to Internal Hard Disks
☐ Other types of hard drives include external hard disks, hard cards, and hard disk cartridges.

Magnetic Tape
☐ Tape drives adapt cassette tape technology to the process of backing up hard disks.
☐ Tape drives cannot replace hard disks because they are a sequential medium, which is inherently slower than a random-access medium.

Other Forms of Tape
☐ Minis and mainframes use reel-to-reel tapes for backup and data transfer.

How Often Should I Back Up?
☐ Backing up is a time trade-off between the time it takes to perform the backup and the time it takes to replace lost work.

Optical Storage Technology
☐ CD-ROM uses the same optical technology as music CDs.
☐ A single CD-ROM disk can store up to 650 MB of data.

Knowing the Facts

True/False

1. A CD-ROM drive is a storage medium.
2. 5¼-inch diskettes are made of mylar, and 3½-inch diskettes are made of aluminum.
3. One reason that 3½-inch diskettes have become more popular than 5¼-inch diskettes is that the smaller diskettes can hold more data.
4. A single hard disk can have several platters.
5. Diskettes should not be removed from the drive unless the drive light is on.
6. The magnetic field around a magnetized paper clip is enough to damage a diskette.
7. The read-write head of a hard disk should never touch the disk surface.
8. *Subdirectory* and *folder* are synonymous terms.
9. Though hard disks have greater capacity, access times for diskettes are less.
10. Hard cards are removable hard disks that can be changed in much the same way as diskettes.

Short Answer

1. Finding data on _____ media is much more time consuming than on random-access media.
2. _____ tape is used for backup and data transfer on minis and mainframes.
3. Some optical media, such as _____ disks, can be read but not written to.
4. _____ allow the user to perform unattended backups of the hard disk onto a single storage unit.
5. On a hard card, the disk is mounted directly on the _____.
6. A hierarchical file structure can be created on a disk using the _____.
7. Though a fingerprint can obscure data on a diskette, it is thick enough to cause a _____ in a hard disk drive.
8. What size diskettes do Macintoshes use?
9. What does the drive light on a diskette drive tell you?
10. Only a _____ should be used to write on a 5½-inch diskette.

Answers

True/False

1. F
2. F
3. T
4. T
5. F
6. T
7. T
8. T
9. F
10. F

Short Answer

1. sequential
2. Reel-to-reel
3. CD-ROM
4. Tape drives
5. controller card or expansion board
6. operating system
7. disk crash
8. 3½-inch diskettes
9. "The diskette is spinning" or "Don't remove the diskette."
10. felt-tip pen

Challenging Your Understanding

1. As technology improves, we will be able to store more and more data on our storage devices. What is the down side of this phenomenon?

2. Look in a computer magazine and determine the cost per megabyte for five hard disks. What are the characteristics that seem to affect the price of a hard disk? What is the best deal you can find?

3. Discuss ways in which the way you use your computer affects how often you should back up your data.

4. Backing up an entire hard disk can take a long time — sometimes hours, if the hard disk is large and you are backing up to diskettes. Under what circumstances might you back up only part of your data? Would these circumstances occur often? See if you can describe a strategy for minimizing the amount of data that you have to back up.

5. Why is CD-ROM becoming such a popular medium? What are the limitations of CD-ROM, and how do these limitations affect the uses for the medium?

Communication Devices

Key Terms

acoustic coupler

baud

bits per second (bps)

bulletin board service (BBS)

bus network

client/server computing
(cooperative processing)

communication error

data bits

diskless workstation

enterprise wide network

fax modem

file server (network server)

full duplex

half duplex

handshake

Hayes-compatible

hierarchical network

host computer

information service

local area network (LAN)

metropolitan area network (MAN)

modem

network interface card (NIC)

node

parity bit

printer server

protocol

ring network

star network

stop bit

terminal

wide area network (WAN)

Objectives

In this chapter you will learn to:

- Identify the four necessary elements of communication and explain the importance of protocol
- Describe how a modem works
- Identify the two types of modem and the speeds at which they can operate
- Describe the settings that must be agreed upon before users communicate via modem
- Explain how a fax is used
- List the advantages and disadvantages of using a fax modem, as opposed to a stand alone fax
- Explain the advantages of networks and the differences among a LAN, a MAN, and a WAN
- Describe the advantages of having a file server and a printer server
- Name and describe four network configurations
- Identify the hardware and software required by computers in a network

Communicating at BVOS

The lifeblood of any healthy enterprise is communication. BVOS is no different. In planning your branch, there is much to consider. Your first priority will be to establish fast, orderly communication systems within your new branch. Only then can you serve your customers with maximum efficiency. You must then establish a link with the main BVOS office in Toronto. A large part of the main office activities concern getting sales data from all of the branches on a daily basis. By getting up-to-the-minute information, the main office personnel can manage inventory levels carefully so that cash is not tied up in overstocked merchandise and customers are not sent away because of underestimated demand.

As you can see, planning your communication systems properly is essential. This chapter will provide important information that will help you make the most of your own personal and professional needs.

What Happens When Communication Occurs?

Before we begin discussing the technology involved with communication systems, it is important that you have a clear understanding of the communication process. A communication system requires four elements: the message, the sender, the receiver, and the channel (Figure 9-1). The message is the picture, words, or data that a sender is trying to deliver to the receiver. The sender is the originator of the message, and the receiver is the intended recipient. The channel consists of the assorted communication devices over which the message is transmitted.

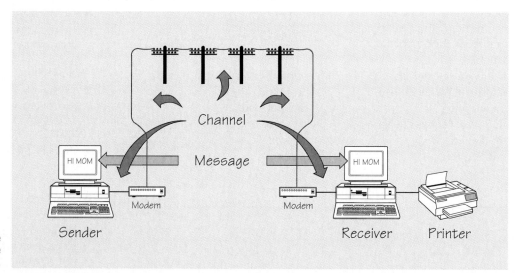

Figure 9-1
The sender transmits the message through the channel to the receiver.

Standards: The Backbone of Computer Communication

One vital ingredient that lets these four elements work together is a set of procedural standards for communication, known as a **protocol**. When people use vocal communication, both the sender and receiver need to use the same language. Likewise, when a sender and a receiver communicate with computers, the receiving computer needs to know in what format the data is being sent.

The Importance of Standards. One of the reasons that protocol is so important in data communication is that it enables errors to be caught and fixed. A **communication error** occurs when the data that was received is not identical to the data that was sent. Just as voice communication is difficult in a noisy room, data communication is error-prone when the channel is experiencing noise. We have all had a telephone conversation interrupted by a click or hum or squeal, or even by the voice of some other person on the same line. These problems in telephone lines can be caused by a device failure, by someone starting a car, by a sun spot, by a water cooler turning on, or by any number of other causes. If a media problem occurs when we are speaking on the phone, the error is usually reported immediately with a simple "Excuse me?" or "Could you repeat that?" If the problem occurs when transmitting data over phone lines, the receiving computer must catch the error. Whatever channel is being used, with proper protocol, the receiving computer should realize that it has received an error and ask the sending computer to repeat the signal.

The Speed of Transmission

When media problems occur in data communication, the errors caused can be huge. The size of a communication error is dependent upon both the amount of time the media problem occurs and the rate at which the data is being transmitted. The speed of transmission is measured either in **baud** or **bits per second (bps)**, two terms that are often used inter-changeably though they are technically different. Baud is the number of changes in the electrical state of the line in one second. Modern transmission techniques pack multiple bits into every change of state, so bps can now be a lot higher than baud.

To get an idea of how big errors can be, let's say we are transmitting data at 19,200 bits per second (bps). When talking on the telephone, if you hear a "tick" on the line that is caused by an error in the phone system, you are hearing something that has a duration of approximately 1/100th of a second. During that 1/100th of a second, 192 bits, or 28 bytes, are being destroyed by the error. *That's this sentence's size!*

Communication Via Modem

When two computer users who are not in close proximity want to communicate or share data, they often do so using phone lines with the help of a modem. A **modem** is a hardware device that, in conjunction with communication software, allows a computer to send or receive data through a telephone system.

How the Modem Works

The word *modem* is actually an acronym for MOdulator/DEModulator. The telephone system was designed to transmit analog voice signals, because that's the way we talk. Computers, however, use digital signals to communicate. To enable computers to use these lines, a device was needed to change a digital signal into an analog signal. That's a modulator. At the receiving end, the data must be changed from analog back to digital — the job of the demodulator. The modem can do both of these functions, but there must be a modem attached to both the sending and receiving computers. Figure 9-2 (on the next page) summarizes how modems are used to transmit data over phone lines.

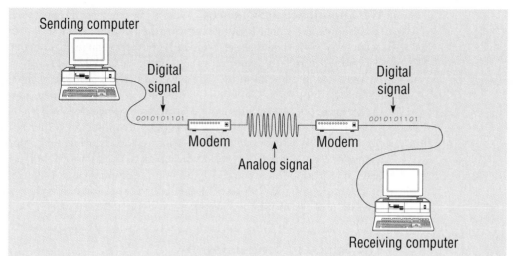

Figure 9-2
The sender's modem modulates the data into an audible (analog) signal. The receiver's modem demodulates the audible signal back into a digital signal that the computer can understand.

Types of Modems

A modem can be internal or external — inside or outside the system unit. An internal modem is mounted on an expansion card that is attached to the motherboard (Figure 9-3a). At one end of the card is a phone jack, into which a standard phone cable can be plugged. An external modem is attached to the motherboard via a serial port (Figure 9-3b). In general, internal modems are less expensive than external modems because the latter require their own power supply, whereas internal modems run off the power supply inside the system unit. External modems are popular with users who don't have available expansion slots in their computers. External modems are also more easily shared among a group of users who need only occasional access to a modem.

Most modems are attached directly to the telephone system using common modular jacks; some use **acoustic couplers** to transmit over the standard telephone handset. The telephone handset is placed into the coupler, which is attached to a serial port on the computer. Modems with acoustic couplers transmit at slower speeds than those that are directly connected. However, they are useful for portable computers that may have to go where there is no modular jack.

Modems can transmit at a variety of speeds. Older models operate at 300, 1200, or 2400 bits per second. Newer models work at 4800, 9600, 14,400, or 19200 bps. As telephone companies install more advanced equipment, even greater speeds may become practical. Most users purchase modems that will operate at at least 2400 bps, and many are now buying much faster models. Your need for speed depends on how you will be using your modem. If you are going to use it only once in a while, or if you are transferring files of moderate size, buying a high-speed modem is probably a waste of money. Speed becomes more valuable if you are transferring graphics or if you will be using the modem every day. As with many types of hardware, if you are not looking for the latest technology, finding used equipment can be extremely cost efficient.

Using a Modem

Modems are programmable, controllable devices that must be used with a piece of communication software. Many modems for microcomputers are **Hayes-compatible**. Hayes is a long-time manufacturer of modems and has designed a language that controls its modems.

(a)

(b)

Figure 9-3
(a) An internal modem;
(b) an external modem.

The Hayes command set has been adopted by other modem manufacturers. No matter what type of modem you buy, make sure it is Hayes-compatible.

To use a modem, you must first load your modem or communication software. Next, you need to make sure that your modem is set up in the same way as the modem that you want to communicate with. There are several settings that you need to check. Figure 9-4 shows the Settings menu for ProComm Plus, a popular communication package.

The Transmission Rate. Both sending and receiving modems need to transmit at the same speed. Often this is not an issue, because most modem software can automatically detect the transmission rate of incoming signals. However, you may need to set your modem to send at a slower speed than it is capable of if the receiver's modem has a maximum baud rate that is less than yours. Most modems are downward-compatible, so you usually don't need to worry about not being able to communicate just because the other user's modem can operate faster or slower. For instance, a 9600-bps modem can send or receive at 2400-bps if that is the maximum the other modem can use.

Figure 9-4
This menu controls several important communication settings. The sender and receiver's settings must be the same before proper communication can occur.

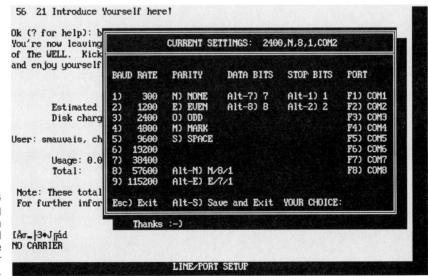

Transmission Modes.   Modems transmit in two modes. **Half duplex** mode refers to the transmission of data in both directions, but only one direction at once. **Full duplex** refers to the ability to send and receive simultaneously.

Data Bits.   The number of **data bits** tells the software how many bits of data to send in each set. Normally, microcomputers send either seven or eight bits of data in a string.

Stop Bits.   At the end of each string of data, the modem sends either one or two stop bits. The **stop bit** simply signals the receiving computer that the sequence of bits has ended.

The Parity Bit.   The **parity bit** provides a way for the receiving computer to know if there were any errors in communication. If the parity bit is used, it is set to either **even parity** or **odd parity**. With even parity, the sending computer manipulates the parity bit so that each string of data has an even number of ls. For example, the sequence of bits, 10001100, has an odd number of 1s. The sending computer would set the parity bit to 1 to bring the total number of 1s up to four, an even number. If a computer receives a string of data for which the parity bit is not correct, it asks the sending computer to repeat the string.

Making the Call.   Once you have made sure that the settings are the same for both modems, you are ready to connect. To do so, you simply instruct your modem software to dial the phone number of the receiving computer. When the other modem answers, each of the two modems sends a small set of data called a **handshake**. The handshake formally establishes the link by testing the settings and ensuring a valid connection.

What happens next depends on the computer you have called. Often, the modem software of the receiving computer prompts you for identification. Then you may be presented with a menu of choices. Menu interfaces are common with modem software. The most common actions performed with modem software are sending and receiving files. To send a file to another user, computer system, information service, or bulletin board, you generally choose "Upload" from a menu. To obtain (receive) a file, you choose "Download." After telling the other computer that you want to upload or download a file, you use your own modem software to initiate the transfer. The transfer itself must adhere to a particular protocol. Common data transfer protocols for microcomputers include Xmodem, Ymodem, Kermit, and many others. Most modem software is capable of adhering to several different protocols.

Using a Bulletin Board Service

Through their modems, users can connect and communicate with bulletin board services (BBSs) and information services such as Prodigy and CompuServe. A **bulletin board service**, or **BBS,** is a forum in which users can trade information on a certain subject. The BBS is run from a central computer, which users call and connect to. To access a BBS, you simply adjust your communication software to the correct line settings and call the service's phone number. Once the connection is made and the user is on-line, he or she can read messages sent by others or leave new messages. Some services have a flat subscription rate that you pay each month; others bill by the amount of time you stay on-line.

Some BBS's allow you to read and participate in on-line conferences on a myriad of subjects. Other bulletin boards focus on specific subjects, ranging from Star Trek to electrical engineering.

Using an Information Service

Information services are on-line companies that allow you to do many things, from shopping and banking to booking an airline reservation or searching for certain types of news. Information services often include their own bulletin boards and conferencing capabilities. Electronic mail (E-mail) is available with many information services. Connecting to an information service and paying for your connect time is much like connecting to a bulletin board. Because the range of services offered is usually much broader, information services generally cost more than bulletin board services.

Table 9-1 lists a few of the well-known BBSs and information services, the type of service they offer, and their connection settings. The column labeled PDS tells you the type of parity (E = even, O = odd, N = none), the number of data bits, and how many stop bits they use. For example, "N81" indicates that you should set your modem for no parity bit, eight data bits, and one stop bit.

PROCOMM PLUS (tm) Dialing Directory

NAME		NUMBER	BAUD	PDS	D	P	SCRIPT	PROTOCOL	TERMINAL	MODEM
1- DEANS OFFICE	NJ	201-279-7048	2400	N81	F	0			ANSI	MODEM
2- PC CONNECTIONS	DC	202-547-2008	2400	N81	F	0			ANSI	MODEM
3- BRUCE'S BAR &GRILL	CT	203-236-3761	2400	N81	F	0			ANSI	MODEM
4- HH-INFONET	CT	203-246-3747	2400	N81	F	0			ANSI	MODEM
5- ROCKY ROAD	CT	203-791-8838	2400	N81	F	0			ANSI	MODEM
6- GOLDEN SPRINGS BBS	AL	205-238-0012	2400	N81	F	0			ANSI	MODEM
7- PRO-TECH BBS	AL	205-452-3897	2400	N81	F	0			ANSI	MODEM
8- CYCLONE BBS	AL	205-974-5123	2400	N81	F	0			ANSI	MODEM
9- ARCHMAGE BBS	WA	206-493-0401	2400	N81	F	0			ANSI	MODEM
10- 28 BARBARY LANE	WA	206-525-2828	2400	N81	F	0			ANSI	MODEM
11- BARBEQUED RIBBS	WA	206-676-5787	2400	N81	F	0			ANSI	MODEM
12- NORTHERN LIGHTS	ME	207-766-5808	2400	N81	F	0			ANSI	MODEM
13- COASTAL DOS USER	ME	207-797-4975	2400	N81	F	0			ANSI	MODEM
14- GREATER BOISE BBS	ID	208-332-5227	2400	N81	F	0			ANSI	MODEM
15- INVENTION FACTORY	NY	212-431-1194	2400	N81	F	0			ANSI	MODEM
16- FRIENDS TOO	NY	212-489-0516	2400	N81	F	0			ANSI	MODEM
17- DATACOM	NY	212-496-7946	2400	N81	F	0			ANSI	MODEM
18- MAC HACers	NY	213-546-9640	2400	N81	F	0			ANSI	MODEM
19- NEWTOWN SQUARE	PA	215-356-8623	2400	N81	F	0			ANSI	MODEM
20- NEXUS BBS=	PA	215-364-5662	2400	N81	F	0			ANSI	MODEM
21- THE HARBOR	PA	215-372-2788	2400	N81	F	0			ANSI	MODEM
22- PHILLY GAMERS=	PA	215-544-3757	2400	N81	F	0			ANSI	MODEM
23- KUTZTOWN CONN=	PA	215-683-9038	2400	N81	F	0			ANSI	MODEM
24- TMC BBS	PA	215-694-1534	2400	N81	F	0			ANSI	MODEM
25- THE CORE	PA	215-XXX-8113	2400	N81	F	0			ANSI	MODEM
26- PC-OHIO	OH	216-381-3320	2400	N81	F	0			ANSI	MODEM
27- AMCOM	OH	216-526-9840	2400	N81	F	0			ANSI	MODEM
28- RUSTY & EDIE'S	OH	216-726-0737	2400	N81	F	0			ANSI	MODEM
29- ASK FRED'S BBS	OH	216-783-9632	2400	N81	F	0			ANSI	MODEM
30- RIVER CITY NETWORK	IN	219-237-0651	2400	N81	F	0			ANSI	MODEM

Copyright (C) 1987,91 Datastorm Technologies, Inc.

Table 9-1
Some popular information services and BBSs.

Fax Modems

The facsimile machine, or fax, has become an indispensable part of modern business. A modern stand alone fax machine (sometimes called a Group III fax) is like a scanner and a printer attached to a modem. To use a fax machine (Figure 9-5 on the next page):

1. The sender types in the telephone number of the receiving fax.

2. The sender feeds the printed pages that need to be sent into the fax machine.

3. The sender's fax scans the document, and the modem in the sender's fax modulates the dark and light spots on the paper into audible signals.

4. The receiver's fax machine demodulates the data and recreates the image.

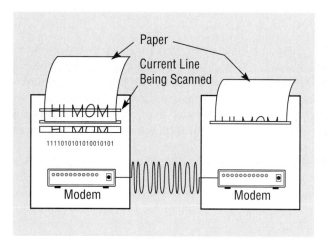

Figure 9-5   The process of faxing a document includes scanning an image line by line and then sending the results of the scan via modem.

Figure 9-6   A stand alone fax machine.

The scanning, transmission, and printing stages happen in such rapid succession that the receiver's fax machine prints the document at almost the same time it is scanned. Fax technology has come a long way in the past 20 years. It continues to advance with better resolution output and faster transmission. A modern stand alone fax machine is shown in Figure 9-6.

A **fax modem**, also called a fax board, is a computer peripheral that accomplishes the same goal as the stand alone fax. Rather than sending printed documents, however, you are able to send data files. Like a modem, the fax modem must be controlled by fax software that is loaded into RAM.

To send a fax using a fax modem, you generally begin by opening a document using a standard application program, such as a spreadsheet or a word processor. You then "print" the document to the fax rather than the printer (Figure 9-7). The fax software creates a bitmap of the document and sends the data to the fax modem line by line. The receiving fax interprets

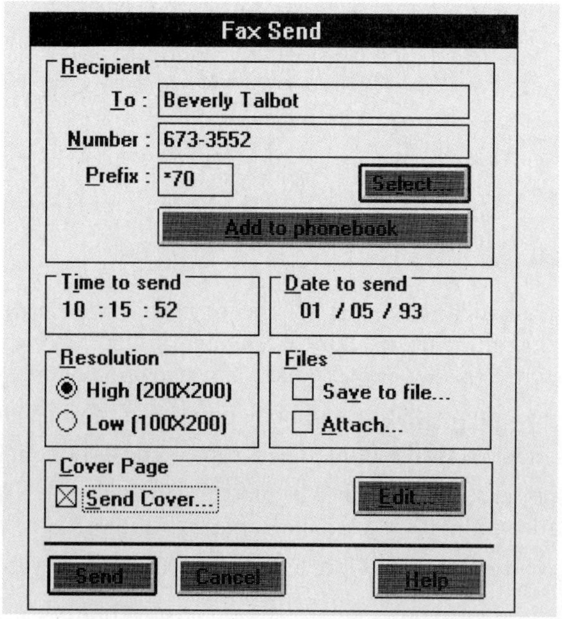

Figure 9-7
This dialog box appears when you "print" to a fax modem using WINFAX, a fax program for Windows.

Fax Send

Recipient
To : Beverly Talbot
Number : 673-3552
Prefix : *70   Select...

Add to phonebook

Time to send   Date to send
10 : 15 : 52   01 / 05 / 93

Resolution   Files
◉ High (200X200)   ☐ Save to file...
○ Low (100X200)   ☐ Attach...

Cover Page
☒ Send Cover...   Edit...

Send   Cancel   Help

the data the same way it would a fax from a stand alone machine. If the fax modem is receiving a fax, it accepts the data and creates a bitmap of the page. The user can then view the file on screen or print it with whatever printer is attached to the system. Like modems, fax modems can be either internal or external.

There are both advantages and disadvantages to fax modems compared to stand alone fax machines. The biggest advantage of the fax modem is the price. Fax modems start at less than $100. In addition, the resolution of a fax that is created directly from an electronic file is generally better than one that is scanned from a piece of paper. Finally, you can save time and paper by not having to print out a document before faxing it.

The advantage of a stand alone fax is primarily that most print faster than fax modems, although fax modems are catching up. Printing a bit-mapped image through your computer can be very slow. Some of the more expensive fax software programs include OCR capabilities, so you can recreate a text document before you print. The text document you create will print much faster than the bitmap. The stand alone fax, however, prints as it receives the data. In addition, you will sometimes need to send a document that exists only on paper. A fax modem must be accompanied by a scanner to send hard copy.

Comprehension Questions

1. If you are transmitting data at 2400 bps and your communication is interrupted for .05 seconds, how much data needs to be retransmitted?

2. What information must be included in the pamphlet that CompuServe (a popular information service) gives to users who want to become subscribers of the service?

3. What style of chassis is least likely to accommodate an internal modem?

Using What You Know

1. Compare prices for a 2400-bps and a 9600-bps modem. What is the difference in price for otherwise comparable capabilities?

2. In addition to taking orders over the telephone, BVOS will take orders by fax. Does it make more sense to have a stand alone fax or a fax modem? Why?

3. Under what circumstances would it be helpful to have both a fax modem and a stand alone fax?

Networks: Communicating Without Phone Lines

Modems are used for communicating via telephone lines, but a different technology is used for communication at closer distances. A **local area network** (**LAN**) is used to connect computers that are located within the same room, building, or complex. Each of the computers attached to a LAN is called a **node**. With a LAN, a company can buy a single expensive printer or a scanner that everyone can share without having to purchase individual peripherals for every machine. Another advantage of LANs is that they can be used to help people work together. Networks allow users to schedule meetings more efficiently, share documents more rapidly, and simply communicate, either one to many or many to one, instantaneously.

Hardware Connections: What Networks Are Made Of

The reason that computers within a LAN can communicate so much more quickly is that they are directly connected to each other. The most common way to connect computers in a LAN is with special wires or cables. A variety of types of wire or cable are used, including twisted-pair wires (such as standard telephone wire), coaxial cables (such as those used by cable television companies), and fiber-optic cables. These three types of cables are shown in Figure 9-8.

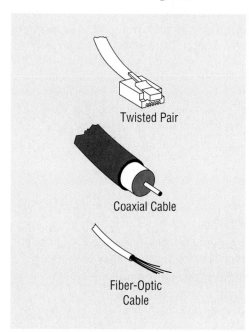

Twisted Pair

Coaxial Cable

Fiber-Optic
Cable

Figure 9-8
The three most common types of cables used in LANs.

Various types of media have different characteristics that affect their capacity for data. Twisted pair wires are the cheapest medium, but standard telephone wire can carry only two signals simultaneously — one signal in each direction. Coaxial cables, on the other hand, can carry almost 100 signals at once, and fiber-optic cables can carry thousands.

In addition to "hardwired" LANs that use wires or cables, there is a trend toward wireless LANs that transmit data using electromagnetic waves, including visible light, infrared, and microwaves. The advantage of such media is simply that no wires are needed, so a major cost of setting up or modifying a LAN can be eliminated. The disadvantage is that, so far, transmission speeds are not as high as with hardwired systems.

As they eliminate the need for hardwired networks, communication by electromagnetic waves is also expanding the LAN to the point that it can no longer be described as local. In the past, LANs usually operated within a single office building. Networks that spanned greater distances required telephone lines and were called **wide area networks**, or **WANs**. WANs are capable of spanning the globe, because they use communication satellites to transmit across large distances (Figure 9-9).

Figure 9-9
Using satelite communications, users attached to LANs, or merely using modems, can communicate around the world.

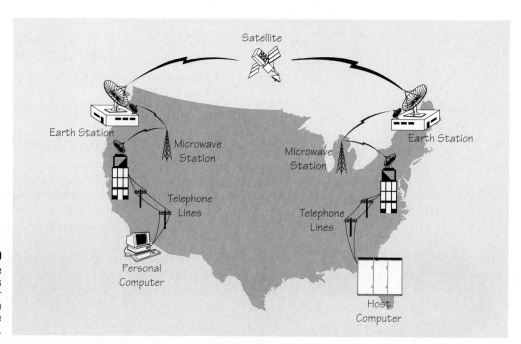

Satellite

Earth Station

Microwave
Station

Microwave
Station

Earth Station

Telephone
Lines

Telephone
Lines

Personal
Computer

Host
Computer

Similar technology, when combined with electromagnetic waves such as microwaves, can transmit signals across town. For example, a company with two buildings one mile apart can use antennas or dishes, similar to the dishes used to receive cable television signals. With a dish on top of each building pointed at the other building (Figure 9-10), the company can expand its LAN into an **enterprise wide network** (also called a **metropolitan area network**, or **MAN**).

File Servers: The Network's Electronic File Cabinet

A **file server**, also called a **network server**, is a fast computer with a large amount of secondary storage, to which all of the other computers in a network have access for data storage and retrieval. A typical file server is shown in Figure 9-11. The file server stores programs and data files shared by the users on the network. File servers can substantially reduce the cost of personal computers on a network, because each computer need not have its own large hard drive. In addition, use of a file server facilitates sharing data, because the data is stored centrally. A single change to a file stored on a file server allows everyone on the LAN to use the most current version of the data. Finally, file servers also provide a single point of backup of user data. Because most of the data will be stored on a file server, a single backup procedure will protect the data resources of all LAN users.

Nodes connected to a file server can be diskless workstations. A **diskless workstation** has its own processing components and generally a keyboard (possibly a mouse or some other input device as well) and a monitor, but it lacks any storage device of its own. When this type of computer is turned on, it looks to the file server for the operating system. All of the applications and data files used by a diskless workstation are also held on the file server.

Increasingly, file servers are replacing mainframes. They perform many of the same functions and are less expensive to purchase and maintain. However, a file server can cause legal problems if it is abused. It is tempting to buy a single copy of a program, place it on a file server, and allow all of the LAN users to share the single copy. This practice is illegal. Most software is licensed to run on a single processor, so only one copy of the program can be running at a time. To address the problem, many software companies sell LAN packages that allow users to buy the right for a fixed number of users to use a single copy of the software. Site licenses are also gaining popularity for similar reasons. A site license authorizes the copying, distributing, and use of software within a single designated facility or jurisdiction.

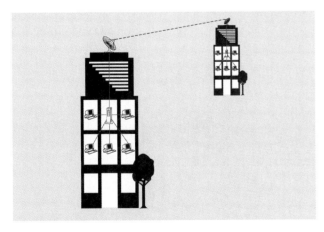

Figure 9-10 Wireless communications have led to the development of the enterprise wide network, in which employees in different buildings can communicate as if their computers were hardwired together.

Figure 9-11 A network file server

Client/Server Computing

Client/server computing, also known as **cooperative processing**, involves using two or more networked computers to perform an application task. For example, one computer might contain a database, while another computer might have the user interface that allows users to manipulate the database. By segregating the activities of these computers, each can be optimized for that particular activity. The database computer (the server) can have a large, fast hard disk, while the user computer (the client) has a high-resolution color graphics monitor and a mouse. This approach to networking allows the strengths of each system to complement the other. As computers become more and more powerful and are interconnected with other kinds of computers, client/server computing may become the standard application architecture.

Printer Servers

Another common type of server is the **printer server**. A printer server (or network printer) allows multiple users to take advantage of a single printing device. High-speed printers, printers with large amounts of RAM, printers with special fonts or paper stock, and color printers are often used as printer servers. This is a cost-effective way to provide the maximum flexibility of printer support while purchasing just a few expensive devices.

The greatest disadvantage of printer servers is that, because of their frequent use, they often require more maintenance than their desktop counterparts. Also, accessing the printer can be a challenge. If users on three floors of a building are sharing a laser printer, the users whose offices are not on the same floor as the printer must leave their desks to retrieve their output. Also, sensitive documents can be compromised when printed on a network printer, because of the easy access afforded to users of the printer.

Network Configurations

Local area networks can be set up in a number of configurations. The most popular are the bus, star, hierarchical, and ring networks.

Bus Networks.   The oldest form of LAN is the **bus network**. The microcomputers in a bus network are connected to a common wire, called the **bus**, through which each computer can transmit and receive data. This arrangement is especially common in relatively small networks. It is a simple, noncentralized way to share peripherals and data in an office. A diagram of the bus network is shown in Figure 9-12.

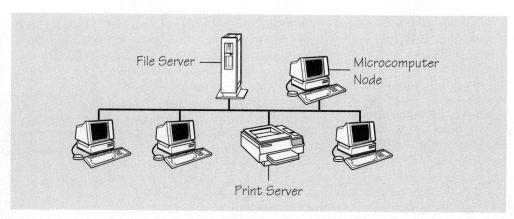

Figure 9-12
A bus network

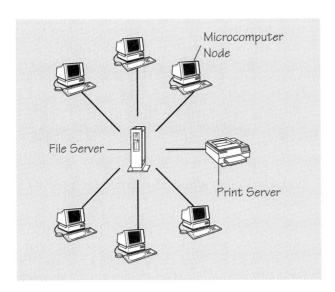

Figure 9-13
A star network.

Star Networks. In a **star network**, each node is connected directly to a central device called a *hub*. As shown in Figure 9-13, all network traffic is routed through the hub to each network node. The hub can be a simple routing device or a centralized host computer.

With a centralized network organized around a host computer, it is also common for the nodes to be terminals, rather than computers. A **terminal** is simply an input and output device that relies entirely on the host computer for processing. Terminals are especially common on mainframe systems.

If the central computer is a mini, mainframe, or even a powerful microcomputer that is heavily relied on for processing, it is referred to as the **host computer**. If the central computer is used primarily as a storage device, it is a file server.

The star network is especially well suited for a small company with a relatively large database to which many employees need access. In this case, the file server is sometimes called the *database server*. Each of the computers in the network can run the database software, and yet all can share the central database.

It is not necessarily true that all of the peripherals in a star network are connected to the host computer or file server. Often, less expensive peripherals, such as dot matrix printers and modems, are connected directly to the node computer.

Hierarchical Networks. Larger computer networks sometimes use another centralized arrangement, called a **hierarchical network** (Figure 9-14). This arrangement is similar to the star network, except that there are more than two levels in the system. In other words, the host computer has several smaller computers linked to it, and these are hosts to yet smaller computers or terminals. These mid-level computers could be specialized computers that help control the terminals, or general purpose minicomputers. For example, a large company's mainframe might be linked to several minicomputers, and these might be connected to micros, diskless workstations, and terminals.

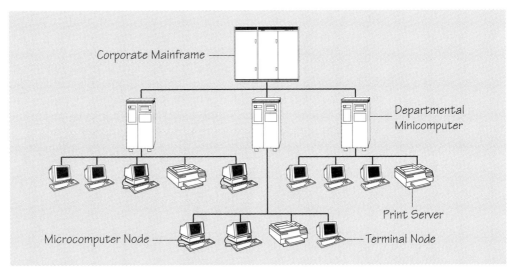

Figure 9-14
A hierarchical network.

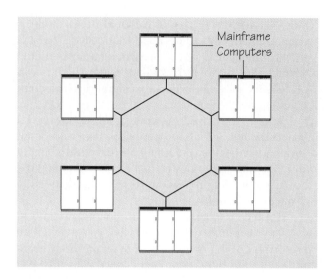

Mainframe
Computers

Figure 9-15

A ring network. Each of the mainframes in this ring could be the host computer of a smaller, centralized LAN.

Ring Networks. The fourth arrangement for a network, shown in Figure 9-15, is a decentralized system called a **ring network**. As the name implies, each of the computers in a ring network is connected to two others, so that data can be passed all the way around in a circle. In a ring network, a message sent by one computer must travel around the ring until it reaches the correct destination.

Network Software and Interface Boards

As with communication over the phone lines, communication in a network requires an expansion board within each computer, plus software to control the communication. The expansion board is called a **network interface card**, or **NIC**. The NIC performs the tasks of sending and receiving data through whatever wires or cables are used in the network. The NIC generally has a port at one end for attaching the wire or cable.

The NIC is controlled by the computer's CPU with the help of network software. In general, network software adheres to one of the major network protocols, such as Ethernet, Token Ring, or LocalTalk. These protocols are also referred to as *access methods*. The most widely used pieces of network software are made by Novell. Macs, however, come with AppleTalk, which adheres to LocalTalk access methods, though it can be adapted to Ethernet or Token Ring systems.

Wireless Computers

Wireless computers are not new. Police vehicles have long had computers that allow police officers instantaneous access to information about people and vehicles. These systems are attached to a radio that sends and receives data through the airways. Now this type of technology is moving into the office in the form of wireless LANs.

Local area networks do not always require a wire to connect nodes on the network. New telecommunications technologies allow users to connect to a LAN without installing wire. These computers exchange information using either infrared or radio frequencies. Infrared LANs are located in a room where an infrared receiver can be "seen" from each computer. This line-of-sight access, however, is not required for radio connectivity. For radio LANs, each node in a network contains a small transmitter that is tuned to frequencies received by the host computer. Data is broadcast from both the host and each node. Special rules are needed to make sure that two or more computers don't try to transmit at the same time. For both infrared and radio LANs, the speed of data transmission is almost equivalent to that of wired LANs, although the error rate may be a bit higher.

Comprehension Questions

1. Which is likely to need greater processing speed, a host computer or a file server?
2. Does the use of telephone cable mean that you are using a WAN?
3. What aspect of a MAN makes it similar to a WAN?

Using What You Know

1. Which network configuration is most appropriate for connecting the computers at BVOS?
2. Which computers at BVOS could be diskless workstations? How would this arrangement work?
3. If BVOS were to use a star network, how might this configuration be linked to headquarters to form a hierarchical network?

Summary Points

Communicating at BVOS

☐ Your branch of BVOS requires both internal communication and communication with the central office in Toronto.

What Happens When Communication Occurs?

☐ Communication requires a sender, a receiver, a message, and a medium.

Standards: The Backbone of Computer Communications

☐ A set of standards for communication is called a protocol.

The Importance of Standards

☐ A communication error occurs when the data received is not the same as the data sent.

The Speed of Transmission

☐ Communication speed is measured in baud or bits per second.
☐ The size of a communication error is determined by the duration of the problem and the speed of transmission.

Communication Via Modem

☐ A modem allows computers to communicate through the phone lines.

How the Modem Works

☐ A modem modulates digital signals and demodulates analog signals.

Types of Modems

☐ Modems can be internal or external.
☐ Modems operate at 300, 1200, 2400, 4800, 9600, or 14,400 bps.

Using a Modem

☐ Modems can connect directly to a telephone wire or use an acoustic coupler.
☐ Modems should be Hayes-compatible.

The Transmission Rate

☐ After the modem software is loaded, the bps rate must be set to agree with the bps rate of the other computer.

Transmission Modes

☐ In half duplex communication, data goes in only one direction at a time; in full duplex, data travels back and forth simultaneously.

Data Bits

☐ The number of data bits tells the software how many bits to send in each set.

Stop Bits

☐ The stop bit informs the receiving computer of the end of each set of data bits.

The Parity Bit

☐ The parity bit provides a check for communication errors.

Making the Call

☐ When the modem reaches another modem, they establish communication with an audible handshake.
☐ Uploading is sending a file to another computer; downloading is retrieving a file from another computer.

Using a Bulletin Board Service

☐ Bulletin board services are electronic forums in which users can share information.

Using an Information Service

☐ Information services are similar to BBSs, except that they tend to include a broader range of services, such as news, electronic shopping, and E-mail.

Fax Modems

☐ A fax allows one person to send a scanned image to another.
☐ A fax modem works like a stand alone fax but transmits files rather than hard copy to another fax.
☐ Fax modems cost less than stand alone faxes and have better resolution.
☐ A stand alone fax prints faster and accepts printed pages.

Networks: Communicating Without Phone Lines

☐ LANs allow users in an office to collaborate closely.

Hardware Connections: What Networks Are Made Of

☐ LANs are usually linked with twisted-pair wires, coaxial cables, or fiber optic cables.
☐ Some LANs use electromagnetic waves to communicate, and therefore do not require wires.
☐ Networks that include telecommunication are called WANs.
☐ Networks that transmit data across town using electromagnetic signals are called MANs.

File Servers: The Network's Electronic File Cabinet

☐ File servers offer an economical way for a group of computers to have access to a large storage device.
☐ Use of a file server can pose a legal problem if users do not purchase network versions or site licenses for software.

Client/Server Computing

☐ The client/server design allows the various parts of a network to cooperate in accomplishing tasks by taking advantage of the strengths of each part.

Printer Servers

☐ A printer server offers an economical way for a group of computers to share an expensive printing device.

Network Configurations

Bus Networks

☐ Computers in a bus network are all attached to a common wire, called the *bus*.

Star Networks

☐ Star networks are a centralized configuration with a host computer or file server.
☐ Diskless workstations in a star network can operate without storage devices.
☐ Terminals are nodes that rely entirely on the host computer for their processing needs.

Hierarchical Networks

☐ Hierarchical networks have more than one level of host computer.

Ring Networks

☐ A ring network requires that messages travel around the ring to the desired destination.

Network Software and Interface Boards

☐ A microcomputer attached to a network requires a network interface card.
☐ The NIC is operated by network software, which usually adheres to one of the common protocols.

Wireless Computers

☐ Networks can now transfer data through infrared waves or radio frequencies and thereby avoid the problems of installing wires around an office.

Knowing the Facts

True/False

1. A modem is capable of converting analog signals to digital, and vice versa.
2. A modem can be part of a network.
3. Modems are internal devices; fax modems are external.
4. Both a modem and a fax modem require software.
5. A file server is an economical way to share a large storage device.
6. For one computer to fax a message to another, each would need a fax modem.
7. When used by computers, telephone signals are digital.
8. A bus network is the most complicated network design.
9. Each node of a network requires processing devices.
10. The ring network is the most common configuration for microcomputers.

Short Answer

1. What does LAN stand for?
2. A set of standard rules for communication is called a _____.
3. Communication requires four elements: a sender, a receiver, a message, and a _____.
4. The most efficient centralized network for a small company is the _____ configuration.
5. A monitor and keyboard linked to a host computer is called a _____.
6. In hardwired networks, _____ cables can carry more data than either coaxial cables or twisted-pair wires.
7. What does NIC stand for?
8. To convert a faxed image into text, a computer must have _____ software.
9. To _____ is to send a file to a remote computer; to _____ is to receive a file from a remote computer.
10. The _____ bit provides a way for a receiving computer to know if there was a communication error.

Answers

True/False

1. T
2. T
3. F
4. T
5. T
6. T
7. F
8. F
9. F
10. F

Short Answer

1. local area network
2. protocol
3. channel
4. star
5. terminal
6. fiber optic
7. network interface card
8. OCR
9. upload; download
10. parity

Challenging Your Understanding

1. Why aren't modems used to communicate on a local area network?

2. A network interface card can cost about $400, a network operating system can cost $3,000, a file server can cost $5,000, wiring for 20 computers can cost $2,000, and a printer server and printer can easily cost $1,000. How do you think business managers justify the expense of creating a local area network?

3. If data is transmitted at 2400 bps and the data travels at the speed of light (186,000 miles per second), how long is a single byte, in miles?

4. A popular saying in the computer business is "The most secure computer is the one that does the least I/O." In a telecommunications network, security is often a problem. How can you make a network as secure as possible?

5. Is a cable television network similar to a local area network, a wide area network, or a metropolitan area network? Why?

Operating Systems

Key Terms

access privileges
BIOS
compatible
cooperative multitasking
device
DOS
Finder
middleware
multitasking
multithreading
operating system (OS)
OS/2
portable
preemptive multitasking
System file
Unix
Windows
Windows NT
workstation

Objectives

In this chapter you will learn to:

- Name and describe the three primary responsibilities of an operating system
- Explain the purpose of BIOS
- Describe how file fragmentation occurs
- Define multitasking
- Describe the two main capabilities of a multiuser OS
- Explain the difference between compatibility and portability
- Describe the advantages and disadvantages of using DOS, the Macintosh operating system, Windows NT, Unix, and OS/2 2.0

Operating Systems at BVOS

Turning back to the scenario we have followed throughout this book, this chapter completes the process of purchasing hardware and software for Buena Vista Office Supply. If you have been completing the exercises, you will have made critical purchasing decisions related to all major aspects of the computer system by the time you finish this chapter.

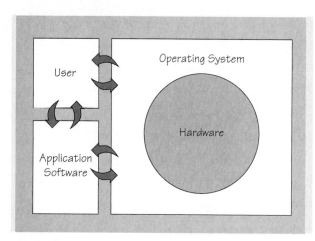

Figure 10-1

The operating system provides an interface between the hardware, which is the core of the computer, and both the user and the applications.

Primary Responsibilities of the Operating System

Today's operating systems provide a wide variety of convenient user tools and advanced capabilities. Many operating systems have adopted the most popular utility programs and included them in the OS files. Nevertheless, these programs and capabilities are add-ons, and it is important to know the core responsibilities of an operating system.

An **operating system**, or **OS**, is a set of programs that run the computer and provide an interface between the application programs — such as word processors and spreadsheets — and the hardware, as well as between the hardware and the user (Figure 10-1). All applications must communicate with the computer through the operating system. Because it is fundamental to the operation of the computer, the operating system must always be the first set of programs loaded into a microcomputer's memory. The programs that make up an operating system can be grouped into one of three primary responsibilities:

- device management
- file management
- memory management

Device Management

Each peripheral (the monitor, the keyboard, and so on) that is attached to the CPU, whether through the motherboard or a port, is called a **device**. Device is just a synonym for peripheral that we use when talking about the operating system.

The CPU of a microcomputer doesn't know how to use all the devices that are attached to it — in fact, it doesn't necessarily even know the devices exist. In order for the CPU to use these devices and use them properly, it needs some instructions.

Some of the instructions that the CPU needs are located in a special program called **BIOS**, which stands for Basic Input/Output System. On a PC, BIOS is located in a ROM chip. When the computer is turned on, BIOS performs diagnostic procedures to test the system resources. First, BIOS tests to see if the RAM chips are functioning properly. Next, BIOS searches for devices and tells the computer where they are. Finally, as shown in Figure 10-2, BIOS provides instructions for interpreting keyboard characters and sending them to the monitor or to the storage devices.

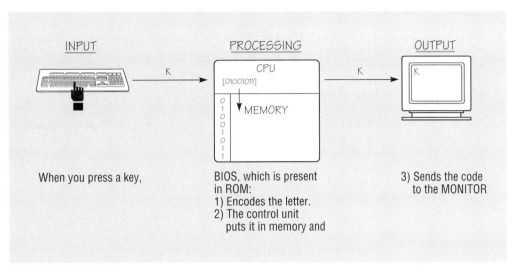

Figure 10-2
One of the functions of BIOS is interpreting input from the keyboard.

Although BIOS tells the CPU where the devices are, the CPU still needs instructions to use the devices properly. Some of these instructions are included in the operating system's device management programs. The amount of device management provided by the OS varies dramatically from one OS to another. On the Macintosh, the devices are centrally controlled by the OS. DOS, however, provides a minimal amount of device management. Because device management isn't tightly controlled by DOS, developers of application software for DOS systems are forced to include the rest of the device management that is required. So, although one of the responsibilities of an OS is device management, the whole responsibility is spread among the BIOS program, the OS, and the application software.

Memory Management

In addition to BIOS, the computer's ROM chip includes a "bootstrap" routine that tells the CPU to look for the operating system in storage and load it into RAM. After the bootstrap routine is completed, the OS takes sole responsibility for telling the CPU how to use RAM for holding all of the data and programs that are needed (Figure 10-3). For example, if the user wants to load an application program, he or she issues an appropriate command to the OS. The OS finds the application program and identifies where in RAM the program should be put. The program can't be put just anywhere; the OS is already occupying some part of RAM, and more space is necessary for loading data files or other pro-

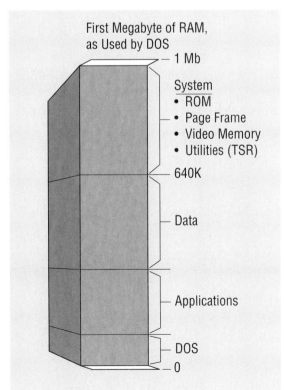

Figure 10-3
When using DOS, the first megabyte of memory can be thought of as a stack. DOS is at the bottom because it is loaded first; then comes the application, and finally the data. Software to access the monitor, plus several small utility programs, are kept in a separate area above 640 K.

grams. Once the application file is loaded, the operating system must keep track of data files that are loaded and modified from within the application. When the user quits a program or closes a data file, the OS clears that area of RAM.

File Management

Besides managing memory, the OS must keep track of everything in storage. Each disk that the computer accesses has a set of files on it. The files may be organized into a directory structure. The directory structure and the location of each file is located in a special place on the disk. If the disk was formatted on a PC using DOS, the location of each file is contained in the FAT, or File Allocation Table. The operating system creates this table on every disk when the disk is formatted (actually, DOS creates two of them, just to be safe), accesses the information in it whenever a file needs to be retrieved from storage, and updates the information anytime data is written to the disk. In essence, the operating system acts as a librarian for the CPU.

Knowing where files are stored on disk can be extremely difficult, especially if a file has been modified a number of times. Say a data file consisting of a letter to a client is originally stored in three adjacent sectors on a disk. Over time, other files are stored on the disk, until there are no more empty areas next to where the letter is stored. Then the user modifies the letter. The modifications don't fit with the rest of the file, so they are placed somewhere else on the disk. The operating system then has to keep track of two separate areas for the same file. Every time the file is modified, the same process can take place. Keeping track of such fragmented files is subject to error, and accessing them is time consuming for the computer. A disk maintenance (or optimizer) utility can be used to reorder the files properly or "defragment" them. Figure 10-4 shows the results of defragmenting a hard disk using Norton Utilities.

Comprehension Questions

1. Which one of the operating system's primary responsibilities is in charge of sending data to a modem?
2. Why must BIOS be read by the computer before the operating system is?
3. What do you think a defragmentation utility does?

Using What You Know

1. What types of computers might not need operating systems?
2. Does the operating system for a diskless workstation require storage management programs? Why or why not?
3. In the top screen of Figure 10-4, why are there unused disk areas between areas that are being used?

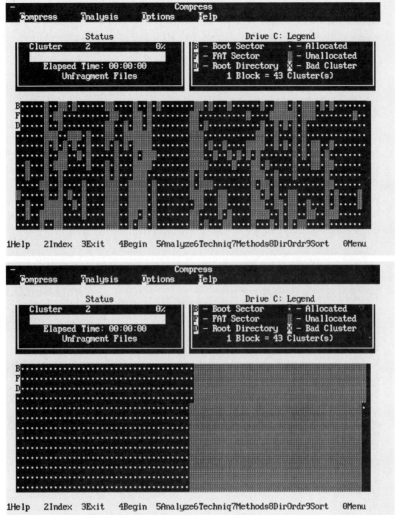

Figure 10-4
When you use a defragmentation program, you are shown a diagram of the disk. The top screen shows the diagram before defragmentation, and the bottom screen after.

Types of Operating Systems

Operating systems have evolved over the years in response to changes in user demands and hardware capabilities. Not only have many utilities been layered on top of the programs that handle the essential responsibilities of the operating system, but new programs have also been added to handle more advanced capabilities. Some of these capabilities have existed on mainframe computers for many years . As microcomputers have become more powerful, the operating systems designed for them have adopted capabilities traditionally associated with mainframe computers. Whether or not you actually need these capabilities will depend on how you intend to use your computer.

Singletasking and Multitasking Operating Systems

One of the biggest buzzwords in the current battle for the operating system throne is multitasking. **Multitasking**, which used to be called multiprogramming, is the ability to run several programs at the same time.

Multitasking is made possible by the differences between processing speed and input or output speed. The microprocessor works very quickly, while I/O devices tend to operate more slowly. When you are typing, for example, the time between each letter you press seems like ages to the CPU. During that interval, it may be able to execute thousands of machine instructions in some other program. Even much faster I/O operations, such as writing data to a disk, allow the CPU plenty of time to execute other instructions. Multitasking operating systems take advantage of these gaps by focusing the power of the CPU on several programs at once.

Multitasking operating systems are further broken down into cooperative multitasking and preemptive multitasking. These are highly technical differences, but they make it possible to distinguish between one OS and another. Essentially, **preemptive multitasking** is more efficient than cooperative multitasking, because the former allows whichever program needs the microprocessor must to go ahead and use it. **Cooperative multitasking** simply divides the CPU's time equally among the programs that are using it. Windows 3.1, shown in Figure 10-5, performs cooperative multitasking.

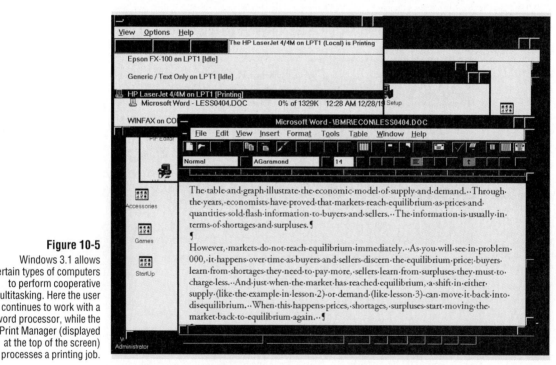

Figure 10-5
Windows 3.1 allows certain types of computers to perform cooperative multitasking. Here the user continues to work with a word processor, while the Print Manager (displayed at the top of the screen) processes a printing job.

Single- and Multiple-User Operating Systems

Some computers can interact with only a single user, while other computers can support multiple users. Single-user operating systems have relatively simple device management programs because they can concentrate on a single keyboard and a single monitor. Multiple-user operating systems are more complicated because they must keep track of all the requests each user makes. For example, one user may be entering an inventory request at the same time another user is reading an E-mail message. As shown in Figure 10-6, the operating system must keep track of input from one and output from the other. A host computer, especially one with terminal nodes, needs to handle multiple-user requests.

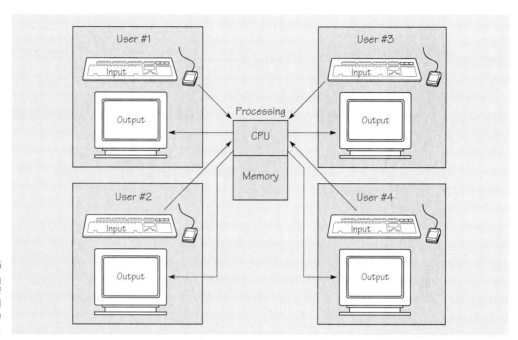

Figure 10-6
A multiuser operating system must keep track of input, processing, and output from more than one user at the same time.

Another important function of a multiuser operating system is managing the **access privileges** afforded to each user. On a multiuser computer, each user normally must enter the system with a "logon" command, such as the one shown in Figure 10-7. The computer then prompts the user for an identification number and possibly a password. The computer associates this identification with certain privileges: Often the user is allowed a fixed amount of storage space and access to specific files or programs. Controlling access privileges thus allows a company to limit the use of valuable resources and protect sensitive files. A network file server's operating system must be able to manage access privileges.

Figure 10-7
On this Novell network, users must issue the LOGIN command followed by their name. The operating system then prompts the user for an identification number, which does not appear on the screen when it is typed. If the identification number is correct, the user is given specific access privileges.

```
Running on DOS V5.00

Attached to server FS-ZA
01-21-93     12:22:27 PM

C:\>f:login brad
Enter your password:
Device LPT1: re-routed to queue PRINTQ_TOP on server FS-ZA.

Shell version: 3.22 Std
Previous setting: SHOW DOTS=OFF     Changed to ON

H:\HOME\BRAD>
```

Single- and Multiple-Processor Operating Systems

Although it is rare for microcomputers, minis and mainframes can have many central processing units. In fact, some very large computers, such as those used to predict the weather or explore for oil, can have thousands of CPUs. These sets of chips are called *multiprocessors* or *parallel processors*. A parallel operating system is used to coordinate the parallel processors and provide communication between them. Each of the processors also has a small operating system.

Portable and Nonportable Operating Systems

With respect to hardware, software can be judged by its compatibility and its portability. A program that is **compatible** with a given machine will run on that machine. A machine that is compatible with another machine can run the same software. Compatibility has been an issue among hardware manufacturers for years, especially in the IBM-compatibles arena. Traditionally, software was written to run on a certain type of machine, and manufacturers of similar machines had to worry about compatibility.

A program that is **portable** can be run on many different machines. Whereas compatibility is often an issue for hardware manufacturers, portability is becoming an issue with software developers. This issue is likely to grow in importance, especially as the Unix operating system gains a foothold in the microcomputer operating system market.

In the late 1960s, a programmer named Ken Thompson, who worked at Bell Laboratories, wanted to move a program from an expensive General Electric computer to a less expensive minicomputer made by Digital Equipment Corporation. Although the DEC equipment offered a good hardware environment for running Thompson's program, it lacked the kind of software support needed to continue his work. Thompson created **Unix** as a set of routines to support the DEC system.

Although the original Unix system was written in assembly language, a subsequent version used a language called "B," which Thompson developed in 1970. B was extended and refined by Dennis Ritchie, another Bell Labs programmer. The resulting language was C. Unix was rewritten in C in 1973.

The major reason for rewriting Unix in C was the desire to move it to a wider range of machines. Only a small portion of Unix is written specifically for a certain computer. The rest — the part written in C — is easily transferred from one machine to another. This portability requires changing the small parts of the program that are written for a particular computer and then recompiling the C portion of the operating system.

Today, efforts to create portable operating systems are in full swing. In addition to the work that has occurred and continues to occur on Unix, Microsoft and IBM are working on operating systems that are portable. There is a greater advantage than simply being able to move the operating system from one type of machine to another. Portability in an OS makes application programs more portable as well. For example, right now it is not possible to use a word processor like Microsoft Word for the Mac on a PC. If Word was written for a portable OS, however, it would run on any computer that could run the portable OS.

Middleware

A new type of software, called **middleware**, attempts to shield users from the complexity of computer systems by providing a layer of software between the application and the operating system. Middleware is a layer of software that integrates disparate technologies. Some people use the analogy of a glue that binds certain pieces of software together.

Middleware simplifies the process of connecting various software products, regardless of whether or not these products compete with or adhere to a given set of standards. As a result, developers and users don't have to deal with all the diversity that results from multivendor configurations and can instead focus on their own technology or applications.

Comprehension Questions

1. Some operating systems accomplish multitasking by allocating short, successive blocks of time to each program that is running. What type of multitasking do you think this is — cooperative or preemptive?

2. Do the computers attached to a file server need a multiuser operating system? Why or why not?

3. Say you already own a set of application programs and hardware devices. Now you need an OS. Is your primary concern the compatibility or the portability of the OS?

Using What You Know

1. Would the stockroom workers at BVOS benefit from a multitasking OS? Why or why not?

2. Which computer at BVOS requires a multiuser OS?

3. As president, how important is the portability of the OS you use at BVOS?

Popular Operating Systems

During the 1980s, two operating systems got most of the attention. DOS was the overwhelming market leader because it had become the standard operating system for all PCs (IBMs and compatibles). The operating system for the Mac also got a lot of attention because it won users by pioneering the possibilities of the user-friendly graphical user interface.

Today, the operating system market is in much greater disarray. While still popular, the Macintosh doesn't command much more or less of the market than it did several years ago, but the DOS market has fragmented. To some extent, this fragmentation has been the result of the Mac's popular operating system. PC users made it clear that they wanted a GUI. More important, however, DOS was designed for the PCs of the 1980s, most of which used the 8088 or 286 chip. Both of these are 16-bit chips, and DOS is a 16-bit operating system. The 386 and 486, however, are 32-bit chips. A 16-bit operating system cannot take full advantage of their capabilities.

Several contenders are vying for the gap created by DOS's shortcomings. The first to enter the race was IBM's OS/2, which first hit the market in 1987. The early versions didn't gain widespread use, but IBM is pressing hard with version 2.0, released in 1992. Another competitor is Unix, which has moved from being a minicomputer OS down to the micro level with the introduction of the 32-bit chip. Finally, Windows NT, which, with Windows 3.1, already has a significant market share, is trying to dominate the market as Microsoft's 32-bit replacement for DOS.

Let's look more closely at each of these operating systems, beginning with the old standard, DOS.

DOS

Microsoft's Disk Operating System, or **DOS**, was developed for IBM and released in 1981. Microsoft Corporation got its start a few years earlier when Bill Gates dropped out of Harvard to form the company with his high school friend Paul Allen (Figure 10-8). They began their business by writing versions of BASIC for the first microcomputers. In 1980, IBM decided to hire the young company to create an operating system for entry into the microcomputer market. When the IBM PC came out a year later, it was an immediate success, and the operating system became a success with it.

As the compatibles market grew, two nearly identical versions of the operating system emerged: PC-DOS was the version licensed by IBM to be packaged on its machines; MS-DOS was Microsoft's proprietary version that was sold to compatibles vendors. Largely through the sales of DOS, Microsoft established itself as the most influential software company. Paul Allen has since left Microsoft to form his own software company, the Asymetrix Corporation. Bill Gates, still the head of Microsoft, has gone on to become the richest man in the United States. In 1992, Mr. Gates, in his mid-thirties, was worth about $8 billion.

Over the years, DOS has matured. It started as a minimalist operating system — what you needed in order to run a PC (Figure 10-9). It grew to include a wide array of utilities. It also grew to keep up with hardware developments, such as the hard disk and 3½-inch diskettes. Today, DOS still represents the minimum requirements of an operating system. The reason, though, is that DOS remains the market-share leader. To beat the leader, an operating system must offer more in terms of features, portability, and compatibility.

Figure 10-8
Paul Allen and Bill Gates, founders of Microsoft, which became the world's largest software company, largely through the sales of DOS.

```
B:\>format b:
Insert new diskette for drive B:
and press ENTER when ready...

Checking existing disk format.
Saving UNFORMAT information.
Verifying 1.44M
Format complete.

Volume label (11 characters, ENTER for none)?

    1457664 bytes total disk space
    1457664 bytes available on disk

       512 bytes in each allocation unit.
      2847 allocation units available on disk.

Volume Serial Number is 3F34-07EC

Format another (Y/N)?
```

Figure 10-9
Most users access DOS from the command line. Here, the user has entered the FORMAT command to reformat the disk.

Here are a few of the advantages and disadvantages of using DOS:

Advantages

- *A huge market base.* For more than 10 years, DOS has been the market-share leader. If you use DOS, you are part of the biggest microcomputer community in the world. In addition, DOS is the industry standard. Even though DOS is losing its lead in the market, new operating systems for PCs still try to make their systems DOS-compatible. New users of other OSs can still use their old DOS applications and files, and DOS users are never cut off from the movement toward more powerful operating systems.

- *The most applications to choose from.* Because DOS dominated the market for so long, thousands of applications and utilities have been written for it. This situation gives users a great deal of flexibility when choosing the right tool for the job.

- *A fast platform for text-based work.* Most of the recently developed operating systems are built around a graphical user interface (GUI). DOS, however, is a text-based system, meaning that it is meant to manage text characters rather than graphical elements. For users who do not want a GUI — whether because of a personal preference or because their systems slow down under the added requirements of a graphical system — DOS is fast and efficient.

- *Can be used with 16-bit chips.* Although the vast majority of the computers sold today include the 386 and 486 32-bit architecture, there are plenty of 286, and even 8088, machines still in the workplace. The reason is that these machines are more than adequate for basic, everyday word processing and spreadsheet needs. If this is all you intend to do with a computer, you can pick up a used machine and a copy of DOS for very little money.

Disadvantages

- *Limited memory management.* One of the major complaints about DOS is that it cannot access more than 1 MB of memory without special software. Many of today's applications require more. Using Windows 3.1 alone requires far more than 1 MB.

- *Lack of a fully integrated GUI.* Confirmed DOS users will tell you that DOS has a GUI, the DOS Shell, which can be run in either graphics mode or text mode (Figure 10-10).

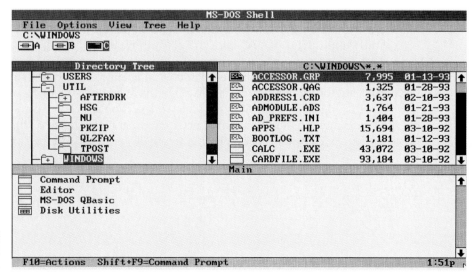

Figure 10-10
The DOS Shell, an optional graphics environment.

This is true, and the DOS Shell is significantly more intuitive, and therefore easier to learn, than the original command-line interface. The operating system as a whole, however, is not graphically based, but text based; the GUI is just an add-on feature. This means that applications running under DOS are usually text based, though they may have graphics modes. This aspect of DOS cannot be called a flaw, because many users prefer the speed and efficiency of text based applications. New users, however, seem to prefer working in graphic environments.

- *Lack of a standard interface.* Ever since the Mac gained a foothold in the market, there has been a move toward interfaces that have a standard look to them. The advantage here is that users can learn new programs more quickly because many aspects of using each program are the same. Windows and Windows NT are perfect examples of how PC interfaces have followed the Mac's lead. DOS, however, remains much more open-ended. A software developer creating a DOS application can create any type of interface. This freedom makes it more difficult to move from one application to another.

- *Cannot perform multitasking.* By itself (without the addition of a graphic environment such as Windows or Deskview 386), DOS is a single-tasking operating system. For many types of computer use, this limitation may not be a problem. However, users who want to either run one program in the background while they use another or load several applications at once so they can switch quickly between them will find DOS cumbersome.

Users frustrated with DOS have been predicting the demise of the operating system for years. Ironically, some aspects of this highly volatile industry don't change nearly as quickly as the experts expect. The reason is the stability of the "installed base," that is, the existing computer systems. There are more computers running DOS than any other operating system in the world. Even though most of the new equipment may be better served by a more powerful OS, DOS will maintain a major presence in the market for several more years.

The Macintosh's System Software

Although the operating system for the Macintosh is called the **System file**, many Mac users aren't even aware of it. The reason is that the System file, a 32-bit operating system, works in conjunction with the **Finder**, an extremely well-designed GUI that insulates the user from the real responsibilities of the operating system (Figure 10-11). The Finder manages the System by using a series of graphical images. For instance, to delete a file from the Macintosh, you simply drag the file into an icon representing a trash can. The Finder manages applications and controls the icons, Clipboard, and Scrapbook functions.

The Macintosh, which was released in 1984, has maintained a similar interface throughout its history. The most recent version of the operating system, System 7, looks very much like the original system, although the recent version is far more powerful. Operating system advancements on the Macintosh have closely paralleled those on the PC. The reason is that the Mac remains a major competitor to the PC, even though the two systems are, in many respects, incompatible.

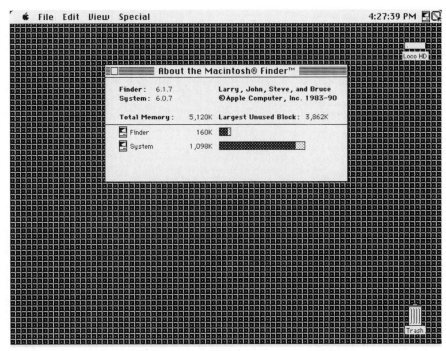

Figure 10-11
The Macintosh and its operating system, which is controlled by the System file and the Finder.

Here are some of the advantages and disadvantages to using the Macintosh and its resident operating system.

Advantages

- *A consistent, "friendly" interface.* The Mac's operating system forces the applications that run under it into a familiar look. As shown in Figure 10-12 on the next page, each one has a set of pull-down menus across the top of the screen, and many of the menus are the same. Consequently, Mac applications are relatively easy to learn, at least in comparison to DOS applications. Historically, ease of use has been the Mac's biggest selling point.

- *A fully integrated graphics interface.* Every program that runs on the Mac is in graphics mode all the time. This feature is an added level of consistency that sets the System apart from DOS, where you can be unexpectedly switched into and out of graphics mode.

- *Continuing efforts at compatibility with DOS machines.* DOS-based machines are not able to run Macintosh applications, but the opposite is less and less true. In recent years, Apple has worked hard to accommodate business users by building in the ability to run PC software. The first step was to include the SuperDrive, which can read DOS-formatted disks. More recently, Apple has made it possible to install PC boards in the Mac and thereby run DOS applications.

- *Multitasking.* Recent versions of the System are able to perform cooperative multitasking, though they are not capable of full, preemptive multitasking.

- *Simplicity of moving data between applications.* Another feature that the Mac's operating system pioneered was the "Clipboard." The Clipboard is a holding pen for data that has been cut or copied from an application. Once the data is in the Clipboard, it can be pasted into another application. This capability makes it possible, for

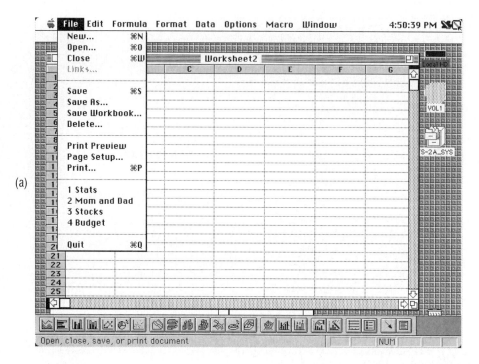

(a)

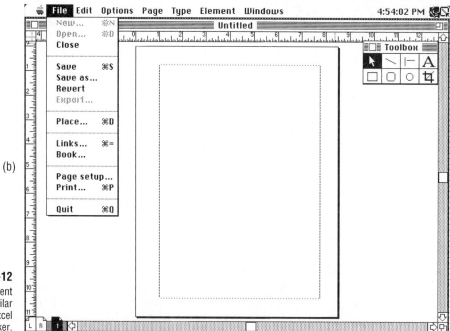

(b)

Figure 10-12

Two very different programs with a similar look: (a) Microsoft Excel and (b) Aldus PageMaker.

instance, to copy a graph created in a spreadsheet into a business report created with a word processor (Figure 10-13 on the next page). With subscribe and publish features, it is also possible to create dynamic links on the Mac. With a dynamic link, material that has been copied into another document will change if the original document is altered. For example, say you create a bar graph showing the amount of your power bill each month. You then copy the graph into a memo to your employees about saving

(a)   (b)

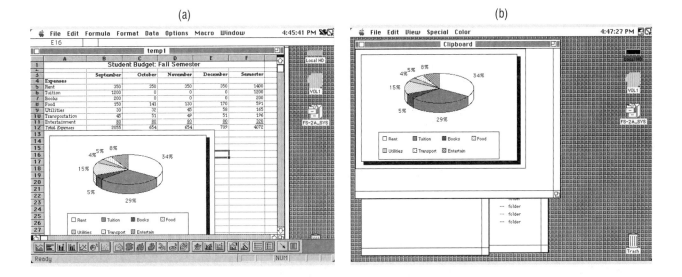

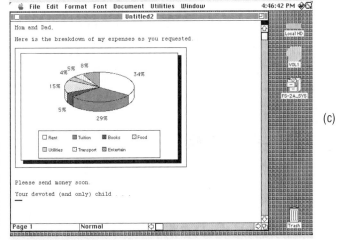

(c)

Figure 10-13

(a) A graph is created in Microsoft Excel.
(b) The graph is copied into the Clipboard.
(c) The graph is pasted into a memo written in Claris MacWrite II.

electricity. Before you give the memo out, you get another power bill and add it to your spreadsheet, which automatically adds it to your graph. If you had created a dynamic link, the graph in your memo would be updated automatically as well.

- *High-quality on-screen graphics.* Creating and manipulating graphic images is made easy by the Mac's high-quality video output.

Disadvantages

- *Inability of PCs to run Mac software.* Despite Apple's efforts to accommodate DOS software, most PC machines cannot run Mac software. For the Mac user, this means that the majority of the business community cannot access Mac software and, more important, data that is formatted for the Mac. Incompatibility has been Apple's biggest stumbling block with the Mac.

- *Expense.* The other major drawback of using the Mac is the price of the machine. Because of the competition from compatibles, the cost of technology on the PC has steadily declined. The same is not true of the Macintosh, where compatible machines are not available. As a result, for a given amount of processing power, storage capacity, and input and output devices, it is cheaper to buy a PC than a Mac.

Looking at the disadvantages mentioned above, you can see that they aren't directly related to the Mac's operating system. The operating system is difficult to fault: It has always been ahead of its time.

Microsoft Windows 3.1 and Windows NT

In 1985, Microsoft released **Windows** as a way to give DOS a Mac-like interface. The name Windows comes from the program's ability to maintain different viewing areas on the screen (Figure 10-14). Each window can contain a different application. Users can switch back and forth between windows with the click of a mouse button.

Windows gives DOS users the ability to work in a graphic environment and still have access to all of the regular DOS applications. They can also use Windows applications, programs specifically designed to operate under Windows. Like the programs designed for the Mac, Windows programs all have a similar look (Figure 10-15). Another advantage of Windows over DOS alone is the ability to move data quickly between applications. Finally, Windows permits a certain level of multitasking. The level of multitasking that is possible depends on the type of machine being used and the mode that Windows is run in.

The problem with Windows is that it must run under DOS. Therefore, Windows is still largely limited to a 16-bit system, and it cannot directly address more than 1 MB of memory. To take advantage of the true power of the 32-bit chips, Microsoft is finalizing **Windows NT** (NT stands for "New Technology"). Windows 3.1 is really just a high-powered shell for DOS but Windows NT is a true operating system. NT is still compatible with DOS because it can use any DOS applications, but DOS is not present in the system. Thus, NT will be Microsoft's replacement for DOS in the 32-bit market.

When purchasing software related to these products, it is critical to distinguish between Windows and Windows NT. You can rely on NT to run applications designed for DOS-dependent Windows, but not vice versa. Also, programs written specifically for NT will generally be faster and more efficient than those written for DOS-dependent Windows.

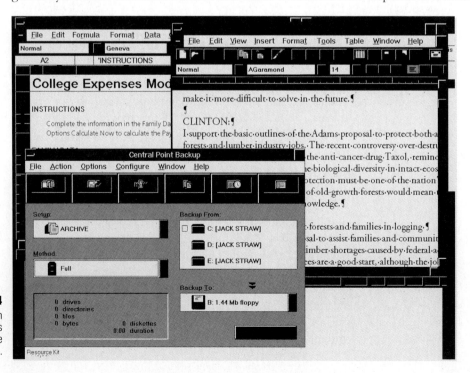

Figure 10-14
In Windows, the user can keep several applications visible on the screen at the same time.

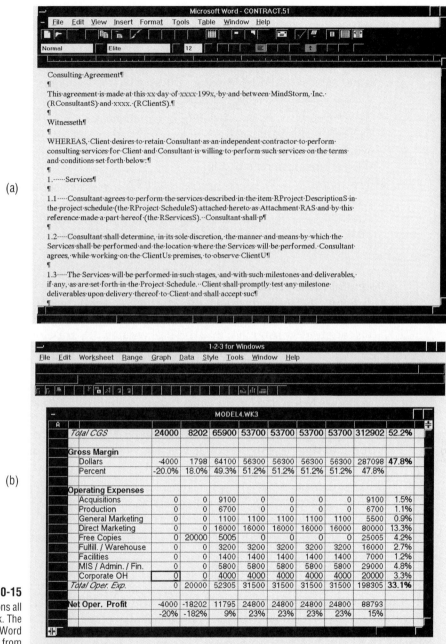

Figure 10-15
Windows applications all have a similar look. The screen in (a) is from Word for Windows; (b) is from Lotus 1-2-3 for Windows.

Here are some of the potential advantages and disadvantages of Windows NT.

Potential Advantages

- *32-bit processing.* The biggest advantage of NT over DOS is that the operating system is designed to take advantage of the 32-bit processing capabilities of 386 and 486 chips.

- *Full preemptive multitasking.* NT is able to perform the highest level of multitasking, allowing applications to use the CPU when they need it most. This is a step up from DOS-dependent Windows, which could perform only cooperative multitasking.

- *Direct access to 4 gigabytes of memory.* Like the other 32-bit operating systems, NT is not subject to the 1 MB barrier under which DOS suffers. NT memory access is therefore faster and more efficient.

- *Excellent data exchange capabilities.* As with the versions of Windows that run under DOS, NT is able to move data between applications quickly and easily. Windows and Windows NT are even able to create dynamic links between files using Windows' OLE (Object Linking and Embedding).

- *The ability to use DOS applications and DOS-dependent Windows applications.* NT is upward-compatible, so users can keep their old Windows programs, as well as their old DOS programs. DOS is, after all, a Microsoft product. The company is likely to make every possible effort not to leave its old customers out in the cold, no matter how much it wants to sell new versions of its application software.

Potential Disadvantages

- *Extensive hardware requirements.* The biggest complaint about NT is the amount of memory that it requires. Prior to the new 32-bit operating systems, few microcomputers for business had more than 4 MB of memory. Because of software like NT, old users are being forced to add memory, and machines with 8 or 16 MB are becoming the norm.

- *A complicated GUI.* Although the complaint is subjective, many users say that NT, like Windows before it, is more difficult than it needs to be. Perhaps the most specific criticism is that the File Manager is not a fully integrated part of the interface. Users must first open the File Manager before they can move, copy, or delete files. Other software vendors have responded to these complaints by creating shells for NT. The Norton Desktop for Windows NT, for example, is one of these shells.

Windows NT has a big advantage in the battle over 32-bit systems, simply because of the success of Windows 3.0 and 3.1. The program does face formidable challengers. Nevertheless, the installed base has shown its force before in the OS war, and Microsoft's presence in the market may be more important than any technical issues.

Unix

The oldest operating system competing for today's market is actually not DOS but Unix. For years, Unix has been touted as "the operating system of the future," but it has yet to gain a large portion of the PC or Macintosh market.

As noted before, Unix was originally developed at AT&T for one of its minicomputers. AT&T licensed the software to universities, and the students at these schools modified and improved the code. The University of California at Berkeley was especially influential in the evolution of the operating system. Some of the improvements were integrated back into AT&T's version of Unix, while others became part of other versions. The number of developers involved with Unix is one of the factors that has made the system so powerful.

Although Unix has yet to gain a large following among business microcomputer users, it does command the lion's share of the workstation market. A **workstation** is a high-powered microcomputer (or a single-user minicomputer) that is used for scientific, engineering, or technical applications. Many workstations are equipped with top-of-the-line graphics capabilities to meet the needs of today's computer-assisted design (CAD) software. Currently, more than three quarters of all workstations use some version of Unix. Figure 10-16 shows one version.

Here are the advantages and disadvantages of using Unix:

Advantages

- *32-bit processing.* Like its competitors and unlike DOS, Unix is a 32-bit operating system.

- *Portability.* Unix is currently the most portable operating system available for micro-computers. With relative ease, a given version of Unix can be adapted to any number of micros, minis, or mainframes.

- *Multitasking.* Like the other 32-bit OSs, Unix is capable of multitasking.

- *Multiuser capabilities.* Unlike Windows NT or OS/2, Unix is able to manage multiple-user requests. This may prove to be a powerful advantage for Unix as more small businesses adopt sophisticated networks.

- *Well-developed networking capabilities.* Because it has always had multiuser capabilities, Unix's networking features are well developed and standardized.

- *Direct access to 4 gigabytes of memory.* Like NT and OS/2 2.0, Unix is not burdened by the 1 MB DOS barrier.

- *Fewer system requirements than Windows NT or OS/2 2.0.* Some versions of Unix will run reliably on systems with 4 MB of RAM. NT and OS/2 both require at least 6 MB for full functionality.

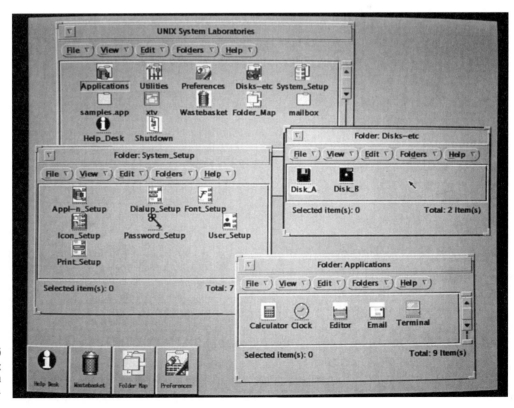

Figure 10-16
Unix System V, by Unix Software Laboratories (a division of Bell Labs).

Disadvantages

- *Competing versions of the software.* Although the number of developers made Unix a powerful operating system, it also led to multiple versions. Unix was originally an AT&T product, but many other companies now market versions of Unix. These companies include such major computer vendors as Sun Microsystems, IBM, Hewlett-Packard, and NeXT. Standards are beginning to emerge, but they are not yet sufficiently stable to satisfy the business community, where compatibility is a high priority.

- *Lack of compatible application software.* Perhaps the biggest disadvantage of using Unix is the lack of business application software that has been written for it. This problem is compounded by the number of versions of Unix, since a program written for one version will not necessarily work on any other version. As standards emerge for Unix, this disadvantage could eventually disappear.

It remains to be seen whether Unix is really the OS of the future. The largest factors in Unix's success are likely to be the existence of top-quality applications for business and compatibility with the DOS and Windows software that is currently so prevalent.

OS/2

In 1987, IBM, with help from Microsoft, released the first version of **OS/2**, the operating system specifically designed to take advantage of the newer Intel chips, beginning with the 286. OS/2 was heralded as a great leap forward because it brought multitasking to the PC. Some industry experts predicted the quick demise of DOS in the face of competition that had superior capabilities. OS/2's reception in the market, however, was lukewarm, to a large extent because of the program's size and lack of applications developed to take advantage of its advanced features.

With OS/2 2.0, IBM made its entrance into the 32-bit OS market (Figure 10-17). IBM is now in a head-to-head race with Windows NT. Unix is in the race as well, so we can safely assume that this market will be unstable for quite some time.

Here are the advantages and disadvantages of using OS/2 2.0:

Advantages

- *32-bit processing.* Like NT and Unix, OS/2 takes advantage of the 32-bit Intel chips, the 386 and the 486.

- *Ability to perform preemptive multitasking.* Like Unix and Windows NT, OS/2 is able to do the highest form of multitasking.

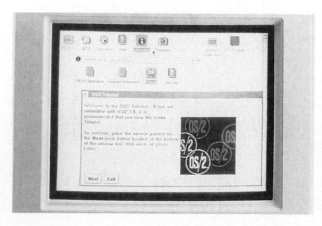

Figure 10-17
OS/2 2.0, IBM's competitor in the 32-bit operating systems market

- *Ability to run DOS and DOS-dependent Windows applications.* To tap into the DOS and Windows markets, IBM has made it possible to run all DOS applications, as well as DOS-dependent Windows applications. OS/2 was the first to include this feature; the software came out a year before NT.

- *Mac-like GUI.* The OS/2 GUI more closely resembles the Mac interface than the NT GUI does. Many of the most common tasks, such as deleting and printing files, can be done simply by moving icons on the screen, a technique called "drag and drop." For example, a file can be deleted by moving its icon to a trash icon.

- *Ability to run applications in "protected mode."* Starting with the 286, it is possible to set up areas in RAM that will not interfere with each other. Using this feature is known as *running applications in protected mode.* In protected mode, if there is a problem with one application, it can be restarted without restarting the whole computer. Although Windows has now adopted this feature, OS/2 incorporated it years before with the first version of the software.

- *No 1 MB barrier.* Like NT and Unix, OS/2 is not subject to the DOS 1 MB barrier.

Disadvantages
- *Few existing 32-bit applications.* IBM's biggest hurdle is a lack of software that will take advantage of the new 32-bit system. Thousands of developers are working on programs for 32-bit OS/2, but it takes time to build up a substantial arsenal.

- *Extensive system requirements.* Like NT, OS/2 2.0 needs at least 6 MB of RAM to run reliably. This requirement is forcing users to add memory to their existing systems or purchase new computers.

- *Difficult installation.* Many early adopters of OS/2 2.0 have complained that the installation process is a headache. Once it is accomplished, however, most users seem more than satisfied with the software's performance.

- *Training old users to operate a new interface.* To win the OS war, IBM needs to convince DOS and Windows users that they should switch to OS/2. Where Windows is already entrenched, this is a difficult feat, because the path of least resistance is to switch to NT.

OS/2 beat Microsoft in the race to release a 32-bit operating system — a wise tactical move. Moreover, OS/2 2.0 is a vast improvement over the earlier versions of the software. But while OS/2 was being revamped, Windows 3.0 and 3.1 took a huge share of the high-end PC market. Now IBM is faced with the formidable task of winning those users over to its OS. As we have said before, the excellence of IBM's product may not be as big a factor as the simple fact that Microsoft dominates the OS market. Time will tell.

Comprehension Questions

1. What aspect of DOS has led to the war among NT, OS/2, and Unix?
2. Which company is the biggest player in the PC software market?
3. What two factors made it imperative that OS/2 2.0 could run DOS and DOS-dependent Windows applications?

Using What You Know

1. Our discussion of 32-bit operating systems is necessarily tentative because this book went to print before the final version of Windows NT was released. Who appears to be winning the war over the 32-bit systems?

2. Compare prices between OS/2 and Windows NT. Make sure the prices you find are for the start-up version of the software, rather than for the upgrade.

3. With the previous purchasing decisions you have made in mind, which operating system would you choose for BVOS?

Summary Points

Operating Systems at BVOS

☐ This chapter completes the process of buying hardware for BVOS.

Primary Responsibilities of the Operating System

☐ The minimum requirements of an operating system are device, file, and memory management.

Device Management

☐ Before the OS is loaded, BIOS checks the RAM chips and looks for devices.
☐ After the BIOS is read, device management is handed over to the OS, though some of this responsibility may be shared with the application software.

Memory Management

☐ After the bootstrap routine tells the CPU to load the OS into RAM, all memory management is handled by the OS.

File Management

☐ The OS acts as a librarian for the CPU, keeping track of where files are stored on the disk.
☐ File management becomes much more complicated when modifications to files causes them to be fragmented.

Types Of Operating Systems

☐ Operating systems for micros are now able to accomplish some of the same capabilities as those of mainframes.

Singletasking and Multitasking Operating Systems

☐ The ability to run more than one program at once is made possible by the difference between processing speed and I/O speeds.
☐ Multitasking OSs are broken down into preemptive and cooperative systems; preemptive systems are more efficient.

Single- and Multiple-User Operating Systems

☐ Multiple-user OSs must keep track of multiple and simultaneous I/O requests.
☐ Most multiple-user OSs also manage the access privileges of the users.
☐ A file server's multiuser OS must be able to manage access privileges.

Single- and Multiple-Processor Operating Systems

☐ Some large computers have many CPUs in them and require a parallel operating system to handle the parallel processors.

Portable and Nonportable Operating Systems
☐ A compatible program can run on a given machine; a compatible machine can run the same software as another machine.
☐ A portable program can be used on different machines.
☐ Unix, which was first developed at AT&T, was the first portable operating system.

Middleware
☐ Middleware establishes an interface between the operating system and the applications.

Popular Operating Systems
☐ The dominance that DOS held in the OS market during the 1980s is giving way to a period of intense competition between the 32-bit operating systems for the PC.

DOS
☐ Microsoft became the biggest player in the software industry by creating the operating system for IBM's first PC and the compatibles market.

Advantages
☐ DOS has the advantage of having the largest market base, having the most applications to choose from, being a fast platform for text-based applications, and not requiring 32-bit chips.

Disadvantages
☐ DOS can only directly address 1 MB of RAM; it lacks a fully integrated GUI and a standard interface; and it cannot perform multitasking without the help of other software.

The Macintosh's System Software
☐ The Mac is most popular with users seeking a computer that is easy to operate and with "power users" who need high-quality graphics.

Advantages
☐ The Mac has a consistent, friendly GUI; it is capable of multitasking and trading or sharing information between applications; and it has high-quality video output.
☐ Apple makes it as simple as possible to use DOS-based data and programs on the Mac.

Disadvantages
☐ The major disadvantages of purchasing a Mac are its expense and the inability of most PCs to run Mac programs or load Mac-formatted data.

Microsoft Windows 3.1 and Windows NT
☐ DOS-dependent Windows was originally created as a GUI shell for the PC.
☐ Windows NT is Microsoft's 32-bit replacement for DOS.

Potential Advantages
☐ NT performs 32-bit processing and preemptive multitasking; it eliminates the 1 MB barrier; it has excellent data exchange capabilities; and it can run DOS and DOS-dependent Windows applications.

Potential Disadvantages
☐ NT requires more memory than most older machines have.
☐ Some users complain that Windows is harder to use than it needs to be.

Unix
☐ Unix is touted as the OS of the future, but it has yet to command a large portion of the business market.

☐ Over three quarters of all workstations use some form of Unix.

Advantages

☐ Like NT and OS/2, Unix is multitasking and is not hindered by the 1 MB DOS memory barrier.
☐ Unix is also a portable, multiuser system; it does not require as much RAM as NT or OS/2; and it has well-developed and standardized networking capabilities.

Disadvantages

☐ Competing versions of Unix make compatibility a problem.
☐ Unix does not yet have as formidable an arsenal of business applications as the other OSs.

OS/2

☐ The early versions of OS/2 were not a great success, but OS/2 2.0 is now in the race for the lead of the 32-bit operating systems.

Advantages

☐ OS/2 2.0 has advantages similar to those of NT, though its interface may be easier to use.

Disadvantages

☐ Compared to NT, the disadvantages of OS/2 are mainly difficult installation, lack of software designed specifically for it, and the fact that much of its target market is already using DOS-dependent Windows.

Knowing the Facts

True/False

1. BIOS must be read before the operating system can be loaded into RAM.
2. BIOS is stored permanently on the RAM chip.
3. DOS can perform preemptive multitasking; OS/2 can perform cooperative multitasking.
4. Multitasking is the modern term used to describe multiprogramming.
5. Unix was originally developed at AT&T.
6. The many developers who worked on Unix have made it a highly compatible operating system.
7. Prior to Windows NT, Windows required DOS to be running in the background.
8. The Macintosh's System file is the core of a 16-bit operating system.
9. A PC is more likely to be able to run Mac software than the other way around.
10. Software designed for Windows NT will run on DOS-dependent Windows, but the opposite is not true.

Short Answer

1. What are the three primary requirements of an operating system?
2. What is the term used to describe a file that is located in nonadjacent sectors on a disk?
3. What capacity must the operating system of a host computer on a network have?
4. What was the first major portable operating system?
5. What operating system is used by more than 75 percent of today's workstations?
6. What operating system pioneered the possibilities of being user friendly?
7. The existence of _____ has made it cheaper to buy a PC than a Macintosh of similar power.
8. One complaint with OS/2 and Windows NT is the amount of _____ required to run these pieces of software.
9. The Mac allows the user to create dynamic links using the publish and subscribe features. A similar capability is possible with Windows using _____.
10. Historically, the biggest factor in the OS war has been _____.

Answers

True/False

1. T
2. F
3. F
4. T
5. T
6. F
7. T
8. F
9. F
10. F

Short Answer

1. device, file, and memory management
2. fragmented
3. It must be a multiuser OS or have the ability to manage multiple I/O requests.
4. Unix
5. Unix
6. The Mac's System
7. compatibles
8. memory
9. OLE (Object Linking and Embedding)
10. market share, or the installed base

Challenging Your Understanding

1. Is it possible to select the wrong operating system for a computer? What are the most important things to think about when choosing an operating system?

2. Should an operating system come standard with a computer when you buy it? Why or why not?

3. Why must all multiuser operating systems be multitasking?

4. What does a multiprocessing operating system have to do that is different from a multitasking operating system?

5. Why is the user interface often a concern for the operating system rather than the application software?

Unit III Project

Tracking Computer Prices for the LAT Newsletter

Los Alamos Technology (LAT) is a business that monitors developments in the computer industry. Companies around the world use the services of LAT analysts to anticipate changes in the computer industry and to help make plans for incorporating new technologies that are being developed into their strategic plans. For example, a large express mail company used information provided by LAT to incorporate hand-held computers into their delivery business and gain a substantial edge over their competition.

Lisa Bunker is the lead analyst for the microcomputer industry focus group. The purpose of this group is to analyze and forecast developments specifically related to desktop microcomputers used in business. While browsing through reams of data that LAT routinely collects concerning developments in microcomputers, it occurred to Lisa that there must be hundreds of small businesses that would pay for information about the current prices and capabilities of microcomputers. She formulated the idea of producing and selling a newsletter that detailed the prices and capabilities of microcomputers and microcomputer components. Lisa presented her ideas to the LAT board of directors and was encouraged to create a prototype newsletter to present to the board at its next monthly meeting. The board authorized Lisa to assign you for the next month to gather data and help produce the prototype.

Using popular microcomputer magazines such as *PC Magazine* and *Byte*, your job is to find the price and feature list of the "average" microcomputer for sale over the past twelve months. What does it include? How much does it cost? What is the average cost per component if the components were purchased independently? Use a graph to depict your findings and then, using this information, help Lisa anticipate developments in microcomputers a year from now.

Organizational Solutions

Unit IV

With the end of Unit III you have put your major purchasing decisions behind you. As president of your BVOS branch, you have bought the necessary hardware and software for your new business. You have already hired most of your employees. Now it is time to build your computer system.

Building a computer system at a business means much more than setting up the hardware and loading the software onto a hard disk. The real work of building the system is creating the information systems that serve the information needs of the company. This is a complex process that involves designing the databases that will store data related to a company's operation and establishing the means for getting raw data into and processed data out of the database.

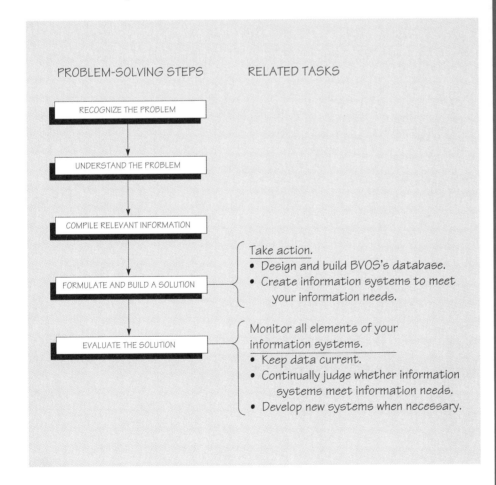

Figure IV-1   In this unit, we will focus on steps 4 and 5 of the problem-solving process.

To demonstrate how information systems are established, we begin with a close look at databases, the core of data around which most information systems are built. Then, we define and categorize the many information systems that use the database, as well as a few that do not. Finally, we examine the steps involved in developing an information system.

In the two previous units, we focused on steps 2, 3, and 4 of the problem-solving methodology. In this unit, our primary emphasis will be on step 4, though we will have a few things to say about step 5, evaluating the solution. Figure IV-1 illustrates how this unit fits into the problem-solving process.

Managing Databases

Key Terms

alphanumeric field
binary field
button
database
database administrator
data dictionary
date field
field
field name
field type
file
flat-file database
graphic field
hierarchical database
hypermedia database
indexing
logical field
memo field
network database
numeric field
query
record
query language
relation
relational database
report
sorting
stack
time field

Objectives

In this chapter you will learn to:

■ Describe the differences between how a paper-based office organizes data and how a computerized office organizes data

■ Explain the relationships among the three elements that make up a database

■ Name the five main types of fields

■ Explain the importance of database structure

■ Describe each of the five common database structures

■ Explain the advantage of a relational structure over a hierarchical, network, or flat-file structure

■ Describe how a hypermedia database differs from a traditional database

■ Differentiate between sorting and indexing

■ Give examples of how a database can be queried

■ Name and describe the five goals of a database

■ Describe the role of the database administrator

■ Describe how databases can affect personal privacy

Managing Data at BVOS

With this chapter, we turn our attention to the fourth element of the computer system: data. The BVOS inventory database is the living core of the business. It is a record of all daily transactions, including items in stock, items ordered by customers, and items on order from the regional distributor. In this chapter, we look at the concept of a database: how it is created, how it can be structured, and how software can be used to manage it.

Managing Data in a Paper-Based Office

Before the proliferation of computers in business, data was kept in the form of written records. Organization of data was largely determined by the ubiquitous file cabinet: Data was stored on forms and other documents, which were organized into folders, which were grouped into hanging folders, which fit into file drawers.

Maintaining this organizational system required the continual creation and proper storage of paper records. For example, if BVOS were a paper-based office, every new customer who ordered supplies would need to fill out a new customer form. One copy of the form would be filed, as shown in Figure 11-1. Another copy would have to go to the inventory manager, who would use the data for accounting purposes. Still another copy would go to the stockroom workers so they could fill the order and give it to the delivery drivers.

Finding a given piece of data in such a system would require finding the right piece of paper. If you were to look in the file cabinet, you would have to look through the hierarchy of drawer, hanging folder, file folder, and documents, and hope the document had been correctly filed. Collecting a set of data that wasn't all filed together might mean finding each desired element separately. If two people needed access to the same data, they had to either share it or make duplicates of it.

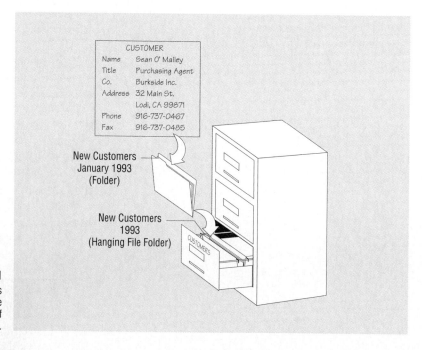

Figure 11-1
The paper-based office is heavily dependent on the organizational structure of the filing cabinet.

Managing Data in the Computer Age

The introduction of the computer allowed for the creation of the **database**, in which data is stored and organized electronically. Managing data with a computer is less time consuming, more reliable, and more flexible than managing data with a file cabinet. Rather than writing or typing data onto forms that are then filed, office workers key data into a computer. The data is organized automatically according to how the database has been set up. Finding a given piece or set of data is often just a matter of asking the computer program for it.

For example, in the computer-based BVOS office, entering data about a new customer is easy. When a new customer calls with an order, BVOS salespeople can take the order, just as they would take any other order. The only difference is that, in a computerized database, when the salesperson enters a business name that has not been entered before, the database management system prompts the salesperson for data that usually appears on the order form automatically, such as the business address and the telephone number (Figure 11-2).

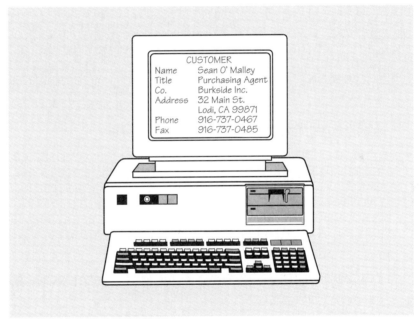

Figure 11-2
The filing cabinet has been surpassed by the capabilities of the electronic database.

Once the data is in the database, it can be available to different workers at the same time. If the inventory manager is doing billing at the same time that a stockroom worker is filling the order, no problem: The data from the order can appear on both computers simultaneously. What's more, if the inventory manager needs to find out how many boxes of paper have been ordered during the past month, she can simply ask the database management system to display the information. The organization of data can be flexible enough to answer that question, and many others, immediately.

Creating a Database

The most critical phase of database management is setting it up. Perhaps the most powerful capability of a good database is the user's ability to write queries to it. A **query** is simply a question. A database query, such as the one shown in Figure 11-3, is a request for data that meets certain criteria. If a database limits the kinds of queries the user can write, it also limits the accessibility of data.

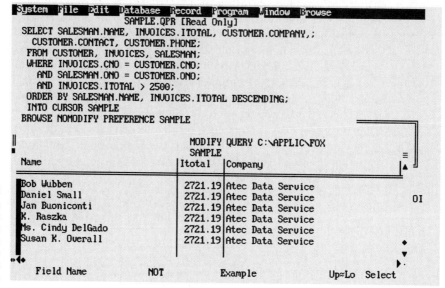

Figure 11-3
The command that begins "Select..." is a database query. The lines at the bottom of the screen are the results, that is, the records that meet its conditions.

The Three Basic Elements of a Database

Recall from Chapter 4 that a database is organized into files, records, and fields. A database is composed of related files. Each **file** holds a set of related records. Each **record** contains data about a thing or an event (Figure 11-4). Within a record, data is organized into **fields** that describe the thing or event. Records about things often refer to a person, a product, or a company. Records containing data about an event often refer to a business transaction. For example, each of the records in a CUSTOMER file at BVOS might contain data about one of

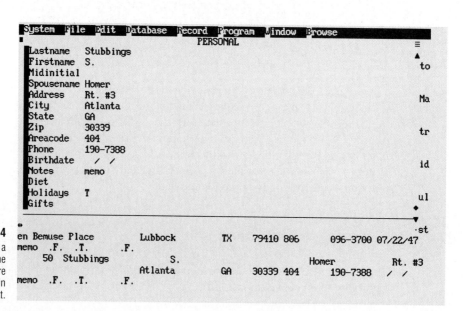

Figure 11-4
A single record in a database shown at the bottom of the screen are multiple records in columnar format.

the businesses that has ordered office supplies. Another file named STOCK might contain data about each order that has been placed with the regional distributor.

Within a database file, each of the records has the same set of fields (Figure 11-5). For example, each record in the CUSTOMER file would contain fields for the name of the business, the street address, the telephone number, a contact name, and the BVOS business account number.

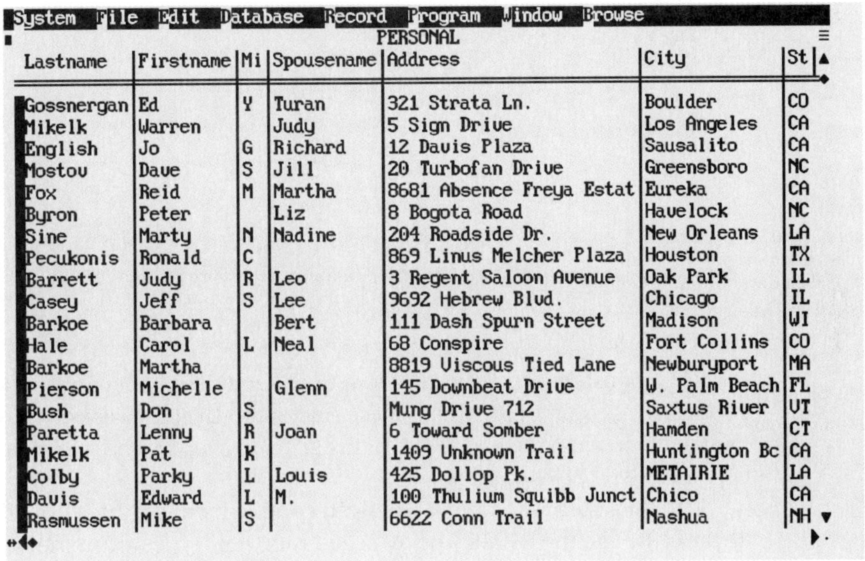

Lastname	Firstname	Mi	Spousename	Address	City	St
Gossnergan	Ed	Y	Turan	321 Strata Ln.	Boulder	CO
Mikelk	Warren		Judy	5 Sign Drive	Los Angeles	CA
English	Jo	G	Richard	12 Davis Plaza	Sausalito	CA
Mostov	Dave	S	Jill	20 Turbofan Drive	Greensboro	NC
Fox	Reid	M	Martha	8681 Absence Freya Estat	Eureka	CA
Byron	Peter		Liz	8 Bogota Road	Havelock	NC
Sine	Marty	N	Nadine	204 Roadside Dr.	New Orleans	LA
Pecukonis	Ronald	C		869 Linus Melcher Plaza	Houston	TX
Barrett	Judy	R	Leo	3 Regent Saloon Avenue	Oak Park	IL
Casey	Jeff	S	Lee	9692 Hebrew Blvd.	Chicago	IL
Barkoe	Barbara		Bert	111 Dash Spurn Street	Madison	WI
Hale	Carol	L	Neal	68 Conspire	Fort Collins	CO
Barkoe	Martha			8819 Viscous Tied Lane	Newburyport	MA
Pierson	Michelle		Glenn	145 Downbeat Drive	W. Palm Beach	FL
Bush	Don	S		Mung Drive 712	Saxtus River	VT
Paretta	Lenny	R	Joan	6 Toward Somber	Hamden	CT
Mikelk	Pat	K		1409 Unknown Trail	Huntington Bc	CA
Colby	Parky	L	Louis	425 Dollop Pk.	METAIRIE	LA
Davis	Edward	L	M.	100 Thulium Squibb Junct	Chico	CA
Rasmussen	Mike	S		6622 Conn Trail	Nashua	NH

Figure 11-5
This database file is displayed as a list. Each row is one record. The column headings indicate the fields that appear in every record.

Defining the Fields

Before any data can be entered into a database file, each of the fields that make up a record must be defined. Figuring out which fields to include can be critical. Unnecessary fields should be avoided; they waste both disk space and the time it takes to key data into them. At the same time, it is important not to omit any essential fields and to divide compound fields into their principal parts.

For example, say you are setting up the CUSTOMER database at BVOS (Figure 11-6 on the next page). In doing so, you find that some of the businesses that order from Buena Vista have P.O. boxes, and some do not. Rather than enter the P.O. box in an ADDRESS field, you decide to create a separate POBOX field. You reason that correspondence and billing should go the P.O. box, while deliveries should go to the street address. Besides, if BVOS ever needs to use a third-party delivery service, such as Federal Express or UPS, they will not be able to deliver to the P.O. box. Another important decision you make is to break up ADDRESS into STREET, CITY, STATE, and ZIP. After all, P.O. boxes still require the city, state, and ZIP code. Also, there may be instances in which BVOS wants to sort customers by ZIP code to save on postage fees (the Post Office charges less for bulk mail that is presorted by ZIP code).

After deciding which fields need to be included in the database, you need to decide on each field's name, size, and type. The **field name** is the label linked to a field. It should accurately describe the data that will go in that field. At the same time, a field name should be as short as possible without compromising the descriptiveness of the name. As an example, in a PERSONNEL database, LAST may be a better field name than LAST_NAME, simply because it is shorter. LN, however, might leave someone wondering what data is supposed to go in the field.

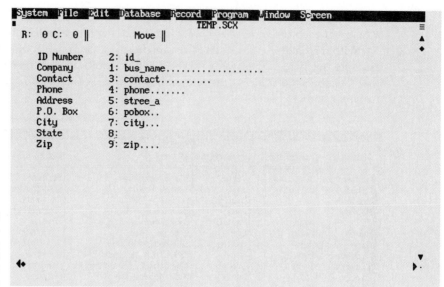

Figure 11-6
A blank form for your
CUSTOMER file. To set up
the file, you must define
the name, length, and type
of each field.

The next step is to define the length of each field. In general, a field should be just long enough to accommodate the longest data entry. In some cases, you will know exactly how long the field should be. STATE, for instance, can always be two characters long. With other fields, you will have to guess.

The third step is to define the **field type**, which indicates how the data in the field can be processed by the DBMS. The most common field types are numeric, alphanumeric, logical, date, and time. In addition, memo and binary fields are sometimes included. The INVOICE file shown in Figure 11-7 includes several of these types .

Numeric Fields. **Numeric fields** contain numbers that can be used in calculations. For example, a PRICE field would be defined as numerical so that the data in it could be added or subtracted from other prices or dollar amounts. A QUANTITY field in an inventory database is another example of a numeric field.

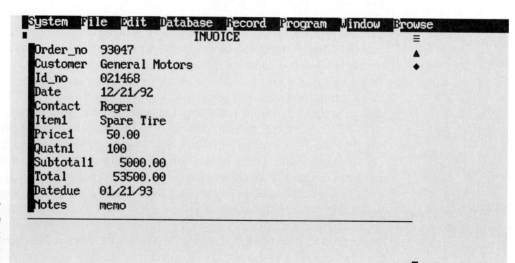

Figure 11-7
This file includes four of
the major field types:
numeric, alphanumeric,
date, and memo.

Alphanumeric Fields. An **alphanumeric field** can contain virtually any symbol on the keyboard: numbers, letters, punctuation, and so on. Fields such as NAME and ADDRESS would be defined as alphanumeric. In addition, a field like ID# (which contains a Social Security number or business identification number) would also be defined as alphanumeric, even though it consists entirely of numbers, because the numbers would never be used in calculations.

Logical Fields. **Logical fields** consist of a single character, which is used to specify a logical condition true or false. For example, PAID? might be a logical field on an electronic purchase order. The field would accept one of only two characters, Y or N (for *yes* or *no*). The contents of the field could be used in if-then conditions to figure total billing for a customer at the end of the month.

Date and Time Fields. **Date fields** and **time fields** allow users to enter a date or time in a standard format. The computer converts the date or time to a number that it can use to make comparisons. Thus, the contents of a DATE_PURCH (date purchased) field can be subtracted from a DATE_PAID field to determine if a customer owes a late payment charge.

Other Fields. **Memo fields** are text-based fields that allow users to enter notes. **Binary fields** and **graphic fields** can contain someone's photograph or fingerprints. Databases used by state motor vehicle departments often include these two fields.

Creating a Data Dictionary. Setting up a data dictionary for your database management system helps ensure data integrity and accuracy. A **data dictionary**, according to Freedman's *The Computer Glossary*, is itself a database — one that contains the name, type, range, source, and authorization access for every data element in another database or set of databases. It also provides information about which applications use the data and how. The data dictionary can be used as an information system for management and documentation, or it can be used to actually control the operation of the database management system.

Designing the Database Structure

After you decide which fields to include in a database, give them names, and decide their size and type, your next step is to decide on the structure of the database. This decision may be the most important one in the entire set-up process, because it will have a profound affect on the accessibility of the data. The decision should go hand in hand with the database software (the DBMS) that you choose. Database packages have very different capabilities in terms of creating various types of structures.

There are five common database structures: hierarchical, network, relational, flat-file, and hypermedia.

Hierarchical Databases. The **hierarchical database**, the oldest and simplest structure, most closely resembles the file cabinet system of organization. The structure, when diagrammed, looks like a family tree (Figure 11-8 on the next page). Each record and file can be related to only one parent, though it can be related to many children. This structure is the most rigid type of database: It is difficult to change and difficult to query. Setting up such a database requires defining all the hierarchical relationships in advance by linking the records in different files. Retrieving a piece of data requires either knowing where the data is stored in the hierarchy or wading through a lengthy search process.

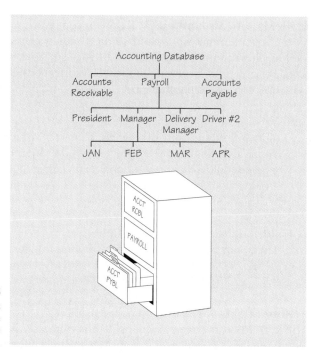

Figure 11-8
A hierarchical database is
organized in much the
same way as files in a file
cabinet.

The hierarchical structure is no longer as widely used as it once was, and it is most often found on mainframe databases. Nevertheless, it is appropriate for certain types of data, such as personnel databases in large corporations, where each employee has a specific place within a group, department, and division. To access data about a specific employee, you would first identify the division, department, and group in which the person works. However, storing data in this way would make it difficult to search for all of the employees that, for example, had salaries over $30,000 per year. Doing so would require searching through every branch of the hierarchical tree.

Network Databases.   The network structure is related to the hierarchical structure but is slightly more flexible. In the **network database**, which is shown in Figure 11-9, records in one file can be linked to several records of another file. This arrangement works well for systems in which people or events belong to several groups simultaneously. For example, in a database that keeps track of student scheduling at a school, each student might be enrolled in six different classes. Using a network arrangement would allow you not only to ask what students are in a particular class, but also to ask what classes a particular student is in. Nevertheless, other types of queries, such as finding all students with a 3.0 minimum grade-point average, would still be difficult to complete.

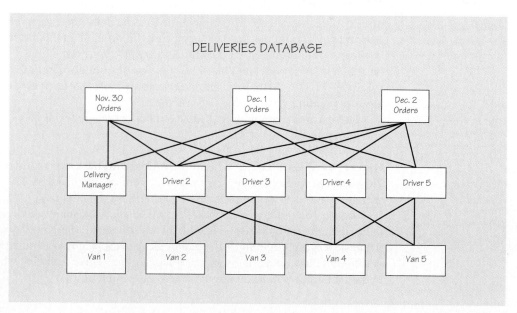

Figure 11-9
A network database.

Relational Databases. To overcome the accessibility problems associated with hierarchical and network databases, many modern databases adhere to the relational model, an example of which is diagrammed in Figure 11-10. The relational database was developed at IBM by E. F. Codd in 1971. In a **relational database**, data is stored in tables, which are called **relations**. Each relation equals a single file. The fields in the file make up the columns of the table, and the records make up the rows. The data in any two tables that share a common field can be compared, and the data in each is accessible from the other. For example, the key field that links data about people in many government databases is the Social Security number.

Customer File

BUS #	NAME	CONTACT	ADDRESS	ADDRESS	CITY	ST	ZIP	PHONE
0011	Asym	M. Fong	1 Broad	1 Broad	SF	CA	941212	726-3400
0012	Attas	Z. Zimmer	17 Market	17 Market	SF	CA	94118	713-2233
0013	Bayre	S. Payne	456 16th	456 16th	SF	CA	94118	655-0220
0014	Best	M. Stiles	72 Taylor	72 Taylor	SF	CA	94123	456-0020

Orders File

ORDER #	DATE	NAME	ITEM 1	QTY 1	ITEM 2	QTY 2	ITEMS
0723	11-28	Vacco.	00231	1	26135	25	—
0724	11-28	Storm	01462	10	02217	1	—
0725	11-28	Bayre	07220	1	05146	1	77335
0726	11-28	Westl.	07220	5	23440	10	74096
0727	11-28	Transi.	11420	50	72435	1	—
0728	11-28	Force	51173	1	01105	10	00223

Figure 11-10
The relational model. Files are organized into tables. Data from two files with the same field can be compared and used at the same time.

The relational database offers many capabilities that were not possible with previous structures. Let's use the BVOS inventory database to demonstrate just one of these possibilities (Figure 11-11 on the next page). Say you have created the CUSTOMER file, which contains the names and addresses of all businesses that buy supplies from BVOS. Next you create the ORDERS file, which contains a record of each customer order, including the items ordered, their prices, the date and time of the order, and the name of the company making the order. A record in the ORDERS file is created by a salesperson each time a new order is received. When the printed order is created to accompany the delivery, the printed form contains the data in the order record, plus the name and address of the company so the delivery driver knows exactly where to take the order. The salesperson does not need to fill out the address of the business, however, because the ORDERS file can be compared to the CUSTOMER file through the field that specifies the name of the business. The address that accompanies that business in the CUSTOMER file is then automatically copied onto the printed order form for the customer.

Most of the major DBMS packages marketed for the microcomputer, such as dBASE IV, Paradox, and FoxBase, are capable of creating relational databases.

Flat-File Databases. The flat-file model is a subset of the relational database model, with limited functionality. **Flat-file databases** are organized into tables, but there are no capabilities for comparing the data in common fields between tables (Figure 11-12 on the next page). In other words, flat-file databases are relational databases that consist of a single file.

Customer File

BUS #	NAME	CONTACT	ADDRESS	ADDRESS	CITY	ST	ZIP	PHONE
0011	Asym	M. Fong	1 Broad	1 Broad	SF	CA	941212	726-3400
0012	Attas	Z. Zimmer	17 Market	17 Market	SF	CA	94118	713-2233
0013	Bayre	S. Payne	456 16th	456 16th	SF	CA	94118	655-0220
0014	Best	M. Stiles	72 Taylor	72 Taylor	SF	CA	94123	456-0020

Orders File

ORDER #	DATE	NAME	ITEM 1	QTY 1	ITEM 2	QTY 2	ITEMS
0723	11-28	Vacco.	00231	1	26135	25	—
0724	11-28	Storm	01462	10	02217	1	—
0725	11-28	Bayre	07220	1	05146	1	77335
0726	11-28	Westl.	07220	5	23440	10	74096
0727	11-28	Transi.	11420	50	72435	1	—
0728	11-28	Force	51173	1	01105	10	00223

DELIVERY STATEMENT

Bayrest Mattress
456 16th
San Francisco, CA 94118
(415) 655-0220

Order #: 0725
Date of order: Nov. 28, 1993

Item		Qty.	Price
Desklamp	07220	1	12.95
File Cab.	05146	1	45.50
File Fold	77335	50	22.75
Sub tot.			81.20
Tax			6.54
Total			87.74

Figure 11-11
The DELIVERY STATEMENT combines data from two relations, the CUSTOMER file and the ORDER file.

Flat-file DBMSs are common among integrated software packages, such as Microsoft Works and Claris Works. In addition, many spreadsheet packages include database capabilities, but these capabilities are limited to creating flat-file structures.

There are many cases in which a flat-file structure is sufficient. For example, if you wanted to create an inventory of the valuable items in your home, you could create it with a flat-file structure. The file could contain one record for each item, with fields for the item name, where it was purchased, the purchase date, and the cost.

Employees

Soc. Sec. #	L. Name	F. Name	Phone	Address	City	Zip
523-41-0727	Lee	Tory	253-7720	5 Blue Ct.	Sausalito	94252
711-73-2486	Yep	Lisa	741-0231	42A Greer	Fremont	95110
141-71-5901	Sorensen	Scott	741-5960	103 Pleasant	San Mateo	94335
224-05-9207	Malecki	Gwen	525-6609	9230 48th Ave.	San Francisco	94116
293-21-7720	Vasquez	Raul	821-5137	4320 Mission	Daly City	94017
566-02-5572	Drobnis	Gloria	741-5532	2 Glenellen	Daly City	94012

Figure 11-12
The flat-file model is similar to the relational model, but only one file is accessible at a time.

Hypermedia Databases.   Hypermedia software is actually a form of DBMS, although there are significant differences between **hypermedia databases** and the other structures we have mentioned. The most well-known hypermedia package is HyperCard, a version of which is supplied with every Macintosh. A similar package available for the PC is Linkway.

In HyperCard, each file consists of a set of cards called a **stack**. A card is therefore the HyperCard equivalent of a record, but there are many important differences. Rather than being a group of fields, a card is a graphical area that can include fields, text, or graphic images.

In addition to the freedom afforded the person creating each card, the flexibility of a HyperCard database is enhanced by the ability to create buttons. A **button** links one card to another card in the same stack or a different stack. When a user clicks on a button with the mouse, the card that it is linked to is immediately displayed. It is even possible to link a button to a sound file that plays a recording.

The uses for hypermedia software are many and varied. One of the most popular is in education; hypermedia databases can be used as teaching tools that allow maximum freedom for the student. For instance, Broderbund Software publishes a geometry tutorial written in HyperCard. The student steps through the stack, clicking on buttons to request examples or to watch animated graphic displays. The software can test the student's knowledge and automatically reteach concepts that were not mastered.

Macintosh software manuals are now often provided in the form of HyperCard stacks. Users can look up subjects in an electronic index and click on the subject they need help on. When reading a definition on screen, users can click on highlighted words to get help on terms they don't understand or of which they aren't sure.

Comprehension Questions

1. What basic fact about database structure guarantees that a table in a relational database is always neatly rectangular?
2. In what way is a hypermedia database similar to a relational database?
3. Are date and time fields more like alphanumeric fields or numeric fields? Why?

Using What You Know

1. Describe two flat-file databases that you could set up for your personal use at BVOS (that is, not connected to the central inventory database).
2. The PERSONNEL file at BVOS contains the following fields: LAST, FIRST, MI, M/F, POBOX, STREET, CITY, STATE, ZIP, AREACODE, TEL#, DOB (date of birth), and SSN (Social Security number). Name the field type for each and give a brief justification (one sentence) for each answer.
3. Describe one way that you might use a hypermedia database at BVOS.

Using a Database

Knowing how to use a database to obtain information is a valuable skill. Unfortunately, there are so many database models and so many methods for getting information out of them that covering this topic completely is beyond the scope of this book. There are, however, a few techniques that you should know about: sorting and indexing, querying, and generating reports.

These three techniques are most appropriate for relational and flat-file databases. They do not apply directly to hypermedia databases.

Sorting and Indexing

One valuable capability of a database is the user's ability to obtain lists of related data. With a database, you could generate such a list in a matter of seconds.

The danger in generating a list is that, unless you specify otherwise, the database will list the records in the order in which they were entered. Often, this order is not particularly useful. A more appropriate list order can be generated by sorting or indexing the records.

In **sorting** the records in a database, you are actually changing their sequence. Say you add a record to the CUSTOMER database file each time a new customer orders supplies. When you enter the new customer, the DBMS adds the new record to the end of the file. If you were to sort the file alphabetically by the names of the businesses, the order of the records in the file would change. The DBMS actually rewrites the file onto the storage medium in the new order.

Indexing is a more flexible method for rearranging the appearance of records, because indexing does not actually change the order of the records. Instead, an indexed group of records represents a temporary order created according to the alphabetical or numerical order of one or more fields. To avoid rewriting the data file, the DBMS creates a second file, which stores the indexed field in the desired order, with pointers that tell the location of each record in the actual data file. Most DBMSs are capable of maintaining several indexes, so the user can quickly display a number of arrangements.

Querying the Database

Querying a database allows the user to obtain specific information that meets desired criteria. The simplest type of data query is the search. In a search, the user asks the DBMS to find a specific record or data item. More complicated queries generally involve collecting a set of records that are related in some way.

The best way to understand the possibilities of a data query is to see a few examples. The example shown in Figure 11-13a is written for dBASE in the fourth-generation query language that is used with DBMSs. A **query language** is any high-level language that is built into a DBMS for the purpose of interacting directly with the database. Figures 11-13b and 11-13c demonstrate creating a query by example in Approach, a Windows-based DBMS.

Generating Reports

A database cannot be printed as simply as a document created in a word processor. Printing a database requires generating a **report** using the DBMS's report writer (Figure 11-14 on page 252). Before a report can be printed, the user must state exactly what information should appear in it and how it should be arranged. Often, the creation of a report is done in conjunction with data obtained using an index (or sort), a query, or both.

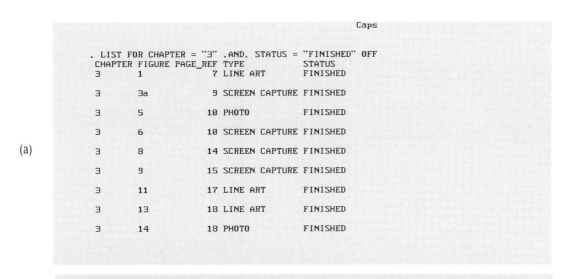

(a)

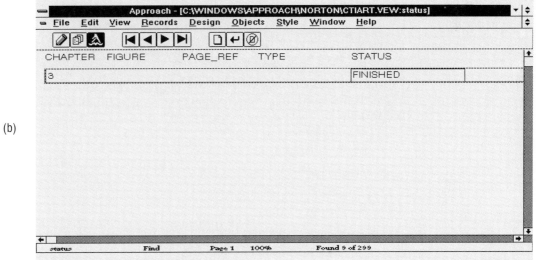

(b)

(c)

Figure 11-13

(a) The query language built into dBASE IV is a relatively intuitive 4GL. Each of these screens shows (b) a query and (c) its results.

CHAPTER 7 ART FIGURES STATUS REPORT

CHAP#	FIG#	PAGE	TYPE	STATUS	DESCRIPTION
7	1	46	LINE ART	FINISHED	IBM 101 keyboard.
7	2	46	LINE ART	FINISHED	Alphanumeric keys.
7	3a	47	LINE ART	FINISHED	Mac SHIFT, OPTION and COMMAND keys.
7	3b	47	LINE ART	FINISHED	IBM 101 SHIFT, CONTROL and ALTERNATE keys.
7	4	48	LINE ART	FINISHED	Function keys.
7	5	49	LINE ART	FINISHED	Cursor control keys.
7	6	49	LINE ART	FINISHED	Numeric keypad.
7	7	50	LINE ART	FINISHED	Keyboard lights.
7	8	50	PHOTO	FINISHED	Data entry employee.
7	9	51	PHOTO	FINISHED	TONY ergonomic keyboard.
7	10	51	LINE ART	FINISHED	Person at computer showing healthy position.
7	11	53	PHOTO	FINISHED	Some mice.
7	13	55	PHOTO	FINISHED	Powerbook.
7	14	55	PHOTO	FINISHED	Light pen.
7	15	55	PHOTO	FINISHED	Digitizer tablet.
7	16	56	PHOTO	FINISHED	Customer using touch screen.
7	17	58	PHOTO	FINISHED	Flatbed scanner.
7	18	59	PHOTO	FINISHED	Bar code reader.
7	20	62	LINE ART	FINISHED	Schematic of screen as grid of pixels.
7	21	62	LINE ART	FINISHED	Cathode ray tube diagram.
7	22	63	LINE ART	FINISHED	Side views of CRT and flat-panel.
7	23	64	LINE ART	FINISHED	LCD pixels with and without current.
7	24	64	PHOTO	FINISHED	Various monitors.
7	25	65	PHOTO	FINISHED	Some Mac monitors.
7	26	71	LINE ART	FINISHED	9 pin vs. 24 pin print.
7	27	71	PHOTO	FINISHED	A common dot-matrix printer.
7	28	72	LINE ART	FINISHED	Ink-jet printer.
7	29	72	LINE ART	FINISHED	Laser printer.
7	30	72	PHOTO	FINISHED	Laser printer.
7	31	73	PHOTO	FINISHED	Close-up of outputs of 24-pin NLQ dot matrix, 300 dpi ink-jet and 600 dpi inkjet.
7	32	76	TEXT FIG	FINISHED	The word PostScript in various fonts.

Figure 11-14

To create a report, the user of a database manager must identify exactly what the report should include and how it should be formatted.

The Goals of a Database

With the ability to sort, index, query, and generate reports, the electronic database provides the user with a vastly improved solution over the paper-based office for five major reasons. It improves:

- Data efficiency
- Data integrity
- Access flexibility
- Data independence
- Data security

These advantages are the goals of database management systems. However, not all DBMSs achieve them equally well. For example, the mainframe databases of the 1960s did not provide nearly the same access flexibility as the relational databases that can be created on today's powerful microcomputers using a modern DBMS. Let's examine each of these goals more closely.

Data Efficiency

The first advantage of a database over paper records is that the database can eliminate the replication of information. People in an organization often need the same data at the same time. For example, at BVOS, the inventory manager might be using all of the current month's orders from a certain customer to create an invoice for billing. At the same time, the stockroom might be filling the latest order. The sales office might also need a copy of the latest order to answer questions from the customer. Without an electronic database, every order taken by the sales force would have to be copied immediately so that records could be kept in the sales office, orders could be filled by the stockroom, and billing and inventory could be managed by the inventory manager.

Creating so many copies is both wasteful and time consuming. By storing all records in a central database, multiple copies can be eliminated. The same data can be accessed simultaneously by all departments.

Data Integrity

Beyond being wasteful, keeping multiple copies of data in an office is dangerous. If there are three copies of an order floating around the office, which one is the master copy? If the customer calls back to make a minor change to the order and the copies are already dispersed around the office, should the salesperson find all the copies and make the change to each of them? The biggest problem with data redundancy is that it leads to incorrect, inconsistent, and outdated data.

With a centralized database, however, the salesperson making the change to the order could make the change to the only copy that exists — the master copy in the database. If the order had already been filled by the stockroom, that information would be apparent in the database, and the salesperson would have access to this up-to-date information so that the customer could be informed.

Access Flexibility

A third advantage of using an electronic database is the flexibility with which data can be retrieved. If BVOS were a paper office, the data related to customer orders would be on the order forms filled out by the salespeople. To keep track of how many reams of copier paper had been ordered in the last week, the inventory manager would have to look at all the orders that had been filled out. With a database and a DBMS, however, the inventory manager can retrieve data in whatever form she needs it. If she needs to know how many reams of paper have been ordered, she should be able to determine exactly that, without having to go through all of the other data related to each individual order. In fact, finding such data might require just a few keystrokes.

The biggest improvements in DBMSs over the past 30 years have been toward the goal of access flexibility. As you have seen, the design of the relational database is especially conducive to flexibility. Older hierarchical databases were much less flexible.

Data Independence

Related to the advantage of data flexibility is data independence. Data independence means that the data itself is independent of the database application that uses it. This simply means that the database is not the same thing as the DBMS. The database is the data itself and its organizing structure. The DBMS is the management software and all of the programs that have been created with it to access the database. Data independence allows the user to add, delete, and change data within a database, without affecting the programs that have been written to access the database.

Data Security

The final goal of the DBMS is the ability to control who can access data. This ability is valuable in keeping data from being intentionally or inadvertently changed and in keeping sensitive data hidden from view. For example, the only people who should be allowed to create or change a customer order at BVOS are the salespeople. Allowing anyone else to change an order could lead to errors in filling the order. As another example, you and your inventory manager should be the only people who have access to employee wages. By limiting access privileges, employees could access an employee database to find out someone's phone number, but they could be prevented from seeing that person's salary. Today, organizations can be held financially or criminally liable if sensitive data about employees or customers is stolen or misused.

The Role of the Database Administrator

In the information age in which we live, the database of a company can be its most valuable asset. Therefore, a database needs to be managed and cared for as a critical component of the business. Large companies that can afford a full-time employee for the job often hire a **database administrator** (Figure 11-15). Even smaller businesses find it valuable to appoint the role of database administrator to a single person.

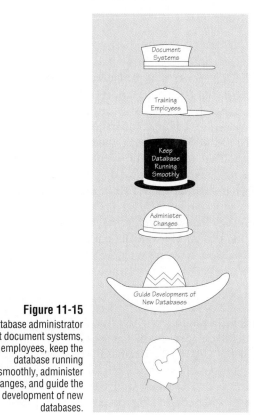

One of the major responsibilities of this job is documenting the various database systems used in the organization. This documentation lists what data is available, how it is accessed, how it is formatted, and what programs use it. The database administrator also provides training to employees who need to use the database.

In addition to documentation and employee support, the database administrator is charged with monitoring and tuning the database to keep it running smoothly and quickly. Databases, especially those with high transaction volumes, can become cluttered with old data fields. In most database systems, when a record is deleted, it is simply marked as being deleted, but the space that the record took up on the hard disk is still reserved. Periodically, the database administrator must repack and reindex the database to improve performance. If this is not done, it takes longer and longer for data to be retrieved from the system.

Any major changes that need to be made to the database are either handled or supervised by the database administrator. Supervising changes involves investigating what programs or departments will be affected by the change and notifying the relevant users. If someone requests a change that will adversely affect certain programs or the work of certain employees, the database administrator must arbitrate the conflicts.

Finally, the database administrator guides the development of new databases and new database applications. It is always important for new applications to make the best possible use of an existing database. When it comes to creating new databases, the administrator's knowledge is a valuable resource, and this person should be consulted in creating the most efficient and accessible design.

Figure 11-15
The database administrator must document systems, train employees, keep the database running smoothly, administer changes, and guide the development of new databases.

Database Threats to Personal Privacy

The power of the database has unleashed an incredible array of business opportunities. The ability to keep track of large amounts of data and the ability to link database files in a relational structure has spawned — among other ventures — the mailing list industry. Mailing lists are incredibly valuable to businesses because they can help target customers. On the other hand, the same industry is often abhorred by consumers because it is responsible for a large percentage of all junk mail and unsolicited phone calls.

People often find getting onto a mailing list a mysterious phenomenon. Consumers may suddenly receive a barrage of solicitations without knowing why. Often, it is because they have subscribed to a magazine, filled out an application for a commercial product or service, or completed a warranty card for a new product. Many consumers believe that filling out the warranty registration card included with many products is the only way to guarantee service. In fact, however, if a warranty exists, it is in effect when you purchase a product, and the bill of sale or receipt acts as proof of purchase. The purpose of warranty cards is to help companies collect data about who is buying their products. Once they have collected this data, they can sort, query, and even sell it to other companies without the consumer's knowledge.

The availability of information can affect your life in much more serious ways than mere junk mail and phone calls. Some companies keep credit histories on virtually every adult in the country. When you apply for a loan or a credit card or try to rent a house, you can be sure that someone will check your credit history. Employers run credit checks and criminal history investigations to judge the honesty of potential employees. Doctors can see if a patient has ever sued another doctor for malpractice. Landlords can check a database to see if another landlord has ever filed a complaint against a prospective tenant.

Minor data entry errors or slight misunderstandings can make these records grossly inaccurate, but they are nevertheless used to make important decisions. Though it is difficult to avoid mailing lists and corporate databases completely, it is worthwhile to monitor new developments. Infringements on personal privacy are a growing concern, and privacy law is expanding to keep up with advancements in database technology. There is even some momentum toward creating a fundamental right to privacy with an amendment to the Bill of Rights. Professor Lawrence Tribe, a noted legal scholar at Harvard University, has proposed just such an amendment (Table 11-1).

Table 11-1
Lawrence Tribe's proposed amendment to the Constitution.

Professor Lawrence Tribe's proposed 27th amendment:
This Constitution's protections for the freedoms of speech, press, petition, and assembly, and its protections against unreasonable searches and seizures and the deprivation of life, liberty, or property without due process of law, shall be construed as fully applicable without regard to the technological method or medium through which information content is generated, stored, altered, transmitted, or controlled.

Comprehension Questions

1. What are the pros and cons of filling out a registration card for a new piece of software?
2. What steps must be taken to print an alphabetical list of customers whose ZIP code is 94121?
3. Are programming skills required of the database administrator? Why or why not?

Using What You Know

1. What major field of study in college would qualify a person to be a database administrator?
2. How does the growing power of LAN servers help to make advanced database capabilities more feasible for small businesses?
3. Describe three ways in which data security will be a critical issue for the BVOS inventory database.

Summary Points

Managing Data at BVOS
☐ The BVOS inventory database is a vital record of daily transaction for the business.

Managing Data in a Paper-Based Office
☐ Data in a paper-based office is organized in files that are placed in folders within a file cabinet.

Managing Data in the Computer Age
☐ The computer allows data to be organized in databases, which are more flexible, more reliable, and require less labor than a paper-based system.

Creating a Database
☐ A database that has been set up well will come close to achieving the five goals.

The Three Basic Elements of a Database
☐ A database is subdivided into files, records, and fields.
☐ Each record contains data about a thing or an event, and every record in a file contains the same fields.

Defining the Fields
☐ A balance must be struck to include all necessary fields without wasting space or time.
☐ Field names should be both descriptive and short.
☐ Fields should be just long enough to accommodate the longest entry.

Numeric Fields
☐ Numeric fields contain numbers that can be used in calculations.

Alphanumeric Fields
☐ Alphanumeric fields can contain any keyboard symbol and cannot be used in calculations.

Logical Fields
☐ Logical fields contain a single character to specify a true or false condition.

Date and Time Fields

☐ Date and time fields allow data to be entered in their standard formats, but also allow the data in the fields to be compared.

Other Fields

☐ Memo fields and binary or graphic fields allow notes, photos, and graphics to be entered.

Creating a Data Dictionary

☐ A data dictionary is a database that helps organize another database.

Designing the Database Structure

☐ The structure of a database has a profound effect on the accessibility of the data.

Hierarchical Databases

☐ The hierarchical structure is the most rigid, following the file-cabinet model.

Network Databases

☐ The network structure is similar to the hierarchical, but multiple links to records in other files are allowed.

Relational Databases

☐ Relational databases organize files into tables; tables with common fields can be compared so that data in one is accessible to another.

☐ Most modern DBMS packages adhere to the relational model because it is more flexible than previous models.

Flat-File Databases

☐ The flat-file structure also relies on tables of data, but no comparisons can be made between files.

Hypermedia Databases

☐ Hypermedia software packages, such as HyperCard, are used to create stacks of cards, which can include fields, text, or graphics.

☐ Cards in a stack can be linked with buttons.

Using a Database

Sorting and Indexing

☐ Sorting a file rearranges the actual order of the records in the file.

☐ Indexing a file creates an index that lists an alternate arrangement that can be displayed.

Querying the Database

☐ Data is selectively displayed with a query, which finds data that meets certain criteria.

Generating Reports

☐ For a database to be printed, the user must generate a report.

☐ Reports are often created in conjunction with indexes and queries.

The Goals of a Database

☐ The goals of a DBMS are maximizing the five advantages that the database has over a paper-based system.

Data Efficiency

☐ A database allows for a single electronic copy of data, which can be shared among users, thus reducing data redundancy.

Data Integrity

☐ The centralization of data in a database leads to more correct, consistent, and current data.

Access Flexibility

☐ A good DBMS allows data to be retrieved in the form in which it is needed.

☐ The biggest improvements in DBMSs have been in access flexibility.

Data Independence

☐ Data independence is the separation of the data from the programs that use it.

Data Security

☐ A DBMS should enable the person who sets up the database to control who has access to it.

The Role of the Database Administrator

☐ An organization's database administrator manages and maintains the company's databases.

☐ The administrator's duties often include documenting the database, training employees, repacking and fine-tuning the database, making employees aware of changes, arbitrating conflicts, and helping with the development of new databases.

Database Threats to Personal Privacy

☐ The power of the database has spawned the direct mail industry, as well as other information-dependent businesses.

☐ The availability of information about people can dramatically affect their lives, and the field of privacy law is growing to keep up with increasing database power.

Knowing the Facts

True/False

1. Maximizing data integrity means ensuring that data is correct, consistent, and current.
2. Greater redundancy of data leads to greater data integrity.
3. The size of a field should represent the average between the largest and smallest data items that will be entered in that field.
4. Access flexibility with a relational database is generally better than with a network database.
5. In a large company, all reports should be generated by the database administrator to ensure data integrity.
6. The simplest type of data query is the search.
7. Filling out a warranty registration card has no effect on whether or not a product is under warranty.
8. A flat-file database may contain any number of files.
9. Sorting is more cumbersome than indexing, because sorting creates a second file that contains the field being sorted.
10. For a database to be printed, a query must be generated.

Short Answer

1. _____ databases are a type of relational database that does not allow comparisons between tables.
2. E. F. Codd developed the _____ for IBM in 1971.
3. A version of _____, a hypermedia software package, comes with every Macintosh.
4. The _____ industry has been spawned by the capabilities of modern DBMSs.
5. Improvements in data integrity are possible with reductions in data _____.
6. Limiting access privileges is one way to improve data _____.
7. The field type of a field containing a street address should be _____.
8. A _____ field (indicate type) lists whether a condition is true or false.
9 What database structure most closely resembles the organization of a file cabinet?
10. A _____ is a data search or a request for data that meets a given criteria or set of criteria.

Answers

True/False

1. T
2. F
3. F
4. T
5. F
6. T
7. T
8. F
9. F
10. F

Short Answer

1. Flat-file
2. relational database
3. HyperCard
4. mailing list
5. redundancy
6. security
7. alphanumeric
8. logical
9. hierarchical
10. query

Challenging Your Understanding

1. One of the most challenging problems facing data processing managers is the question of when to remove data from a database. After all, you cannot keep data around forever. It becomes too difficult to manage and it eventually becomes irrelevant. What rules would you use to remove data from a database?

2. Can you think of any data that should not be collected in a database? Give some examples and the consequences of storing that data.

3. The relational database design creates a flexible database that can be used to answer questions that may arise in the future, as well as those at hand. Why is this advantage important? Why can't users specify all of the required information before a database is constructed?

4. Sorting is the most common activity performed on a business computer. Why is sorting more common than querying?

5. Your telephone number is not your property. The number is "owned" by the telephone company. A company can own database hardware and software, but the ownership of the data is less clear. Think about a database that contains information about consumer purchase behaviors. Who owns the data in that database — the consumers or the company that collected the data? Why?

Information Systems for Business

Key Terms

accounts payable
accounts receivable
computer-aided design (CAD)
computer-aided manufacturing (CAM)
decision support system (DSS)
demand reports
downsizing
E-mail
exception reports
flaming
general ledger
information system
job displacement
job enlargement
just-in-time (JIT) manufacturing
management information systems (MIS)
middle-level managers
operations managers
outsourcing
payroll
performance monitoring
scheduled reports
quality control
upper-level managers
voice mail

Objectives

In this chapter you will learn to:

- Define the term *information system*
- Identify the three levels of management and describe the types of information required by each
- Describe operational information systems and give examples of them in production and accounting departments
- Describe management information systems and decision support systems
- Explain how E-mail works and identify its advantages and disadvantages
- Describe voice mail
- Explain how computerized information systems relate to quality control, job displacement, job enlargement, and performance monitoring
- Identify the advantages of downsizing and outsourcing

Information Systems in Large Businesses

Throughout this book, we have focused on the needs of Buena Vista Office Supply to explain how computers are used in business. In these last two chapters, we look more closely at larger businesses. Corporations and large organizations are complex enough to require highly developed information systems to coordinate their activities. In this chapter, we look at the full range of information systems that exist to give you a better idea of how computers and technology support all aspects of a large company.

What Is an Information System?

The term **information system** has two meanings, depending on who you ask for the definition. If you ask computer users in business, they may give you the more narrow definition. Users tend to think of an information system is a means of obtaining information from a company's database. The information system includes the database itself, the means for getting data into the database, and the application programs that get data out in a useful format. If you ask an information systems (IS) professional, however, he or she may give you a more general definition: An information system is a path or set of established paths along which data travels through an organization.

For the most part, these two groups — general business users and IS professionals — are talking about the same thing. The most talked-about kinds of information system are those in which data is generated at the operations level of a business, collected in a database, and processed so that managers can glean information from it and make decisions. The broader definition, however, also includes information systems, such as electronic mail, in which data and information do not necessarily move up through the levels of management. Most of this chapter addresses information systems as defined by the first group. At the end of the chapter, however, we discuss these other types of information system that do not fit into the narrower definition.

Levels of Management and Their Needs for Information

To understand the purpose of an information system, it is helpful to see a standard diagram showing the levels of management in a company. A large business can be thought of as a pyramid, resting on a large foundation (Figure 12-1). This foundation represents the operations level of the company, which consists of workers organized into departments. There are five basic departments in many companies:

- The production department produces goods.
- The marketing department sells the goods that the production department makes, or it sells services.
- The research department develops new products or services and improves old ones.
- The personnel department hires new employees.
- The accounting department coordinates the financial needs of the company, including billing customers, paying for raw materials, and paying employees.

The pyramid that sits on top of this base of departments and their employees are the managers that run the company. The pyramid is divided into three levels:

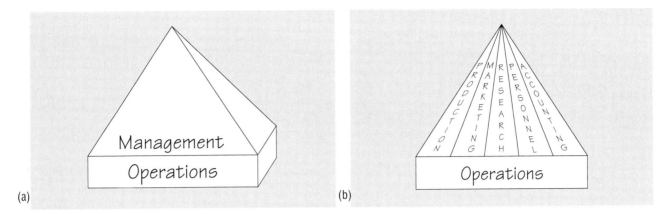

(a)   (b)

Figure 12-1
(a) Management is like a pyramid resting on the foundation of operations. (b) The operations and management levels are divided into departments.

- **Operations managers** supervise the daily operation of the company.
- **Middle-level managers** track operations over time and develop tactical plans to meet the objectives of upper-level management.
- **Upper-level managers**, or executives, oversee the entire company, monitor profits and losses, and determine the company's future by developing business strategies.

Each type of manager needs different kinds of information. Operations managers need information systems that allow them to keep track of details. Operations managers in production departments need to keep track of inventory (or availability of personnel, in the case of a service organization). Operations managers in accounting departments need to watch cash flow. The information systems that support these and other operations managers focus on the present and the immediate future. These managers make relatively structured decisions; certain sets of data require certain decisions. For example, when an operations manager in a production department finds that the inventory of raw materials has shrunk to a certain level, the manager orders new raw materials.

Middle-level managers need information systems that give them more long-term data. They do not need to monitor every minute aspect of their departments, but they need to synthesize a wide range of factors to make tactical decisions. Middle-level managers often require reports that summarize operational conditions or track them over time. They make more open-ended, less structured decisions than those made by operations managers. They combine facts, gained from the information systems that serve them, with their own expertise to carry out the strategies dictated by executives.

Upper-level managers make relatively unstructured decisions; they require more intangible factors, such as personal experience and company goals and strategies, so their need for information can vary greatly. They must always be concerned with long-term growth. Upper-level managers also tend to be more concerned with the relationships between departments than are middle-level managers, who still function at the departmental level.

As you move up the pyramid, managers need an increasing amount of data from outside the organization — data about competitors, customers, markets, and the economy — as well as more and more summarized information from within the organization.

Comprehension Questions

1. If the whole country were considered one company, how could the U.S. Postal Service be considered an information system?

2. Would the Postal Service fit the narrow or broad definition of an information system?

3. What level of manager is likely to use information about the sales strategies of competitors?

Using What You Know

1. Describe where the various employees of BVOS fit into the business model described in the previous section.

2. You might say that BVOS has two main departments. What are they, and who works in them?

3. We named the five most common business departments, but there are many others. Name three other types of departments.

Information Systems for Operations Managers

The information systems that exist for operations managers, which are sometimes called transaction processing systems or electronic data processing systems, are as many and as varied as the managers' departments and the duties. To give you a general sense of what operational information systems do, let's look at two types and how they use computers.

Production Systems

When a production department generates a tangible good such as shoes or airplane engines, as opposed to a service such as advertising, the department performs a manufacturing process. Manufacturing a product involves the movement of raw materials through a process that transforms them into finished goods. For some products, the process can be incredibly complex. Imagine the production process in manufacturing an automobile. Computers are integrated into the manufacturing process at three levels: design, manufacturing, and inventory control.

CAD. **Computer-aided design**, or **CAD,** programs are used in both production and research departments to create electronic models of products before they are produced. CAD is often performed by users at expensive workstations with advanced input devices, such as light pens and digitizer tablets. With a CAD system, a designer can draft a product, create specifications for each part, and even test its functionality and strength (Figure 12-2). The result of a CAD design is a set of working drawings, a database that describes every dimension of every part of the product, and even a list of materials needed to make the product.

CAM and Robotics. Once a product has been designed using a CAD system, the database created by CAD can be used by a **computer-aided manufacturing**, or **CAM**, system. CAM actually has two meanings. The more colorful type of CAM is robotics: numerical control devices and process control devices. Recall that a robot is a computer that uses numerical input to create physical output. The simplest types of robots are actually numerical control devices. These are standard pieces of machinery, such as drills and lathes, that can be controlled with numerical input — sometimes coming directly from a CAD system — rather than operated manually (Figure 12-3). More advanced industrial robots are specifically designed to perform such duties as packing boxes, painting cars, and welding metal parts.

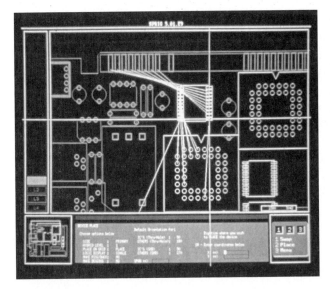

Figure 12-2 This electrical diagram was drawn using CAD software. The model is held in memory as a database.

Figure 12-3 This drill is referred to as a numerical control device because it is controlled with CAM software rather than operated manually.

Process control takes automation one step further by controlling a series of manufacturing steps, such as stages along an assembly line, with the help of a computer.

CAM and Inventory Management.   The other meaning of CAM involves using a computer to manage inventory. This type of CAM isn't as colorful as industrial robots, but it fits the strict definition of the term *information system* rather than the broad one. In some manufacturing processes, where computers have been extensively integrated, a CAM system can use the CAD database and list of materials to manage the inventory of raw materials needed for production and finished goods.

The most critical component of inventory management is forecasting when the inventory of raw materials will be depleted. Raw materials for the production process don't just appear on the delivery dock of a company. Someone must order them and schedule delivery. Raw materials that are not ordered on time or not delivered on time can jeopardize an entire production process.

The traditional method for dealing with this problem was to keep plenty of raw materials in inventory at all times. However, the more inventory a company has on its shelves, the more capital investment it has tied up in the production process. One alternative to keeping lots of raw materials inventory in stock is a technique mastered by Japanese companies called **just-in-time (JIT) manufacturing**. With a well-managed JIT system, a company runs out of raw materials just as the new supply arrives.

Accounting Systems

Computers were first used in business as tools for accounting. In fact, the machine that Hollerith created to help tabulate the 1890 census results was later manufactured and sold as an accounting device. Modern accounting information systems affect every part of the company and every level of management. Every accounting information system includes at least four databases:

- **Accounts receivable** keeps track of who owes the company money, how much they owe, and when the money is due.
- **Accounts payable** keeps track of who the company owes money to, how much is owed, and the terms of the debt.
- **Payroll** keeps track of the wages owed to each employee, plus insurance and retirement deductions, Social Security, and tax withholdings. The payroll system is actually a type of accounts payable that recognizes the company's short-term debt to employees.
- The **general ledger** integrates and summarizes the data in the other three systems.

Every one of these subsystems can be made more efficient with the help of computers. In fact, software is available to help businesses set up each of them. At the operations level, this software helps organize the information to aid in data entry and routine payments and billing. At higher management levels, the systems are used to create a number of accounting reports, including balance sheets, profit and loss records, and reports indicating the true cost of goods sold.

Information Systems for Middle and Upper Management

Middle-level and upper-level managers deal less with data input and more with process output and summaries of data entered at the operational level. In large corporations, the information systems designed to meet the needs of middle-level managers are sometimes called *management information systems*, although the same term is also used to mean any information system. Upper-level managers rely on *decision support systems* to help them generate business strategies.

Management Information Systems

A **management information system (MIS)** is an established process for generating reports that serve the needs of middle-level managers. Very little data goes into a company's database at this level of management. Middle managers obtain data from the databases in an effort to monitor and steer the company.

The role of the middle manager is served by three types of reports. **Scheduled reports** (Figure 12-4a) are generated regularly to keep middle managers abreast of the routine operations of the business. **Exception reports** (Figure 12-4b) are created in response to an unusual event or set of circumstances. Finally, **demand reports** (Figure 12-4c) are requested by middle managers when they want to see a specific set of data that is not displayed in other reports.

Decision Support Systems

Because upper-level managers make relatively unstructured decisions, the information systems that support them, called **decision support systems (DSS)**, tend to be oriented less toward reports and more toward generating answers to open-ended questions, such as questions about the efficacy of closing a factory or opening a new one. Like middle managers, executives get data out of a database rather than putting it in. But the data that upper-level managers get out of the database is not typically presented in standard formats. The format is more often tailored to answer the question being asked.

```
********************************************************************************
DATE:  2/05/93              UNITED TECHNOLOGIES INC                 PAGE:  1

                       JOB COST / MEMO ACCOUNTING

BRANCH:  SAN FRANCISCO                          DATES:  1/01/93 - 1/31/93
********************************************************************************

FILE NUMBER        REVENUE             ACTUAL COST          PROFIT
-----------        -------             -----------          ------
0048700            349.83                 299.83             50.00
0048701            232.00                 143.70             88.30
0048702            437.64                 322.64            115.00
0048703            833.07                 431.91            401.16
0048704            328.58                 313.99             14.59
0048705            374.51                 324.51             50.00
0048706            409.79                 359.79             50.00
0048707            981.31                 931.31             50.00
0048708            687.86                 637.86             50.00
0048709          1,103.40                 921.97            181.43
0048710          3,389.78               3,025.80            363.98
0048711            876.99                 755.99            121.00
0048712            494.00                 345.50            148.50
0048713            760.78                 642.29            118.49
0048714            474.63                 359.63            115.00
0048715            496.35                 391.35            105.00
0048716            360.56                 344.03             16.53
0048717              0.00                 180.44            180.44-
0048718            325.80                 311.58             14.22
0048719          1,111.90               1,153.22             41.32-
0048720            144.00                  31.15            112.85
0048721          1,002.58                 844.08            158.50
0048722            373.88                 225.38            148.50
0048723          2,713.46               2,570.11            143.35
0048724            510.16                 460.20             49.96
0048725            326.73                 276.73             50.00
0048726            318.41                 268.41             50.00
0048727            435.53                 302.53            133.00
```

```
********************************************************************************
DATE:  2/05/93              UNITED TECHNOLOGIES INC                 PAGE:  1

                       JOB COST / MEMO ACCOUNTING

BRANCH:  SAN FRANCISCO        EXCEPTION:  PROFIT < 0     DATES:  1/01/93 - 1/31/93
********************************************************************************

FILE NUMBER        REVENUE             ACTUAL COST          PROFIT
-----------        -------             -----------          ------
0048717              0.00                 180.44            180.44-
0048719          1,111.90               1,153.22             41.32-
0048734          1278.85                1328.90              50.05-
0048737            278.18                 293.97             15.79-
0048749            129.52                 284.52            155.00-
0048776          1,200.04               1,347.21            147.17-
0048781             76.55                 199.55            123.00-
0048782            172.41                 222.00             49.69-
0048801          1,500.32               1,506.75              6.43-
0048822             16.80                 185.30            168.50-
0048835              0.00                 186.40            186.40-
0048849            293.23                 473.00            180.77-
0048855            150.00                 225.33             75.33-
0048861            457.25                 460.45              3.20-
0048891            889.59                1010.80            121.21-
0048897            135.76                 235.70             99.94-
```

```
********************************************************************************
DATE:  2/05/93              UNITED TECHNOLOGIES INC                 PAGE:  1

                          A / R AGING REPORT

CUSTOMER TYPE:  TRADE CUSTOMER    FOR PERIOD ENDING:  02/93       TIME:  15:36:42
********************************************************************************

CUSTOMER CODE & NAME      PHONE#        CREDIT LIMIT

                                                               AGED BALANCE
        INVOICE # & DATE  INVOICE AMOUNT  BALANCE      0-30     31-60      61-90
--------------------------------------------------------------------------------

ABM341   ABM SYSTEMS      2124985983    5,000

  2345       1/13/93      568.34        568.34       568.34
  2467       1/18/93      345.87        345.87       345.87
  2491       1/23/93      448.43        448.43       448.43

         ****CUSTOMER TOTALS            1362.64      1362.64
              PERCENT OF TOTAL                       100

AHM656   A & H MANUFACTURING 4153459438 20,000

  1945      12/20/92      431.35        431.35                  431.35

         ****CUSTOMER TOTALS            431.35                  431.35
              PERCENT OF TOTAL                                  100

BRA198   BRAMBLEBUNT INC   2138476377   5,000

  1533      11/15/92       20.00         20.00                             20.00
  1562      11/15/92      200.00-       200.00-                           200.00-
  1961      12/20/92      635.64        635.64                  635.64
  1974      12/21/92      513.17        513.17                  513.17

         ****CUSTOMER TOTALS            968.81                 1148.81    180.00
              PERCENT OF TOTAL                                 118.6       18.6-

BRS233   BRANT SHIPPING    7072927689   17,000

  2231       1/6/93       476.50        476.50       476.50
  2301       1/8/93       261.23        261.23       261.23

         ****CUSTOMER TOTALS            747.73       747.73
              PERCENT OF TOTAL                       100

BTC346   BUILDTECH         2128476398   4,000

  1550      11/15/93      602.94        602.94                             602.94

         ****CUSTOMER TOTALS            602.94                             602.94
              PERCENT OF TOTAL                                             100
```

Figure 12-4
Examples of (a) a scheduled report, (b) an exception report, and (c) a demand report.

Decision support systems provide a user-friendly interface so that upper-level managers can obtain specific data without having to use the programming capabilities of the DBMS. In addition to the company's databases, the DSS may also have access to spreadsheet programs, statistical analysis programs, and analytical graphics software.

Comprehension Questions

1. What level of manager is likely to use a report comparing advertising costs to sales levels?

2. CAD is often used by both production and research departments. Can the same be said of CAM? Why or why not?

3. Why is JIT manufacturing more difficult to manage than traditional methods of inventory control?

Using What You Know

1. Describe what transactions are recorded in accounts receivable and accounts payable at BVOS.

2. Why do you think the user interface for a DSS tends to be friendlier than that of an MIS?

3. If you wanted a DSS for your work at BVOS, what kinds of information would you want to be able to get out of it?

Enterprise-Wide Information Systems

As we noted earlier in the chapter, not all information systems fit the narrow definition. The information systems we have discussed so far serve to automate business functions and to provide data so that managers can make informed decisions. With these types of systems, data is input at the operations level and travels up the pyramid to be used by managers. There are, however, less structured types of information systems that are used simply to communicate information. The most common types of information systems for communication are electronic mail and voice mail.

E-Mail

If a company has a network, it can be more efficient and more convenient for employees to communicate using the network rather than using memos and other paper-based methods of communication. Electronic mail, commonly called **E-mail**, is an information system that allows computer users to write, send, and read messages, such as the one shown in Figure 12-5, using a computer network. Local area networks allow workers within a business to send messages around the office. Wide area networks allow computer users at opposite ends of the country to trade messages.

Using E-Mail. To use E-mail, the person with whom you want to communicate must also have access to an E-mail system. Quite often, a user begins by entering a log-in identification and perhaps a system address, rather than his or her name. (Other systems require the user's

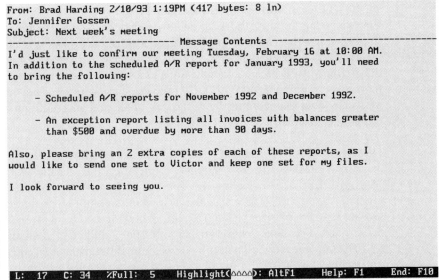

Figure 12-5

E-mail systems make cooperation and communication around the office much easier.

```
From: Brad Harding 2/10/93 1:19PM (417 bytes: 8 ln)
To: Jennifer Gossen
Subject: Next week's meeting
---------------------------- Message Contents -----------------------------
I'd just like to confirm our meeting Tuesday, February 16 at 10:00 AM.
In addition to the scheduled A/R report for January 1993, you'll need
to bring the following:

    - Scheduled A/R reports for November 1992 and December 1992.

    - An exception report listing all invoices with balances greater
      than $500 and overdue by more than 90 days.

Also, please bring an 2 extra copies of each of these reports, as I
would like to send one set to Victor and keep one set for my files.

I look forward to seeing you.



 L:  17   C: 34   %Full:  5    Highlight(▵▵▵▵): AltF1    Help: F1    End: F10
```

password.) The system address is a set of numbers and letters that identifies the electronic location of the user. As soon as you log in, the E-mail system tells you whether you have any messages waiting. If you do, you can read them, print them, save them, delete them, or forward them to another person.

To send a message, you must know the name or user ID and perhaps address of the person to whom you are sending the message (Figure 12-6). Some E-mail systems have directories that let you look up a person's address by looking up a last and first name. You type your message after you address it. If several people need to read the message, you can send the same message to several users simultaneously.

Advantages of E-mail.   E-mail has many advantages. Probably the most important is the speed of communication and the quality of detail that such a system permits. E-mail messages

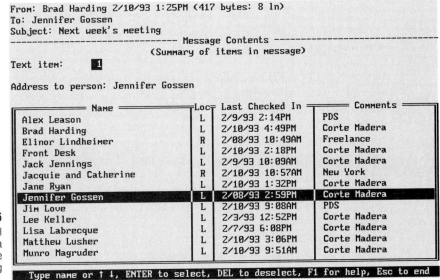

Figure 12-6

Sending an E-mail message is merely a matter of composing the message and knowing where you want to send it.

```
From: Brad Harding 2/10/93 1:25PM (417 bytes: 8 ln)
To: Jennifer Gossen
Subject: Next week's meeting
---------------------------- Message Contents -----------------------------
                   (Summary of items in message)

Text item:      █1

Address to person: Jennifer Gossen

  ====== Name ======= ┬Loc┬ Last Checked In ═══ ═══ Comments ═══
  │ Alex Leason        │ L │ 2/9/93  2:14PM  │ PDS            │
  │ Brad Harding       │ L │ 2/10/93 4:49PM  │ Corte Madera   │
  │ Elinor Lindheimer  │ R │ 2/08/93 10:49AM │ Freelance      │
  │ Front Desk         │ L │ 2/10/93 2:18PM  │ Corte Madera   │
  │ Jack Jennings      │ L │ 2/9/93  10:09AM │ Corte Madera   │
  │ Jacquie and Catherine│ R │ 2/10/93 10:57AM │ New York     │
  │ Jane Ryan          │ L │ 2/10/93 1:32PM  │ Corte Madera   │
  │ Jennifer Gossen    │ L │ 2/08/93 2:59PM  │ Corte Madera   │
  │ Jim Love           │ L │ 2/10/93 9:08AM  │ PDS            │
  │ Lee Keller         │ L │ 2/3/93  12:52PM │ Corte Madera   │
  │ Lisa Labrecque     │ L │ 2/7/93  6:08PM  │ Corte Madera   │
  │ Matthew Lusher     │ L │ 2/10/93 3:06PM  │ Corte Madera   │
  │ Munro Magruder     │ L │ 2/10/93 9:51AM  │ Corte Madera   │

  Type name or ↑ ↓, ENTER to select, DEL to deselect, F1 for help, Esc to end
```

can be sent across the country cheaply and in a matter of seconds. They also tend to eliminate "telephone tag" because the recipient does not need to be present for the message to be sent. In businesses, this capability allows managers to react quickly to changes both within the business and in the marketplace. In addition, E-mail increases the amount of useful information that can be exchanged. Finally, E-mail messages tend to be more complete and accurate than voice communication. If an employee can sit down and thoughtfully compose a message rather than convey the message verbally, the message is more likely to contain all of the information that the sender needs to convey.

Disadvantages of E-mail.   E-mail can also cause problems. Because it is so easy to send an E-mail message, users sometimes write messages hastily, without developing their messages fully or considering the consequences of their messages. For example, say a company announces a pay raise that is lower than employees are expecting. A disgruntled worker may fire off a message to a manager saying things that he or she would not say in a face-to-face discussion. This is an example of a phenomenon called **flaming**.

The tendency toward flaming points to the differences between the dynamics of E-mail and those of face-to-face communication. It's easier to tell someone how you really feel when you don't have to deal directly with the person's reaction. And because the two people are not face to face, they are less able to gauge the effect of their words on each other. They cannot transmit and interpret important communication cues, such as tone of voice and body language. Certain forms of communication, such as sarcasm and humor, often do not travel well in E-mail. But remember that once you send an E-mail message, it's irretrievable, just like the letter you drop in a mailbox. And also remember that, in the workplace at least, you will have to face your E-mail correspondents sooner or later.

Another concern about the use of E-mail is that of privacy. Because messages are stored temporarily in a central database, the individuals that manage the database can have access to the messages. Several lawsuits have been filed against companies for alleged invasion of privacy in e-mail. The companies often contend that the E-mail system, like other computer technology, is the property of the company, and the company has a right to regulate its use. The plaintiffs believe that their rights to privacy and free speech have been violated. With public E-mail systems, the federal government now requires that the carrier maintain the privacy of the communication. However, no clear mandate has been set for private communication systems. Thus it is best to avoid intimate revelations in E-mail. Delete sensitive messages when you no longer need them.

Voice Mail

A **voice mail** (sometimes called V-mail) system is a computer-based system by which the user of a standard telephone can send, receive, store, or redirect voice messages. A voice mail system is more than an answering machine. When coupled with an automatic call distribution system, callers can control the direction of their calls through an organization. Voice menus are often used to provide options from which the caller can select. A voice mail menu might say: "Press 1 for new orders; press 2 for billing inquiries; press 3 for shipment status; or press 4 to talk to an operator." When calling a specific person who is not at his or her desk, the caller is able to either leave a message or redirect the call to an operator or another employee. Voice mail systems also allow users to forward their incoming calls to phones in other offices.

The primary advantage of voice mail is that it provides an efficient method for a business to communicate with the rest of the world. Anyone with a push-button phone can call in and generally either reach who they want or leave a message without involving an operator. In addition to providing customers and clients easy channels for communication, a voice mail system saves the company the labor costs of manually handling every incoming phone call.

One disadvantage of some voice mail systems is not being able to edit a message as you can with E-mail. With some systems, you can, however, erase a message that you have just recorded and start over. A more important disadvantage is the impersonal nature of the system in comparison to operator-directed calls. Many people prefer to have a human being help them get through to the right person at a company and take their messages.

Related Business Issues

The use of information systems in both small and large businesses has had a profound effect — both good and bad — on employment, consumer products, and, of course, the way that companies manage their affairs. In this section, we look at a few of the most important effects of information systems.

Quality Control

The basic idea of **quality control** is to measure and compare goods and services. Information systems related to quality control maintain current and historical data about such factors as sales or production targets, failure and reject rates of manufactured parts, and customer satisfaction. Managers use these kinds of data to make judgments about the effectiveness of production and marketing techniques, as well as about their employees.

Total quality management, or TQM, is a methodology for establishing, measuring, and implementing quality performance measures from one end of the production process to the other. TQM looks not only at the production systems, but also at the human systems. From customer service to the factory floor, the focus is on the use of top-quality parts, processes, and people.

Job Displacement and Job Enlargement

From the business's point of view, one of the most persuasive arguments for automating a business function is the reduction in the workforce. For example, between 1972 and 1977, computerization at AT&T allowed the company to eliminate 50,000 workers from the payroll, even though demand for telephone service was increasing.

Job displacement as a result of computer technology has both positive and negative effects. The obvious negative effect is the unemployment that can result from automating business functions. If you look more closely at this phenomenon, however, you will find that not as many jobs are lost as you might think. When systems are automated, jobs are created at computer hardware, software, and services companies. Jobs are also created for information systems professionals who create and manage the new systems. The key to keeping or getting a job often depends on the computer skills you have and your ability to learn new ones.

Another effect of computerization is the changing responsibilities of the workforce. In general, reducing the workforce at a company requires more of the employees who are not displaced, an effect called **job enlargement**. Computers allow fewer managers to supervise more workers and fewer workers to produce more goods. Companies are finding that as new computer systems are introduced, the companies must provide effective retraining so their workers learn to handle their increased responsibilities. This effect can be either good or bad, depending on the nature of the change, the feelings of the employees, and how employers manage the change. Some people resent having their job descriptions change to include a host of new responsibilities. Others find that, with automation, their jobs include less drudgery and more interesting work.

Finally, one of the leading benefits of computerization is the decreased cost of consumer goods. When a company can save money by automating some processes, some of the savings pass on to consumers in the form of lower prices.

Performance Monitoring

Computers are multifaceted. While allowing a clerk to electronically file documents, a computer can also track how many documents per hour the clerk is filing. By comparing the output from each employee, operations and middle-level managers can distribute awards or mete out warnings or punishment.

This **performance monitoring** can happen with or without the worker's knowledge. In some cases, performance monitoring can be an effective way to boost productivity. In other cases, however, it can have severe effects on the social and psychological reactions of the employee because it is so intrusive. At a warehouse owned by a large grocery chain, for example, employees were monitored according to how long it took them to bend over and move one box! If workers begin to resent the monitoring system, the system can decrease morale and, in turn, decrease productivity.

Downsizing and Outsourcing

When considering the benefits of automating a process or creating an information system, the central question asked by executives is whether or not the new system justifies its own cost. This is a tough question. Analyzing return on investment requires calculating the profit that a system makes relative to its costs. If the rate of return is greater than the prevailing interest rate, the system is deemed a success. Computerized information systems, however, are difficult to cost justify. The cost of hardware and software is easy to figure, but the benefit is much more difficult to pinpoint.

One of the ways companies are decreasing their information systems costs is reducing, or **downsizing**, the function of the central information system. Downsizing involves distributing the computer resources throughout an organization and then coordinating information exchange in a centralized fashion. For example, before downsizing, a marketing department's information system is stored in the company's mainframe. After downsizing, it is stored in a smaller departmental computer, which is often a file server. (A file server is a high-speed computer in a local area network that stores programs and data files shared by users on that network.)

In a downsizing situation, telecommunications systems are used to share data between departments. Downsizing reduces the cost of a centralized information systems department by moving the costs onto the departments that use the systems. Downsizing is therefore one way to make users more responsible for the resources they use.

Another popular technique for decreasing the costs of computing is **outsourcing**. Instead of employing a full-time, in-house computer operations staff, a company hires a computer service company to manage, maintain, and service a networked computer system. The client company owns the hardware and software but outsources the service and support. Outsourcing makes sense for companies that do not require a full-time network manager but find it impractical to expect an employee with other responsibilities to handle such a specialized job.

Comprehension Questions

1. How does sending a file via modem differ from sending a message across the country using an E-mail system?
2. Describe an information system that accomplished both performance monitoring and quality control.
3. In the short term, which do you think saves a company more money, downsizing or outsourcing?

Using What You Know

1. Describe a voice mail menu for customers and clients who call BVOS.
2. Describe the ways in which BVOS might use an E-mail system.
3. Describe how information systems could be used at BVOS to maintain quality control.

Summary Points

Information Systems in Large Businesses

☐ Complex organizations require highly developed information systems to coordinate their activities.

What Is an Information System?

☐ The narrow definition of an information system is that it provides a means for managers to obtain information from a company's database.
☐ The more general definition is that an information system is an established path or set of paths along which information can travel through an organization.

Levels of Management and Their Needs for Information

☐ A company can be diagrammed as a pyramid of managers on top of a foundation of operations-level workers.
☐ Workers are often organized into five basic departments: production, marketing, research, personnel, and accounting.
☐ Managers are divided between three levels: operations managers, middle-level managers, and upper-level managers.
☐ Each level of management needs different kinds of information to make different kinds of decisions.
☐ Operations managers make structured, immediate decisions; middle-level managers make less structured, tactical decisions; and executives make unstructured, strategic decisions.

Information Systems for Operations Managers

Production Systems

☐ Manufacturing is performed by a production department that creates a tangible good.

CAD

☐ CAD is used by production and research departments to design and test products.

CAM and Robotics

☐ One meaning of CAM is the use of a CAD database for robotics, numerical control, and process control.

CAM and Inventory Management

☐ Another meaning of CAM is the use of a computer to manage inventories of raw goods and finished products.

☐ Just-in-time manufacturing is a technique for keeping just enough stock of raw materials on hand.

Accounting Systems

☐ Accounting systems include at least four databases: accounts receivable, accounts payable, payroll, and the general ledger.

Information Systems for Middle and Upper Management

Management Information Systems

☐ Management information systems generate scheduled, exception, and demand reports to help middle-level managers make tactical decisions.

Decision Support Systems

☐ Decision support systems allow upper-level managers to obtain information in a variety of formats, depending on the requiremets of the decision being made.

Enterprise-Wide Information Systems

☐ Some types of information systems, rather than serving the specific needs of managers, simply create communication channels in an organization.

E-Mail

☐ E-mail allows users connected to a WAN or LAN to send written messages to each other.

Using E-Mail

☐ Using E-mail may or may not require specifying a system address of your own computer and knowing the address of the receiving computer.

☐ E-mail messages are stored in a database until the recipient accesses the system, at which time they can read, print, save, delete, or forward each message.

Advantages of E-mail

☐ E-mail is fast, cheap, and effective.

Disadvantages of E-mail

☐ E-mail can be subject to invasions of privacy.

☐ The medium can lead to flaming or other inappropriate types of messages because of the different dynamics of face-to-face and on-line communication.

Voice Mail

☐ Voice mail systems act as electronic operators, allowing callers to direct their own calls and leave answering-machine-type messages. They also provide flexibility to users through call-forwarding and other features.

☐ The primary advantage of voice mail is its efficiency for the business.

☐ The primary disadvantage is the impersonal nature of the system.

Related Business Issues

Quality Control

☐ Managers use computerized quality control techniques to make judgments about production and marketing techniques and about employees.

Job Displacement and Job Enlargement

☐ Job displacement can add to unemployment. It can also save money for a business and thereby raise profitability and lower consumer prices.

☐ Computer skills can help decrease your chances of being displaced and increase your job opportunities.

☐ When employees are displaced by computers, remaining employees find their jobs enlarged.

Performance Monitoring

☐ Performance monitoring systems can boost productivity or deter it by demoralizing workers.

Downsizing and Outsourcing

☐ Determining return on investment for computer systems is difficult because the benefits are difficult to quantify.

☐ One way for companies to save money on computer systems is downsizing, which is the process of moving applications from mainframes to file servers and to other more local computer, thus distributing computing costs more equitably.

☐ Outsourcing involves hiring outside computer specialists to manage, service, and support the computer system when it is not cost effective to maintain that level of expertise in-house.

Knowing the Facts

True/False

1. Personnel departments usually handle the accounting systems of large companies.

2. Middle-level managers make strategic decisions; upper-level managers make tactical decisions.

3. Middle-level managers need data that spans a greater period of time than the data required by operations managers.

4. Executives tend to make decisions that are more structured than those made by operations managers.

5. CAM can mean either robotics or computerized inventory control.

6. Payroll is a type of accounts payable that recognizes a company's short-term debt to employees.

7. Decision support systems are used to generate scheduled, exception, and demand reports.

8. Using E-mail requires that both the sender and the receiver of a message are connected to the same network.

9. Analyzing return on investment requires calculating the profit that a system makes relative to its costs.

10. Forcing departments to buy their own minicomputers, rather than using the company's mainframe, is an example of outsourcing.

Short Answer

1. _____ can lead to a phenomenon called flaming, in which one person insults another when he or she would not ordinarily do so in face-to-face contact.

2. _____ often have user-friendly interfaces that allow executives to obtain specific data without having to use the programming capabilities of a DBMS.

3. Most data that enters a company's database comes in at the _____ level and is analyzed at the management level.

4. An accounting database called the _____ _____ integrates and summarizes the data in payroll and accounts receivable and payable.

5. The first use of computers in business was as tools for _____.

6. With a fully automated manufacturing systems, a _____ database can be used as input by CAM systems to control industrial robots or manage inventory.

7. In_____, a company sells its centralized computer system to a computer services company.

8. _____ manufacturing is a technique used to minimize the amount of inventory that a company keeps.

9. The purpose of _____ is to measure and compare goods and services to make judgments about the effectiveness of production and marketing techniques.

10. Scheduled reports are generated regularly; _____ reports are generated in response to an unusual event or set of circumstances.

Answers

True/False

1. F
2. F
3. T
4. F
5. T
6. T
7. F
8. T
9. T
10. F

Short Answer

1. E-mail
2. Decision support systems
3. operations
4. general ledger
5. accounting
6. CAD
7. outsourcing
8. Just-in-time
9. quality control
10. exception

Challenging Your Understanding

1. When voice mail was first becoming popular, callers frequently complained about leaving messages on computers and not interacting with humans. Now, many callers would prefer to leave a message on a machine rather than talk directly to a human. Can you explain this dramatic shift?

2. Some experts maintain that very few people actually lose jobs to computers. Rather, computers allow fewer workers to do more things, so workers are displaced and not replaced by computers. What do you think?

3. In a JIT system, the manufacturer carries the optimal amount of inventory in stock. Just when the inventory is running out, the new shipment arrives. This requires good relationships with suppliers and substantial information systems resources to coordinate the orders. Given the costs involved, why is this a popular idea?

4. Which level of manager requires the most information from outside the company? Why?

Developing Information Systems

Key Terms

computer-aided software engineering (CASE)
data flow diagram
economic feasibility
feasibility study
garbage in, garbage out (GIGO)
legal feasibility
obsolescence
operational feasibility
prototyping
request for proposal (RFP)
request for quote (RFQ)
schedule feasibility
system flowchart
system analyst
system designer
system development life cycle
technological feasibility

Objectives

In this chapter you will learn to:

- Name and describe the seven steps of the system development life cycle

- Compare the system development life cycle to the programming process and the problem-solving process

- Describe how CASE tools are used in system development

- Identify the importance of user involvement in system development

- Explain the purpose and process of prototyping

- List the ethical responsibilities of the information systems professional

- Describe three common misconceptions about information systems

The System Development Life Cycle

Because they serve the needs of people in a changing environment, information systems act like living organisms. They are conceived and born, they mature and grow old, and they eventually die and are replaced with newer information systems. The **system development life cycle** is typically described as having seven stages:

1. Recognizing the problem
2. Analyzing the current system
3. Designing the new system
4. Developing the new system
5. Installing the new system
6. Evaluating and maintaining the system
7. Recognizing obsolescence

This sequence of stages closely resembles two other sets of stages we have covered: programming and problem solving (Figure 13-1). The resemblance is logical, because an important part of system development is programming, and programming is a means for solving a problem. The resemblance between development of an information system and problem solving makes sense for another reason. Throughout this book, we have used problem solving as a structured method for creating a computer system. Now we are describing an information system rather than just a computer system. The computer system is the heart of an information system, so the processes for establishing both are similar.

Recognizing the Problem

The life cycle of a system begins when the users of a mature information system begin to identify problems in it. For example, say an operations manager for an accounting department is analyzing an accounts receivable system. In doing so, he finds that, on average, account balances go unpaid for 10 weeks. From working at other companies and from knowing the goals of his middle-level manager, he knows that this delay is too long. Unfortunately, the operations manager is unable to simply bill sooner, because the number of orders processed every week is already pushing the limits of the hardware and software currently being used.

This type of problem recognition, in which the user identifies the need for change, is the most common scenario. It generally ends with users writing a formal request to initiate the development of a new system (Figure 13-2). However, problem recognition can come from other sources. If upper managers discover that a competitor has developed an advanced information system to gain a competitive advantage, they may institute a similar change as a competitive necessity.

Once management agrees to initiate a new development cycle, the last step of problem recognition — sometimes considered a separate stage — is often to write a **feasibility study**. This study is a preliminary investigation of the problem to see if the benefits of solving it outweigh the costs of developing a solution. Several kinds of feasibility must be looked at, including technological, economic, legal, operational, and scheduling.

- **Technological feasibility** determines whether the problem can be solved using current technology. Technological feasibility is not always a "yes or no" question. Sometimes, technological innovation may be worth the risks, especially when management is pursuing a competitive advantage.

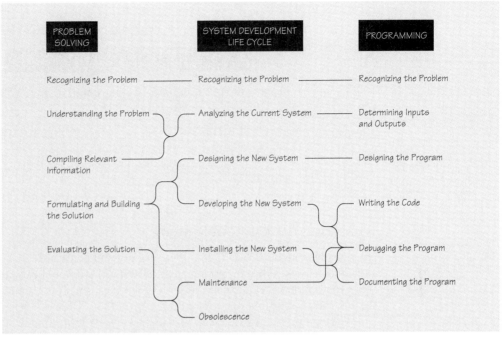

Figure 13-1
The system development life cycle is closely related to the problem solving steps and the programming process.

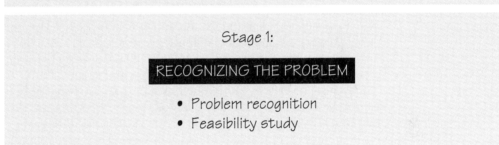

Figure 13-2
The most important phases of stage 1.

- **Economic feasibility** is easy to understand but difficult to determine. The question is simply whether the new system will be worth the money. Unfortunately, it is much easier to determine the costs of a new system than to put a dollar amount on the benefits.

- Business laws and regulations change frequently. As a result, a company must consider the **legal feasibility** of a new information system solution. Because computer applications are always growing, you can expect to see increased legislation affecting the use of computers in business.

- **Operational feasibility** helps determine whether the proposed system will function in the organization. The new system may require restructuring a department. The company might need to hire additional personnel, or the system may displace employees from their current positions. If the new system will be too disruptive, it may not be pursued.

- Finally, **scheduling feasibility** ascertains when the system will be ready for implementation. If the information systems department cannot develop the system in the required time, management may consider an outside vendor. The price of hiring another vendor may, in turn, undermine the economic feasibility of solving the problem.

Stage 2:

ANALYZING THE CURRENT SYSTEM

- List inputs and outputs
- List procedures
- Create data flow diagrams
- Create system flowchart
- Write definition of new requirements

Figure 13-3
Stage 2 of the system development life cycle.

Analyzing the Current System

If a feasibility study shows that a new system will be cost effective, the company begins a detailed analysis of the current information system. At some companies, professionals called **system analysts** specialize in this kind of work. At smaller companies, users of the current system can take on this role.

The analysis stage has several goals, as shown in Figure 13-3. First, the inputs and outputs of the current system are listed; the person doing the analysis documents each type of data that the system requires and the reports or other processed data that the system generates. After documenting inputs and outputs, the system analyst next lists all of the procedures for using the current system. A third goal of the analysis stage is to use the inputs, outputs, and procedures to create data flow diagrams and systems flowcharts, both of which show graphically how data moves through an information system. The difference between the two is that the **data flow diagram** is a broad view of the whole system, including the people who use it. **System flowcharts** detail how data moves through the computer system. These diagrams closely resemble the flowcharts created in programming.

System analysts use several common methods to gather data about the current system. Four of the most common are:

- Interviewing users
- Distributing written questionnaires
- Observing operations
- Collecting output documents and system documentation

In smaller companies, or when a user is doing the system analysis, these methods may not all be necessary. In a larger company, however, the system analyst may have little experience with the work carried on at the operations level of a given department. In this case, the analyst needs to establish as many channels of communication with the users as possible.

The result of the analysis stage is a written, detailed definition of the new system requirements. Like the feasibility study, this report is generally submitted to middle- or upper-level managers before the next stage begins.

Designing the New System

Once the old system has been thoroughly analyzed, the new system must be designed to meet the new requirements. The design stage of the system development life cycle, summa-

Figure 13-4
Stage 3 of the system
development life cycle.

Stage 3:

DESIGNING THE NEW SYSTEM

- Propose design solutions
- Second feasibility study

Figure 13-4
Stage 3 of the system
development life cycle.

rized in Figure 13-4, is similar to the design stage of the programming process. Designing a system, however, is a broader problem because it includes not only software, but hardware, people, and procedures. At this point, an information systems professional, known as the **system designer**, heads the project. The designer may be the same person as the analyst or a new professional with specific experience in this field.

The techniques used in this stage borrow from the previous stages. Normally, the first thing the system designer must do is propose several designs. Each of these is described with the help of data flow diagrams and system flowcharts. In some cases, the system designer uses pseudocode to rough out the design for programs that need to be written or purchased. As you can see, system developers adhere to the principles of structured programming, even though programming is just part of the problem.

After the various proposed alternatives are designed, they are presented to middle or upper managers, who must again consider the feasibility of each solution. Like the feasibility study mentioned in the first stage, this design report must reconsider certain kinds of feasibility, especially economic, operational, and scheduling. The design report should also make a recommendation about which design offers the best solution.

It is possible for this second feasibility study to reveal that the benefits of creating any solution do not outweigh the costs. Despite significant investment in the project at the end of the design stage, it is still better to scrap a design that is too technically difficult, too expensive, or too time consuming than to proceed to the development stage.

Developing the New System

When a final design has been approved, it is time to develop the new system. Development consists of buying necessary hardware and programming or purchasing software (Figure 13-5).

Stage 4:

DEVELOPING THE NEW SYSTEM

- Buying hardware
- Programming or purchasing software

Figure 13-5
Stage 4 of the system
development life cycle.

Buying Hardware. Many new information systems require the purchase of hardware. If a company is moving from a manual to a computerized system, development includes purchasing all of the hardware for the new system. If a company is replacing one computerized system with another, much — if not all — of the old hardware may still be useful. Additional hardware may be required, however. For example, if an inventory control system is being improved with bar-code readers, the existing company or departmental computer may handle this change just fine. In terms of hardware, the company may need to purchase only the bar-code readers themselves.

You are already familiar with most of the issues involved in purchasing hardware, because we covered them in Unit III. When you purchase relatively small or inexpensive equipment, such as bar-code readers or even microcomputers, the techniques and sources you have used throughout this book will serve you well.

In large companies, however, a new information system may require a mainframe or a large number of smaller hardware devices. In such cases, the purchaser has a great deal of money to spend and therefore has some leverage among hardware manufacturers. The developer should send out several **requests for proposal**, or **RFPs**. An RFP is exactly what its name implies: It is a request for a vendor to send a bid offering a hardware solution to the requirements specified in the RFP. The bid includes the description of the solution and the price that the vendor will charge the business developing the system. A company will normally send out several RFPs so that it can compare competing bids and pick the best one.

If a company knows exactly what it wants in the way of a hardware solution, it may send out **requests for quote**, or **RFQs**, rather than RFPs. RFQs identify a specific product and ask for the price at which the vendor is willing to sell it. Judging the best quote is a relatively simple process; however, judging the best proposal requires deciding who best satisfies the requirements as well as offering the best value.

Programming or Purchasing Software. Unlike hardware, which is almost always bought when needed, software can be either bought or created. We have already discussed the program vs. purchase decision in Unit II, so we won't go into detail again here. As with hardware, when purchasing software, a company may want to send out RFPs or RFQs. If the company needs software that is not available in the market, it is more likely to send out RFPs. If the software already exists and the company needs a site license or support service or help with installation, it is more likely to send RFQs.

If a company decides that it is more efficient to develop the software in-house (with programmers who are already employees), the development follows the sequence of the programming cycle.

Structured programming is extremely important here. In all likelihood, the person who writes the program will not be the one who maintains or reworks it later on. If the program is not logically structured and well documented, the second programmer will waste countless hours trying to understand its design. Another reason for structured programming is the ease with which program modules and subroutines can be used in other systems throughout the company. The ability to reuse parts of programs is obviously more cost efficient for a company than building every program from scratch.

Installing the New System

Installing a new information system in a large company (Figure 13-6) is a period of high visibility for information systems professionals. This stage should be approached cautiously and the job carried out thoroughly. To a large degree, the quality of work during installation can determine the long-term worth of the system.

The installation stage has five parts:
- Setup
- Testing
- Documentation
- Conversion
- Training

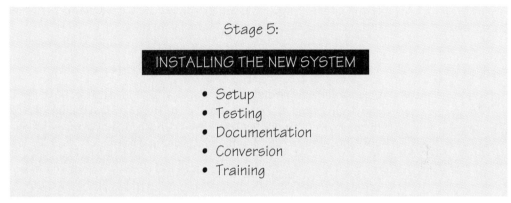

Stage 5:

INSTALLING THE NEW SYSTEM

- Setup
- Testing
- Documentation
- Conversion
- Training

Figure 13-6
Stage 5 of the system
development life cycle

These are not steps; they can take place simultaneously or they can overlap.

Setup. Setting up the new system is a matter of putting together the various parts that have been purchased or developed on site. It can have many aspects, depending on the nature of the new system. In addition to connecting hardware and loading software, setup can include construction to accommodate new hardware or users, rewiring, configuring software to run efficiently on hardware, and many other tasks.

Testing. The biggest part of testing a new system is often testing software developed in-house. This includes debugging the code as well as having employees perform the alpha and beta testing. In addition to testing software, hardware must be checked to see if it works properly, and new procedures should be carried through to see that they produce the desired results.

Documentation. Like a software program, an information system must be thoroughly documented. The internal and external documentation of the programs is part of the development process. The documentation that is part of installation tells how employees are to use all parts of the system. It should cover every procedure the system is designed to perform, how data is entered and by whom, and how and in what form data is retrieved.

Conversion. If the new system requires data from the old system, that data may have to be converted so the new system can understand it. Converting data from a manual system to a computerized system can require a massive amount of data entry. Converting from one software package to another or from one hardware platform to another usually means translating the format. The growth of portable software — especially operating systems — will lessen the difficulty of this type of conversion.

How you execute the conversion from one system to another can spell the difference between success and failure of the new system. If you rip out the old system on Friday and plan to start with the new system Monday morning, you will have problems. Instead, phase the new system in one department at a time or one function at a time.

Training. Perhaps the most critical part of installation is training the employees who will use the system. Motivating people to learn the system is crucial for successful implementation. The training can be performed by one of several groups: representatives of the vendor that sold the system or parts of it; employees from the information systems department who designed and developed the system; or the users who first learned the system and helped test it. In any case, someone or some group must act as the expert and be available for technical support, even after the initial training.

Evaluating and Maintaining the System

Once you have installed the information system, it is fully developed and normal operations can begin as you enter the stage of evaluating and maintaining the system (Figure 13-7). You might expect that all that remains is periodic maintenance to keep the system serving the ever-changing needs of workers and managers.

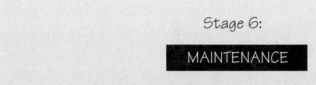

Stage 6:

MAINTENANCE

- Post-implementation evaluation
- Additional development
- Continuous evaluation and maintenance

Figure 13-7
Stage 6 of the system development life cycle.

Actually, though, the maintenance stage begins with a post-implementation evaluation, which is written by users of the new system. In this report, users compare performance with the goals that were identified early in the development process. If the goals were not met, some additional development may be required.

Throughout the normal operating life of the system, other evaluations may be written. Problems that arise are handled by a maintenance group. The cost of maintenance has led companies to realize the value of proper design and development and of this formal developmental process. Simply speaking, a well-designed system is easier and therefore less costly to maintain. And it may save you a lot of money. According to some experts, the cost of maintenance over the entire life of a system roughly equals the cost of development.

Recognizing Obsolescence

No matter how well an information system is designed, the cost of periodic maintenance gradually increases. Each "patch" that a maintenance group adds to a system makes it more cumbersome. Eventually, like an old car, it is no longer worth fixing. Even if the system has not been continually repaired, the advent of new technology may make it more cost efficient to scrap the system than bring it up to date. This is the stage of **obsolescence** (Figure 13-8), when new feasibility studies begin to initiate a new system development life cycle.

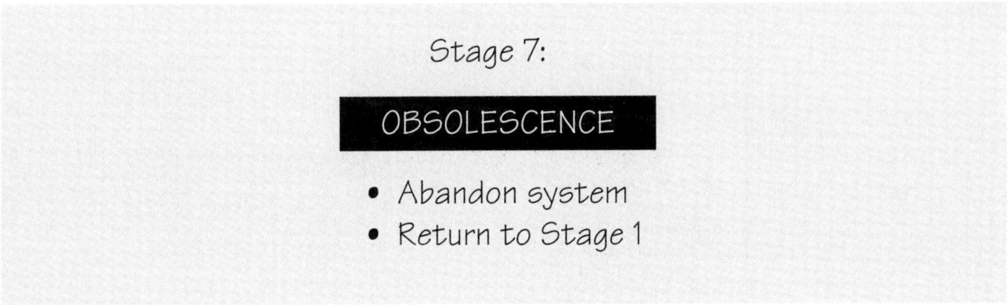

Stage 7:

OBSOLESCENCE

- Abandon system
- Return to Stage 1

Figure 13-8
The obsolescence stage leads back to stage 1 of the cycle.

Comprehension Questions

1. What stage in the system development life cycle has no counterpart in the problem-solving process? Why?

2. Why is the life of a system described as a cycle?

3. Why must data flow diagrams contain symbols that differ from those used in system flowcharts?

Using What You Know

1. At BVOS, who would most likely act as the system analyst in the development of an accounting system?

2. If a company is changing from a manual to computerized accounting system, what do you think is the most costly part of the installation stage?

3. Why is it not necessary to send out an RFP for the LAN server you intend to use at BVOS?

Tools and Techniques for Developing Information Systems

A variety of tools and techniques have been created to help in the analysis and design of information systems.

CASE Tools

One of the most promising tools used to aid system analysts and programmers is called **computer-aided software engineering**, or **CASE**, tool. CASE tools are software packages that help programmers write programs.

CASE packages can include several different tools (Figure 13-9 on the next page). They can help create flowcharts, keep track of program specifications, and generate reports and program documentation. Most also include third- or fourth-generation languages, as well as libraries in which to store subroutines and modules that can be reused. In general, CASE tools support as many facets of the programming process as possible and promote the creation of top-down, structured programs.

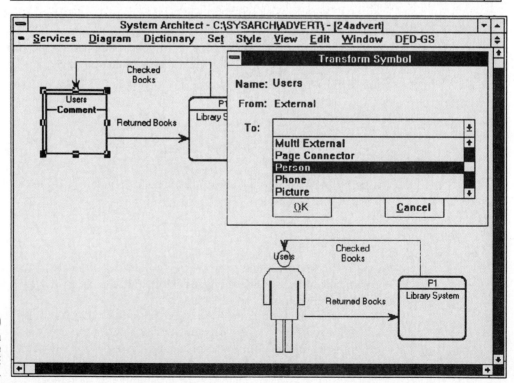

User Involvement

The importance of user involvement in the system development process should not be underestimated (Figure 13-10). It is critical that an information systems professional realize he or she is working for users. These users are generally knowledgeable about the specific application area for which the program is being written. They also have a vested interest in the quality of the system that the information system professional creates. The perspective and interest of the users can be a valuable resource for the IS professional, who, after all, has experience in the fields of programming and system development but may know very little about the complexity of the users' jobs.

Figure 13-10
Perhaps the most crucial ingredient of successful system development is user involvement.

In addition to the users' worth as a resource, users are also customers. In many cases, if they have doubts about the quality of work coming from the information systems department, or if they are displeased with the IS department's responsiveness to their concerns, they can take their problem to an outside vendor. This type of competition can motivate systems professionals to excel at their jobs.

Information system development in Europe is especially oriented toward the involvement of the user. There, users are encouraged to define and even solve system problems. The participative methods they use also tend to be less structured than the system development life cycle described in this chapter.

Prototyping

No matter how hard an analyst may try, sometimes the system that is delivered does not meet the users' expectations. One way of assuring that the user's needs are met is by **prototyping**. This technique involves the creation of a simple program that mimics the operations the user desires. In general, the system evolves through a series of interim steps, with a tremendous amount of user involvement during the process. The first prototype is not a totally functional system, but includes the major system components, so that users see what the new system will do. As the interim steps are carried out, users give their feedback and aid in the evolution of the system. In some cases, the prototype itself grows into the actual system. In others, it is just an increasingly complex model that is rebuilt when the actual system is developed. Today, prototypes can be developed quickly using special programming tools, such as CASE tools. Sometimes, users themselves create the prototype.

Unfortunately, a prototype can give the user an unrealistic view of the complexity of the project. Typically a programmer will create a prototyped system without many of the components required for a corporate information system. For example, a prototyped system may have no security or error-checking routines built in. These components are often some of the most difficult elements of a system to build. Also, if a user is helping to create the prototype, the user will probably get an inaccurate picture of how hard it is to write a program. This can cause some disregard for the efforts of the programmer and analyst.

Ethics and the Information System Professional

Richard Mason, a noted researcher of ethical uses of information technology, states that the information systems professional is responsible for four ethical agendas: privacy, accuracy, property, and access. Privacy is the right of an individual or organization to control the collection, use, and dissemination of identifiable information. The information systems professional is responsible for maintaining the privacy of those whose data is in his or her control. The IS professional is charged with assuring that the data in corporate databases is as accurate as possible and remains secure while it is in the possession of the organization. Property refers to the ownership of intellectual property such as software. Users of information systems are charged with making sure that all software they use is properly licensed. Finally, access refers to access to information technology and data. The IS professional is charged with removing technological barriers between authorized users and the information technologies and data that will help them do their jobs.

Misconceptions About the Information System

There are three prevalent myths surrounding the use of computing technology in business.

The first myth is that computerization always improves efficiency. There are many ways to design an information system. If a system exactly mimics the manual system it replaces, there is no substantive change to the nature of the work, only to who is carrying it out. A better way to design a system is to determine if the business process can be re-engineered using computer technology. In this case, the business function can be improved rather than simply automated. But just as we are able to improve a function with a computer, we can likewise harm a function. The misdiagnosis of a problem or a poor implementation of the design can severely limit the success of the system and even disrupt the operation of the business function.

A common mistake analysts make when designing information systems is failing to take into account the human systems in the organization. When this happens, the most technically perfect solution to a problem may be doomed to failure. Hence, the second myth is that every problem in a system has a purely technological solution. The successful computer analyst wears many hats when designing a system. He or she might be a computer consultant one moment, a business consultant another, and a rhetorical sounding board another. The idea is that the installation of an information system requires the modification of human systems. The modification may be entirely computerized, but it can also be a hybrid of computer systems and manual systems. These hybrid solutions are often the most efficient because they do not force the limitations of the computer onto every systems problem.

Finally, many computer users act as if the computer is always correct. To some individuals, if some piece of information came from a computer, it must be right. These people ascribe to the computer certain characteristics that border on science fiction. Even knowledgeable computer users often feel very confident about the way the technology works. Neither group challenges the assumptions under which the program was designed or the system runs.

In part, this misconception comes from the fact that the use of a computer can add a certain credibility to one's argument. Desktop publishing, presentation graphics, and sophisticated computer models can make an impressive statement during a presentation. Often, though, the style of presentation is more persuasive than the facts. When faced with supposed facts from a computer, remember the most important computer adage: *Garbage in, garbage out*, or *GIGO*. The saying means that the worth of what comes out of the computer is only as valuable or accurate as the data that went in.

Comprehension Questions

1. Does prototyping tend to encourage or discourage user involvement? Why?
2. Why is managing access the sole responsibility of the information systems professional?
3. Explain why protecting intellectual property is not solely the responsibility of the information systems professional.

Using What You Know

1. Compare prototyping to generating pseudocode.
2. Invent three scenarios related to daily operations at BVOS that illustrate each of the common misconceptions about computers.
3. If there is no full-time information systems professional at BVOS, who should oversee the four ethical responsibilities related to that role?

Summary Points

The System Development Life Cycle
☐ The seven stages of the system development life cycle closely resemble the stages in the programming process and the problem-solving process.

Recognizing the Problem
☐ The life cycle typically begins when users run into problems with the existing system.
☐ The cycle can begin with middle- or upper-level managers who are looking for a competitive advantage.
☐ The stage ends with a feasibility study that examines the technological, economic, legal, operational, and scheduling feasibility of finding a solution to the problem.

Analyzing the Current System
☐ The goals of the analysis stage are to list inputs, outputs, and procedures, and to create system flowcharts and data flow diagrams.
☐ The system analyst may use several techniques to gather information, including interviews, questionnaires, observations, and existing documents.
☐ A detailed list of the new system requirements should be written at the end of the analysis stage.

Designing the New System

☐ The system design stage resembles the design stage of the programming process.

☐ Several alternative designs should be developed by the system designer.

☐ Another feasibility study focusing on the feasibility of the solutions is written at the end of this stage.

Developing the New System

Buying Hardware

☐ In a large company, if a detailed solution has not been developed, the company may send out RFPs.

☐ If the company knows exactly what it is looking for, it will send out RFQs.

Programming or Purchasing Software

☐ If a company wants to buy software that does not yet exist, it will send out RFPs.

☐ If the company wants a special deal on existing software, it will send out RFQs.

☐ If the software is being programmed in-house, structured programming is extremely important.

Installing the New System

Setup

☐ Setup can include such jobs as construction and software configuration, in addition to putting hardware together and loading software.

Testing

☐ Testing includes testing the hardware, software, and procedures.

Documentation

☐ The documentation tells the users how to operate the system.

Conversion

☐ Conversion involves moving existing data, work, and procedures from the old system to the new system.

Training

☐ Training of new users can be carried out by programmers, vendors, or other users who helped test the system.

Evaluating and Maintaining the System

☐ Maintenance begins with a post-implementation evaluation that reports whether the system meets the requirements.

☐ Evaluations of a system are written throughout its life, and a maintenance group takes care of problems.

Recognizing Obsolescence

☐ As a system ages, maintenance becomes gradually more expensive, until the system is obsolete.

Tools and Techniques for Developing Information Systems

CASE Tools

☐ CASE tools are sets of programs that help the programmer write programs.

User Involvement

☐ The users' experience and interest in the success of the system should be used as a resource by the information systems professionals.

☐ IS professionals may also be motivated by the fact that users can go to outside vendors.

☐ Companies in Europe tend to use more highly participative and less structured methods in systems development than those in the United States.

Prototyping

☐ Prototyping is a means for more accurately meeting the needs of users by creating a model that mimics the design and function of the desired system.

☐ The model is successively revised with the help of user feedback.

Ethics and the Information Systems Professional

☐ Information systems professionals should be responsible for four ethical agendas: privacy of information, accuracy of data, rights to intellectual property, and appropriate access to the system.

Misconceptions About the Information System

☐ Professionals tend to believe that computerization always improves efficiency.

☐ Computers only improve efficiency if the computer solution is better engineered than the manual solution.

☐ People tend to think that system problems always have computer solutions.

☐ Often, the best solution is a hybrid of manual and computerized systems.

☐ People tend to think that the computer is always right.

☐ Remember: "Garbage in, garbage out."

Knowing the Facts

True/False

1. At small companies, users often play the role of the system analyst.

2. Responses to RFPs are more difficult to evaluate than responses to RFQs.

3. According to some experts, the long-term cost of maintenance roughly equals the cost of development.

4. Training employees to use a new system must be carried out by the programmers who developed the software for it.

5. Prototype systems are developed by users and gradually evolve into the working system.

6. The first feasibility study focuses on the problem, while later ones focus on proposed solutions.

7. The internal and external software documentation generated during the programming process acts as the documentation for the whole information system.

8. Hybrid systems can be more efficient than fully computerized systems.

9. The participative development methods used in Europe tend to be more structured than methods used in the United States.

10. Technological feasibility identifies whether a solution is worth the money it will cost.

Short Answer

1. _____ often include programs for creating documentation, flowcharts, and even module libraries.

2. _____ involves creating a model of the proposed system; the model is presented to users for their feedback.

3. The problem with determining _____ feasibility is that it is much easier to measure the costs of a new system than to put a dollar amount on the benefits.

4. Portable software will lessen the difficulties in the _____ part of the installation stage when one computerized system is being replaced with another.

5. The system flowchart shows how data moves through the computer system; the _____ shows how data moves through the entire information system.

6. The belief that the computer is always right is refuted with the adage "_____."

7. One part of the installation stage, _____, can include construction, rewiring, and configuring software.

8. Companies that have defined system requirements but have not developed a detailed design are likely to send out _____ to potential vendors.

9. Feasibility studies are often conducted at the ends of the "recognizing the problem" stage and the _____ stage.

10. If a company wants to purchase software that is already on the market, it is likely to send out _____.

Answers

True/False

1. T
2. T
3. T
4. F
5. F
6. T
7. F
8. T
9. F
10. F

Short Answer

1. CASE tools
2. Prototyping
3. economic
4. conversion
5. data flow diagram
6. garbage in, garbage out
7. setup
8. RFPs
9. "designing the new system," or design
10. RFQs

Challenging Your Understanding

1. Compare the steps involved in writing a research paper to the steps of the system development life cycle.

2. Some people maintain that the four responsibilities of information system professionals are actually *everybody's* responsibilities. Explain how each of the four could be construed as a responsibility of the BVOS sales force.

3. How does the system development life cycle differ from the problem-solving process?

4. The system development life cycle is ideally suited for creating management information systems, but not quite as well suited for setting up something like an E-mail system. Descibe how the steps of the life cycle might differ for setting up an E-mail system.

Unit IV Project

Selecting an Integrated Accounting System for Michelman Fine Furniture

In 1923 Peter Michelman emigrated to the United States. Peter, a cabinet maker, moved to San Antonio, Texas, to open a cabinetry shop. Peter worked hard, learned the language of business, and prospered. When his sons were teenagers, Peter decided to expand his business to include the sale and manufacture of home furniture. By the late 1950s, Michelman Fine Furniture was one of the leading domestic furniture makers in the country. The company manufactured furniture in Texas, California, Alabama, and South Carolina, and shipped products to retailers in every state in the nation.

Peter retired in 1961 and turned operations over to his eldest son, Erik, who managed the company for 25 years, maintaining its commitment to quality. Erik's daughter, Alyssa, became president and presided over the modernization of the company. She wants to create a microcomputer-based accounting system and to replace the six-year-old minicomputer. The current system is used by six accounting clerks and provides accounting reports and on-line data access to Michelman management.

The new system must run on microcomputers attached to a local area network. The integrated accounting system should have a general ledger, payroll, accounts receivable, accounts payable, and inventory modules. As a chief consultant for a computer services company, you have been hired to evaluate three integrated accounting systems and to suggest which best meets the needs of Michelman Fine Furniture. Using information found in computer magazines, prepare a report detailing your findings for Alyssa. You should assume that Michelman Fine Furniture has no microcomputers and will need to purchase and install them, too. However, before the computers are purchased, Alyssa wants your opinion so that she can purchase the computers after selecting the application software. Consequently, your report should also detail the kinds of computers the system will run on and the operating systems that are supported. Package your report as a total, turnkey solution to the accounting system problem at Michelman Fine Furniture.

Glossary

286 A PC (IBM or compatible) built around the 80286, a 16-bit processor from Intel.

386 A PC built around the 80386, a 32-bit processor from Intel.

486 A PC built around the 80486, a 32-bit processor from Intel.

access privileges Refers to the ability of a multi-user system to control which users can read and write which data.

accounts payable Accounting system that keeps track of who the company owes money to, how much is owed, and the terms of the debt.

accounts receivable Accounting system that keeps track of who owes the company money, how much they owe, and when the money is due.

acoustic coupler A device attached to a modem that sends and receives signals through a standard telephone handset.

Ada The standard programming language for all major federal systems projects. Ada was originally designed for the U.S. Department of Defense. It works well in real-time and batch systems.

alpha version The first version of a software program that is released to a select group of users for testing.

alphanumeric field A type of database field that can contain letters, numbers, punctuation symbols, and other typewriter characters. Data in an alphanumeric field cannot be used in calculations.

alphanumeric keys The area of a computer keyboard that looks like the standard typewriter keyboard.

analog device A machine that represents data with continuously variable physical quantities.

analytic graphics Charts and graphs used to summarize numerical data.

ANSI American National Standards Institute. ANSI code is a popular alternative to ASCII.

antivirus software Utility software used to detect and eradicate computer viruses.

Apple Computer Company Hardware and software company founded by Steve Jobs and Steve Wozniak in 1976. Apple is best known for developing the Macintosh computer.

Apple II Apple Computer's first big success, released in 1977. The Apple II had an open architecture and was released in several different models.

application A task required by a computer user.

application package A piece of application software. The term generally refers to proprietary software.

application software A program that is used to accomplish a specific type of task required by the user.

arithmetic logic unit (ALU) The part of the CPU that works in conjunction with the control unit by handling arithmetic and logical processing.

artificial intelligence A broad field that attempts to endow computers with the ability to think and reason in ways similar to humans.

ASCII American Standard Code for Information Interchange, the most common character code used by microcomputers.

Automated Teller Machine (ATM) A special purpose computer that allows a bank's customers to perform banking transactions.

backing up (archiving) Copying data and software from a computer's hard disk, usually to diskettes or tape, and storing the copy in a safe location.

bar-code reader A scanner capable of reading bar codes, such as the universal product code (UPC) symbol.

BASIC Acronym for Beginner's All-Purpose Symbolic Instruction Code, a third-generation language popular with microcomputer users. Originally created by John Kemeny and Thomas Kurtz.

batch processing Refers to a computer system that stores input for a period of time before processing it in large sets.

baud A unit for measuring the speed of data transmission. Baud measures the number of times that the signal changes electrical states in a single second.

beta version The last pre-final version of a program, which is released to a large group of users for testing.

binary Consisting of only two possible states.

binary code The term used to refer to computer data that is represented using a series of binary numbers.

binary field A type of database field that contains a bitmap; a graphic field.

binary numbering system (Base 2). A numbering system with only two symbols, 1 and 0.

BIOS Basic Input/Output System. A program, usually stored in ROM, that is loaded before the operating system. BIOS controls how the CPU interacts with I/O devices.

bit A binary digit, represented using a single transistor. The smallest unit of computer data.

bitmap An image stored as a grid of dots that represent the pixels on the screen.

bits per second (bps) A unit for measuring the speed of data transmission. Contrast with baud.

bug An error in software or malfunction in hardware.

bulletin board service (BBS) An electronic forum, normally accessed with a modem, in which users trade information by reading and leaving messages.

bus An electronic pathway. The two most common types of bus are the data bus and the address bus.

bus network A network configuration in which all of the computers and peripherals are connected to a single transmission line.

byte Eight bits, grouped together. The byte is a useful unit for measuring data, because it takes one byte to signify a single alphanumeric character.

C A powerful programming language designed by Dennis Ritchie to be portable across several types of computers.

cache A high-speed memory device. A disk cache is a reserved section of RAM that speeds up operations requiring frequent reading and writing to disk. A memory cache is a high-speed buffer between the CPU and memory.

CAM Computer-assisted manufacturing. CAM can refer to the use of robotics and numerical control devices or the use of computers to monitor inventory during manufacturing.

CASE tool A computer-aided software engineering software package that helps programmers write programs.

cathode ray tube (CRT) A special type of vacuum tube that sprays a stream of electrons, which are directed onto a piece of glass that is coated with phosphor. The term CRT is also used to refer to a monitor built around such a vacuum tube.

CD-ROM Compact Disk-Read Only Memory. An optical disk that uses the same laser technology as musical compact disks.

central processing unit (CPU) The part of a computer responsible for controlling the flow of data throughout the computer and for executing program instructions. Sometimes called the brain of the computer.

CGA Color Graphics Adapter. The first type of color graphics adapter that was released with the IBM PC. CGA systems display 320 x 200 pixels (320 horizontally and 200 vertically) in four colors on the screen when the monitor is in graphics mode.

characters per second (cps) A unit for measuring printer speed. The number of alphanumeric characters printed in one second.

chassis The box that houses the system unit.

chip A small piece of silicon that is etched with electrical pathways.

client/server computing A computer information system strategy that uses two or more networked computers to perform an application task.

click A mouse technique of pointing to a place on the monitor and pressing once on the mouse button.

clock speed The number of electronic cycles per second, measured in megahertz. One cycle is the amount of time is takes to turn a transistor on and off again.

clone A microcomputer that is similar in design to the IBM PC and PS/2 and is capable of running the same software.

COBOL Acronym for COmmon Business-Oriented Language, a programming language frequently used for developing business applications. COBOL was formally defined in 1959 by Grace Hopper.

code Programming instructions.

command-line interface A type of user interface in which the user controls the program by typing commands at the keyboard.

communications device A hardware component that enables one computer system to share data with another. Connecting communications devices requires a communications medium, the most common of which are telephone lines, electromagnetic waves, and coaxial, twisted-pair, and fiber-optic cable.

communications error A problem that occurs when the data received is not identical to the data sent.

communications software Application software that manages the transmission of data between one computer and another.

Compaq The first major manufacturer of IBM compatible computers. Compaq remains an important player in the compatibles market.

compatible With respect to programs, the ability to run on a given machine. With respect to hardware, the ability of one machine to run the same software as another machine. Also, see clone.

competitive advantage A business strategy that relies on innovation to gain an edge over the competition.

competitive necessity A technique that is required of a business in order to remain competitive.

compiler A program that translates programming code into machine language. A compiler translates all the code at once before the program can be run.

computer An electronic device for processing data.

computer information systems An organized means of collecting and processing data that makes the data useful to a company.

computer system A collection of hardware, software, data, and people that work together.

computer-assisted design (CAD) Use of a computer system to create high-quality electronic models and exact scaled images.

context-sensitive help Software features that automatically display the relevant help screen depending on the command or procedure that the user is trying to execute.

control unit The part of the CPU that retrieves program instructions from memory, evaluates them, and retrieves data from memory.

cooperative multitasking A multitasking strategy in which the CPU executes different programs by alternating between them at an even rate. Contrast with preemptive multitasking, a more advanced strategy.

copy protected   Refers to software that includes safeguards against software piracy.

cursor   The point on the screen where letters, numbers, or punctuation symbols typed at the keyboard will be entered.

cursor-movement keys   Keys that allow the user to move the cursor around the screen with the keyboard. They include the arrow keys, as well as other keys, such as End, Home, Page Up, and so on.

data   Raw, unprocessed facts that, for a computer, consist of numbers, letters, images, and sounds. The computer accepts data as input.

data bits   A modem setting that tells the software how many bits of data to send in each set. Normally, microcomputers send either seven or eight bits of data in a string when communicating via a modem.

data bus   An electronic pathway between the CPU and other hardware devices, including memory and all peripherals. It is used for transferring data throughout the computer system.

data compression   The use of logical and mathematical methods to minimize the amount of storage space that software or data occupies.

data dictionary   A database that contains data about the fields and access privileges of another database.

data flow diagram   A diagram of an entire information system. In addition to computing steps, such as processing and storage, it includes the users of the system and the data that travels through it.

database   An organized collection of data that allows users to sort entries and query the database manager for data that meets certain criteria.

database administrator   An employee who manages a corporate database.

database file   A group of related records, each of which has the same set of fields.

database management system (DBMS)   A program that allows users to create a database, as well as sort, query, and create reports with it.

date field   A type of data field that contains a date. Data can be entered into a date field in standard date formats (for example, 12/31/93).

debugging   The process of eliminating errors from programming code.

decision support system (DSS)   An information system for executives, which tends to be oriented less toward reports and more toward generating answers to open-ended questions.

desktop model   A computer chassis that is designed to lie flat on a desktop.

desktop publishing (DTP)   Using a computer to create high-quality documents that are ready to be sent to a printer. Although desktop publishing software shares many of the same capabilities as modern word processing software, DTP software specializes in the most advanced features, especially the ability to incorporate a wide variety of typefaces and the ability to combine text and graphics.

device   A peripheral.

digital device   A machine that represents all data as numbers.

Digital Equipment Corporation (DEC)   A hardware company founded in 1957 by Kenneth Olsen. DEC is most famous for the PDP and VAX series of computers.

digitizer tablet   An input device used in conjunction with an electronic stylus. As the user points to places on the tablet with the stylus, the corresponding point on the screen is selected.

directory   An organized listing of files on a disk.

disk crash   Contact between the read-write head and the disk surface in a hard disk. A disk crash results in loss of data where the head touched the disk.

diskette   A round piece of mylar (plastic) coated with ferrous oxide and encased in a square plastic envelope or shell.

diskette drive   The I/O device that is used to access the data on a diskette.

diskless workstation   A networked computer that has its own processing components and generally a keyboard (possibly a mouse or some other input device as well) and a monitor, but lacks any storage device of its own. When this type of computer is turned on, it looks to the file server for the operating system.

documentation   The print material that comes with a piece of proprietary software. Also, print material and explanations of programming code that are created as part of the programming process.

DOS   Microsoft's Disk Operating System, designed for PCs. DOS is the most widely used operating system in the world.

dot matrix printer   An output device that creates images with a set of pins that push an inked ribbon against paper.

dot pitch   The distance between the three colored dots that make up a single pixel on a color monitor.

double-click   A mouse technique of pointing to a place on the monitor and pressing the mouse button twice in rapid succession.

downloading   Retrieving a file from another computer.

downsizing   Reducing the function of the central information systems department and distributing computer resources throughout an organization.

drag   A mouse technique of holding down the mouse button while moving the pointer on the screen.

dynamic link   A cross-reference between data files that allows a single data item to be used in several different files. When the data is changed in one file, the change is reflected in all linked files.

E-mail An information system that allows computer users to write, send, and read messages using a computer network.

EBCDIC Extended Binary-Coded Decimal Interchange Code, a character code used by IBM mainframes.

edit Make changes to a document

EGA Enhanced Graphics Adapter, a system for displaying graphics images on a PC monitor. EGA can produce 16 different colors on the screen, with 640 x 350 resolution.

enterprise-wide network A communications network that includes a group of the computers that are used in the same company, even if the computers are located in separate buildings.

ergonomics The study of the physical relationship between people and machines.

evaluation copy A piece of software that a dealer has provided to customers so they can judge the software before they buy it.

executable file A program.

expansion board A printed circuit board that provides a hardware interface between a peripheral and the motherboard.

expansion slot An electronic connection on the motherboard that allows the user to plug in an expansion board.

expert system A software package that has been created to mimic the human decision-making process in a narrow problem area.

fax modem A computer peripheral that accomplishes the same goal as the standalone fax, except that the user is able to send only files, rather than hard copy.

feasibility study A preliminary investigation of a problem to see if the benefits of solving it outweigh the costs of developing a solution.

field A unit of data, the type of which has been predefined. In most databases (excluding hypermedia databases) all records in a file have the same set of fields.

field name The label linked to a field in a database. If the database is viewed as a table, the field names are usually displayed as the column headings.

field type Describes the kind of data that can be held in a given field. The field type determines the ways in which the database manager can process the data in that field.

fifth-generation language A programming language that combines the easy-to-use aspects of a fourth-generation language with artificial intelligence and expert systems to make the computer even easier to use. Although very few 5GLs are available, one of their primary characteristics is natural language processing (NLP).

file A set of data that the user has given a name to.

file management The process of organizing software and data

in a meaningful way on a hard disk, making frequent backups, and eliminating old files.

file server A fast computer with a large amount of secondary storage to which all of the other computers in a network have access for data storage and retrieval.

Finder A Macintosh operating system file that manages files.

first-generation language A machine language.

flaming Creating an inappropriate or overly emotional message on an E-mail system.

flat-file database A database structure in which data is organized as tables, but only one table can be accessed at a time.

flat-panel display Compact, energy-efficient monitors that are only one or two inches thick. Most often used with laptop computers.

flowchart A structured programming tool that shows the logical progression of processing in a program.

folder Same as subdirectory. The Mac displays subdirectories as folders, which are represented by icons that look like file folders.

font A specific typeface, in a specific size. Some font managers use font to mean typeface.

font manager A utility program used to control what fonts are available for use, which ones can be displayed, and which ones can be printed.

footprint The amount of horizontal space that a computer's chassis occupies.

formatted Refers to a disk that has been mapped into tracks and sectors. A disk is not useable until it has been formatted.

FORTRAN Acronym for FORmula TRANslator, a third-generation language known for being able to perform extensive mathematical manipulations. Developed in 1957 by John Backus.

fourth-generation language A programming language that is more intuitive than a third-generation language. 4GLs are often more specialized than third-generation languages. Some people consider object-oriented languages to be 4GLs.

full duplex Refers to the ability to send and receive data simultaneously.

function keys Keyboard keys marked F1, F2, and so on. Their function is determined by the software being used.

game software A type of application software that allows the computer to be used to play video games.

garbage in, garbage out (GIGO) Saying meaning that the worth of computer system or information system output is only as valuable or accurate as the input.

general ledger Accounting system that integrates and summarizes the data in accounts receivable, accounts payable, and payroll.

general purpose computer A computer designed to solve a variety of problems.

graphic field See *binary field*.

graphic user interface (GUI) A type of user interface in which the program is controlled by using a mouse, trackball, or stylus and digitizer tablet to select items shown on the screen. In addition to text and menus, a graphical user interface usually includes icons that represent programs, data files, and commands.

graphics software Application software that allows the user to create illustrations, diagrams, graphs, or charts.

gray scale Refers to a monochrome monitor that can create varying intensities of the single color.

half duplex Refers to the transmission of data in both directions, but only one direction at a time.

handshake A set of data that formally establishes a communications link by testing the line settings and thereby ensuring a valid connection.

hard copy Printed output. Contrast with *soft copy*, which is displayed on a monitor.

hard disk A large magnetic storage medium, consisting of stacked aluminum platters.

hard disk drive The I/O device that reads and writes data from and to a hard disk.

hard disk management See file management.

hardware The machinery of the computer system. Hardware consists of input, processing, output, storage, and communication components.

Hayes-compatible Refers to a modem that uses the standard command language created by Hayes Microcomputer Products, Inc., the oldest manufacturer of modems for microcomputers.

help features Files, built into the software package, that the user can access while using the software.

Hewlett-Packard A company best known in the computer business for the LaserJet series of printers. HP also makes computers, ranging in size from micros to mainframes.

hierarchical database A database structure in which each record is related to a single parent record, though each can be related to many child records. When diagrammed, the hierarchical structure looks like a family tree.

hierarchical network A network configuration in which the host computer has several smaller computers linked to it, each of the smaller computers can have other computers linked to it, and so on.

high level language A third-, fourth-, or fifth- generation language.

host computer A central network computer that is relied on heavily by the other nodes for processing.

hypermedia database A database structure in which data is organized by cards, each of which can contain fields of any data type, and each of which can be linked to any other card in any other stack.

hypermedia software A subset of the database family that incorporates the advantages of multimedia for conveying information.

IBM Corporation International Business Machines, the largest producer of mainframe machines and one of the major microcomputer manufacturers. Most notably, the manufacturer of the IBM PC, XT, AT, and PS/2, as well as the mainframe System/360 and the OS/2 operating system.

icon A small on-screen picture that represents a program, data file, or command.

impact printer An output device that creates hard copy by striking the paper with an inked element.

indexing Creating an alternate order for the records in a database file. Unlike a sort, an index is not a permanent reordering.

information Processed data; data in context; data plus meaning.

information service An on-line company that allows the subscriber access to a number of services. Information services often include their own bulletin boards and conferencing capabilities. Electronic mail (E-mail) is available with many information services.

information system A set of established paths along which data travels through an organization.

initialized The Mac's term for formatted.

ink-jet printer An output device that creates hard copy images by shooting tiny droplets of ink at the paper.

input device A hardware component that accepts data from the person or machine using the computer and transmits it to the processing devices.

installation With proprietary software, the process of copying software from diskettes to a hard disk. With an information system, the process of setting up the new hardware and software and training the users of the new system.

instruction explosion The increase that occurs in the number of lines of code when a program is translated into machine language.

integrated application package Software that combines a collection of applications in one package with a common interface. Common applications found in an integrated package include a word processor, a database, a spreadsheet, a graphics system, and a communications system.

interactive program Software that requires user input to guide processing. Real-time processing is usually accomplished with interactive programs.

internal font A font built into the printer.

interpreter   A program that translates code into machine language while the program is running.

job displacement   A forced change in employment as a result of the increased use of computers.

job enlargement   Expansion of job responsibilities as a result of computer technology. Often a byproduct of job displacement.

just-in-time manufacturing (JIT)   A manufacturing technique that minimizes inventory by supplying new materials just as the old materials are used up and by supplying just enough output to meet demand.

kilobyte (K)   1,024 (210) bytes.

knowledge   Represented by an understanding of the significance of information.

knowledge engineer   A generic term for an expert systems programmer.

laptop   A portable microcomputer that weighs less than 10 pounds and folds down to the size of a two-inch thick pad of paper. Often used interchangeably with notebook.

laser printer   An output device that uses laser beams to project an image onto a photosensitive drum, where powdered toner is bonded to the paper with heat. The process is similar to that used by photocopiers.

letter-quality print   Refers to a printer that creates characters comparable in quality to typewriter print.

light pen   A light-sensitive, pen-shaped input device that is connected to a video terminal.

liquid crystal display (LCD)   A type of flat-screen monitor that contains a film of liquid crystal between two panes of glass. Wires running through the crystal can make the pixels opaque or transparent.

local area network (LAN)   A group of computers that are located within the same room, building, or complex and connected to each other through cabling or some other method.

logic error   A mistake in a program that does not violate the syntax rules of the language but causes unexpected results.

logic structure   One of several techniques for processing data. The three most common logic structures are the sequence, selection, and loop structures.

logical field   A type of database field that contains a single character, which indicates a logical condition, true or false. There are only two possibilities in a logical field.

loop structure   Also called a DO WHILE or DO UNTIL structure. A logic structure in which a set of processing steps is repeated until a given condition is true or false.

Lotus 1-2-3   The most widely used spreadsheet program, made by the Lotus Development Corporation.

low-level language   Any first- or second-generation language (machine language or assembly language).

machine language   Binary code that is understandable by the computer.

Macintosh   Apple Computer's most successful line of computer. The first Mac was released in 1984. All Macintosh models use the 68000 series of chips from Motorola.

mainframe   A class of large, general purpose computers capable of handling the input, output, and processing needs of many users simultaneously.

management information systems (MIS)   An established process for generating information that serves the needs of middle-level managers.

math coprocessor   An extension to the control unit and the ALU that can help speed up processing of complex calculations.

megabyte (MB)   1,048,576 (220) bytes.

megahertz (MHz)   A unit measuring millions of cycles per second.

memo field   Text-based database fields that allow users to enter notes.

memory   The set of electronic cubbyholes where data and program instructions are stored when the CPU needs quick access to them.

memory chip   An integrated circuit that holds memory and data that is readily available to the CPU.

menu-driven interface   A type of user interface in which the user can control the software by choosing from lists of options that are presented on screen.

metropolitan area network (MAN)   *See enterprise-wide network.*

microcomputer   The smallest class of computers, its CPU consists of a single microprocessor. The majority of microcomputers are intended to be used by only one person at a time.

microprocessor   A computer chip, such as the CPU of a microcomputer, that is capable of processing data.

Microsoft Corporation   The largest and most powerful software company in the world. The developer of DOS, Windows, and several popular application packages, including Microsoft Works, Word, and Excel.

middle-level managers   Managers who track operations over time and develop tactical plans to meet the objectives of upper-level management.

middleware   Software that establishes an interface between application software and the operating system. Middleware shields the user from the complexity of the system.

minicomputer   A class of general purpose computers that are smaller than mainframes but perform similar tasks. They are usually capable of handling the input, output, and processing needs of at least several users simultaneously.

MIPS   Millions of instructions per second. A unit used to measure the processing speed of a computer.

modem Contraction of "modulator-demodulator." A hardware device that allows a computer to send and receive data through a telephone system.

monitor An output device that displays output on a screen.

monochrome Refers to a monitor that displays only one color.

motherboard An electronic circuit board that includes the bus, the CPU, all of the chips for controlling system peripherals, and slots for additional circuit boards. Also called the *system board*.

mouse A pointing device that enables the user to identify a position on the screen by moving a tool around on a horizontal surface, such as a desktop or a mouse pad.

multimedia Refers to the use of several communicative media within a single presentation.

multitasking The ability to run several programs at the same time.

near letter-quality (NLQ) print Refers to a printer that creates characters that are not as sharp as typewriter print but are sharper than standard, 9-pin, dot-matrix print.

network database A database structure in which each record can be related to multiple parent records and multiple child records.

network interface card (NIC) An expansion card that acts as the device interface between a computer and the rest of the network.

network server See file server.

node Refers to each of the computers or terminals in a network.

non-procedural language Flexible programming languages that require less training of the programmer than more traditional procedural languages.

nonremovable storage A storage medium that cannot be removed from the storage device. Most hard disks are nonremovable.

nonvolatile memory A type of memory, the contents of which are not erased when the power supply is shut off.

notebook A light laptop. Laptop and notebook are now often used interchangeably.

numeric field A type of database field that contains numbers, which can be used in calculations.

numeric keypad A group of keys, normally located at the right side of the keyboard, that allow for convenient entry of numbers and mathematical symbols.

object code A machine language version of a program.

operating system A set of programs that run the computer, providing an interface between the programs and the hardware, as well as between the hardware and the user.

operations manager A member of the lowest level of management in a company who supervises its daily operation.

optical character recognition (OCR) A software technique that allows text to be regenerated from a bit-mapped image of alphanumeric characters.

optical disk A storage medium that can be written to and read with light. A CD-ROM disk is an optical disk that can be read from but not written to.

OS/2 A 32-bit operating system from IBM.

output device A hardware component that accepts processed data from the processing devices and returns it as information to the person or machine using the computer.

outsourcing Hiring an outside consulting company to handle responsibilities that were traditionally managed by an internal information systems department.

pages per minute (ppm) A unit for measuring printer speed. The unit measures how many pages of text can be printed in one minute.

palmtop A hand-held microcomputer designed to offer a limited number of features. To date, palmtops do not offer the full functionality of notebook computers.

parallel port A device interface that allows simultaneous transmission of several bits.

parity bit A single bit used in data communications that allows the receiving computer to know if there were any errors in transmission.

payroll An accounting system that keeps track of the wages owed to each employee, plus insurance and retirement deductions, Social Security, and tax withholdings. The payroll system is actually a type of accounts payable that recognizes the company's short-term debt to employees.

PC Although *PC* stands for *personal computer*, the term usually refers to IBM computers and compatibles.

performance monitoring Measuring the output of employees through systems built into the computers they use at work.

peripheral Hardware devices, such as modems, mice, and external disk drives, that connect to the system unit.

pixel Contraction of *picture element*. A pixel, which appears as a dot on a monitor, is the smallest graphic unit on the screen.

point of sale (POS) computer Special purpose computers that were developed to make it easier for large stores to keep track of inventory. They are usually housed in cash registers and attached to scanning devices, such as bar-code readers.

pointing device An input device, such as a mouse, that allows the user to interact with the computer simply by pointing to parts of the screen.

port An I/O device interface, in which an external peripheral can be plugged into the system unit.

portability The ability of programming code to be used on different types of computers.

portable A microcomputer that can be folded up to the size of a briefcase, or smaller.

PostScript A standard, developed by Adobe Systems, for translating CPU output into data that the printer can understand.

power supply A hardware component in the system unit that takes ordinary household AC power and transforms it into DC current, on which the computer operates.

preemptive multitasking A multitasking strategy in which several programs can share the CPU, and the tasks being executed are prioritized, so the most important tasks are executed first. Contrast with cooperative multitasking.

presentation graphics High-quality analytic graphics that use color, multiple typefaces, and 3-D effects.

printer driver A piece of software that translates the CPU's output into codes that the printer understands.

printer server A shared printer in a network.

procedural language A programming language that requires the programmer to be trained in the proper order of actions that the language allows.

processing devices Electronic circuits, the purpose of which are to manipulate data using a written set of instructions.

program A series of instructions that tell a computer how to perform a task. Used interchangeably with *software* or a *piece of software*.

programming The process of creating the instructions the computer can use.

protocol Standards for communication.

prototyping A technique involving the creation of a simple program that mimics the operations desired by the user of an information system.

pseudocode A structured programming technique in which the programmer writes the code without worrying about proper syntax.

public domain Refers to software to which nobody claims a copyright.

quality control Measuring and comparing the output of goods and services to ensure customer satisfaction.

query Literally, *question*. A request for data from a database that meets certain criteria.

query language A high-level language that is built into a DBMS for the purpose of interacting directly with the database.

QWERTY Term used to describe the alphanumeric keys on a keyboard or the way in which the keys are arranged. The term QWERTY comes from the first six characters in the upper-left row of letters.

random access memory (RAM). Volatile memory used to store data and programs to which the CPU needs immediate access.

read-write head The part of a disk drive that reads the magnetic charges on the disk and records new charges when necessary.

real-time processing Refers to a computer system that processes input as soon as it is received.

record A set of fields containing data about a person, place, or event.

register A high-speed memory circuit within the CPU.

relation A table of data. Each column in the table is a field, and each row is a record.

relational database A database structure in which data is organized into tables. If one table contains the same data item as another table, data from both can be accessed at the same time. The relational structure is more flexible than the hierarchical, network, or flat-file structures.

removable storage A storage medium, such as a diskette, that can be removed from a storage device.

report Output from an information system. The most common types are scheduled, exception, and demand reports.

request for proposal (RFP) A request for vendors to send bids offering hardware solutions to a given problem.

request for quote (RFQ) A request for vendors to indicate the price at which they will sell specified hardware or software.

resistor An electronic component that resists the flow of current.

resolution The degree of clarity of images displayed on a monitor or a printed page.

ring network A network configuration in which each computer is linked to two others, so that data can be passed all the way around in a circle.

read-only memory (ROM) Nonvolatile memory that is permanently stored on the motherboard of a microcomputer.

scanner An input device that automates the process of data entry by reading an image and translating it into digital code.

screen saver A utility that, after a specified number of minutes during which no input has been received, causes the screen to go blank or display geometric patterns or moving pictures. As soon as input is received, the screen redisplays whatever was on it before the screen saver was activated.

second-generation language An assembly language. The lowest level of symbolic language.

selection structure Sometimes called an IF-THEN-ELSE structure. A branching structure in which the processing that occurs depends on the outcome of a logical decision that is based on the condition of data.

sequence structure A logic structure in which data is passed from one programming step to the next.

serial port A device interface capable of transmitting only one data bit in each direction at a time.

shareware Software that is distributed free of charge or for a nominal fee. If, after using the software, the customer finds it useful, the customer is required to pay for it.

single in-line memory module (SIMM) Circuit boards that hold memory chips.

simulation software A type of application software that uses the computer to imitate some other device, such as a car, jet, or forklift.

site license The right to copy and use a software product on a specified number of computers.

soft copy Output displayed on a monitor. Contrast with hard copy, which is printed output.

soft fonts Fonts downloaded from the computer to the printer.

software The part of a computer system that tells the hardware how to perform a job.

software piracy Illegal duplication or use of software.

sorting Reordering the records in a database file.

spaghetti code The opposite of a structured program. Spaghetti code is typified by many GOTO statements.

special purpose computer A computer designed to address just one kind of problem.

spreadsheet A grid of rows and columns used to perform calculations on large sets of numbers. Often used to mean spreadsheet software, a program that allows the user to create electronic spreadsheets.

SQL Acronym for structured query language, a fourth-generation language designed for managing databases.

star network A network configuration in which each node is connected directly to a central device called a hub.

stop bit In data communication, a single bit used that signals the receiving computer of the end of a sequence of bits.

storage device A hardware component that accesses magnetic or optical data. A disk drive is a storage device.

storage media Passive pieces of hardware that hold data. Data held on storage media is nonvolatile. A diskette is a storage media.

structured programming An approach to programming in which a logical framework is developed before any code is written.

subdirectory A directory within another directory. A subdirectory can contain files or other subdirectories.

subroutine A set of code in a program that accomplishes a limited task.

supercomputer A class of powerful computers designed to solve large, complex mathematical problems.

surge suppresser A hardware device that keeps electrical surges and spikes from passing from the electrical source (usually a wall socket) to the power supply.

SVGA Super VGA, a graphics system for the PC capable of 1024 x 768 resolution, with 16 colors on the screen at any given time. At lower resolutions, SVGA adapters can display much higher numbers of colors at once.

syntax error A mistake in program code that violates the rules of whatever language the program is written in.

System file The core of the Macintosh's operating system.

system flowchart Detailed diagram showing how data moves through the computer systems that are used in an information system.

system unit The main hardware unit of a microcomputer. It includes the motherboard, ports, and power supply, and frequently the disk drives and sometimes the monitor.

systems analyst Professional who specializes in the detailed analysis of existing and planned information systems.

systems designer Professional who manages the design of a new information system.

systems development life cycle Phases through which an information system goes during its design, development, installation, maintenance, and obsolescence.

tape drive An I/O device for accessing magnetic tape. A tape drive is commonly used for making backup copies of a hard disk.

telephone support A service offered by a software developer through which users can ask questions directly to employees of the manufacturer.

terminal An I/O device that relies entirely on the host computer for processing and storage. The most common type of terminal is just a remote keyboard and monitor.

third-generation language A general purpose symbolic language that is machine independent.

time field A type of database field that contains a time of day. Data can be entered into a time field in standard time formats (for example, 3:45 PM).

timesharing Multiple users sharing the central processing unit of a computer.

toggle switch A key that turns a feature, such as Insert mode, on and off.

top-down design A divide-and-conquer approach to programming in which the programmer breaks the overall objective into smaller and smaller tasks until each is relatively simple.

touch screen A monitor that also accepts input. Users make choices by touching different parts of the screen.

tower model A computer with a chassis designed to stand on one end so it takes up less space on a desk or on the floor.

trackball A pointing device that provides the functionality of a mouse, but doesn't roll around on the desk.

transistor An on/off switch that controls the flow of electricity.

tutorial software A type of application software that teaches a subject by having the student step through a series of screens. Good tutorial software is highly interactive.

typeface A complete set of printed characters that are created with a single style.

Unix A multiuser operating system originally developed by Ken Thompson at Bell Laboratories. Today, Unix is the most popular OS used on workstations.

upgrade A new version of an existing piece of software, generally with additional features.

uploading Sending a file to another computer through a modem or a network.

upper-level managers Also known as executives, they oversee the entire company, monitor profits and losses, and determine the company's future by developing business strategies.

upward compatibility A strategy in the design of hardware that allows new equipment to be attached to the same hardware devices and use the same software as old equipment.

user The person operating the computer system. Sometimes defined as the recipient of processed data or information.

user friendly Referring to a computer or computer software that is easy to use.

user interface A facet of any computer program that controls how the computer accepts data and commands as input, and to some degree, how it presents data as output.

utility A program that aids the internal functioning of the computer. Sometimes classified as a type of application software.

vector A straight line that is designated by its end points.

version One iteration in the evolution of a software package, generally indicated by a number that follows the name of the program.

VGA Video Graphics Array, a graphics system for the PC capable of displaying 200,000 different colors in 640 x 480 resolu-

tion, though only 16 colors can be displayed on the screen at once.

virus A rogue program that attaches itself to a legitimate program and automatically copies itself into other programs.

voice input Refers to computer systems capable of accepting spoken commands or data.

voice mail A computer-based system by which the user of a standard telephone can send, receive, store, or redirect voice messages.

volatile memory Memory that loses its contents when the power supply is shut off. Volatile memory is sometimes called read and write memory.

what-if capability The ability to ask a hypothetical question and consider alternatives simply by entering new data or changing a formula.

wide area network (WAN) A group of computers that are connected through communications devices but are not in close proximity.

Windows A graphic user interface designed by Microsoft for DOS-based computers. Although Windows acts like an operating system, it requires DOS to be running at the same time.

Windows NT Microsoft's 32-bit operating system for computers using Intel's 386 or 486. Unlike Windows, Windows NT is a full-fledged operating system and does not require DOS.

word processing The process of creating text documents on a computer.

word size The number of bits that a computer can process at once. The word size of a CPU is the same as the size of its registers.

WordPerfect The most widely used word processing package, made by the WordPerfect Corporation.

workstation A powerful microcomputer, often designed for scientific research or for architectural or engineering design. Many workstation CPUs are designed around RISC (Reduced Instruction Set Computing) architectures.

write protected Refers to a diskette that can be read but not written to.

Index *

A

access
    flexibility of databases, 253
    methods and protocols, 206
    privileges, 217
    time on hard disks, 180-181
accounting systems, described, 265-266
accounts receivable/payable, accounting systems, 266
acoustic couplers, described, 196
Ada language
    compared, 97f
    described, 102
addressable memory,
    Intel CPU, 133f
Adobe Systems, makes PageMaker and PostScript, 166
After Dark, screen saver, 74f
Aldus PageMaker, 224f
Allen, Paul, founder of Microsoft, 28-29, 220f
alphanumeric fields, described, 245
alphanumeric keys
    keyboard, 148
    (*see also* QWERTY)
alpha version of software, 109
Altair 8800 computer, Micro Instrumentation and
    Telemetry Systems, 28
Altair, microcomputers, 15f
Alternate (Alt) key, on IBM keyboards, 149
ALU (*see* arithmetic-logic unit compared)
Amdahl, mainframe manufacture, 15
American Airlines' Sabre System, described, 32-33
American Express, computer industry, 34
American Hospital Supply Corp., ASAP system described,
    33
American National Standards Institute, described, 92
AMEX (*see* American Express)
analog data, computers, 90-92
analog device, described, 90
analytic graphics, described, 65
Analytic Systems Automatic Purchasing, system by
American Hospital Supply Corp., 33
analyzing current system, life cycle, 280, 282
Anderson Consulting, computer services, 35
ANSI (*see* American National Standards Institute)
antivirus software, described, 72, 73f
Apple Computer, Inc.
    Apple I/II computers, 26, 27f
    computer evolution, 27f
    computers, 25-28
    Mac, 27f
    Mac II, 27f
    Macintosh computers, 127
    PowerBook, 27f
printer production, 30
AppleTalk, by Macintosh, Inc., 206
application packages (*see* application software)
applications, many for DOS, 221-222
application software, 60-86
    compatibility lacking in Unix, 230
described, 47-48
    operating systems, 18
    user groups, 77f
archiving data (*see* backup entries)
arithmetic-logic unit, control unit compared, 125
arrow keys, described, 149
artificial intelligence, described, 69-70
ASAP (*see* Analytic Systems Automatic Purchasing)
ASCII
    described, 92-93
    and OCR, 156
Ashton-Tate, acquired by Borland International, 31
Assembly language
    described, 95
    used in Unix, 218
Asymetrix Corp., created by Paul Allen, 220
AT&T Corp.
    Bell Laboratories invent transistor, 123
    Unix development, 228
    Unix Software Laboratories subsidiary, 229
ATM (*see* automated teller machine)
AutoCAD, microcomputer use, 66f
automated teller machine, described, 11

B

Babbage, Charles, "father of computers," 102
Backspace key, described, 150
backup
    frequency, 186
    making copies, 79-80
    process, 71f
    systems described, 71-72
    tape drives used, 185f
Backus, John, developed FORTRAN language, 98
banks
    ATMs use real-time processing, 54f
    use batch processing, 55
bar-code readers, described, 156
Basic Input/Output System (*see* BIOS)
BASIC language
    compared, 97f
    described, 98
BASIC program, compared with FORTRAN program, 99f
batch processing, described, 54-55
baud, described, 195

f after page number denotes figure reference

N